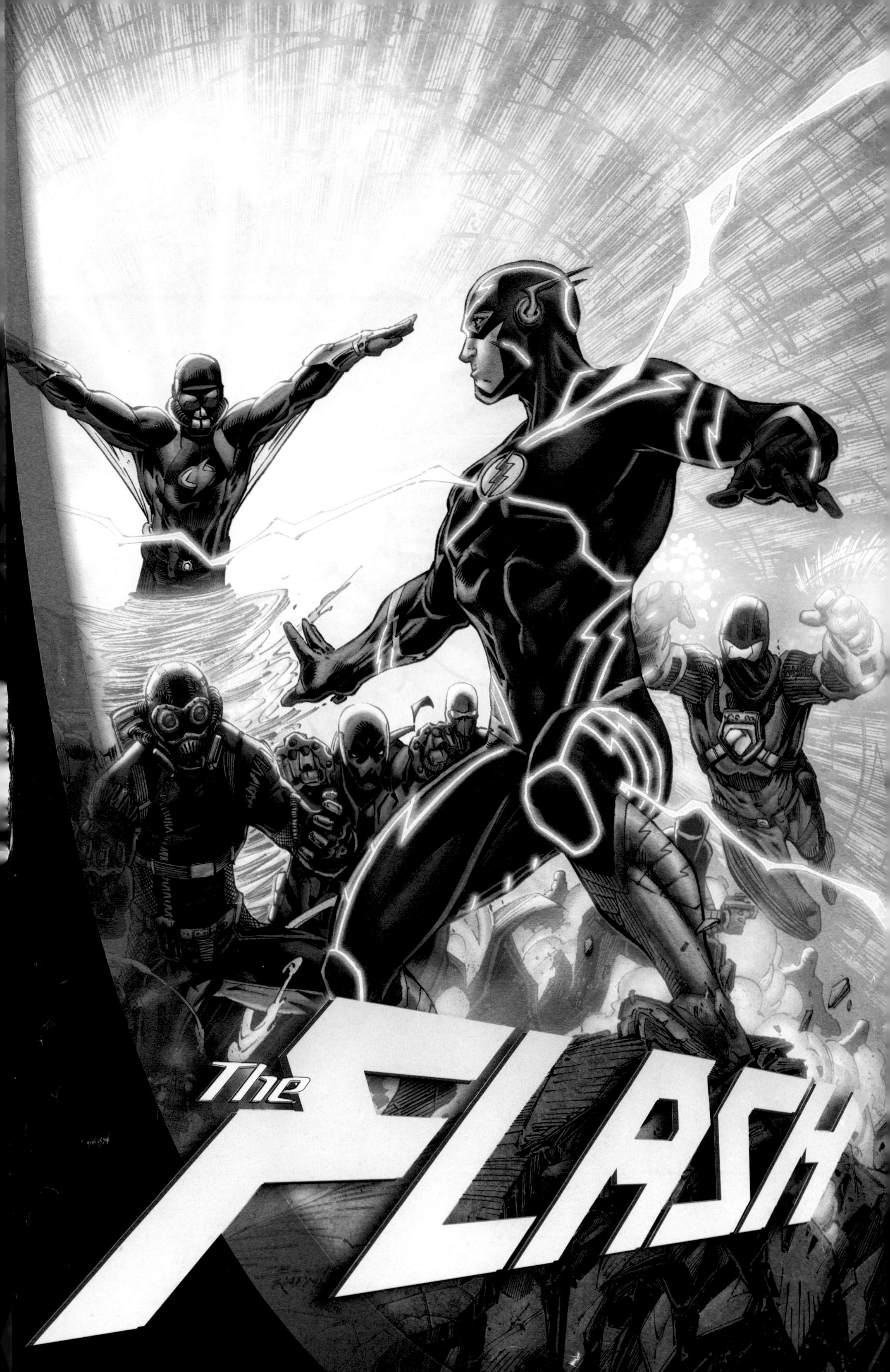
The
FLASH

VOLUME 6 **OUT OF TIME**

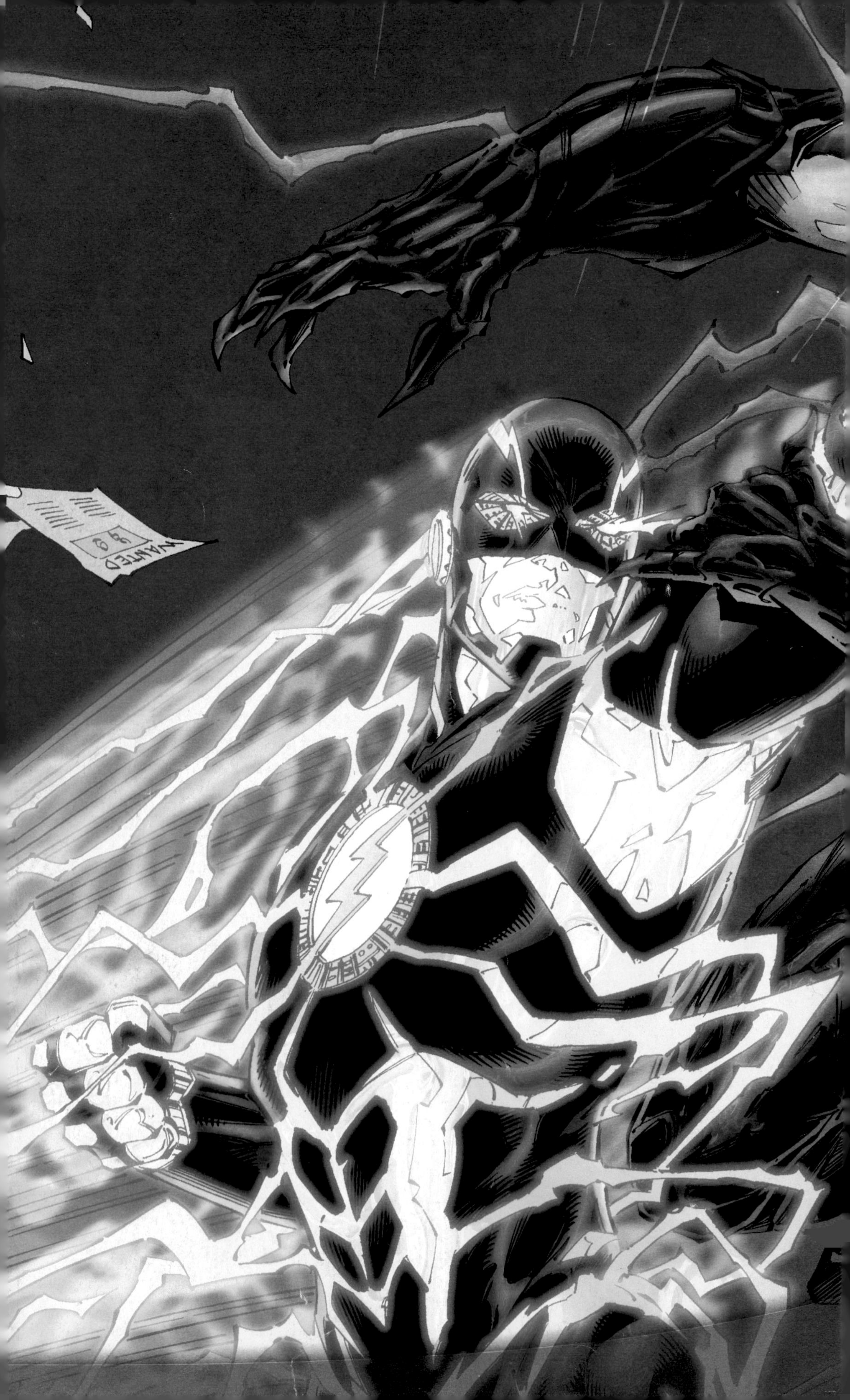
WANTED

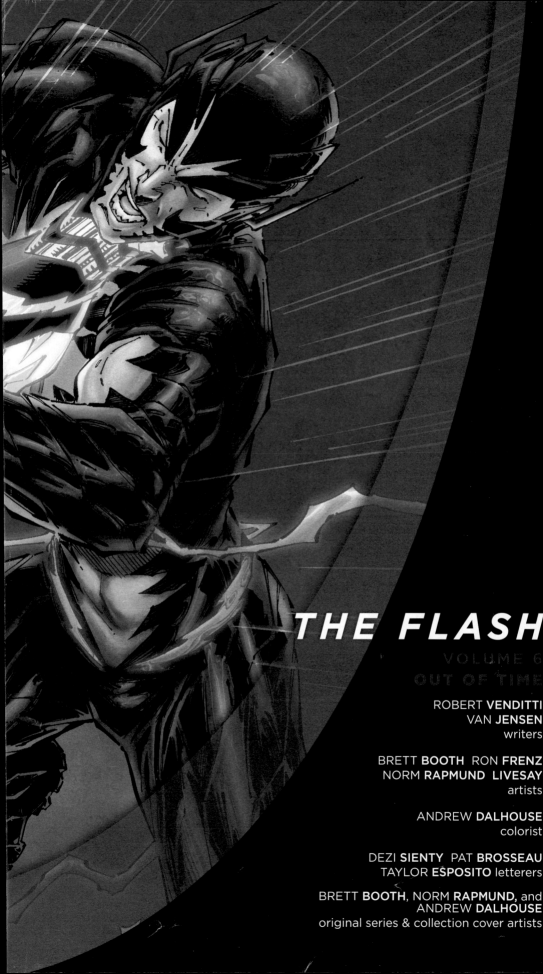

THE FLASH

VOLUME 6
OUT OF TIME

ROBERT **VENDITTI**
VAN **JENSEN**
writers

BRETT **BOOTH** RON **FRENZ**
NORM **RAPMUND LIVESAY**
artists

ANDREW **DALHOUSE**
colorist

DEZI **SIENTY** PAT **BROSSEAU**
TAYLOR **ESPOSITO** letterers

BRETT **BOOTH**, NORM **RAPMUND,** and
ANDREW **DALHOUSE**
original series & collection cover artists

BRIAN CUNNINGHAM Editor – Original Series
KATE DURRÉ AMEDEO TURTURRO Assistant Editors – Original Series
PAUL SANTOS Editor
ROBBIN BROSTERMAN Design Director – Books ROBBIE BIEDERMAN Publication Design

BOB HARRAS Senior VP – Editor-in-Chief, DC Comics

DIANE NELSON President DAN DIDIO and JIM LEE Co-Publishers GEOFF JOHNS Chief Creative Officer
AMIT DESAI Senior VP – Marketing and Franchise Management
AMY GENKINS Senior VP – Business and Legal Affairs NAIRI GARDINER Senior VP – Finance
JEFF BOISON VP – Publishing Planning MARK CHIARELLO VP – Art Direction and Design
JOHN CUNNINGHAM VP – Marketing TERRI CUNNINGHAM VP – Editorial Administration
LARRY GANEM VP – Talent Relations and Services ALISON GILL Senior VP – Manufacturing and Operations
HANK KANALZ Senior VP – Vertigo and Integrated Publishing JAY KOGAN VP – Business and Legal Affairs, Publishing
JACK MAHAN VP – Business Affairs, Talent NICK NAPOLITANO VP – Manufacturing Administration SUE POHJA VP – Book Sales
FRED RUIZ VP – Manufacturing Operations COURTNEY SIMMONS Senior VP – Publicity BOB WAYNE Senior VP – Sales

THE FLASH VOLUME 6: OUT OF TIME

DC Comics, 4000 Warner Blvd., Burbank, CA 91522
A Warner Bros. Entertainment Company.
Printed by RR Donnelley, Salem, VA, USA. 5/15/15. First Printing.

ISBN: 978-1-4012-5427-8

SUSTAINABLE
FORESTRY
INITIATIVE

Certified Chain of Custody
20% Certified Forest Content,
80% Certified Sourcing
www.sfiprogram.org
SFI-01042
APPLIES TO TEXT STOCK ONLY

Library of Congress Cataloging-in-Publication Data

Venditti, Robert.
The Flash. Volume 6, Out of Time / Van Jensen, Brett Booth.
pages cm. — (The New 52!)
ISBN 978-1-4012-5427-8
1. Graphic novels. I. Jensen, Van, illustrator. II. Title. III. Title: Out of Time.

PN6728.F53B884 2015
741.5'973—dc23

2014033188

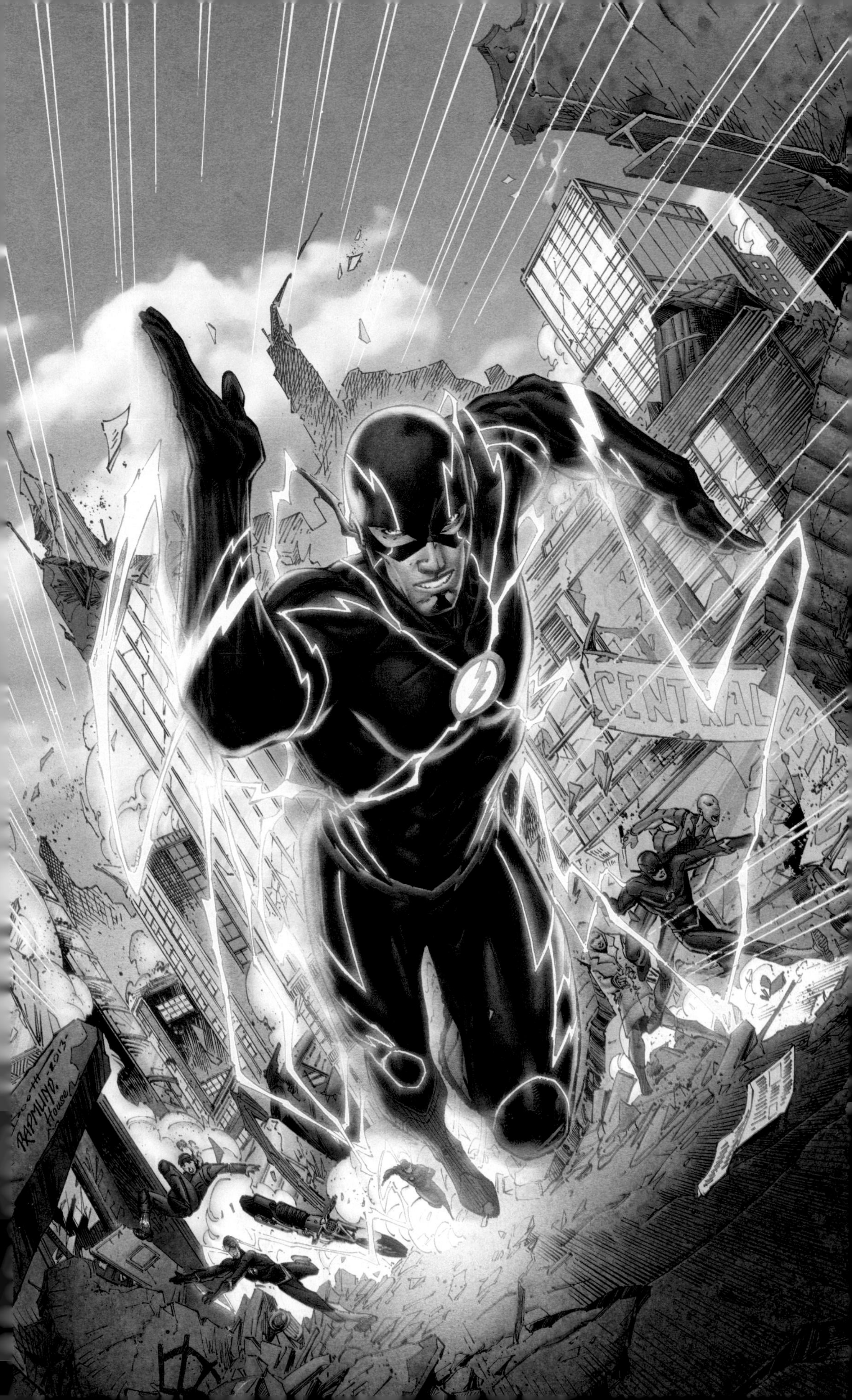
CENTRAL

LOST TIME

ROBERT VENDITTI & VAN JENSEN writers **BRETT BOOTH** penciller **NORM RAPMUND** inker

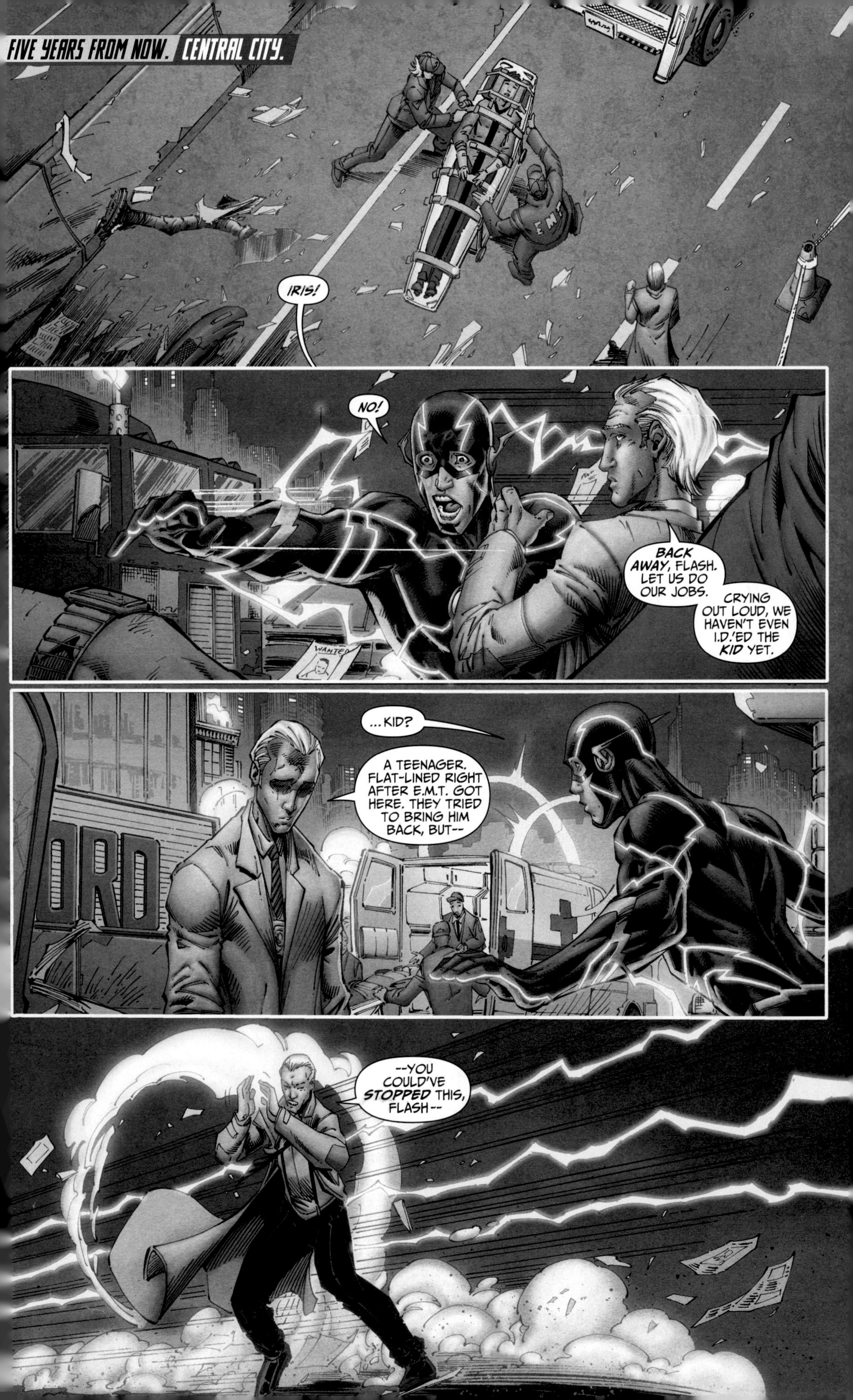
FIVE YEARS FROM NOW.
CENTRAL CITY.
IRIS!
NO!
BACK AWAY, FLASH. LET US DO OUR JOBS.
CRYING OUT LOUD, WE HAVEN'T EVEN I.D.'ED THE KID YET.
WANTED
...KID?
A TEENAGER. FLAT-LINED RIGHT AFTER E.M.T. GOT HERE. THEY TRIED TO BRING HIM BACK, BUT--
--YOU COULD'VE STOPPED THIS, FLASH--

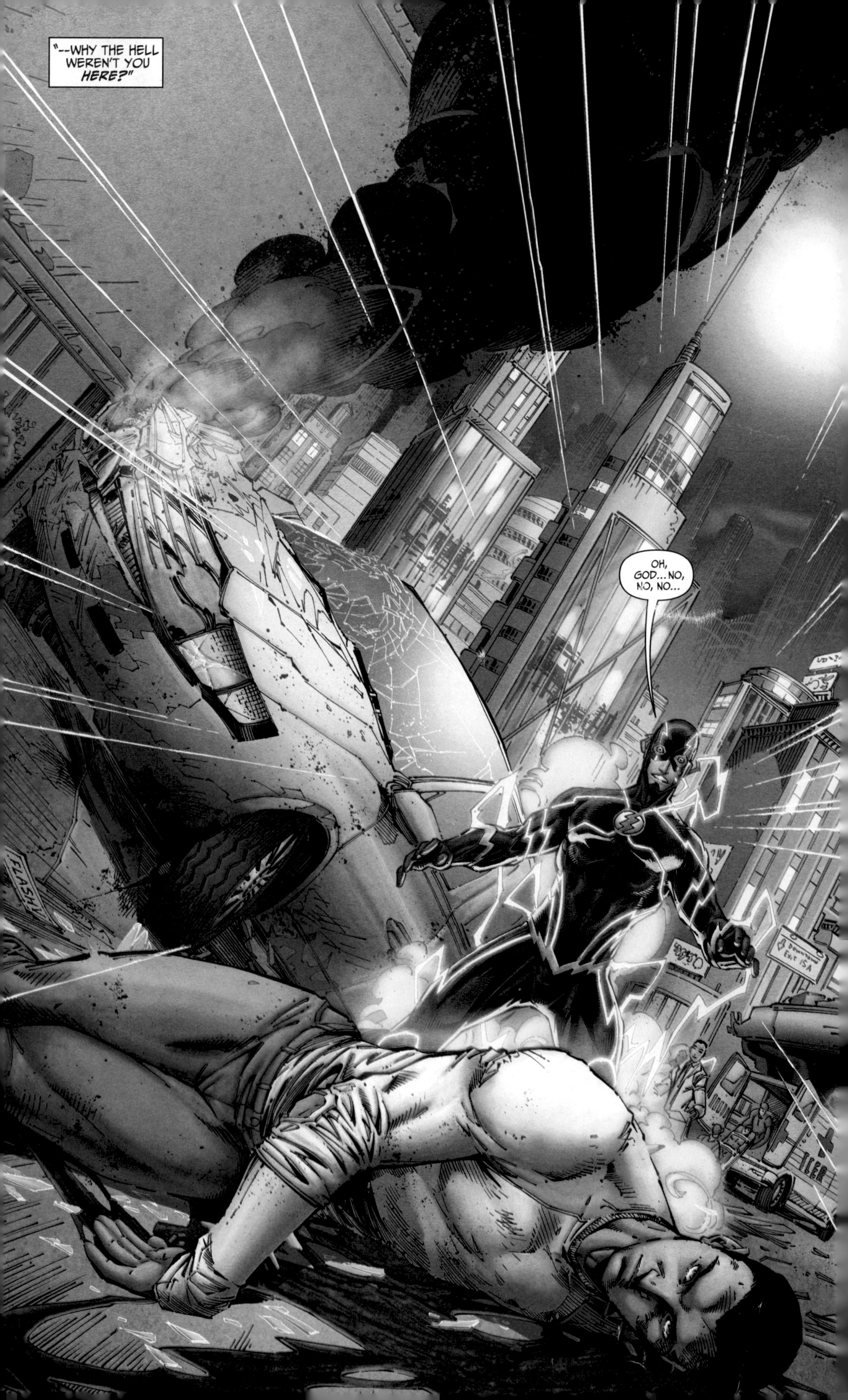
"--WHY THE HELL WEREN'T YOU HERE?"
OH, GOD... NO, NO, NO...
FLASH!

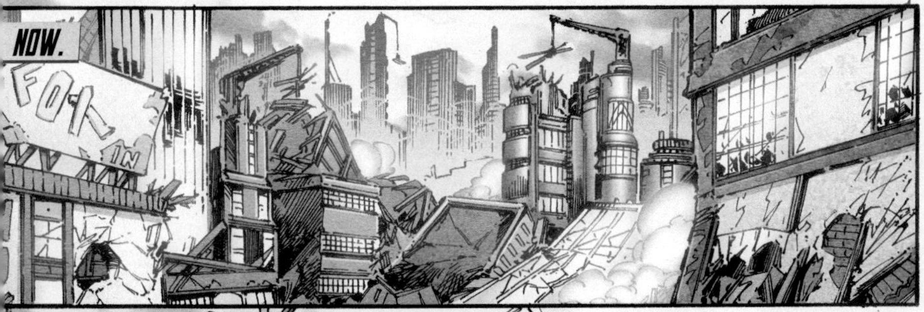
NOW.

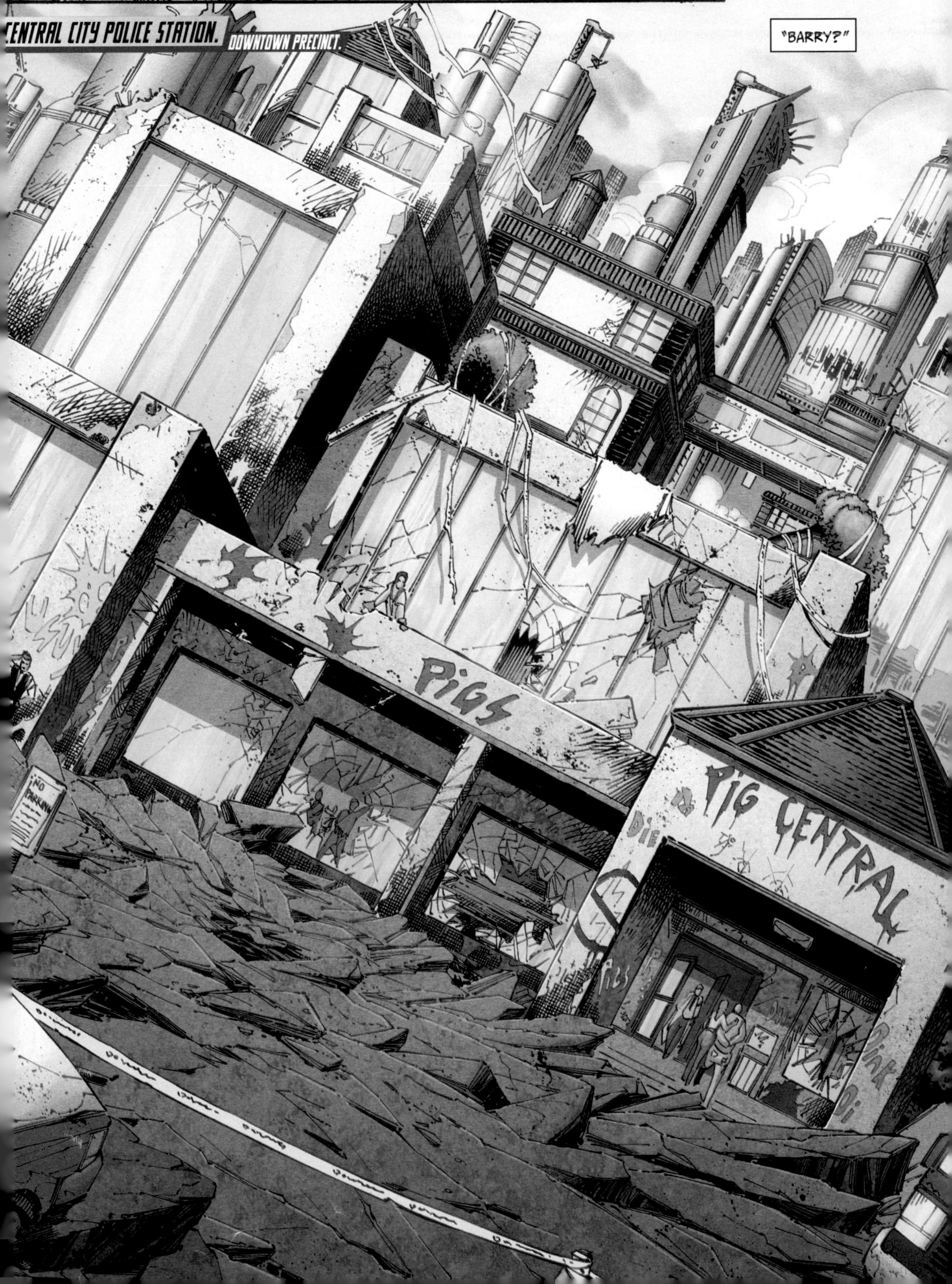
CENTRAL CITY POLICE STATION.
DOWNTOWN PRECINCT.
"BARRY?"
PIGS
PIG CENTRAL
NO PARKING

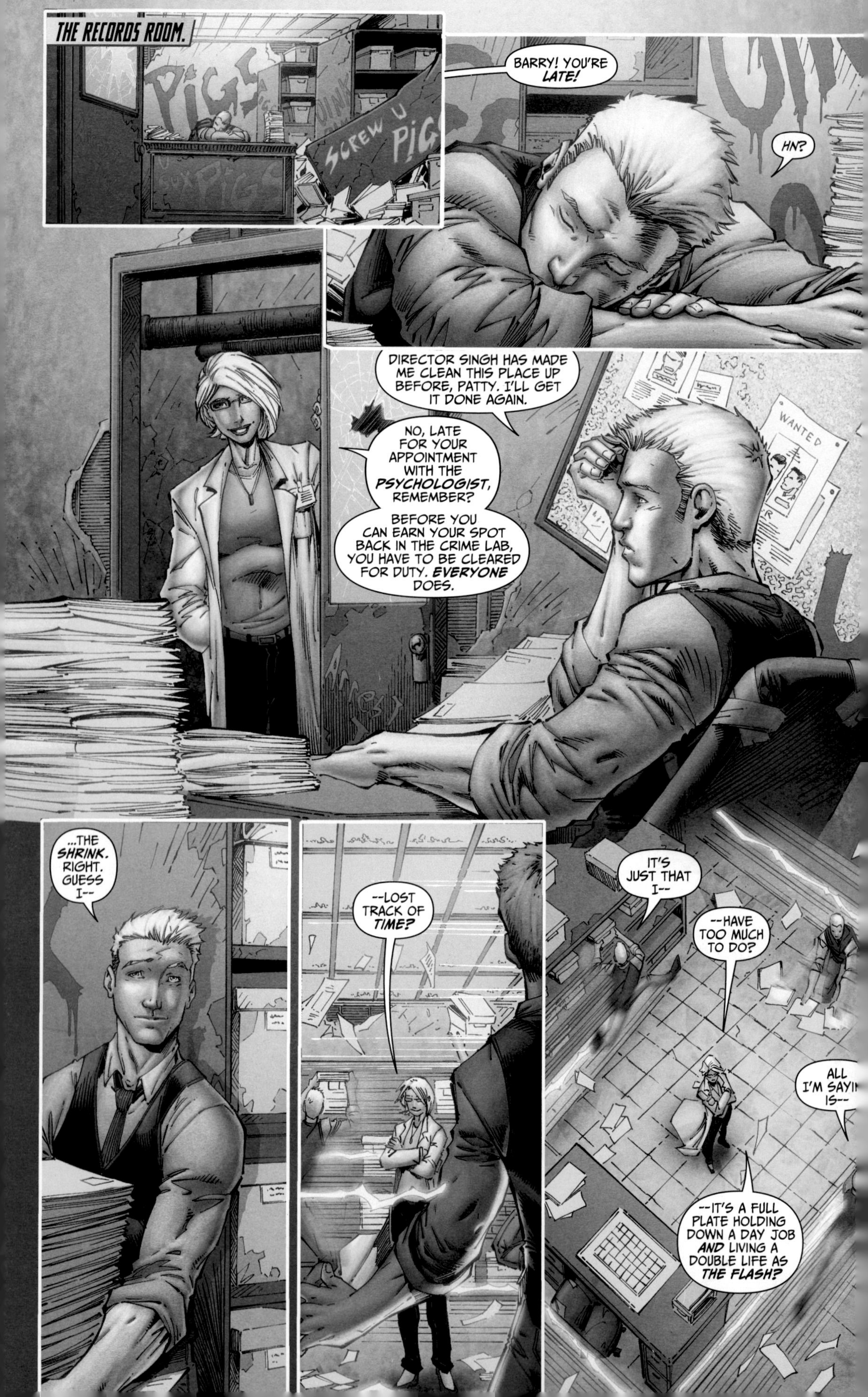
THE RECORDS ROOM.
PIGS
SCREW U PIGS
BARRY! YOU'RE *LATE!*
HN?
DIRECTOR SINGH HAS MADE ME CLEAN THIS PLACE UP BEFORE, PATTY. I'LL GET IT DONE AGAIN.
NO, LATE FOR YOUR APPOINTMENT WITH THE *PSYCHOLOGIST*, REMEMBER?
BEFORE YOU CAN EARN YOUR SPOT BACK IN THE CRIME LAB, YOU HAVE TO BE CLEARED FOR DUTY. *EVERYONE* DOES.
WANTED
...THE *SHRINK.* RIGHT. GUESS I--
--LOST TRACK OF *TIME?*
IT'S JUST THAT I--
--HAVE TOO MUCH TO DO?
ALL I'M SAYIN IS--
--IT'S A FULL PLATE HOLDING DOWN A DAY JOB *AND* LIVING A DOUBLE LIFE AS *THE FLASH?*

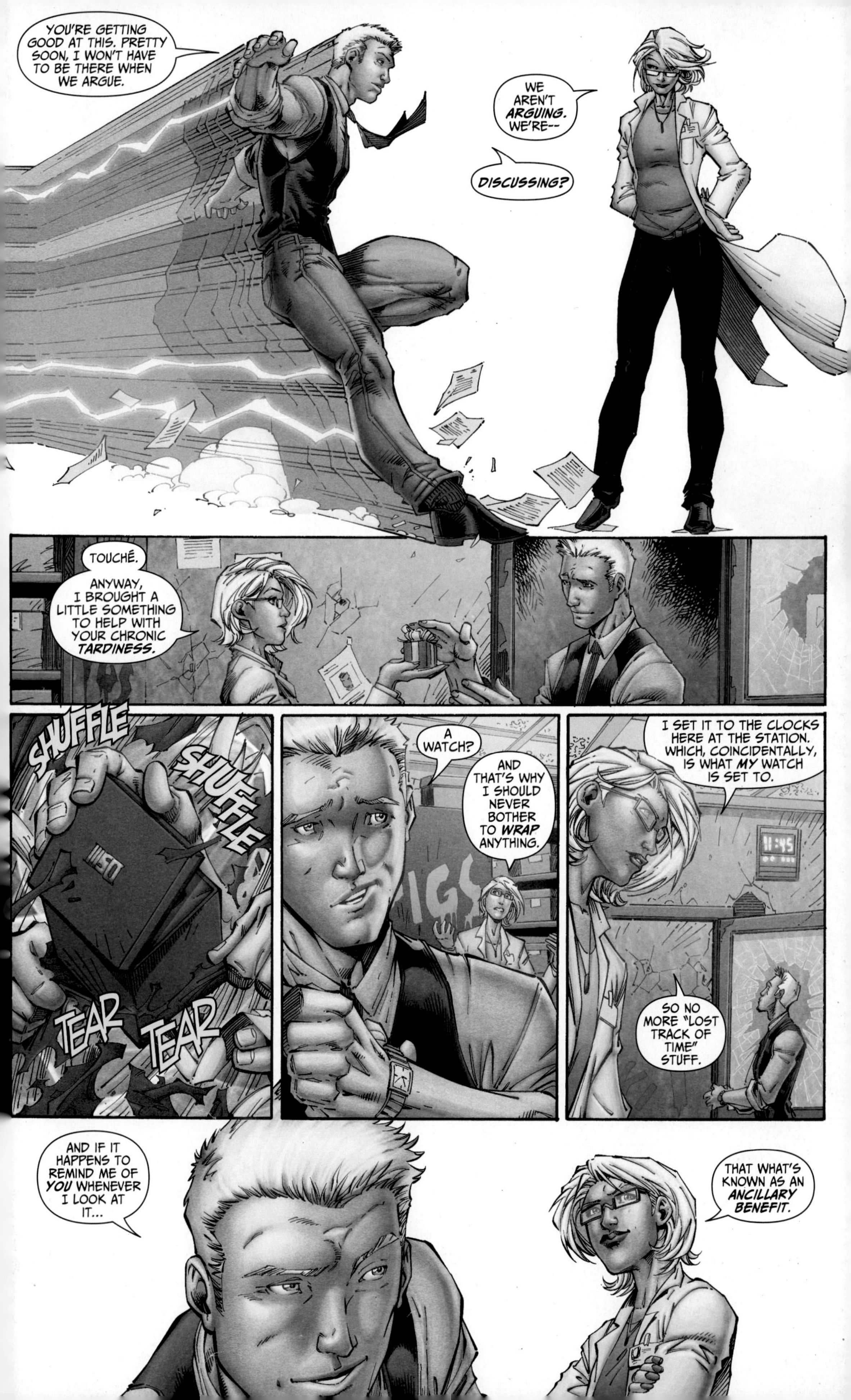
YOU'RE GETTING GOOD AT THIS. PRETTY SOON, I WON'T HAVE TO BE THERE WHEN WE ARGUE.
WE AREN'T ARGUING. WE'RE--
DISCUSSING?
TOUCHÉ.
ANYWAY, I BROUGHT A LITTLE SOMETHING TO HELP WITH YOUR CHRONIC TARDINESS.
SHUFFLE
SHUFFLE
TEAR
TEAR
A WATCH?
AND THAT'S WHY I SHOULD NEVER BOTHER TO WRAP ANYTHING.
I SET IT TO THE CLOCKS HERE AT THE STATION. WHICH, COINCIDENTALLY, IS WHAT MY WATCH IS SET TO.
SO NO MORE "LOST TRACK OF TIME" STUFF.
AND IF IT HAPPENS TO REMIND ME OF YOU WHENEVER I LOOK AT IT...
THAT WHAT'S KNOWN AS AN ANCILLARY BENEFIT.

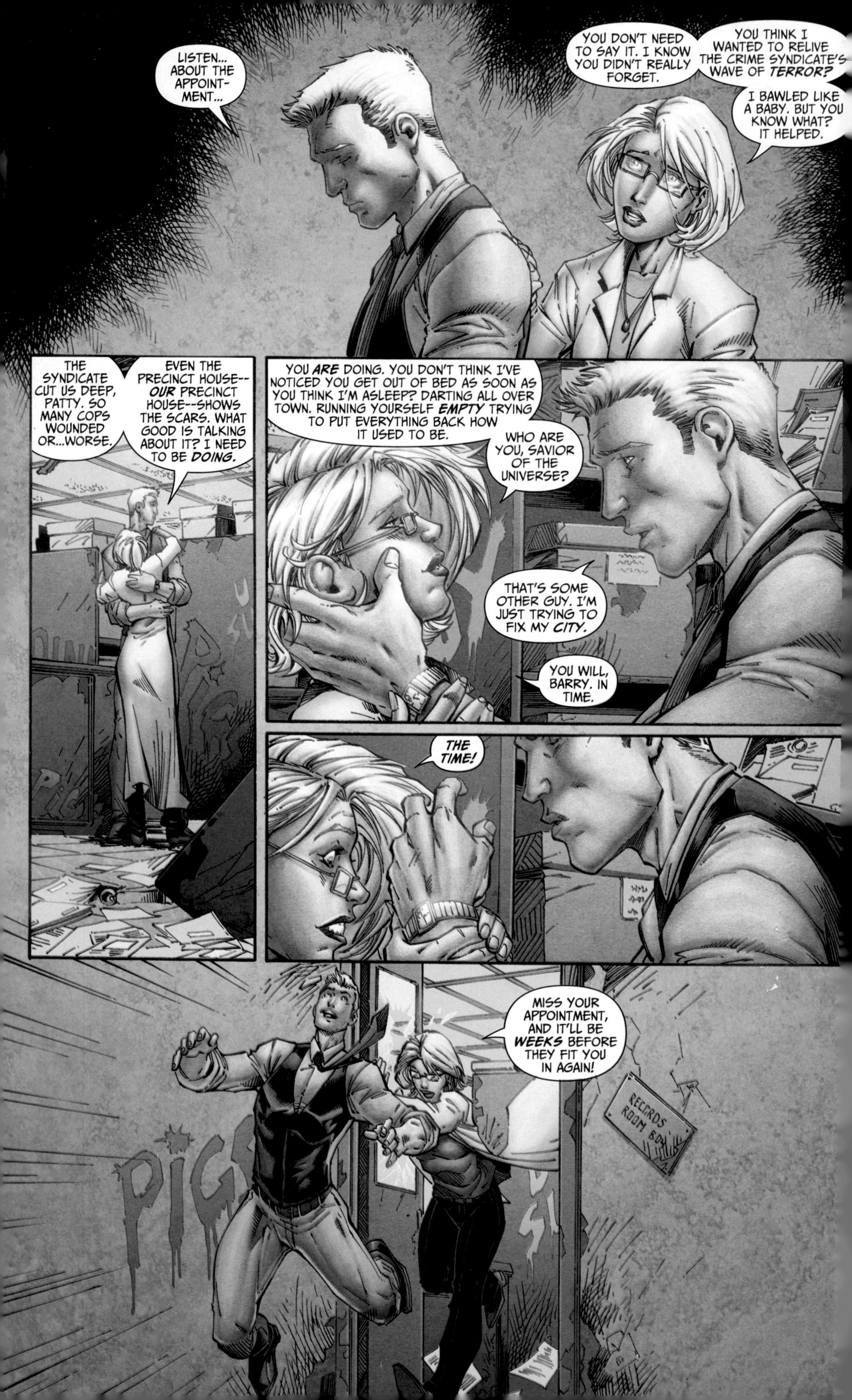
LISTEN... ABOUT THE APPOINT-MENT...
YOU DON'T NEED TO SAY IT. I KNOW YOU DIDN'T REALLY FORGET.
YOU THINK I WANTED TO RELIVE THE CRIME SYNDICATE'S WAVE OF TERROR?
I BAWLED LIKE A BABY. BUT YOU KNOW WHAT? IT HELPED.
THE SYNDICATE CUT US DEEP, PATTY. SO MANY COPS WOUNDED OR...WORSE.
EVEN THE PRECINCT HOUSE--OUR PRECINCT HOUSE--SHOWS THE SCARS. WHAT GOOD IS TALKING ABOUT IT? I NEED TO BE DOING.
YOU ARE DOING. YOU DON'T THINK I'VE NOTICED YOU GET OUT OF BED AS SOON AS YOU THINK I'M ASLEEP? DARTING ALL OVER TOWN. RUNNING YOURSELF EMPTY TRYING TO PUT EVERYTHING BACK HOW IT USED TO BE.
WHO ARE YOU, SAVIOR OF THE UNIVERSE?
THAT'S SOME OTHER GUY. I'M JUST TRYING TO FIX MY CITY.
YOU WILL, BARRY. IN TIME.
THE TIME!
MISS YOUR APPOINTMENT, AND IT'LL BE WEEKS BEFORE THEY FIT YOU IN AGAIN!
PIGS
RECORDS ROOM B04

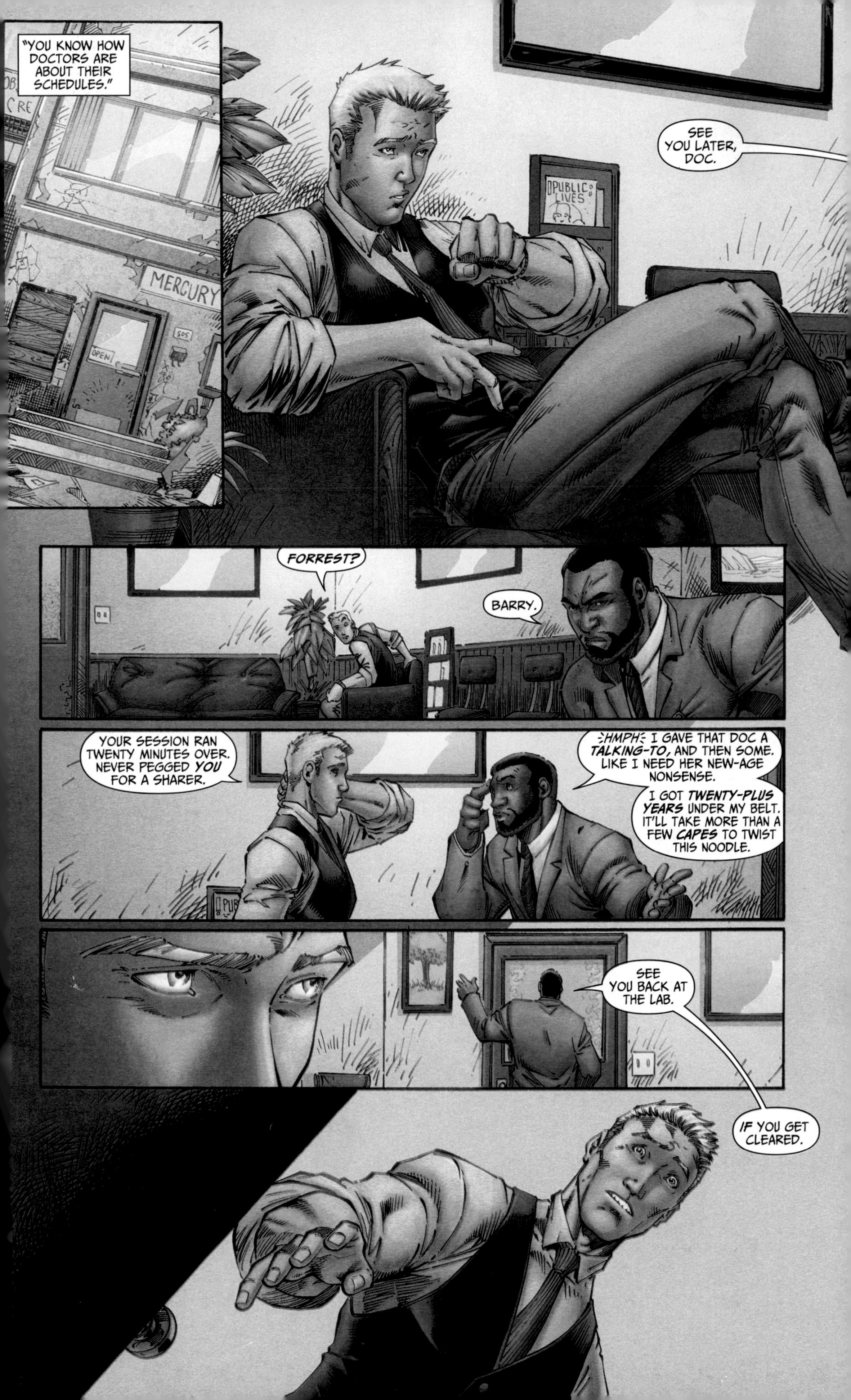

"YOU KNOW HOW DOCTORS ARE ABOUT THEIR SCHEDULES."
MERCURY
OPEN
PUBLIC LIVES
SEE YOU LATER, DOC.
FORREST?
BARRY.
YOUR SESSION RAN TWENTY MINUTES OVER. NEVER PEGGED YOU FOR A SHARER.
HMPH. I GAVE THAT DOC A TALKING-TO, AND THEN SOME. LIKE I NEED HER NEW-AGE NONSENSE.
I GOT TWENTY-PLUS YEARS UNDER MY BELT. IT'LL TAKE MORE THAN A FEW CAPES TO TWIST THIS NOODLE.
SEE YOU BACK AT THE LAB.
IF YOU GET CLEARED.

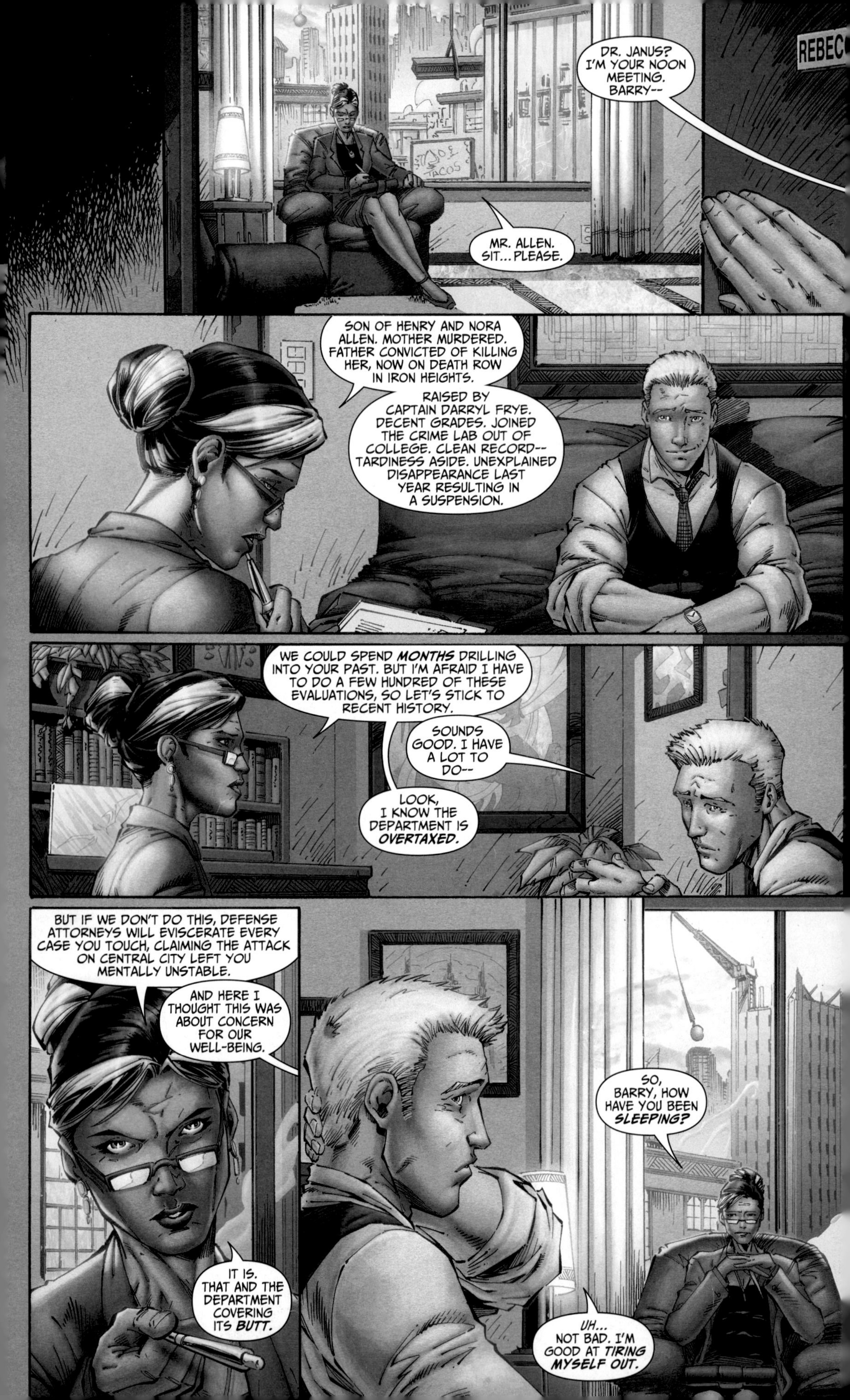
REBEC
DR. JANUS? I'M YOUR NOON MEETING. BARRY--
TACOS
MR. ALLEN. SIT... PLEASE.
SON OF HENRY AND NORA ALLEN. MOTHER MURDERED. FATHER CONVICTED OF KILLING HER, NOW ON DEATH ROW IN IRON HEIGHTS.
RAISED BY CAPTAIN DARRYL FRYE. DECENT GRADES. JOINED THE CRIME LAB OUT OF COLLEGE. CLEAN RECORD-- TARDINESS ASIDE. UNEXPLAINED DISAPPEARANCE LAST YEAR RESULTING IN A SUSPENSION.
WE COULD SPEND *MONTHS* DRILLING INTO YOUR PAST. BUT I'M AFRAID I HAVE TO DO A FEW HUNDRED OF THESE EVALUATIONS, SO LET'S STICK TO RECENT HISTORY.
SOUNDS GOOD. I HAVE A LOT TO DO--
LOOK, I KNOW THE DEPARTMENT IS ***OVERTAXED.***
BUT IF WE DON'T DO THIS, DEFENSE ATTORNEYS WILL EVISCERATE EVERY CASE YOU TOUCH, CLAIMING THE ATTACK ON CENTRAL CITY LEFT YOU MENTALLY UNSTABLE.
AND HERE I THOUGHT THIS WAS ABOUT CONCERN FOR OUR WELL-BEING.
IT IS. THAT AND THE DEPARTMENT COVERING ITS ***BUTT.***
SO, BARRY, HOW HAVE YOU BEEN ***SLEEPING?***
UH... NOT BAD. I'M GOOD AT ***TIRING MYSELF OUT.***

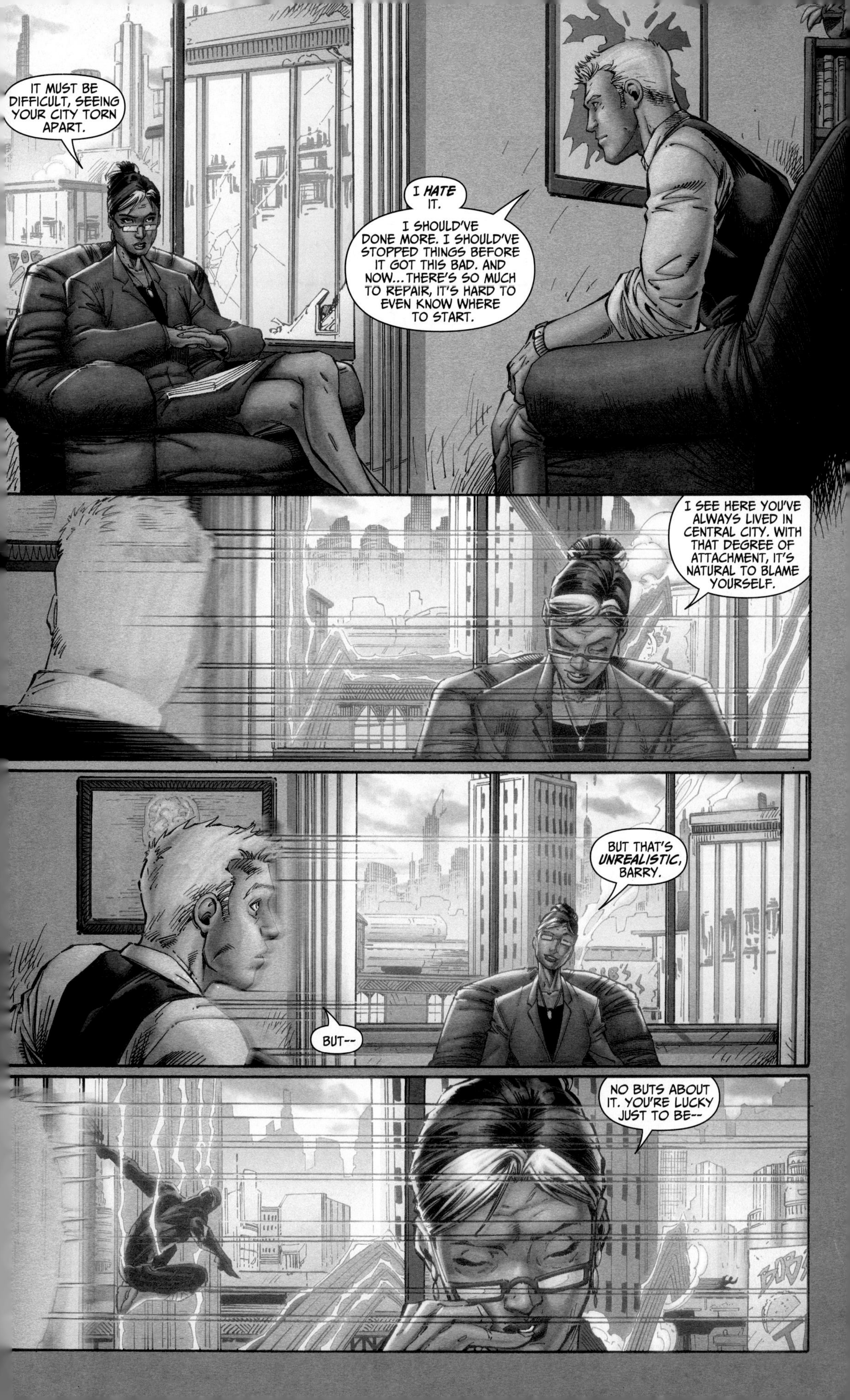
IT MUST BE DIFFICULT, SEEING YOUR CITY TORN APART.
I *HATE* IT.
I SHOULD'VE DONE MORE. I SHOULD'VE STOPPED THINGS BEFORE IT GOT THIS BAD. AND NOW...THERE'S SO MUCH TO REPAIR, IT'S HARD TO EVEN KNOW WHERE TO START.
I SEE HERE YOU'VE ALWAYS LIVED IN CENTRAL CITY. WITH THAT DEGREE OF ATTACHMENT, IT'S NATURAL TO BLAME YOURSELF.
BUT THAT'S *UNREALISTIC*, BARRY.
BUT--
NO BUTS ABOUT IT. YOU'RE LUCKY JUST TO BE--

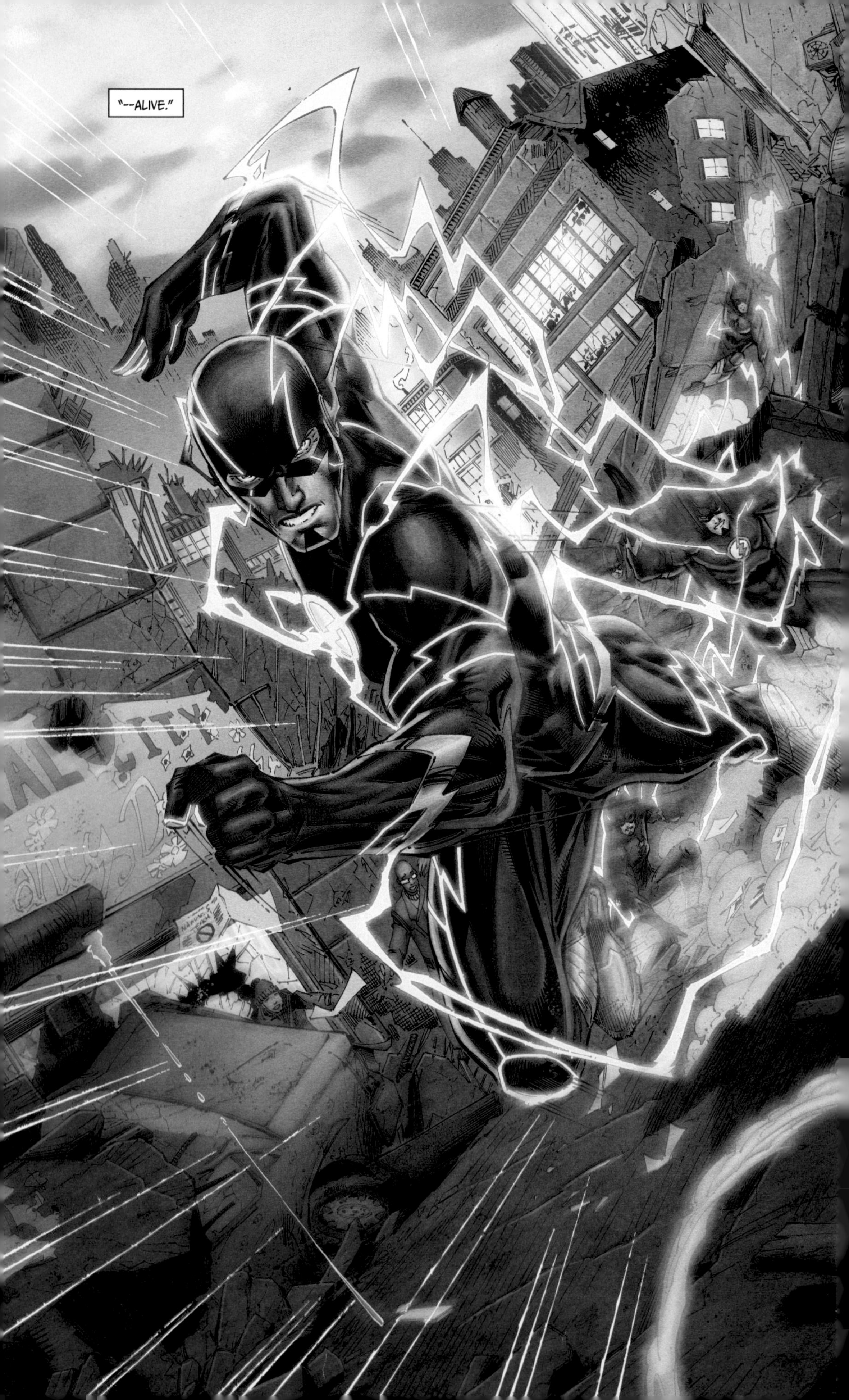
"--ALIVE."

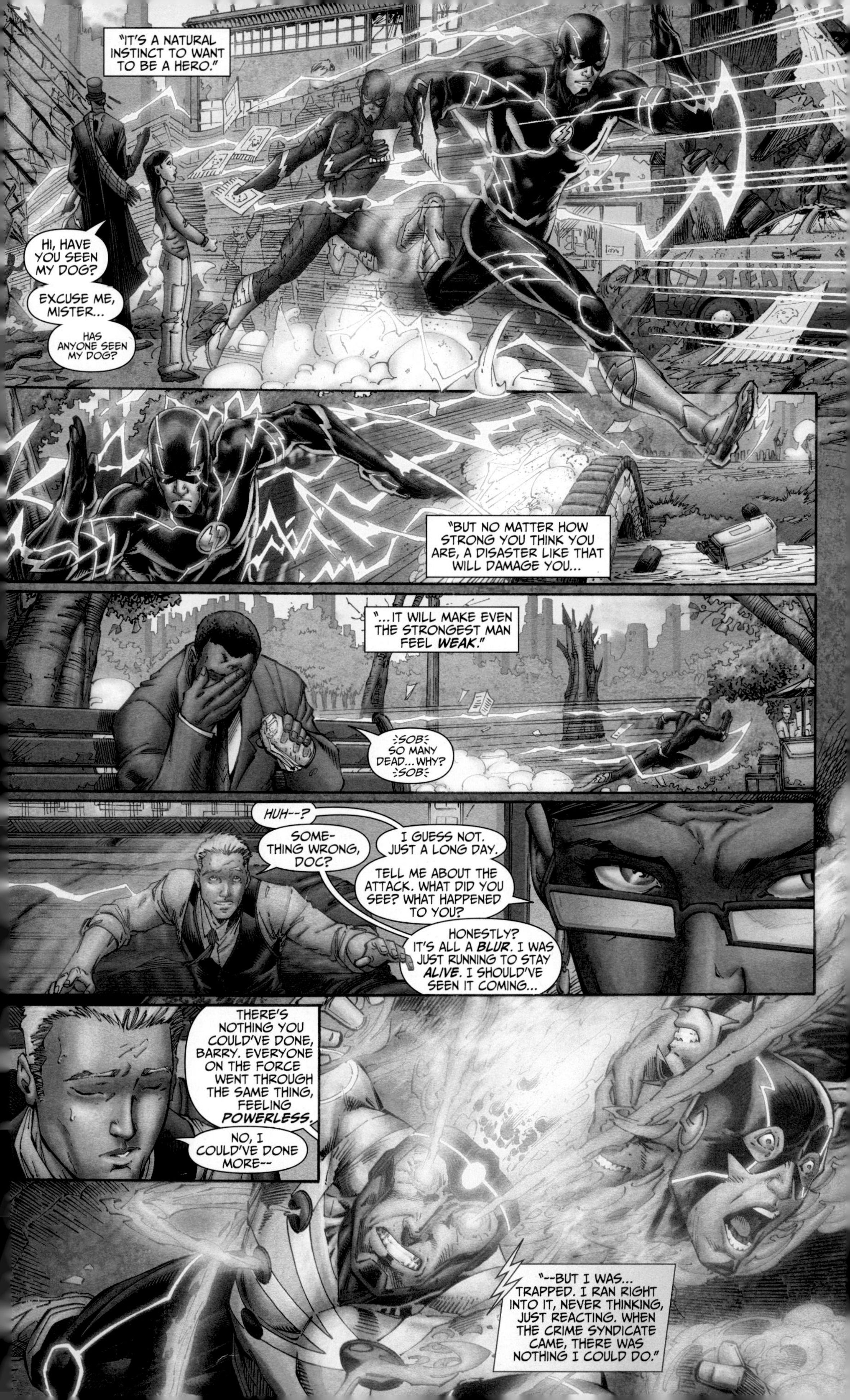
"IT'S A NATURAL INSTINCT TO WANT TO BE A HERO."
HI, HAVE YOU SEEN MY DOG?
EXCUSE ME, MISTER...
HAS ANYONE SEEN MY DOG?
"BUT NO MATTER HOW STRONG YOU THINK YOU ARE, A DISASTER LIKE THAT WILL DAMAGE YOU...
"...IT WILL MAKE EVEN THE STRONGEST MAN FEEL WEAK."
SOB SO MANY DEAD...WHY? SOB
HUH--?
SOME-THING WRONG, DOC?
I GUESS NOT. JUST A LONG DAY.
TELL ME ABOUT THE ATTACK. WHAT DID YOU SEE? WHAT HAPPENED TO YOU?
HONESTLY? IT'S ALL A BLUR. I WAS JUST RUNNING TO STAY ALIVE. I SHOULD'VE SEEN IT COMING...
THERE'S NOTHING YOU COULD'VE DONE, BARRY. EVERYONE ON THE FORCE WENT THROUGH THE SAME THING, FEELING POWERLESS.
NO, I COULD'VE DONE MORE--
"--BUT I WAS... TRAPPED. I RAN RIGHT INTO IT, NEVER THINKING, JUST REACTING. WHEN THE CRIME SYNDICATE CAME, THERE WAS NOTHING I COULD DO."

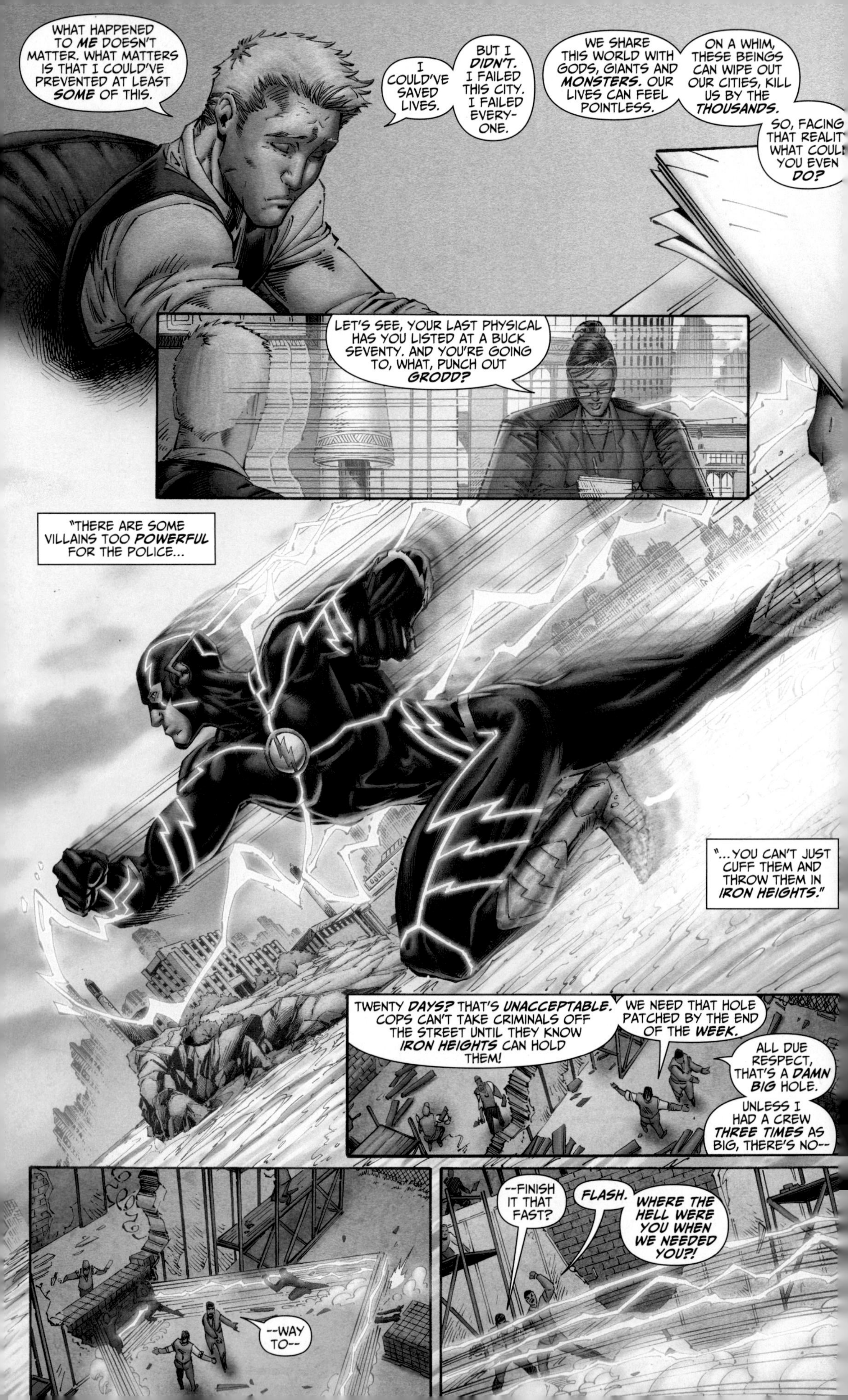
WHAT HAPPENED TO ME DOESN'T MATTER. WHAT MATTERS IS THAT I COULD'VE PREVENTED AT LEAST SOME OF THIS.
I COULD'VE SAVED LIVES.
BUT I DIDN'T. I FAILED THIS CITY. I FAILED EVERY-ONE.
WE SHARE THIS WORLD WITH GODS, GIANTS AND MONSTERS. OUR LIVES CAN FEEL POINTLESS.
ON A WHIM, THESE BEINGS CAN WIPE OUT OUR CITIES, KILL US BY THE THOUSANDS.
LET'S SEE, YOUR LAST PHYSICAL HAS YOU LISTED AT A BUCK SEVENTY. AND YOU'RE GOING TO, WHAT, PUNCH OUT GRODD?
"THERE ARE SOME VILLAINS TOO POWERFUL FOR THE POLICE...
"...YOU CAN'T JUST CUFF THEM AND THROW THEM IN IRON HEIGHTS."
TWENTY DAYS? THAT'S UNACCEPTABLE. COPS CAN'T TAKE CRIMINALS OFF THE STREET UNTIL THEY KNOW IRON HEIGHTS CAN HOLD THEM!
WE NEED THAT HOLE PATCHED BY THE END OF THE WEEK.
ALL DUE RESPECT, THAT'S A DAMN BIG HOLE.
UNLESS I HAD A CREW THREE TIMES AS BIG, THERE'S NO--
--WAY TO--
--FINISH IT THAT FAST?
FLASH.
WHERE THE HELL WERE YOU WHEN WE NEEDED YOU?!

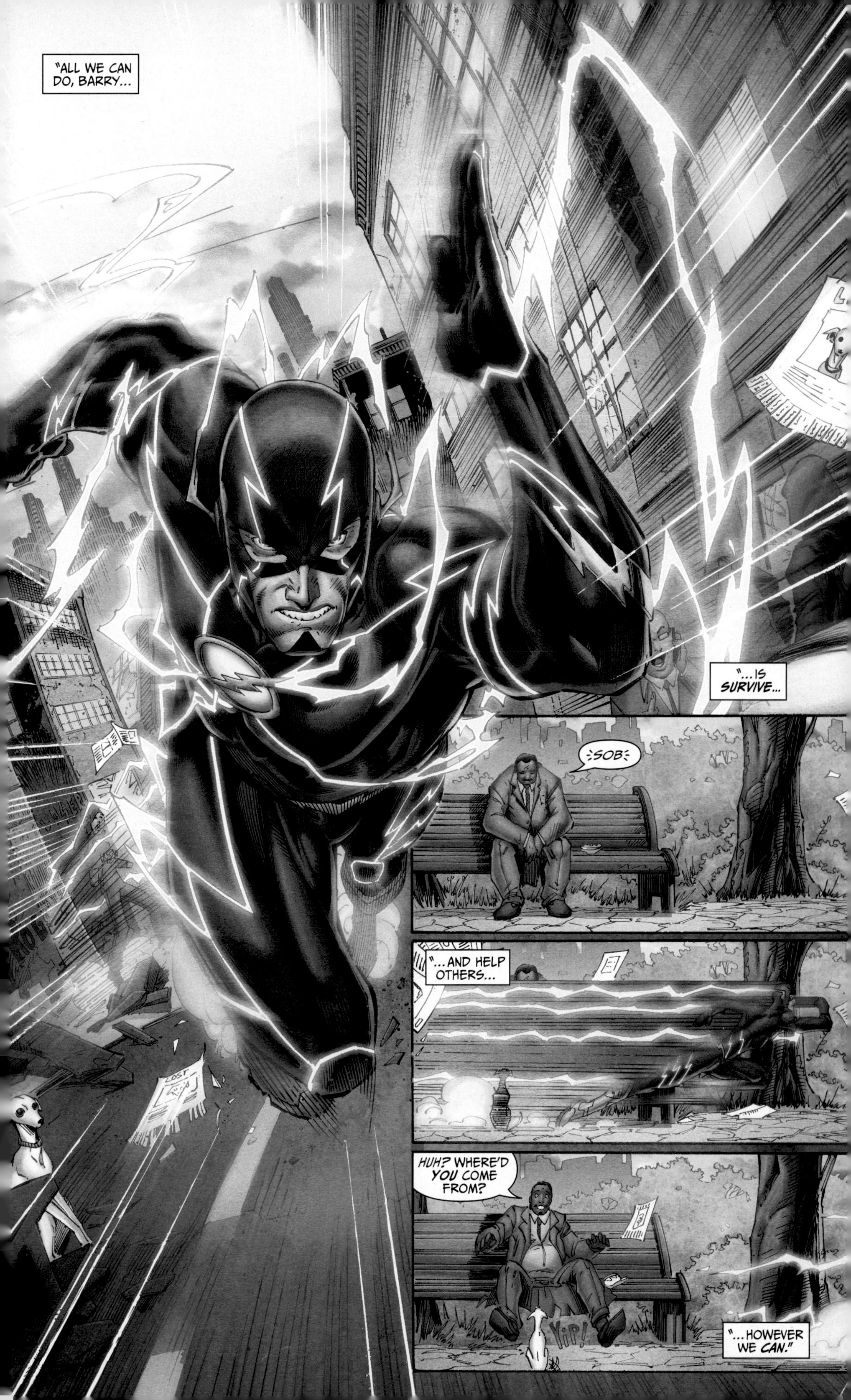
"ALL WE CAN DO, BARRY...
"...IS SURVIVE...
SOB
"...AND HELP OTHERS...
HUH? WHERE'D YOU COME FROM?
YIP!
"...HOWEVER WE CAN."

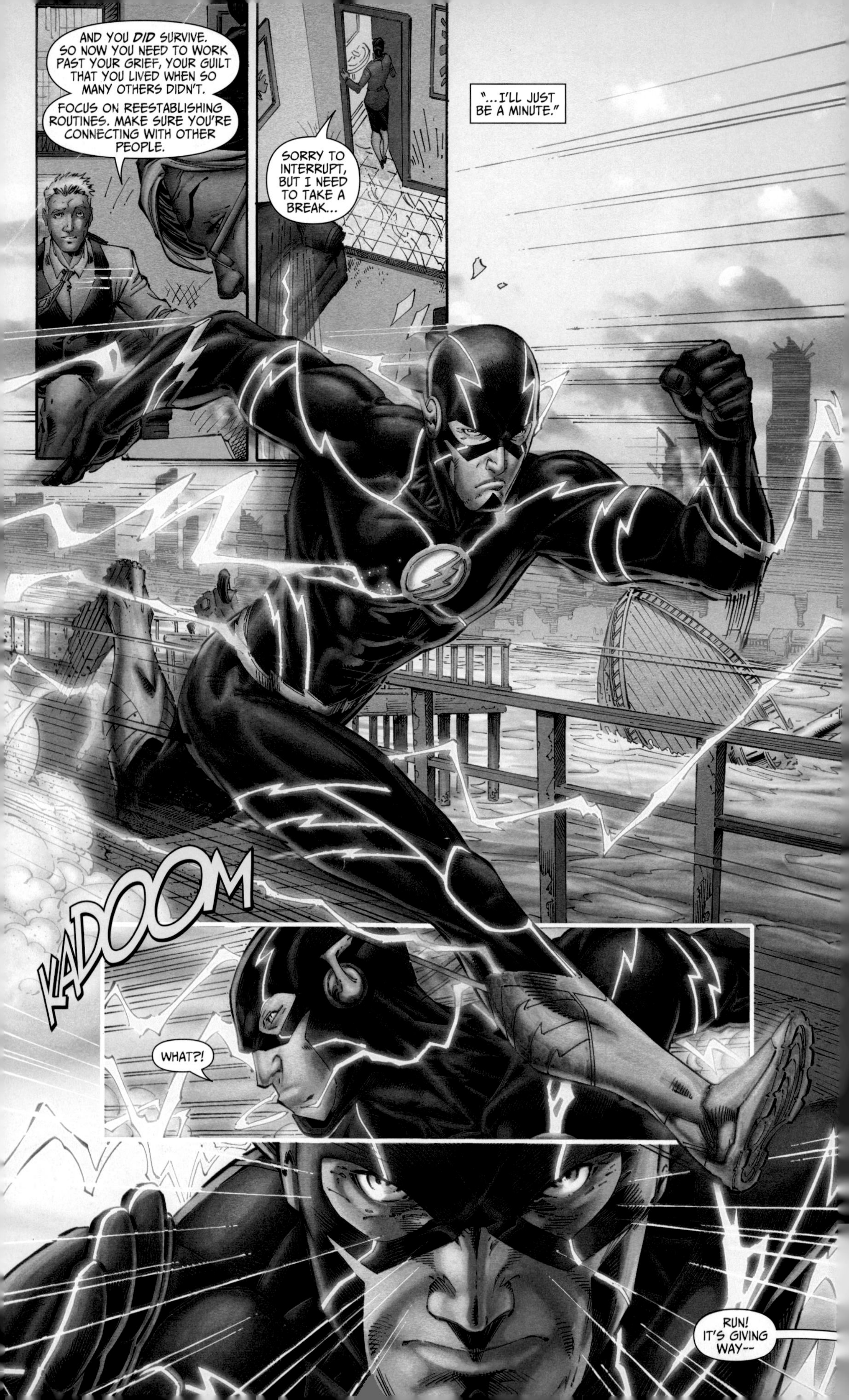
AND YOU *DID* SURVIVE. SO NOW YOU NEED TO WORK PAST YOUR GRIEF, YOUR GUILT THAT YOU LIVED WHEN SO MANY OTHERS DIDN'T.
FOCUS ON REESTABLISHING ROUTINES. MAKE SURE YOU'RE CONNECTING WITH OTHER PEOPLE.
SORRY TO INTERRUPT, BUT I NEED TO TAKE A BREAK...
"...I'LL JUST BE A MINUTE."
KADOOM
WHAT?!
RUN! IT'S GIVING WAY--

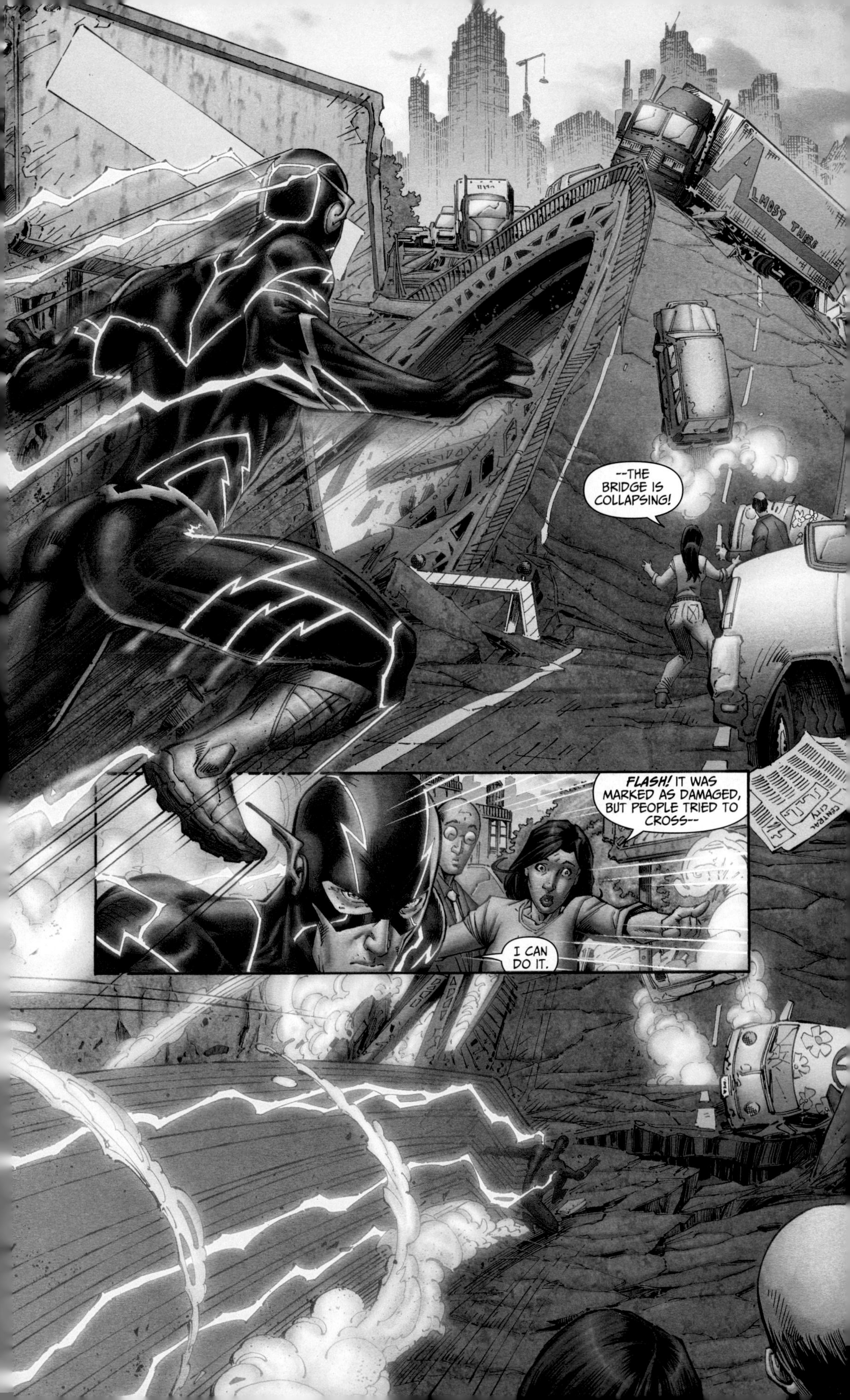
ALMOST THERE
--THE BRIDGE IS COLLAPSING!
FLASH! IT WAS MARKED AS DAMAGED, BUT PEOPLE TRIED TO CROSS--
CENTRAL CITY
I CAN DO IT.

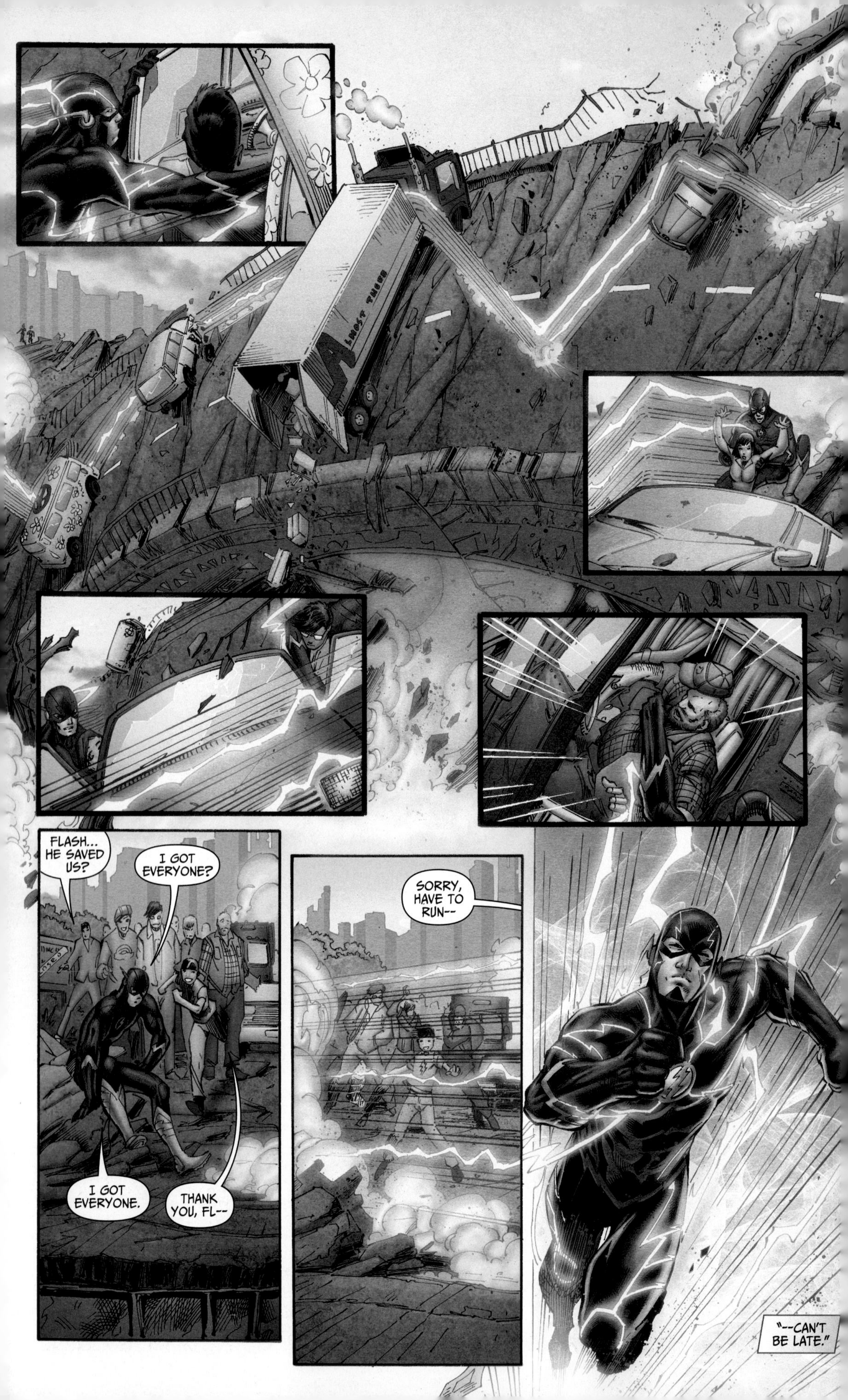
FLASH... HE SAVED US?
I GOT EVERYONE?
I GOT EVERYONE.
THANK YOU, FL--
SORRY, HAVE TO RUN--
"--CAN'T BE LATE."

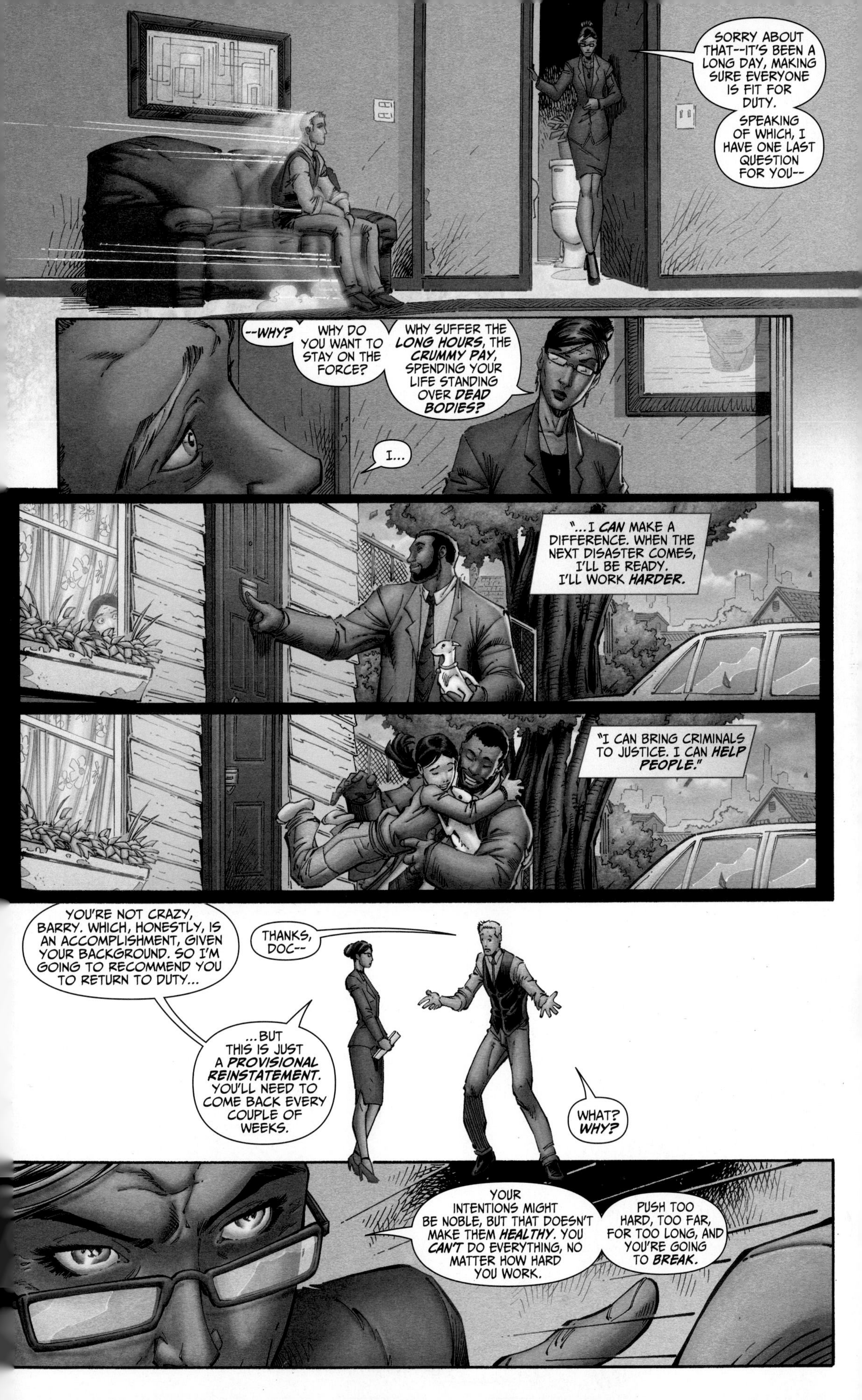
SORRY ABOUT THAT--IT'S BEEN A LONG DAY, MAKING SURE EVERYONE IS FIT FOR DUTY.
SPEAKING OF WHICH, I HAVE ONE LAST QUESTION FOR YOU--
--WHY?
WHY DO YOU WANT TO STAY ON THE FORCE?
WHY SUFFER THE LONG HOURS, THE CRUMMY PAY, SPENDING YOUR LIFE STANDING OVER DEAD BODIES?
I...
"...I CAN MAKE A DIFFERENCE. WHEN THE NEXT DISASTER COMES, I'LL BE READY. I'LL WORK HARDER.
"I CAN BRING CRIMINALS TO JUSTICE. I CAN HELP PEOPLE."
YOU'RE NOT CRAZY, BARRY. WHICH, HONESTLY, IS AN ACCOMPLISHMENT, GIVEN YOUR BACKGROUND. SO I'M GOING TO RECOMMEND YOU TO RETURN TO DUTY...
THANKS, DOC--
...BUT THIS IS JUST A PROVISIONAL REINSTATEMENT. YOU'LL NEED TO COME BACK EVERY COUPLE OF WEEKS.
WHAT? WHY?
YOUR INTENTIONS MIGHT BE NOBLE, BUT THAT DOESN'T MAKE THEM HEALTHY. YOU CAN'T DO EVERYTHING, NO MATTER HOW HARD YOU WORK.
PUSH TOO HARD, TOO FAR, FOR TOO LONG, AND YOU'RE GOING TO BREAK.

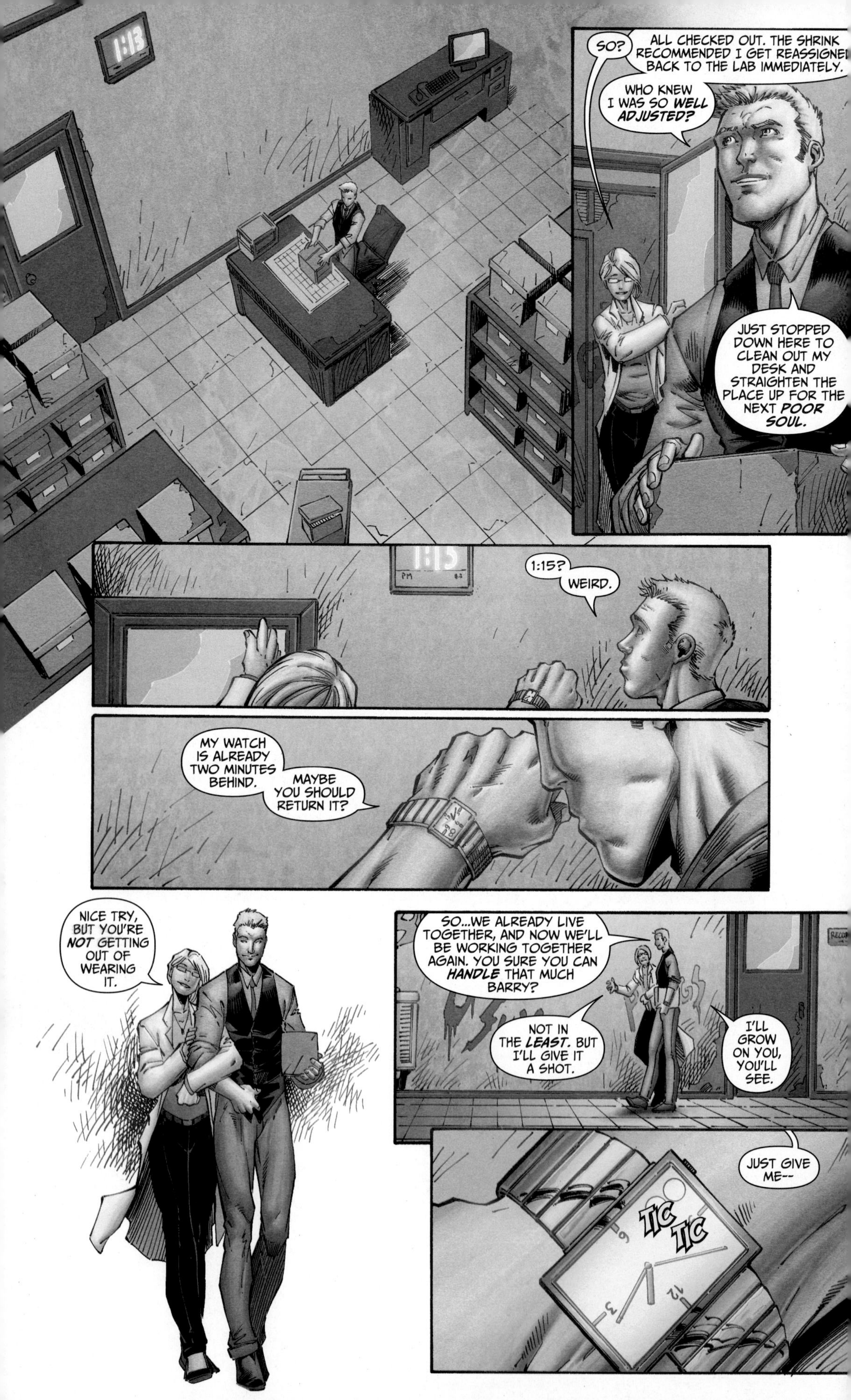

1:13
SO?
ALL CHECKED OUT. THE SHRINK RECOMMENDED I GET REASSIGNED BACK TO THE LAB IMMEDIATELY.
WHO KNEW I WAS SO WELL ADJUSTED?
JUST STOPPED DOWN HERE TO CLEAN OUT MY DESK AND STRAIGHTEN THE PLACE UP FOR THE NEXT POOR SOUL.
1:15
1:15?
WEIRD.
MY WATCH IS ALREADY TWO MINUTES BEHIND.
MAYBE YOU SHOULD RETURN IT?
NICE TRY, BUT YOU'RE NOT GETTING OUT OF WEARING IT.
SO...WE ALREADY LIVE TOGETHER, AND NOW WE'LL BE WORKING TOGETHER AGAIN. YOU SURE YOU CAN HANDLE THAT MUCH BARRY?
NOT IN THE LEAST. BUT I'LL GIVE IT A SHOT.
I'LL GROW ON YOU, YOU'LL SEE.
JUST GIVE ME--
TIC TIC

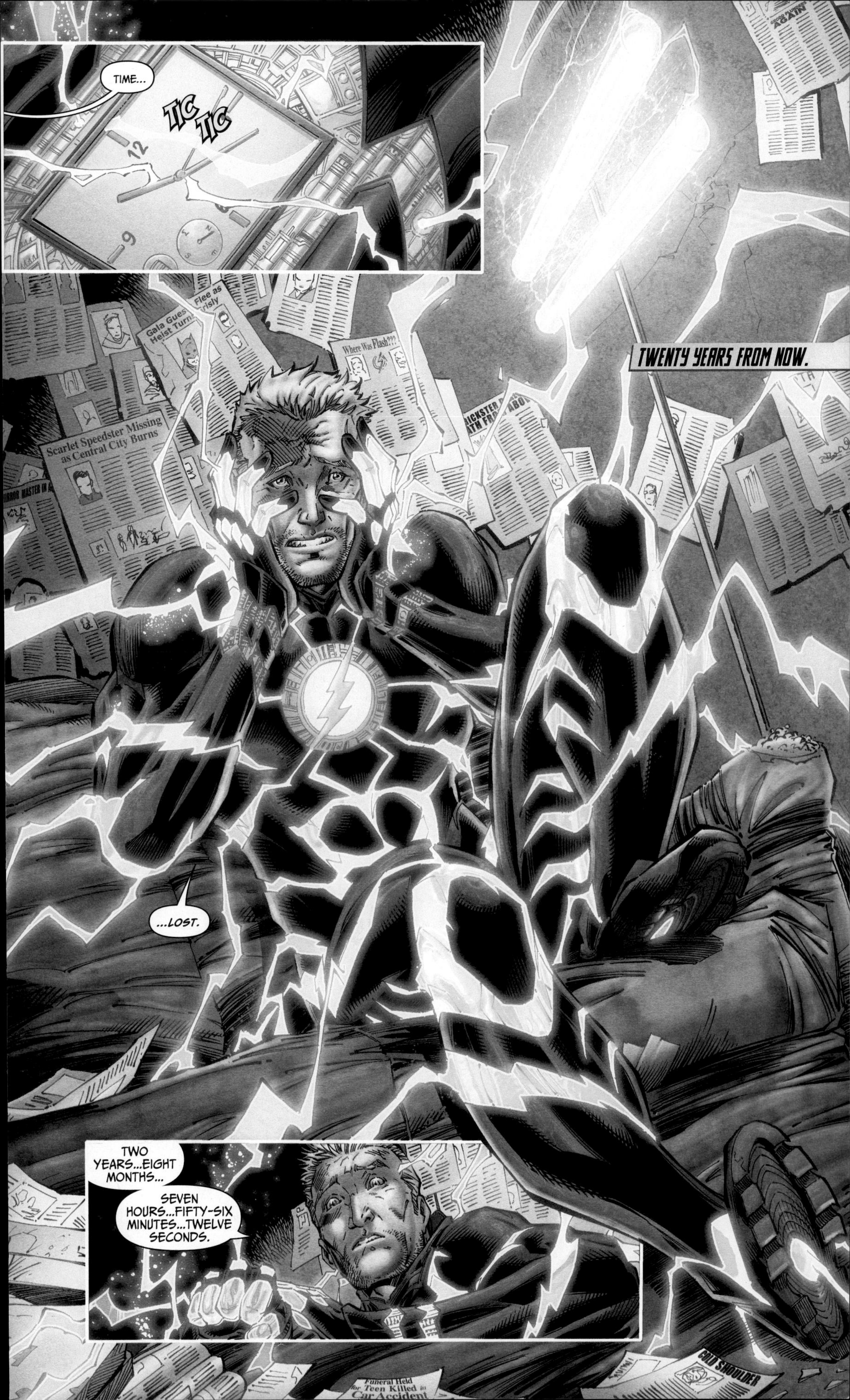
TIME...
TIC TIC
Where Was Flash???
TWENTY YEARS FROM NOW.
Scarlet Speedster Missing as Central City Burns
...LOST.
TWO YEARS...EIGHT MONTHS...
SEVEN HOURS...FIFTY-SIX MINUTES...TWELVE SECONDS.
Funeral Held for Teen Killed in Car Accident

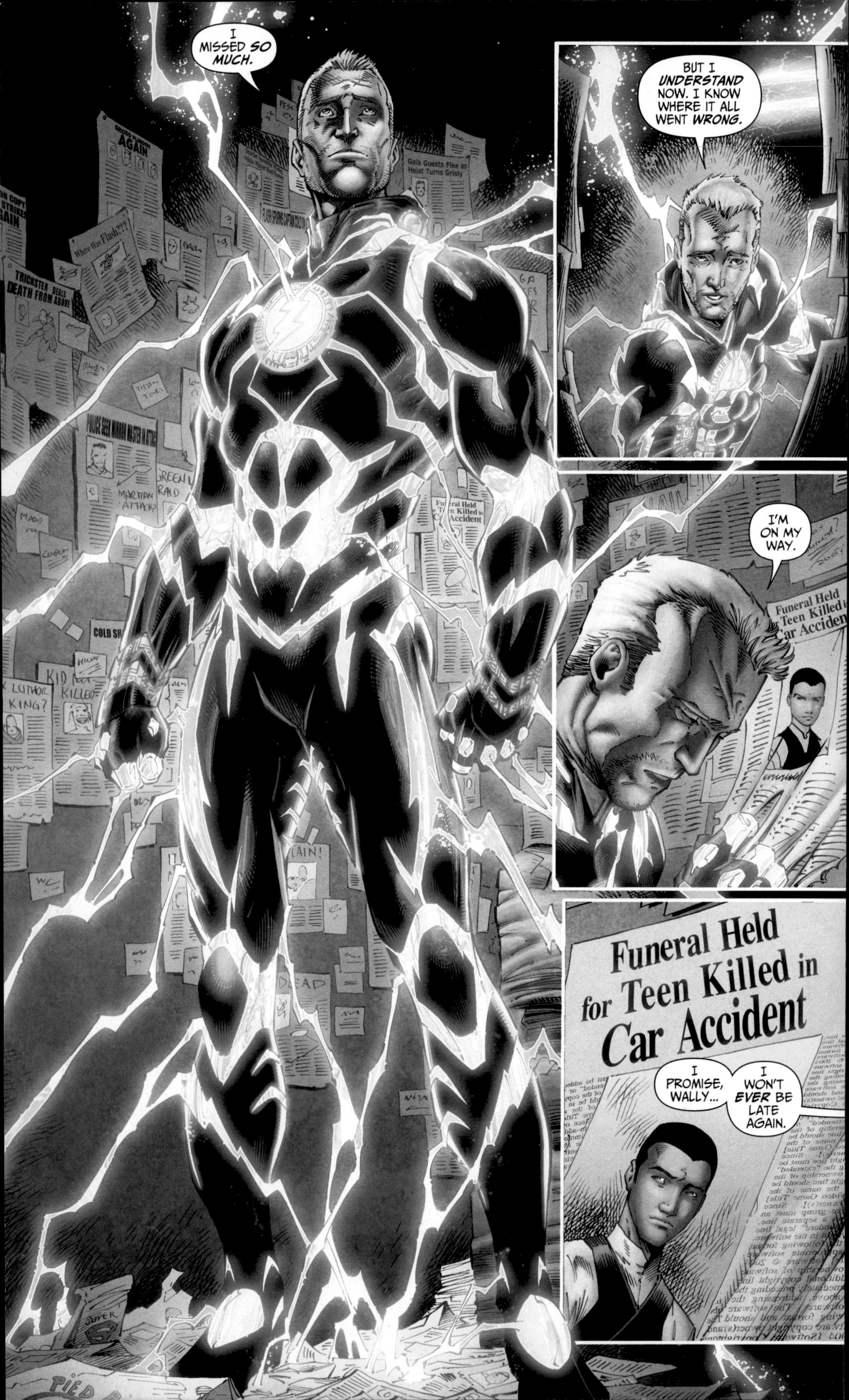
I MISSED SO MUCH.
BUT I UNDERSTAND NOW. I KNOW WHERE IT ALL WENT WRONG.
I'M ON MY WAY.
Funeral Held for Teen Killed in Car Accident
I PROMISE, WALLY...
I WON'T EVER BE LATE AGAIN.

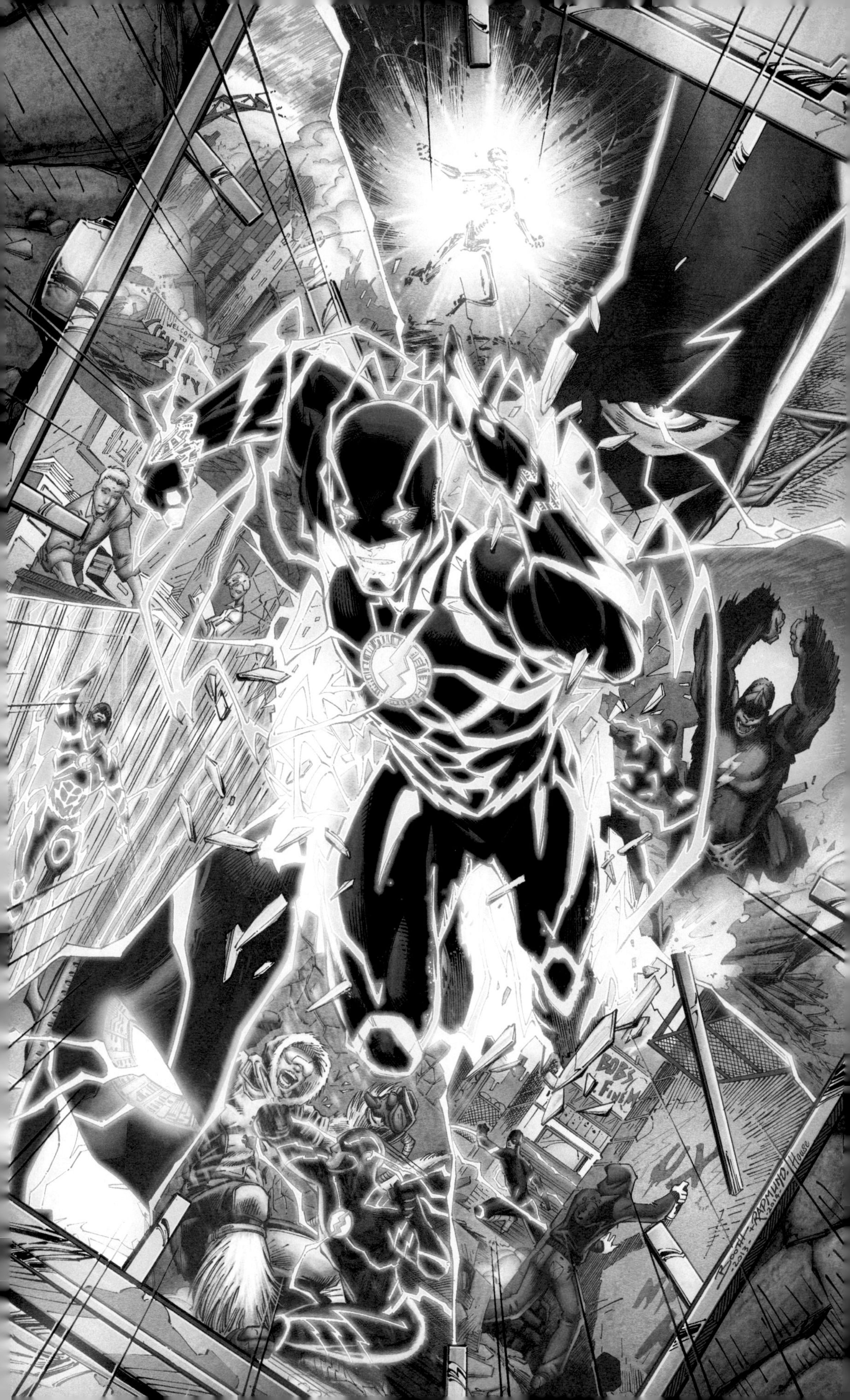
WELCOME TO
BOB'S
BOOTH -2013- + RAPMUND. -2014- House

SLIP

ROBERT VENDITTI & VAN JENSEN writers BRETT BOOTH penciller NORM RAPMUND inker (Future Flash)
RON FRENZ penciller LIVESAY inker (Present Flash)

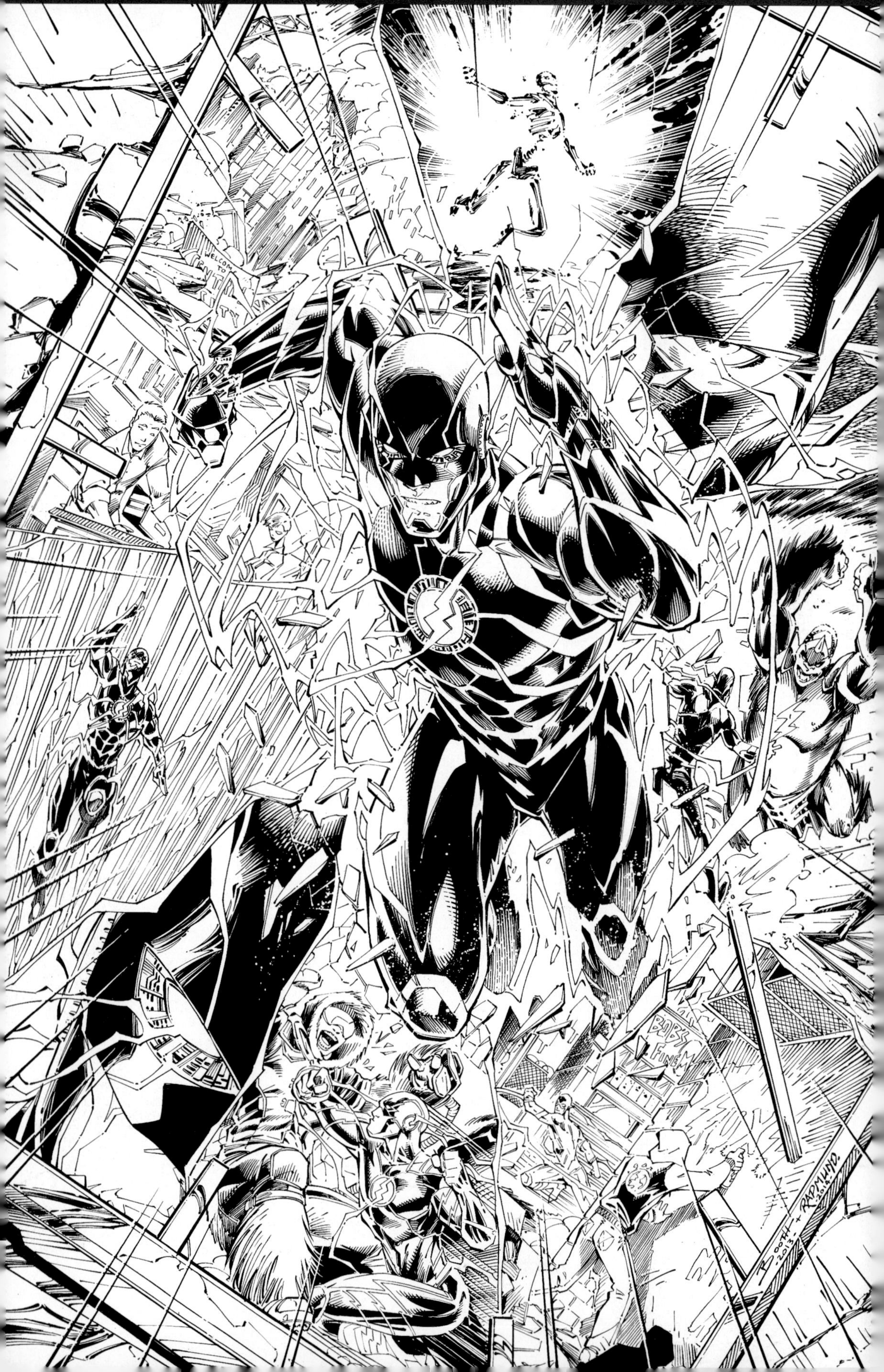
WELCOME TO
BOB'S
RAPMUND. 2014.

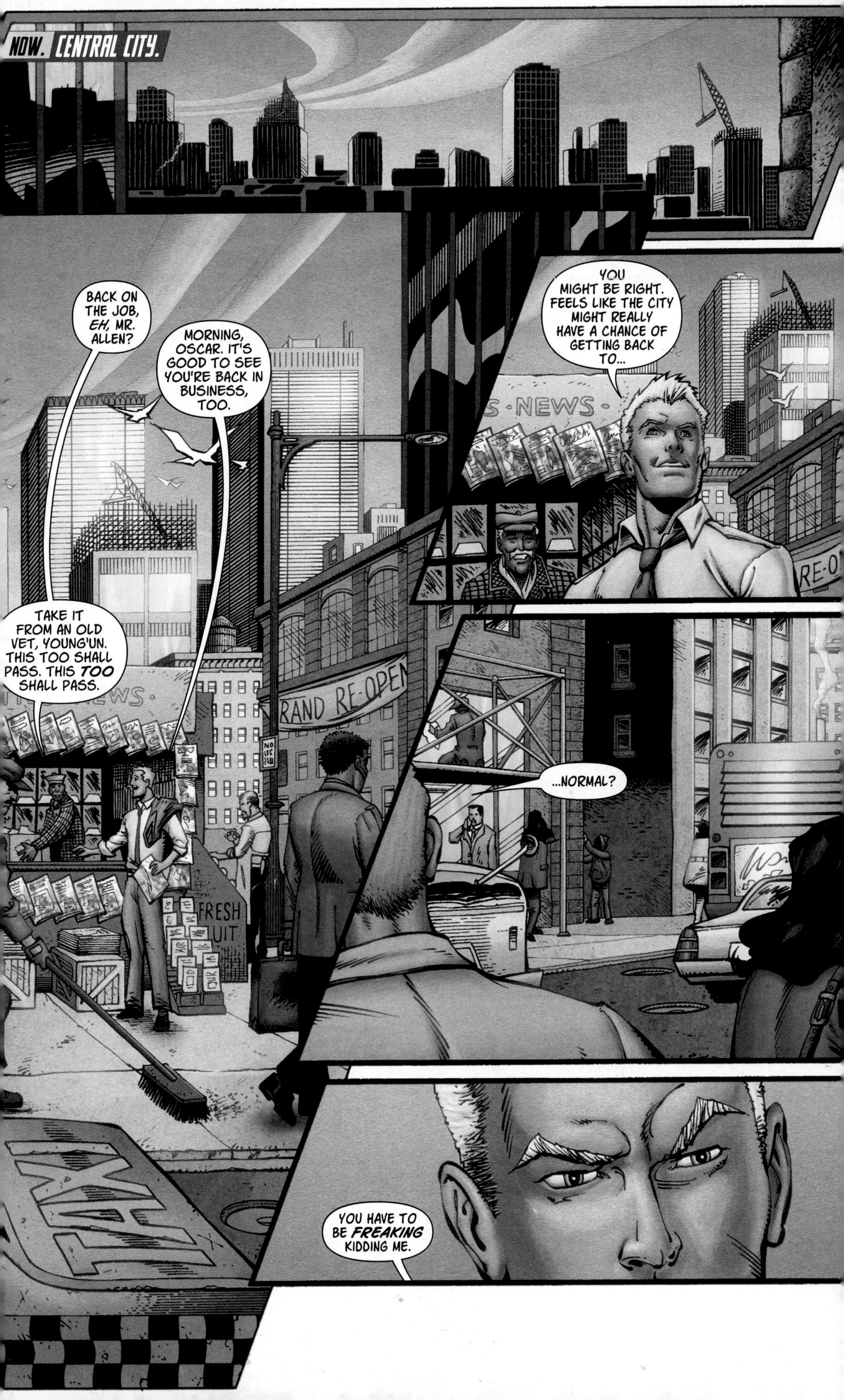
NOW. CENTRAL CITY.
BACK ON THE JOB, EH, MR. ALLEN?
MORNING, OSCAR. IT'S GOOD TO SEE YOU'RE BACK IN BUSINESS, TOO.
TAKE IT FROM AN OLD VET, YOUNG'UN. THIS TOO SHALL PASS. THIS TOO SHALL PASS.
YOU MIGHT BE RIGHT. FEELS LIKE THE CITY MIGHT REALLY HAVE A CHANCE OF GETTING BACK TO...
...NORMAL?
YOU HAVE TO BE FREAKING KIDDING ME.

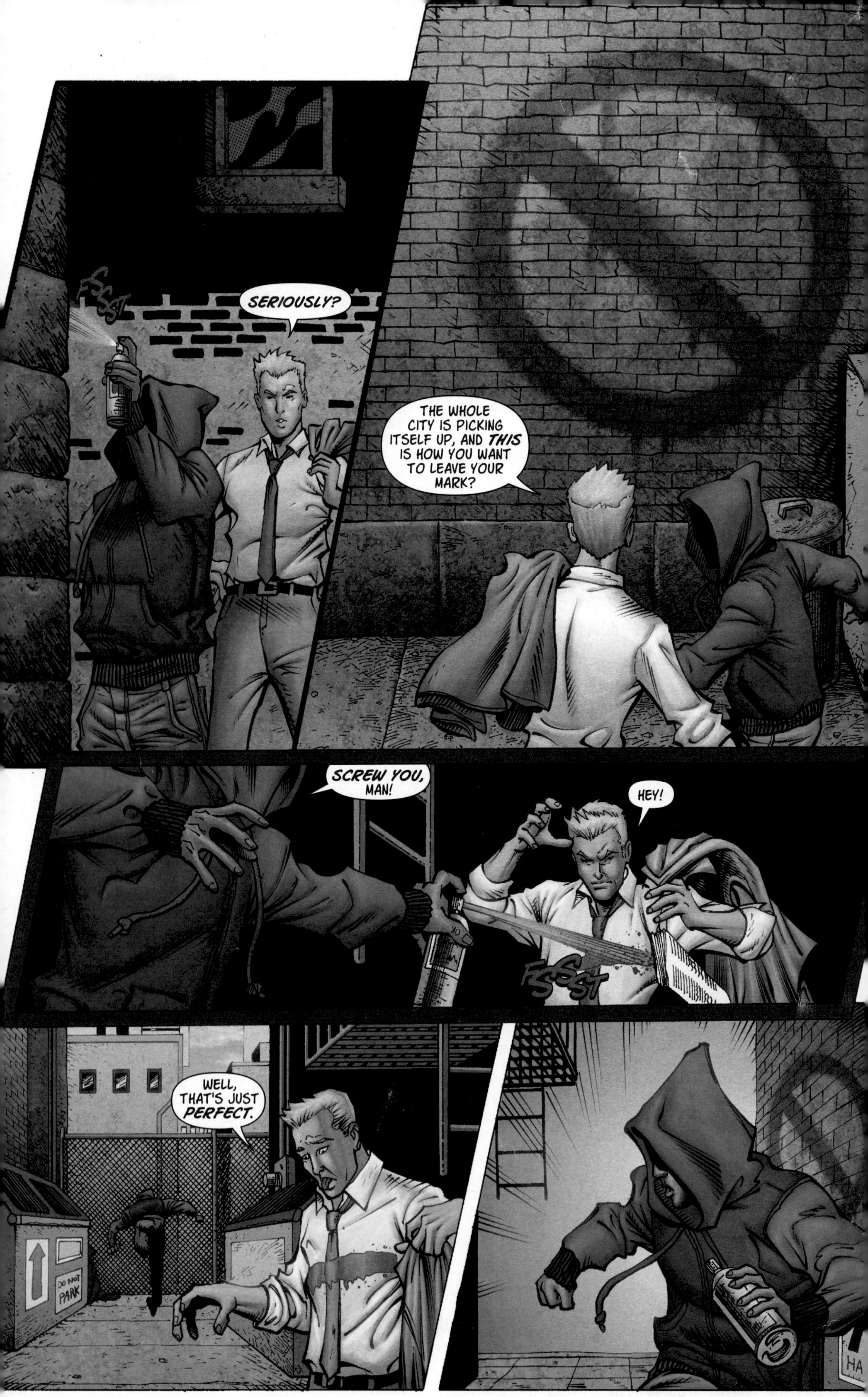
FSSST
SERIOUSLY?
THE WHOLE CITY IS PICKING ITSELF UP, AND THIS IS HOW YOU WANT TO LEAVE YOUR MARK?
SCREW YOU, MAN!
HEY!
FSSST
WELL, THAT'S JUST PERFECT.
DO NOT PARK

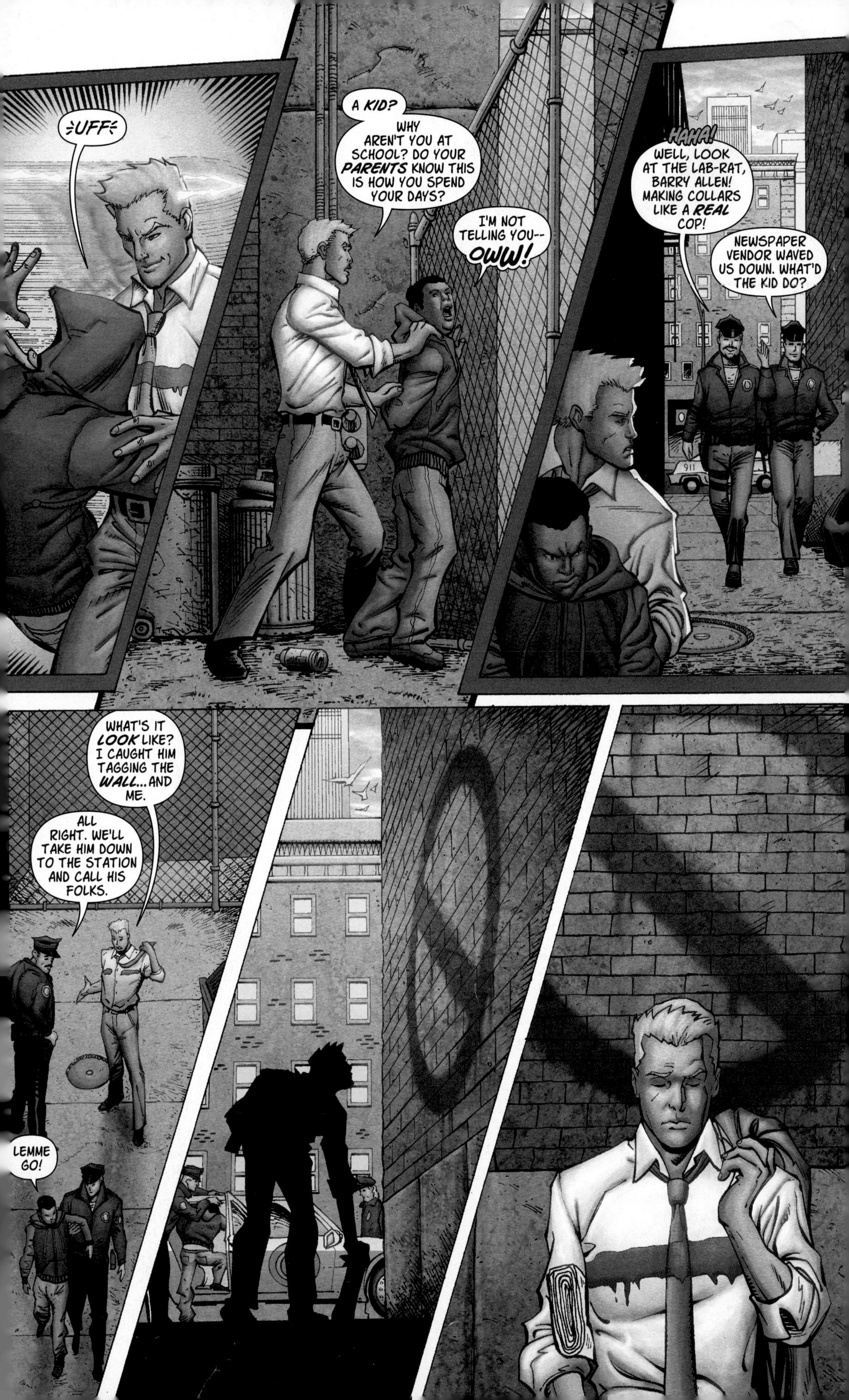
UFF
A KID?
WHY AREN'T YOU AT SCHOOL? DO YOUR PARENTS KNOW THIS IS HOW YOU SPEND YOUR DAYS?
I'M NOT TELLING YOU-- OWW!
HAHA!
WELL, LOOK AT THE LAB-RAT, BARRY ALLEN! MAKING COLLARS LIKE A REAL COP!
NEWSPAPER VENDOR WAVED US DOWN. WHAT'D THE KID DO?
WHAT'S IT LOOK LIKE? I CAUGHT HIM TAGGING THE WALL... AND ME.
ALL RIGHT. WE'LL TAKE HIM DOWN TO THE STATION AND CALL HIS FOLKS.
LEMME GO!

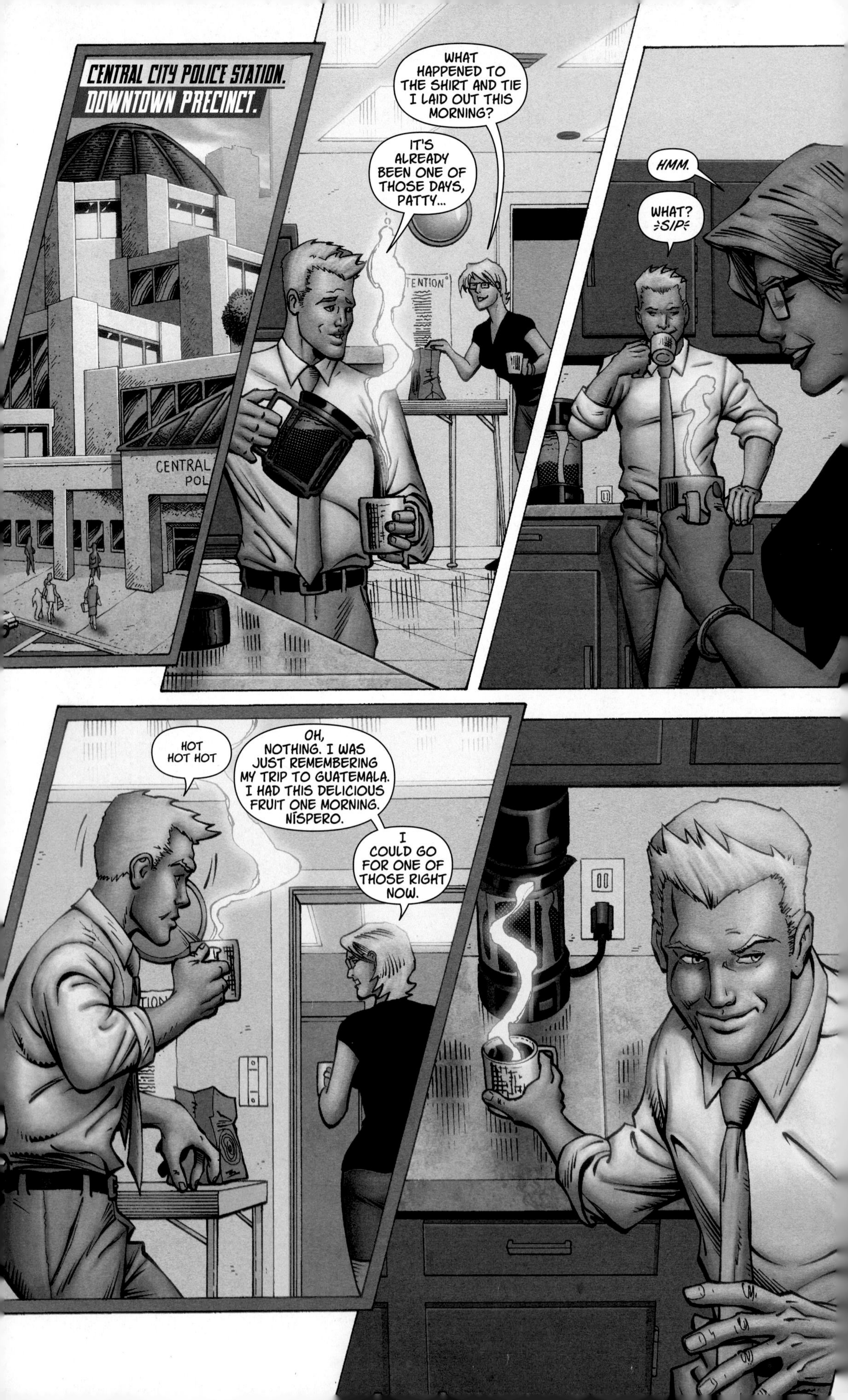
CENTRAL CITY POLICE STATION. DOWNTOWN PRECINCT.
CENTRAL POL
WHAT HAPPENED TO THE SHIRT AND TIE I LAID OUT THIS MORNING?
IT'S ALREADY BEEN ONE OF THOSE DAYS, PATTY...
TENTION
HMM.
WHAT? SIP
HOT HOT HOT
OH, NOTHING. I WAS JUST REMEMBERING MY TRIP TO GUATEMALA. I HAD THIS DELICIOUS FRUIT ONE MORNING. NÍSPERO.
I COULD GO FOR ONE OF THOSE RIGHT NOW.

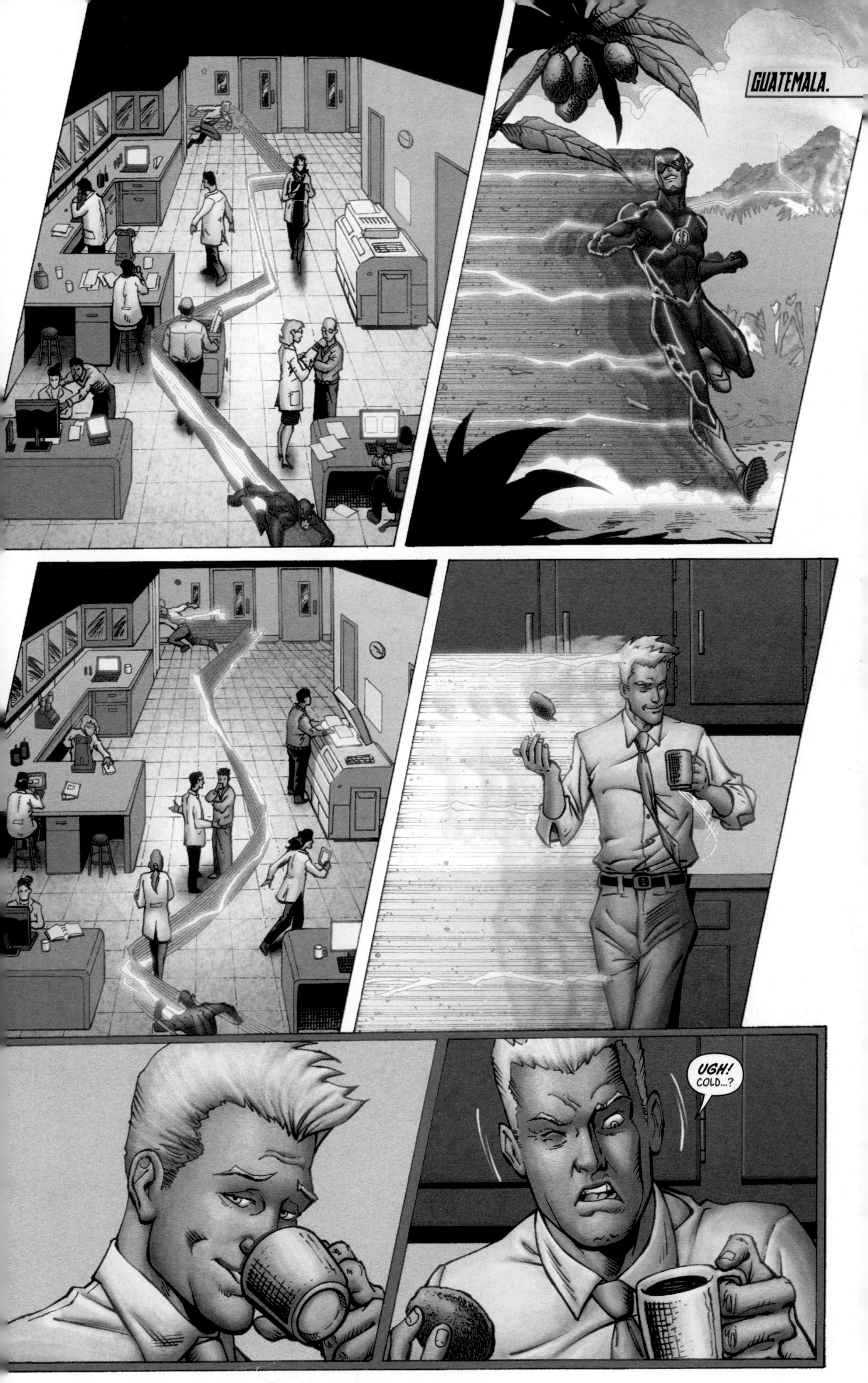
GUATEMALA.
UGH!
COLD...?

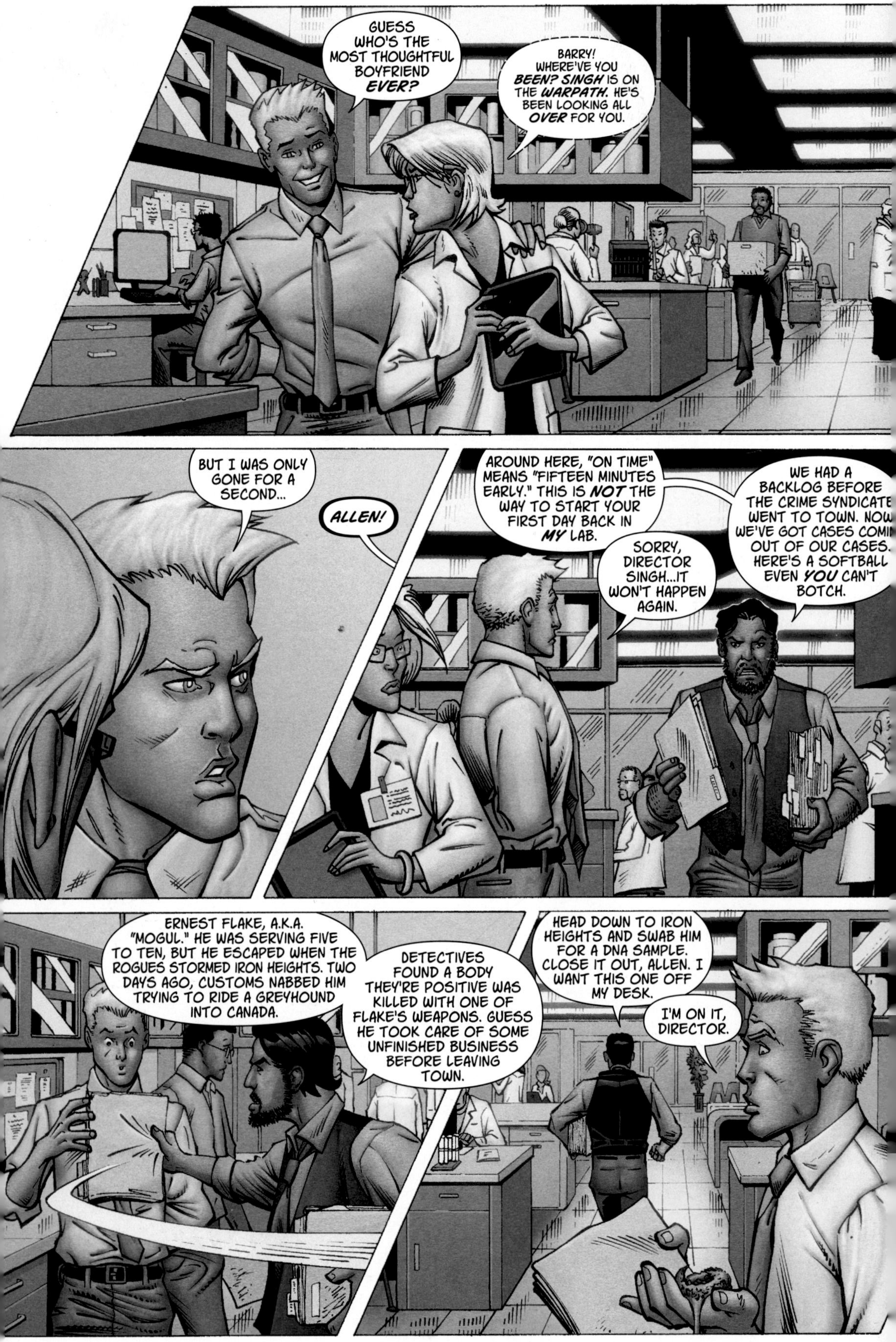
GUESS WHO'S THE MOST THOUGHTFUL BOYFRIEND *EVER?*
BARRY! WHERE'VE YOU *BEEN? SINGH* IS ON THE *WARPATH.* HE'S BEEN LOOKING ALL *OVER* FOR YOU.
BUT I WAS ONLY GONE FOR A SECOND...
ALLEN!
AROUND HERE, "ON TIME" MEANS "FIFTEEN MINUTES EARLY." THIS IS *NOT* THE WAY TO START YOUR FIRST DAY BACK IN *MY* LAB.
SORRY, DIRECTOR SINGH...IT WON'T HAPPEN AGAIN.
WE HAD A BACKLOG BEFORE THE CRIME SYNDICATE WENT TO TOWN. NOW WE'VE GOT CASES COMIN OUT OF OUR CASES. HERE'S A SOFTBALL EVEN *YOU* CAN'T BOTCH.
ERNEST FLAKE, A.K.A. "MOGUL." HE WAS SERVING FIVE TO TEN, BUT HE ESCAPED WHEN THE ROGUES STORMED IRON HEIGHTS. TWO DAYS AGO, CUSTOMS NABBED HIM TRYING TO RIDE A GREYHOUND INTO CANADA.
DETECTIVES FOUND A BODY THEY'RE POSITIVE WAS KILLED WITH ONE OF FLAKE'S WEAPONS. GUESS HE TOOK CARE OF SOME UNFINISHED BUSINESS BEFORE LEAVING TOWN.
HEAD DOWN TO IRON HEIGHTS AND SWAB HIM FOR A DNA SAMPLE. CLOSE IT OUT, ALLEN. I WANT THIS ONE OFF MY DESK.
I'M ON IT, DIRECTOR.

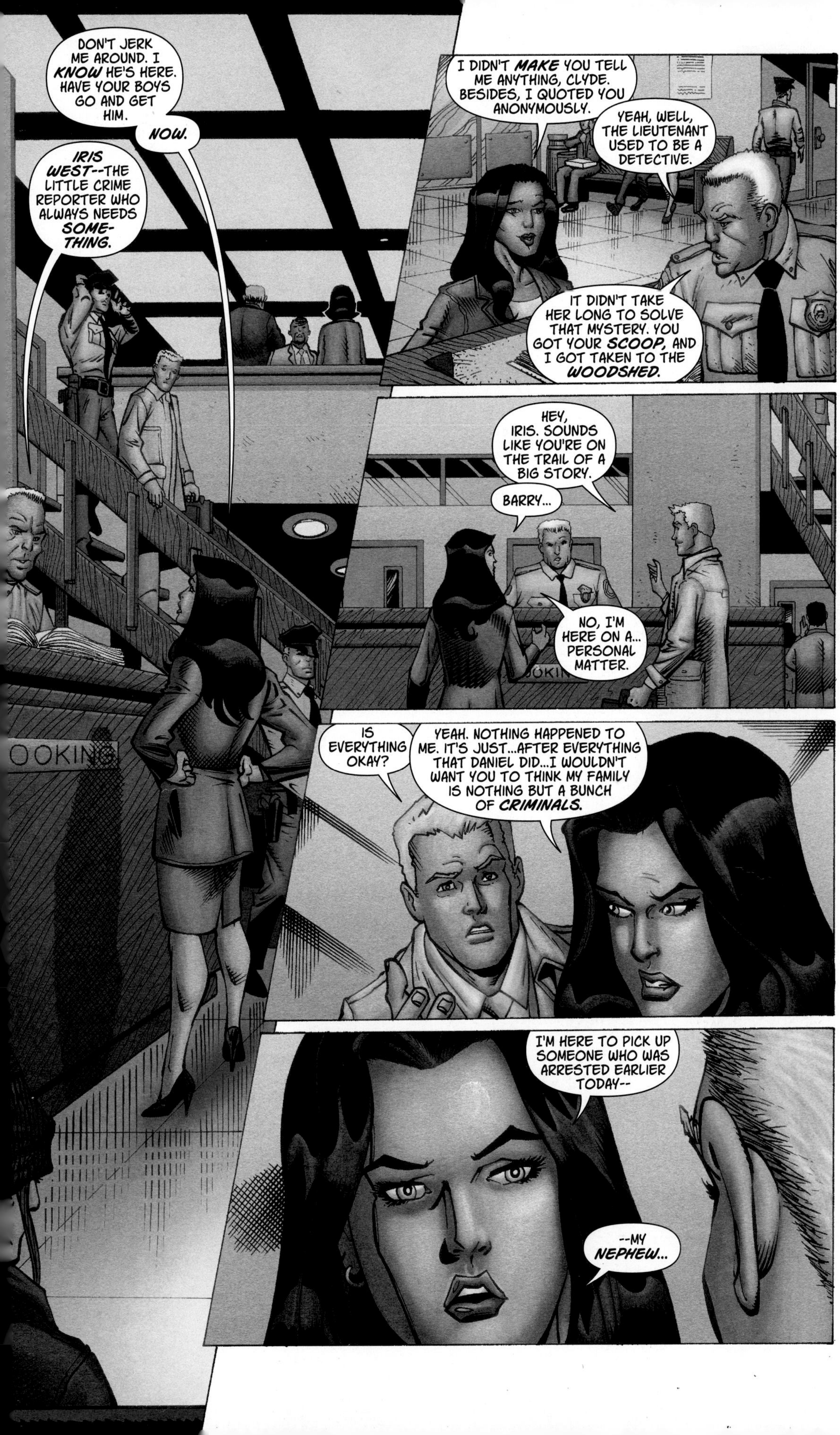

DON'T JERK ME AROUND. I KNOW HE'S HERE. HAVE YOUR BOYS GO AND GET HIM.
NOW.
IRIS WEST--THE LITTLE CRIME REPORTER WHO ALWAYS NEEDS SOME-THING.
BOOKING
I DIDN'T MAKE YOU TELL ME ANYTHING, CLYDE. BESIDES, I QUOTED YOU ANONYMOUSLY.
YEAH, WELL, THE LIEUTENANT USED TO BE A DETECTIVE.
IT DIDN'T TAKE HER LONG TO SOLVE THAT MYSTERY. YOU GOT YOUR SCOOP, AND I GOT TAKEN TO THE WOODSHED.
HEY, IRIS. SOUNDS LIKE YOU'RE ON THE TRAIL OF A BIG STORY.
BARRY...
NO, I'M HERE ON A... PERSONAL MATTER.
IS EVERYTHING OKAY?
YEAH. NOTHING HAPPENED TO ME. IT'S JUST...AFTER EVERYTHING THAT DANIEL DID...I WOULDN'T WANT YOU TO THINK MY FAMILY IS NOTHING BUT A BUNCH OF CRIMINALS.
I'M HERE TO PICK UP SOMEONE WHO WAS ARRESTED EARLIER TODAY--
--MY NEPHEW...

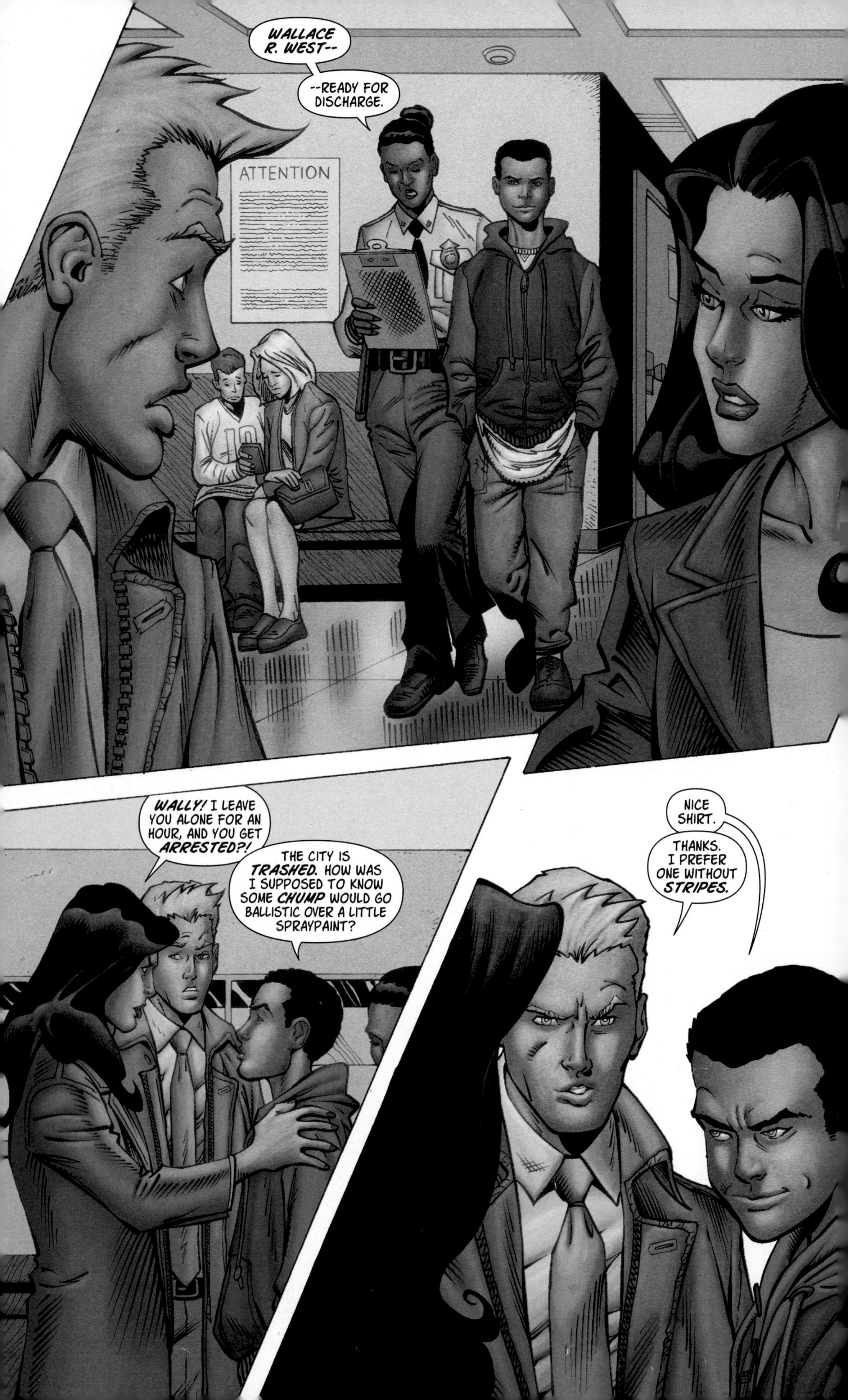
WALLACE R. WEST--
--READY FOR DISCHARGE.
ATTENTION
WALLY! I LEAVE YOU ALONE FOR AN HOUR, AND YOU GET ARRESTED?!
THE CITY IS TRASHED. HOW WAS I SUPPOSED TO KNOW SOME CHUMP WOULD GO BALLISTIC OVER A LITTLE SPRAYPAINT?
NICE SHIRT.
THANKS. I PREFER ONE WITHOUT STRIPES.

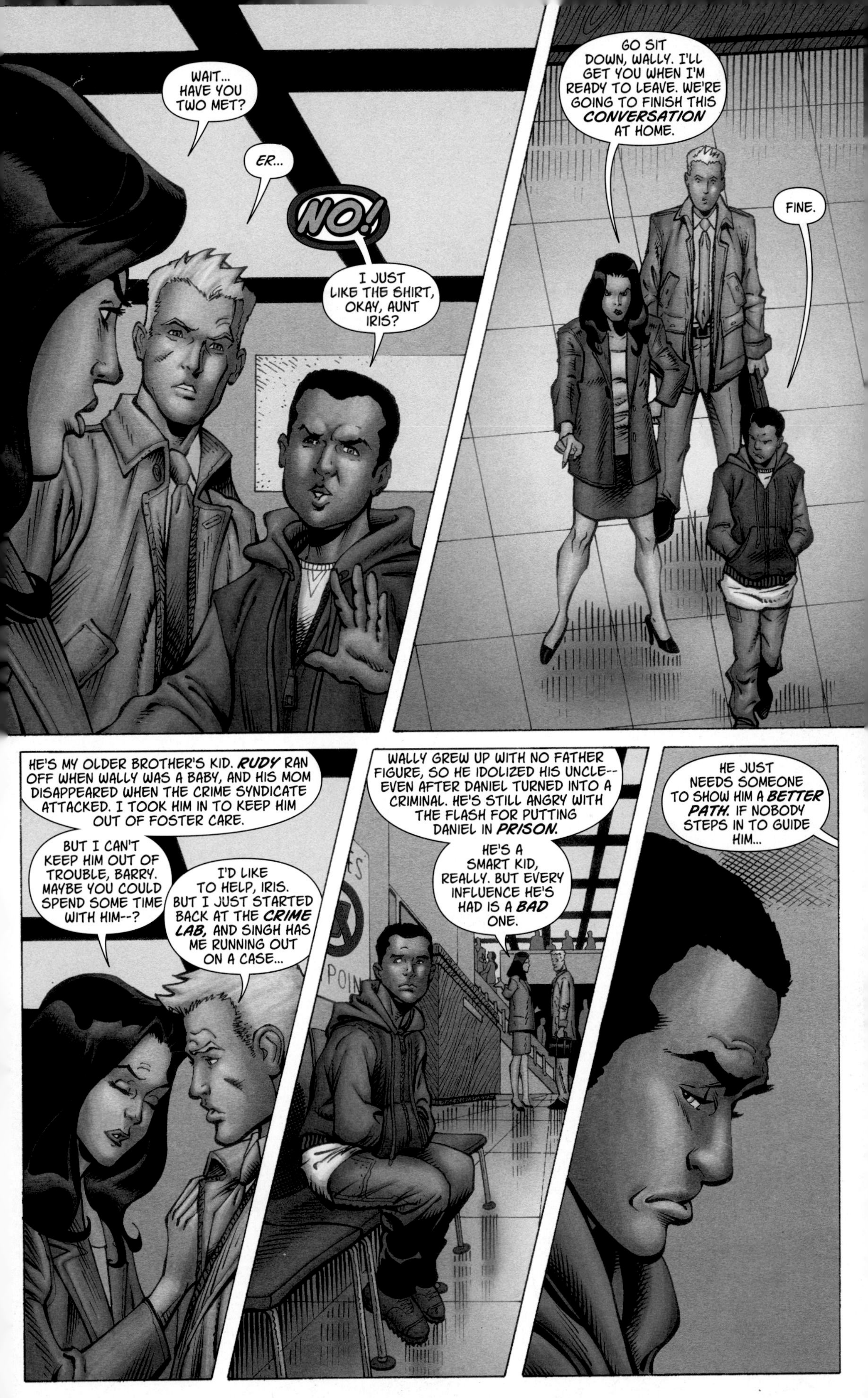

WAIT... HAVE YOU TWO MET?
ER...
NO!
I JUST LIKE THE SHIRT, OKAY, AUNT IRIS?
GO SIT DOWN, WALLY. I'LL GET YOU WHEN I'M READY TO LEAVE. WE'RE GOING TO FINISH THIS CONVERSATION AT HOME.
FINE.
HE'S MY OLDER BROTHER'S KID. RUDY RAN OFF WHEN WALLY WAS A BABY, AND HIS MOM DISAPPEARED WHEN THE CRIME SYNDICATE ATTACKED. I TOOK HIM IN TO KEEP HIM OUT OF FOSTER CARE.
BUT I CAN'T KEEP HIM OUT OF TROUBLE, BARRY. MAYBE YOU COULD SPEND SOME TIME WITH HIM--?
I'D LIKE TO HELP, IRIS. BUT I JUST STARTED BACK AT THE CRIME LAB, AND SINGH HAS ME RUNNING OUT ON A CASE...
WALLY GREW UP WITH NO FATHER FIGURE, SO HE IDOLIZED HIS UNCLE-- EVEN AFTER DANIEL TURNED INTO A CRIMINAL. HE'S STILL ANGRY WITH THE FLASH FOR PUTTING DANIEL IN PRISON.
HE'S A SMART KID, REALLY. BUT EVERY INFLUENCE HE'S HAD IS A BAD ONE.
HE JUST NEEDS SOMEONE TO SHOW HIM A BETTER PATH. IF NOBODY STEPS IN TO GUIDE HIM...

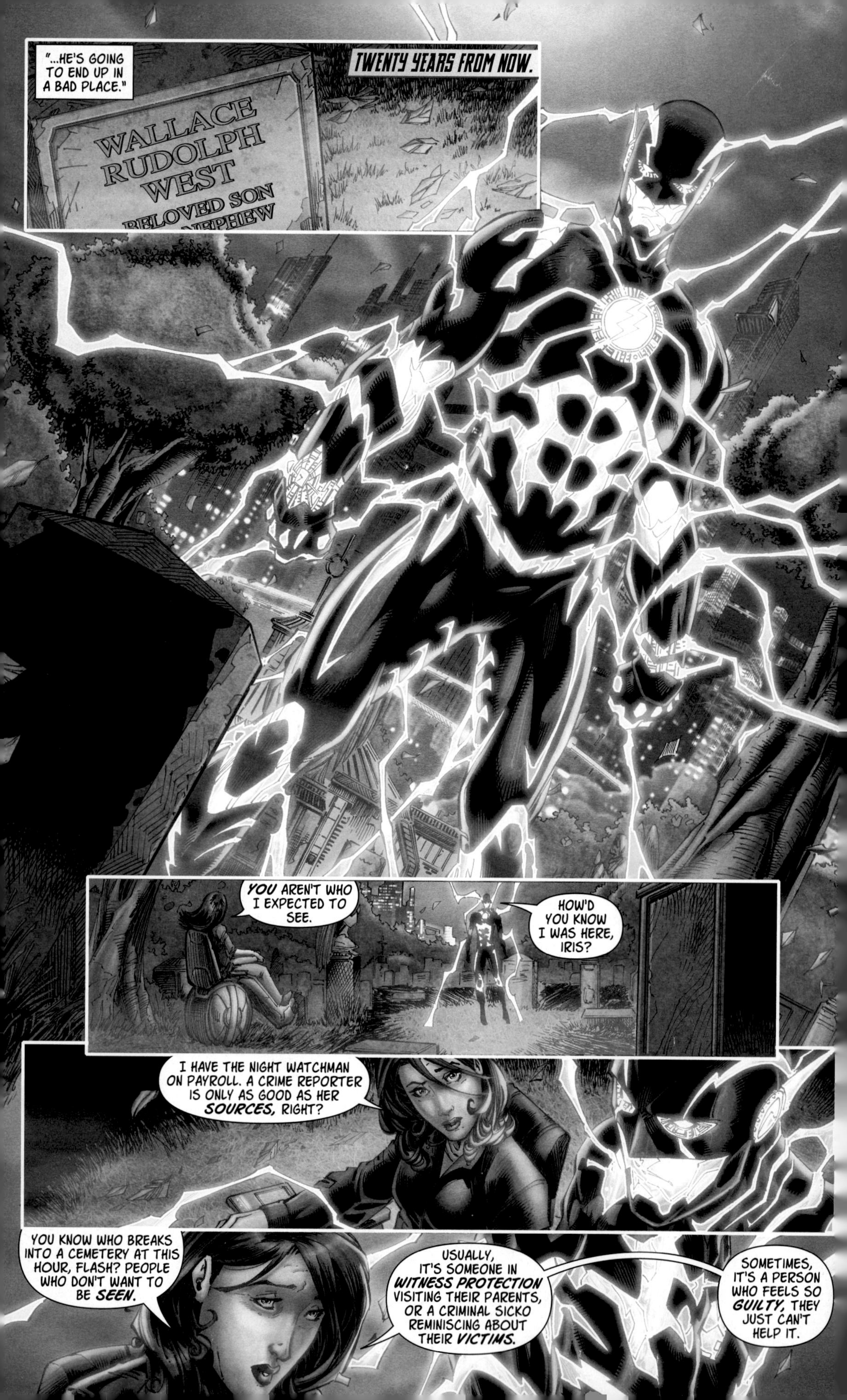
"...HE'S GOING TO END UP IN A BAD PLACE."
TWENTY YEARS FROM NOW.
WALLACE RUDOLPH WEST BELOVED SON
YOU AREN'T WHO I EXPECTED TO SEE.
HOW'D YOU KNOW I WAS HERE, IRIS?
I HAVE THE NIGHT WATCHMAN ON PAYROLL. A CRIME REPORTER IS ONLY AS GOOD AS HER SOURCES, RIGHT?
YOU KNOW WHO BREAKS INTO A CEMETERY AT THIS HOUR, FLASH? PEOPLE WHO DON'T WANT TO BE SEEN.
USUALLY, IT'S SOMEONE IN WITNESS PROTECTION VISITING THEIR PARENTS, OR A CRIMINAL SICKO REMINISCING ABOUT THEIR VICTIMS.
SOMETIMES, IT'S A PERSON WHO FEELS SO GUILTY, THEY JUST CAN'T HELP IT.

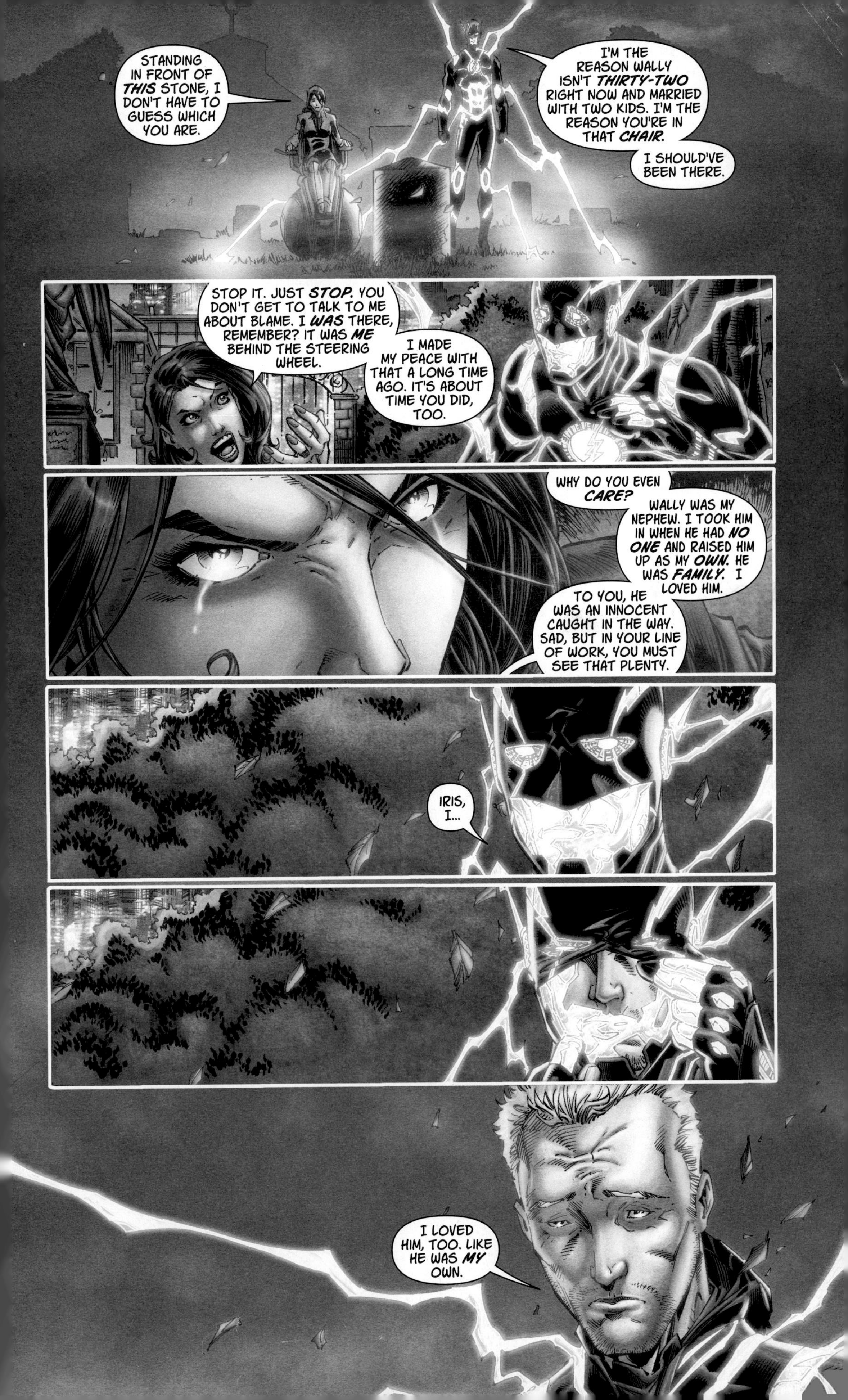
STANDING IN FRONT OF THIS STONE, I DON'T HAVE TO GUESS WHICH YOU ARE.
I'M THE REASON WALLY ISN'T THIRTY-TWO RIGHT NOW AND MARRIED WITH TWO KIDS. I'M THE REASON YOU'RE IN THAT CHAIR.
I SHOULD'VE BEEN THERE.
STOP IT. JUST STOP. YOU DON'T GET TO TALK TO ME ABOUT BLAME. I WAS THERE, REMEMBER? IT WAS ME BEHIND THE STEERING WHEEL.
I MADE MY PEACE WITH THAT A LONG TIME AGO. IT'S ABOUT TIME YOU DID, TOO.
WHY DO YOU EVEN CARE?
WALLY WAS MY NEPHEW. I TOOK HIM IN WHEN HE HAD NO ONE AND RAISED HIM UP AS MY OWN. HE WAS FAMILY. I LOVED HIM.
TO YOU, HE WAS AN INNOCENT CAUGHT IN THE WAY. SAD, BUT IN YOUR LINE OF WORK, YOU MUST SEE THAT PLENTY.
IRIS, I...
I LOVED HIM, TOO. LIKE HE WAS MY OWN.

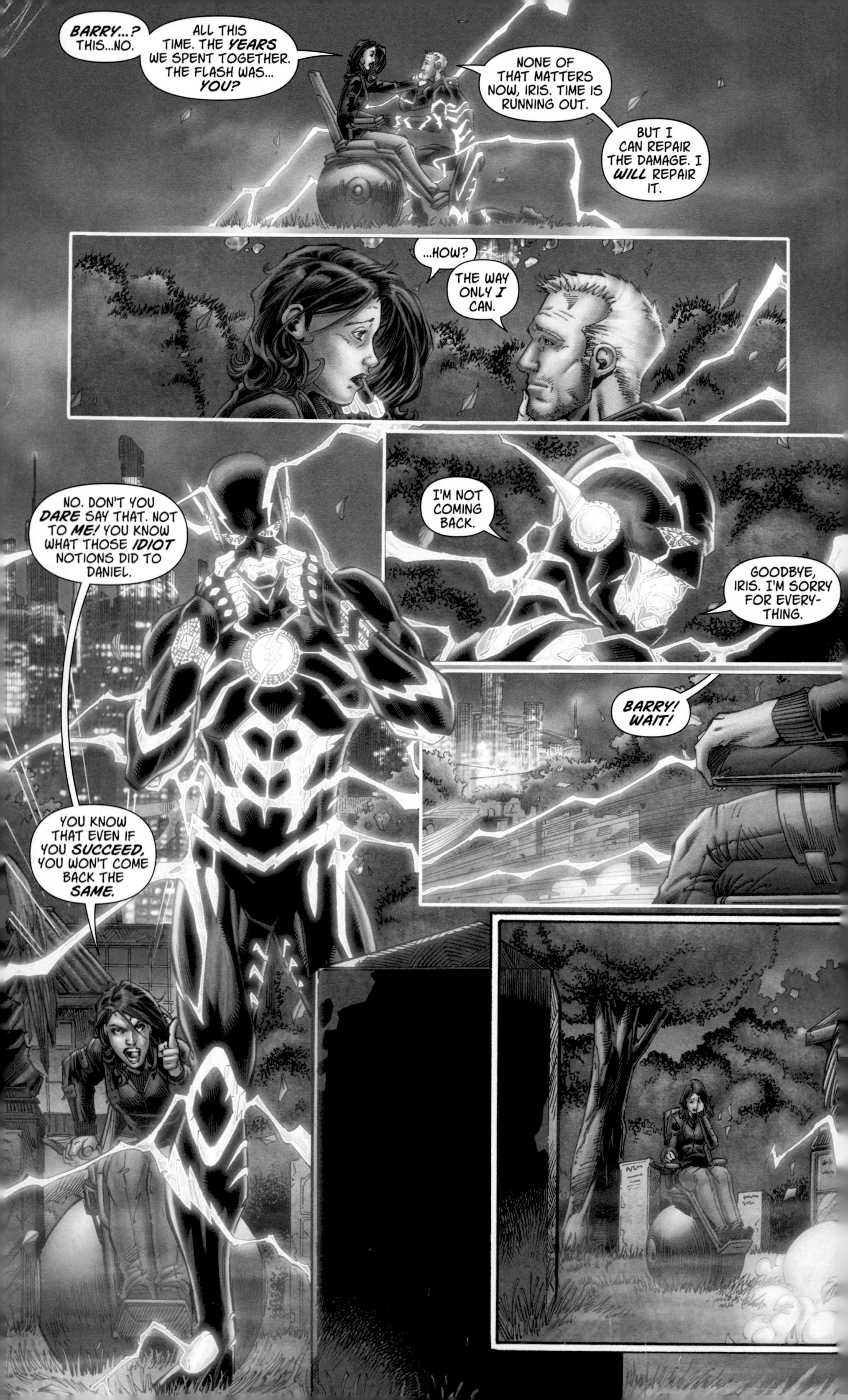
BARRY...? THIS...NO.
ALL THIS TIME. THE YEARS WE SPENT TOGETHER. THE FLASH WAS... YOU?
NONE OF THAT MATTERS NOW, IRIS. TIME IS RUNNING OUT.
BUT I CAN REPAIR THE DAMAGE. I WILL REPAIR IT.
...HOW?
THE WAY ONLY I CAN.
NO. DON'T YOU DARE SAY THAT. NOT TO ME! YOU KNOW WHAT THOSE IDIOT NOTIONS DID TO DANIEL.
YOU KNOW THAT EVEN IF YOU SUCCEED, YOU WON'T COME BACK THE SAME.
I'M NOT COMING BACK.
GOODBYE, IRIS. I'M SORRY FOR EVERY-THING.
BARRY! WAIT!

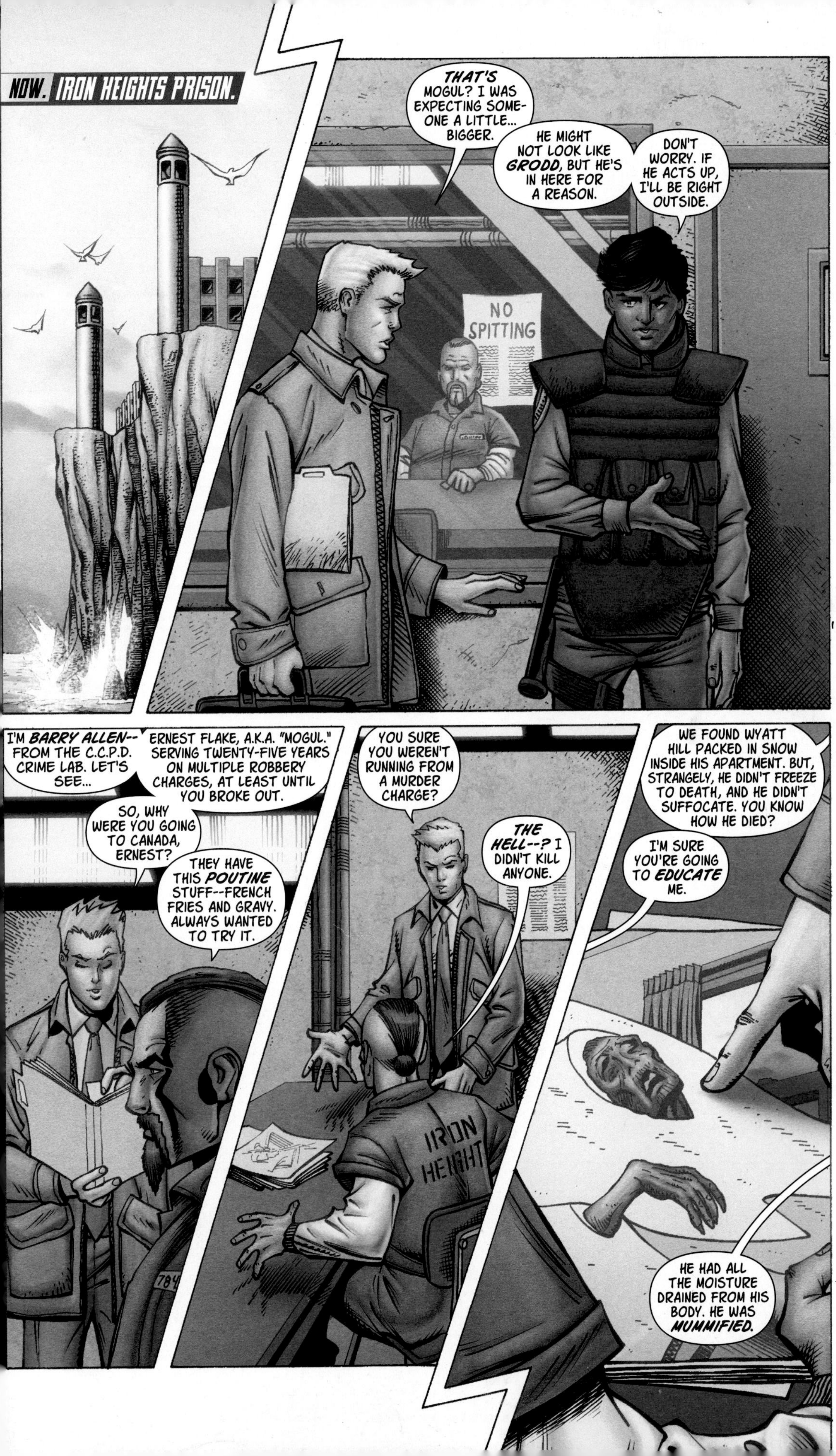
NOW. IRON HEIGHTS PRISON.
THAT'S MOGUL? I WAS EXPECTING SOME-ONE A LITTLE... BIGGER.
HE MIGHT NOT LOOK LIKE GRODD, BUT HE'S IN HERE FOR A REASON.
DON'T WORRY. IF HE ACTS UP, I'LL BE RIGHT OUTSIDE.
NO SPITTING
I'M BARRY ALLEN-- FROM THE C.C.P.D. CRIME LAB. LET'S SEE...
ERNEST FLAKE, A.K.A. "MOGUL." SERVING TWENTY-FIVE YEARS ON MULTIPLE ROBBERY CHARGES, AT LEAST UNTIL YOU BROKE OUT.
SO, WHY WERE YOU GOING TO CANADA, ERNEST?
THEY HAVE THIS POUTINE STUFF--FRENCH FRIES AND GRAVY. ALWAYS WANTED TO TRY IT.
YOU SURE YOU WEREN'T RUNNING FROM A MURDER CHARGE?
THE HELL--? I DIDN'T KILL ANYONE.
IRON HEIGHT
WE FOUND WYATT HILL PACKED IN SNOW INSIDE HIS APARTMENT. BUT, STRANGELY, HE DIDN'T FREEZE TO DEATH, AND HE DIDN'T SUFFOCATE. YOU KNOW HOW HE DIED?
I'M SURE YOU'RE GOING TO EDUCATE ME.
HE HAD ALL THE MOISTURE DRAINED FROM HIS BODY. HE WAS MUMMIFIED.

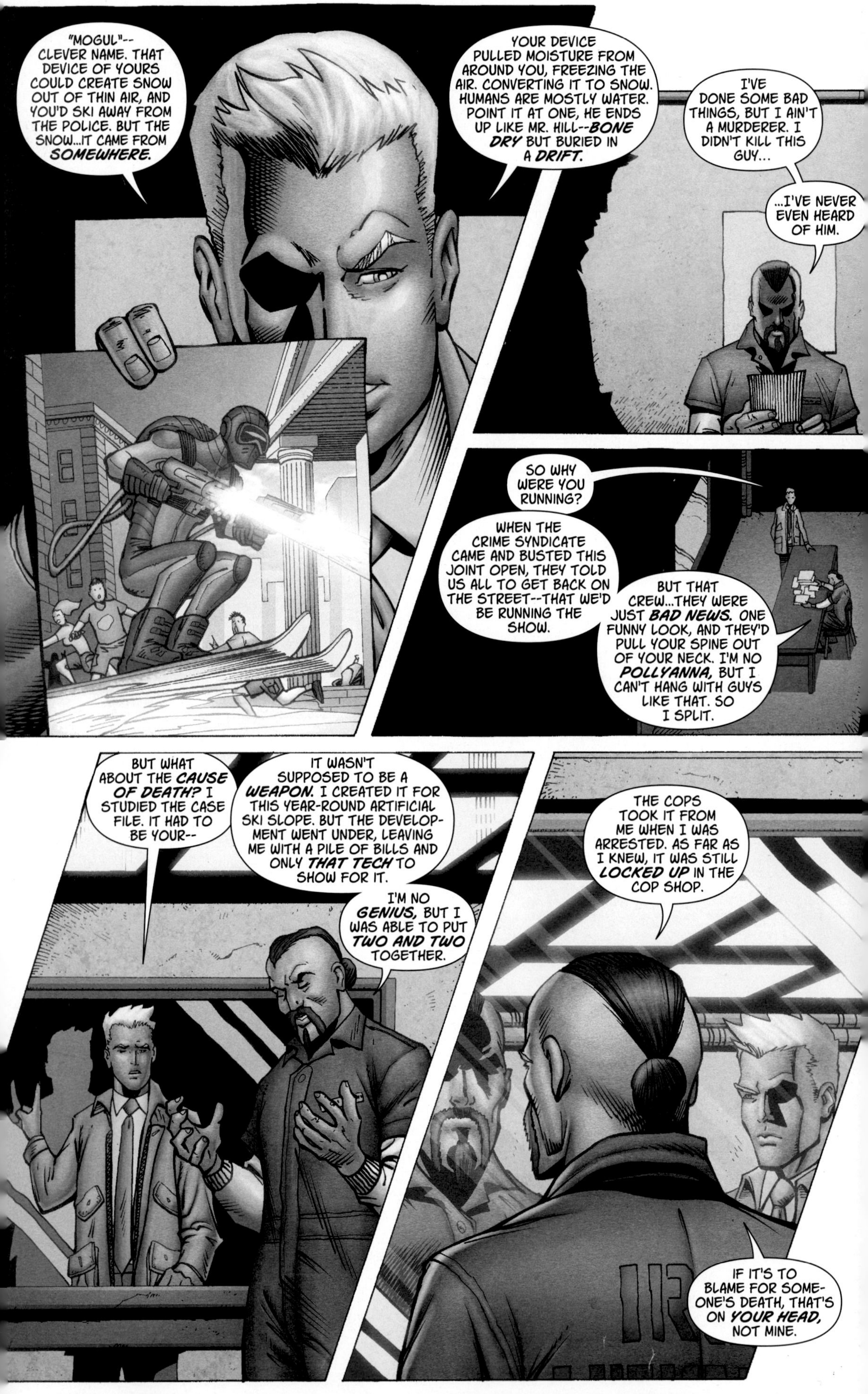
"MOGUL"-- CLEVER NAME. THAT DEVICE OF YOURS COULD CREATE SNOW OUT OF THIN AIR, AND YOU'D SKI AWAY FROM THE POLICE. BUT THE SNOW...IT CAME FROM SOMEWHERE.
YOUR DEVICE PULLED MOISTURE FROM AROUND YOU, FREEZING THE AIR. CONVERTING IT TO SNOW. HUMANS ARE MOSTLY WATER. POINT IT AT ONE, HE ENDS UP LIKE MR. HILL--BONE DRY BUT BURIED IN A DRIFT.
I'VE DONE SOME BAD THINGS, BUT I AIN'T A MURDERER. I DIDN'T KILL THIS GUY...
...I'VE NEVER EVEN HEARD OF HIM.
SO WHY WERE YOU RUNNING?
WHEN THE CRIME SYNDICATE CAME AND BUSTED THIS JOINT OPEN, THEY TOLD US ALL TO GET BACK ON THE STREET--THAT WE'D BE RUNNING THE SHOW.
BUT THAT CREW...THEY WERE JUST BAD NEWS. ONE FUNNY LOOK, AND THEY'D PULL YOUR SPINE OUT OF YOUR NECK. I'M NO POLLYANNA, BUT I CAN'T HANG WITH GUYS LIKE THAT. SO I SPLIT.
BUT WHAT ABOUT THE CAUSE OF DEATH? I STUDIED THE CASE FILE. IT HAD TO BE YOUR--
IT WASN'T SUPPOSED TO BE A WEAPON. I CREATED IT FOR THIS YEAR-ROUND ARTIFICIAL SKI SLOPE. BUT THE DEVELOPMENT WENT UNDER, LEAVING ME WITH A PILE OF BILLS AND ONLY THAT TECH TO SHOW FOR IT.
I'M NO GENIUS, BUT I WAS ABLE TO PUT TWO AND TWO TOGETHER.
THE COPS TOOK IT FROM ME WHEN I WAS ARRESTED. AS FAR AS I KNEW, IT WAS STILL LOCKED UP IN THE COP SHOP.
IF IT'S TO BLAME FOR SOMEONE'S DEATH, THAT'S ON YOUR HEAD, NOT MINE.

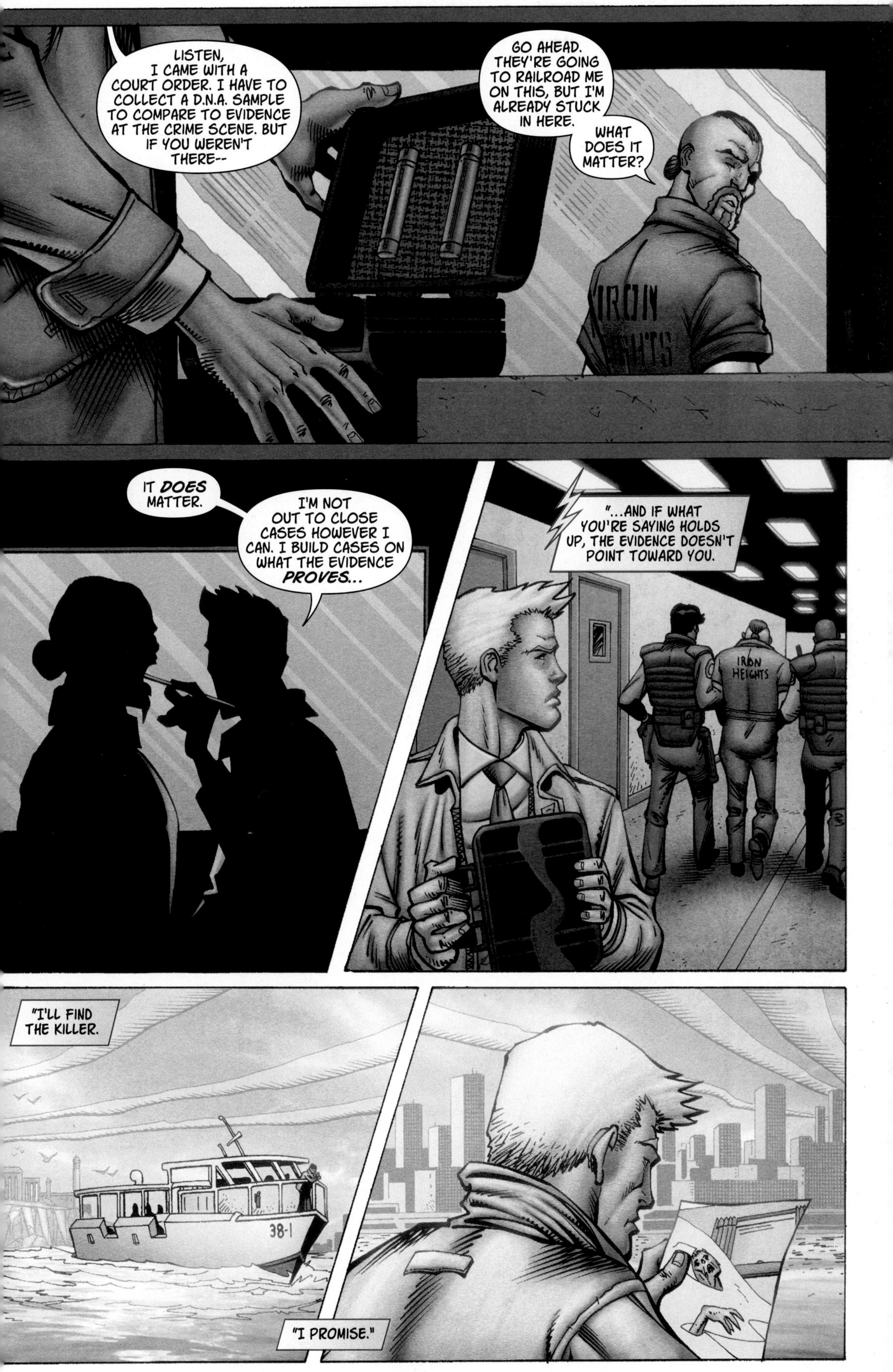

LISTEN, I CAME WITH A COURT ORDER. I HAVE TO COLLECT A D.N.A. SAMPLE TO COMPARE TO EVIDENCE AT THE CRIME SCENE. BUT IF YOU WEREN'T THERE--
GO AHEAD. THEY'RE GOING TO RAILROAD ME ON THIS, BUT I'M ALREADY STUCK IN HERE.
WHAT DOES IT MATTER?
IRON HEIGHTS
IT DOES MATTER.
I'M NOT OUT TO CLOSE CASES HOWEVER I CAN. I BUILD CASES ON WHAT THE EVIDENCE PROVES...
"...AND IF WHAT YOU'RE SAYING HOLDS UP, THE EVIDENCE DOESN'T POINT TOWARD YOU.
IRON HEIGHTS
"I'LL FIND THE KILLER.
38-1
"I PROMISE."

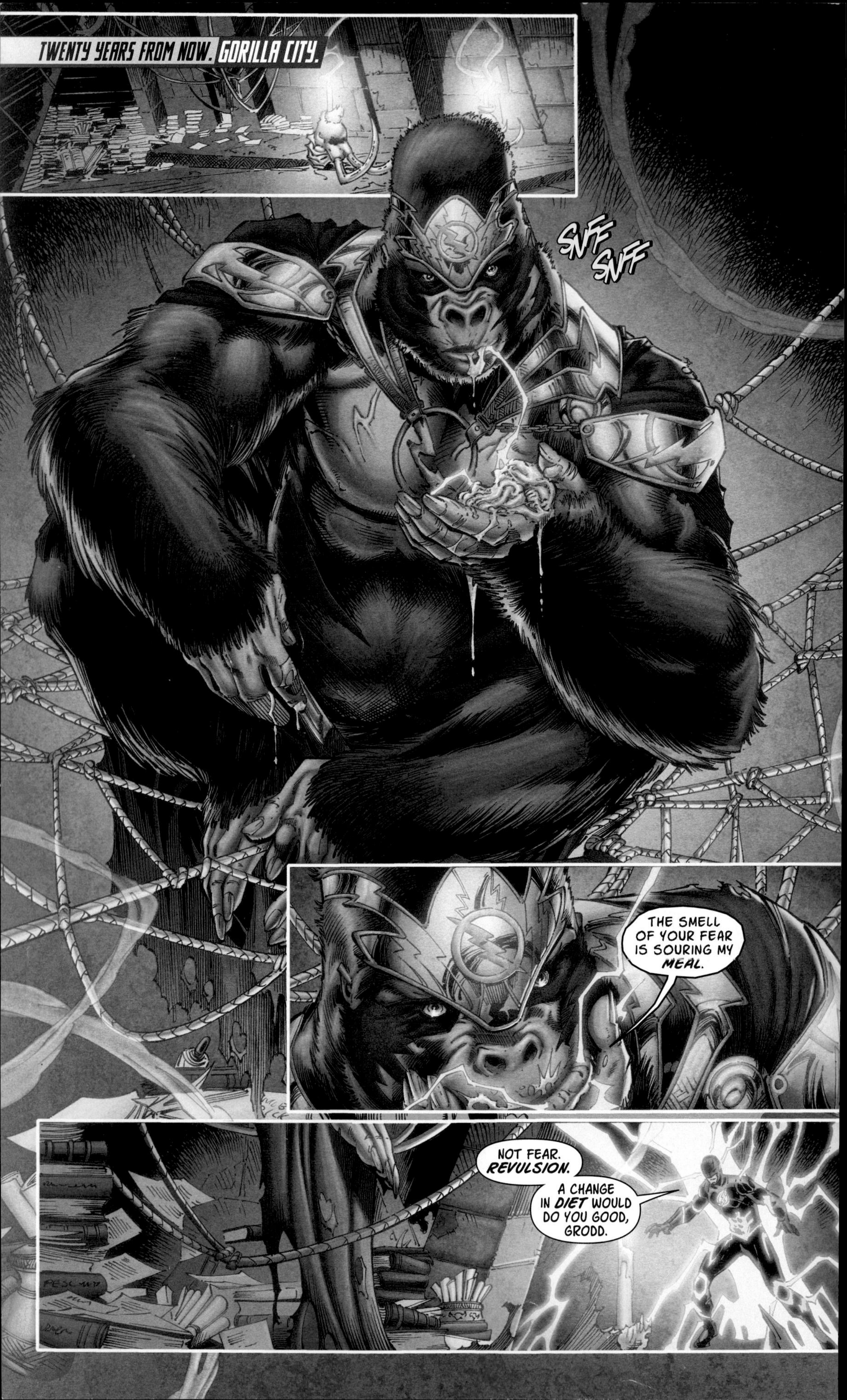
TWENTY YEARS FROM NOW. GORILLA CITY.
SNFF SNFF
THE SMELL OF YOUR FEAR IS SOURING MY MEAL.
NOT FEAR. REVULSION.
A CHANGE IN DIET WOULD DO YOU GOOD, GRODD.

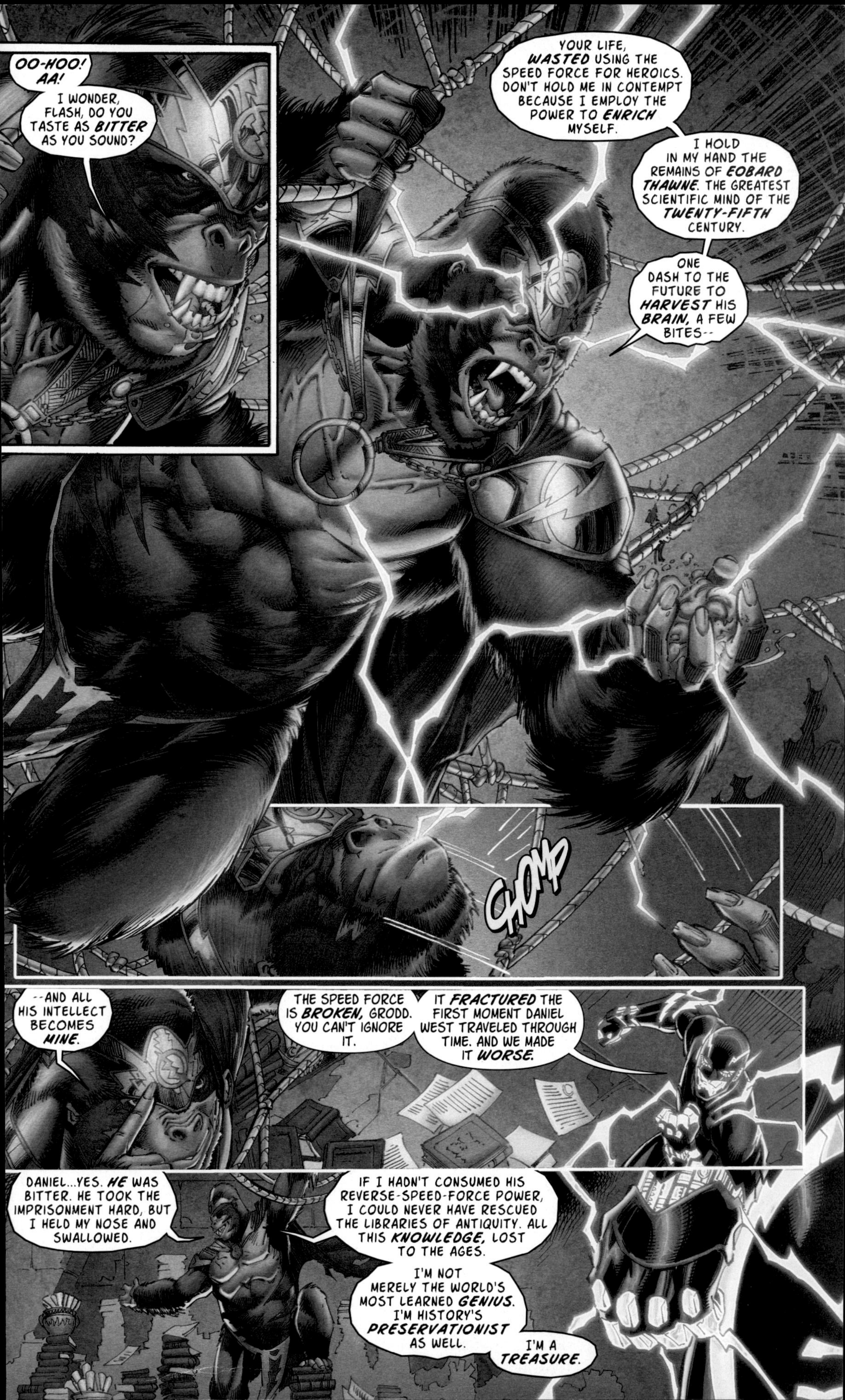
OO-HOO! AA!
I WONDER, FLASH, DO YOU TASTE AS BITTER AS YOU SOUND?
YOUR LIFE, WASTED USING THE SPEED FORCE FOR HEROICS. DON'T HOLD ME IN CONTEMPT BECAUSE I EMPLOY THE POWER TO ENRICH MYSELF.
I HOLD IN MY HAND THE REMAINS OF EOBARD THAWNE. THE GREATEST SCIENTIFIC MIND OF THE TWENTY-FIFTH CENTURY.
ONE DASH TO THE FUTURE TO HARVEST HIS BRAIN, A FEW BITES--
CHOMP
--AND ALL HIS INTELLECT BECOMES MINE.
THE SPEED FORCE IS BROKEN, GRODD. YOU CAN'T IGNORE IT.
IT FRACTURED THE FIRST MOMENT DANIEL WEST TRAVELED THROUGH TIME. AND WE MADE IT WORSE.
DANIEL...YES. HE WAS BITTER. HE TOOK THE IMPRISONMENT HARD, BUT I HELD MY NOSE AND SWALLOWED.
IF I HADN'T CONSUMED HIS REVERSE-SPEED-FORCE POWER, I COULD NEVER HAVE RESCUED THE LIBRARIES OF ANTIQUITY. ALL THIS KNOWLEDGE, LOST TO THE AGES.
I'M NOT MERELY THE WORLD'S MOST LEARNED GENIUS. I'M HISTORY'S PRESERVATIONIST AS WELL.
I'M A TREASURE.

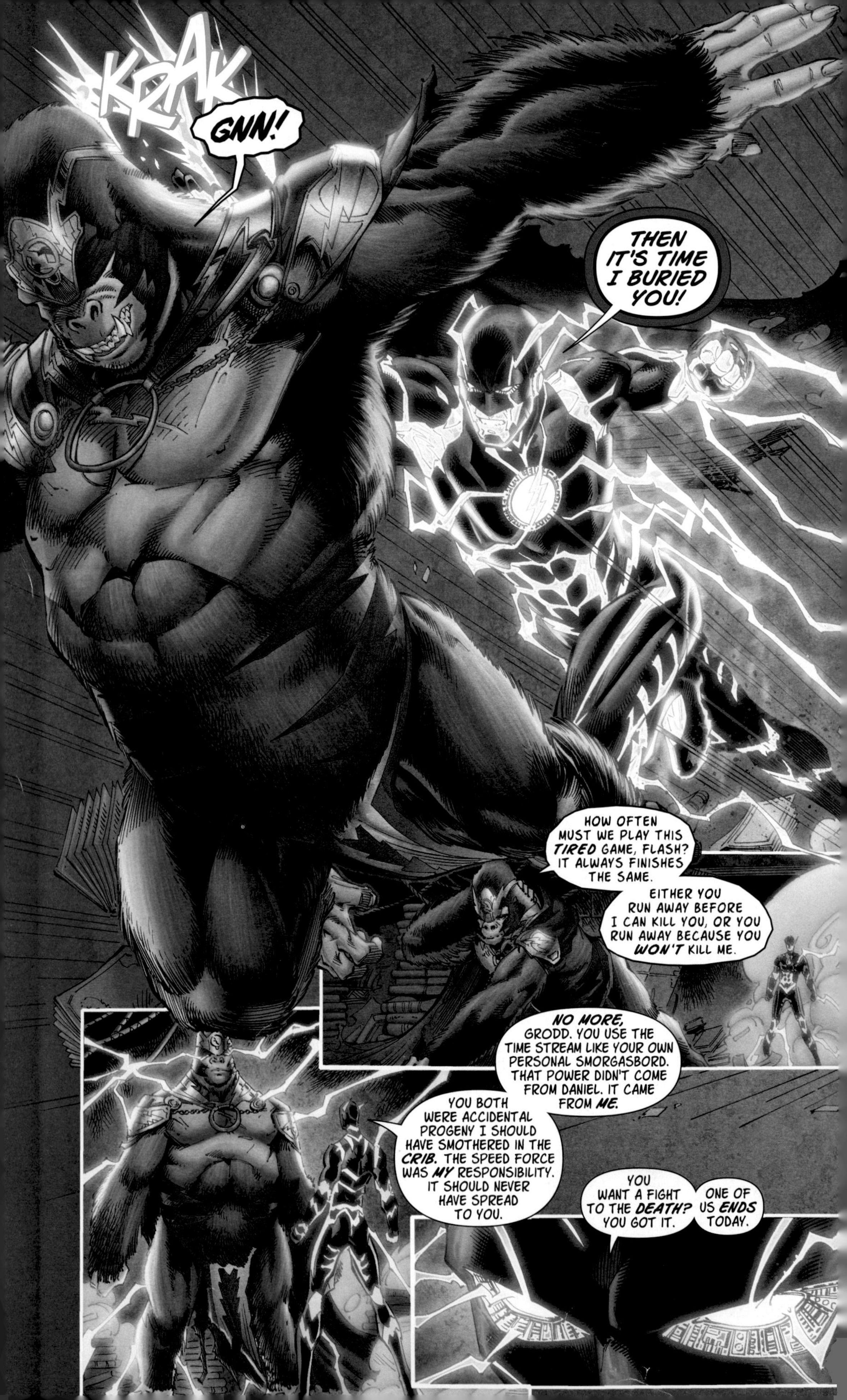
KRAK
GNN!
THEN IT'S TIME I BURIED YOU!
HOW OFTEN MUST WE PLAY THIS TIRED GAME, FLASH? IT ALWAYS FINISHES THE SAME.
EITHER YOU RUN AWAY BEFORE I CAN KILL YOU, OR YOU RUN AWAY BECAUSE YOU WON'T KILL ME.
NO MORE, GRODD. YOU USE THE TIME STREAM LIKE YOUR OWN PERSONAL SMORGASBORD. THAT POWER DIDN'T COME FROM DANIEL. IT CAME FROM ME.
YOU BOTH WERE ACCIDENTAL PROGENY I SHOULD HAVE SMOTHERED IN THE CRIB. THE SPEED FORCE WAS MY RESPONSIBILITY. IT SHOULD NEVER HAVE SPREAD TO YOU.
YOU WANT A FIGHT TO THE DEATH? YOU GOT IT.
ONE OF US ENDS TODAY.

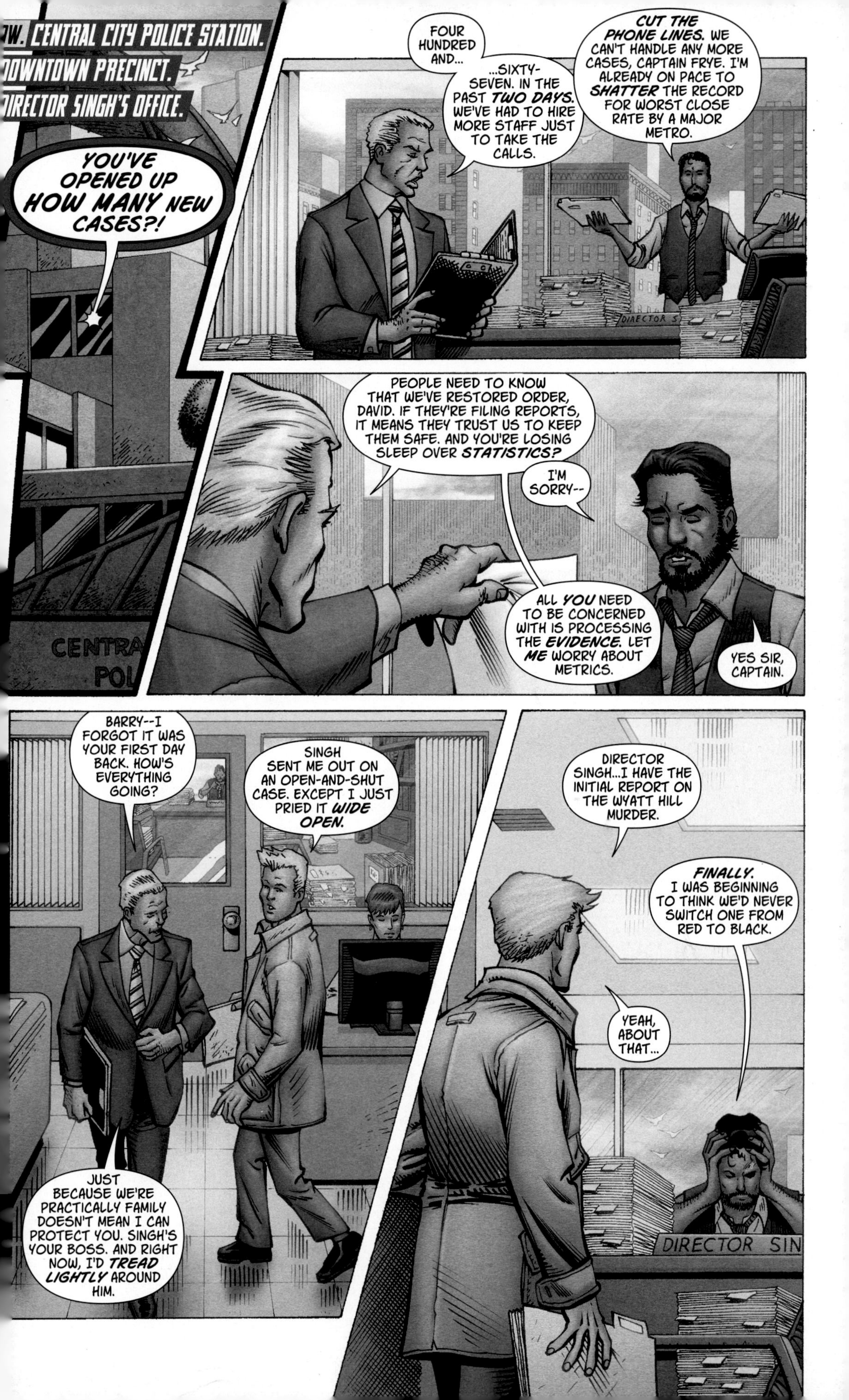
NOW. CENTRAL CITY POLICE STATION.
DOWNTOWN PRECINCT.
DIRECTOR SINGH'S OFFICE.
YOU'VE OPENED UP HOW MANY NEW CASES?!
FOUR HUNDRED AND...
...SIXTY-SEVEN. IN THE PAST TWO DAYS. WE'VE HAD TO HIRE MORE STAFF JUST TO TAKE THE CALLS.
CUT THE PHONE LINES. WE CAN'T HANDLE ANY MORE CASES, CAPTAIN FRYE. I'M ALREADY ON PACE TO SHATTER THE RECORD FOR WORST CLOSE RATE BY A MAJOR METRO.
PEOPLE NEED TO KNOW THAT WE'VE RESTORED ORDER, DAVID. IF THEY'RE FILING REPORTS, IT MEANS THEY TRUST US TO KEEP THEM SAFE. AND YOU'RE LOSING SLEEP OVER STATISTICS?
I'M SORRY--
ALL YOU NEED TO BE CONCERNED WITH IS PROCESSING THE EVIDENCE. LET ME WORRY ABOUT METRICS.
YES SIR, CAPTAIN.
BARRY--I FORGOT IT WAS YOUR FIRST DAY BACK. HOW'S EVERYTHING GOING?
SINGH SENT ME OUT ON AN OPEN-AND-SHUT CASE. EXCEPT I JUST PRIED IT WIDE OPEN.
JUST BECAUSE WE'RE PRACTICALLY FAMILY DOESN'T MEAN I CAN PROTECT YOU. SINGH'S YOUR BOSS. AND RIGHT NOW, I'D TREAD LIGHTLY AROUND HIM.
DIRECTOR SINGH...I HAVE THE INITIAL REPORT ON THE WYATT HILL MURDER.
FINALLY. I WAS BEGINNING TO THINK WE'D NEVER SWITCH ONE FROM RED TO BLACK.
YEAH, ABOUT THAT...

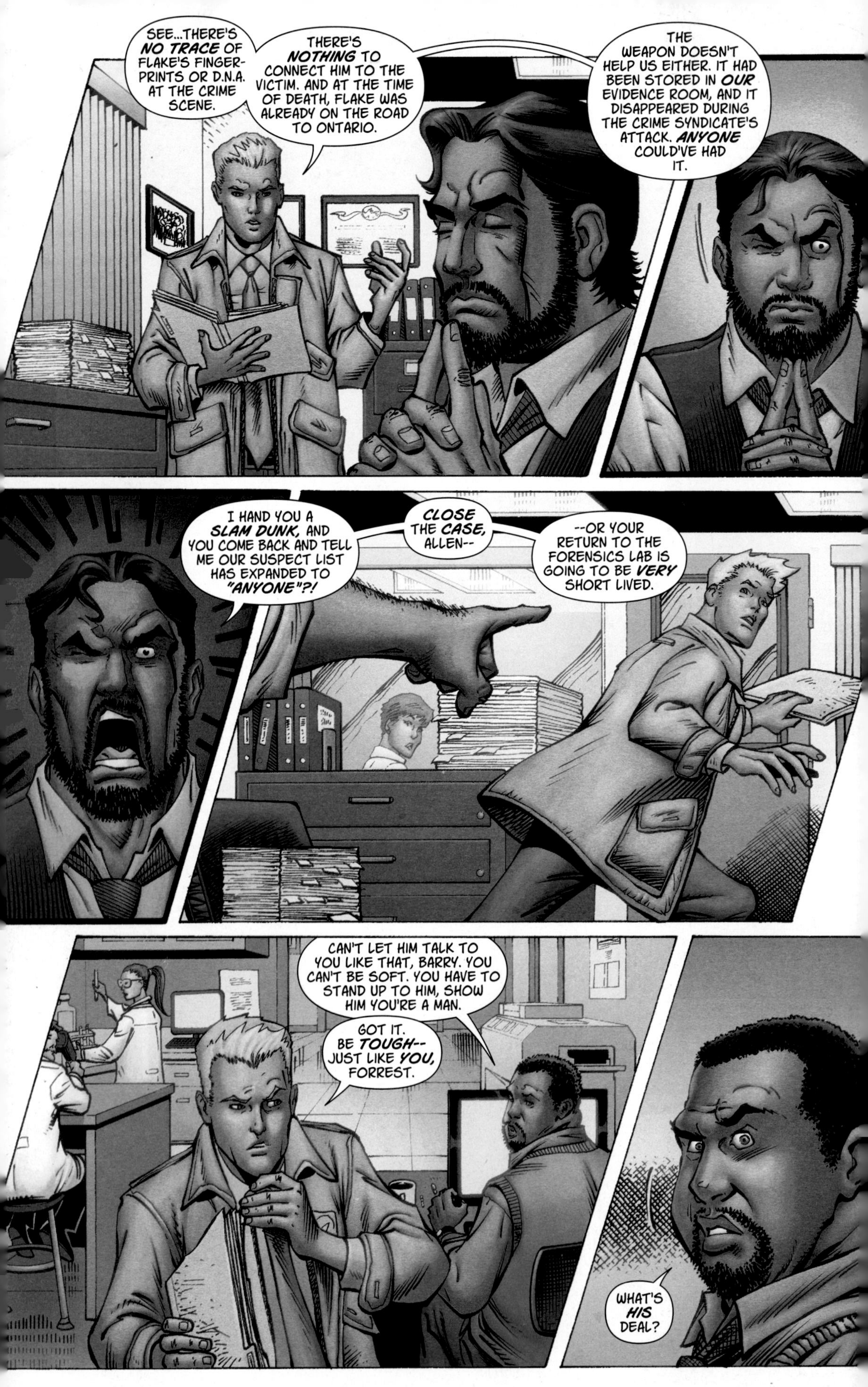
SEE...THERE'S NO TRACE OF FLAKE'S FINGER-PRINTS OR D.N.A. AT THE CRIME SCENE.
THERE'S NOTHING TO CONNECT HIM TO THE VICTIM. AND AT THE TIME OF DEATH, FLAKE WAS ALREADY ON THE ROAD TO ONTARIO.
THE WEAPON DOESN'T HELP US EITHER. IT HAD BEEN STORED IN OUR EVIDENCE ROOM, AND IT DISAPPEARED DURING THE CRIME SYNDICATE'S ATTACK. ANYONE COULD'VE HAD IT.
I HAND YOU A SLAM DUNK, AND YOU COME BACK AND TELL ME OUR SUSPECT LIST HAS EXPANDED TO "ANYONE"?!
CLOSE THE CASE, ALLEN--
--OR YOUR RETURN TO THE FORENSICS LAB IS GOING TO BE VERY SHORT LIVED.
CAN'T LET HIM TALK TO YOU LIKE THAT, BARRY. YOU CAN'T BE SOFT. YOU HAVE TO STAND UP TO HIM, SHOW HIM YOU'RE A MAN.
GOT IT. BE TOUGH-- JUST LIKE YOU, FORREST.
WHAT'S HIS DEAL?

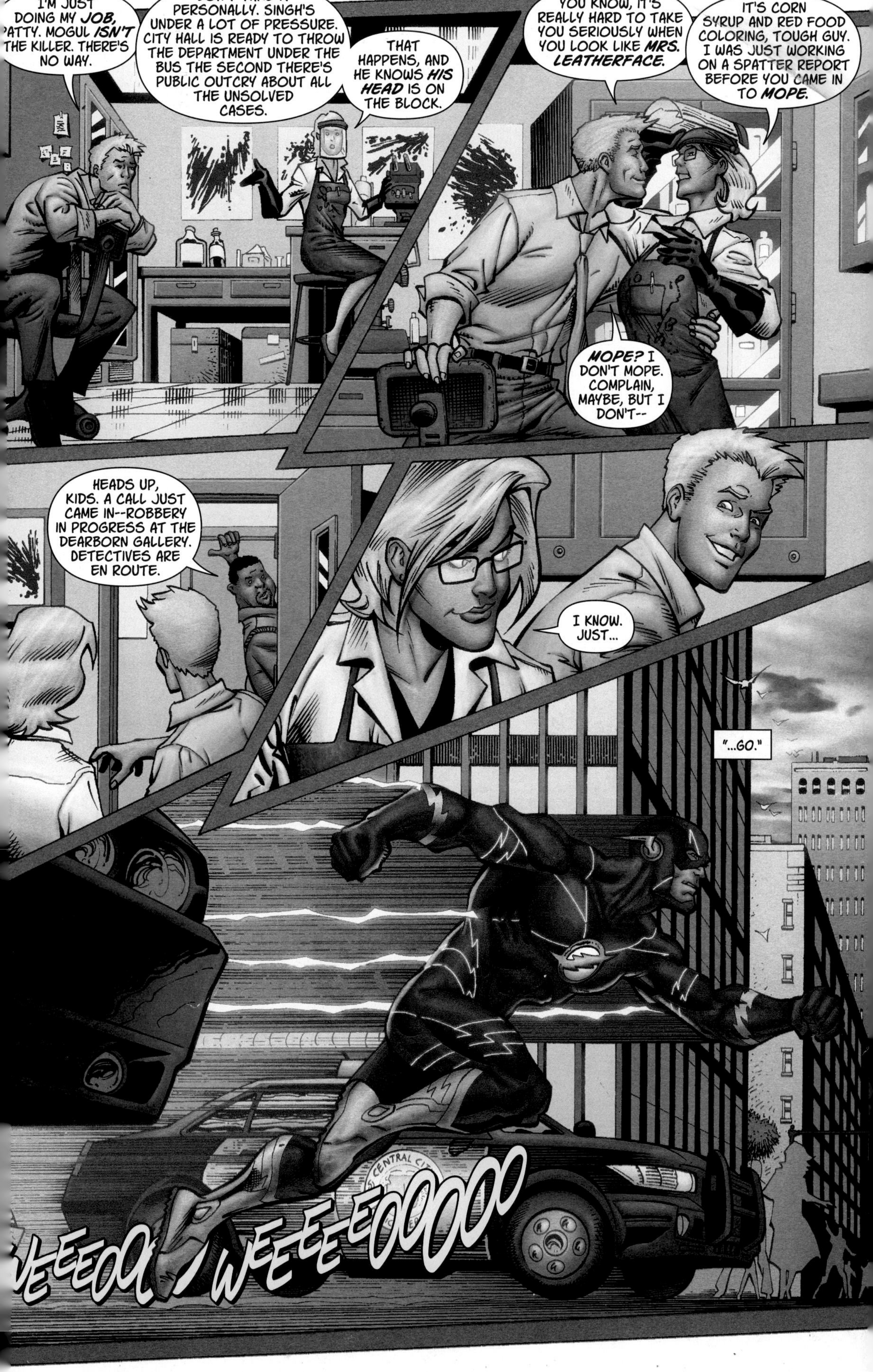

I'M JUST DOING MY JOB, PATTY. MOGUL ISN'T THE KILLER. THERE'S NO WAY.
DON'T TAKE IT PERSONALLY. SINGH'S UNDER A LOT OF PRESSURE. CITY HALL IS READY TO THROW THE DEPARTMENT UNDER THE BUS THE SECOND THERE'S PUBLIC OUTCRY ABOUT ALL THE UNSOLVED CASES.
THAT HAPPENS, AND HE KNOWS HIS HEAD IS ON THE BLOCK.
YOU KNOW, IT'S REALLY HARD TO TAKE YOU SERIOUSLY WHEN YOU LOOK LIKE MRS. LEATHERFACE.
IT'S CORN SYRUP AND RED FOOD COLORING, TOUGH GUY. I WAS JUST WORKING ON A SPATTER REPORT BEFORE YOU CAME IN TO MOPE.
MOPE? I DON'T MOPE. COMPLAIN, MAYBE, BUT I DON'T--
HEADS UP, KIDS. A CALL JUST CAME IN--ROBBERY IN PROGRESS AT THE DEARBORN GALLERY. DETECTIVES ARE EN ROUTE.
I KNOW. JUST...
"...GO."
CENTRAL CITY
WEEEOOO WEEEEOOOOOO

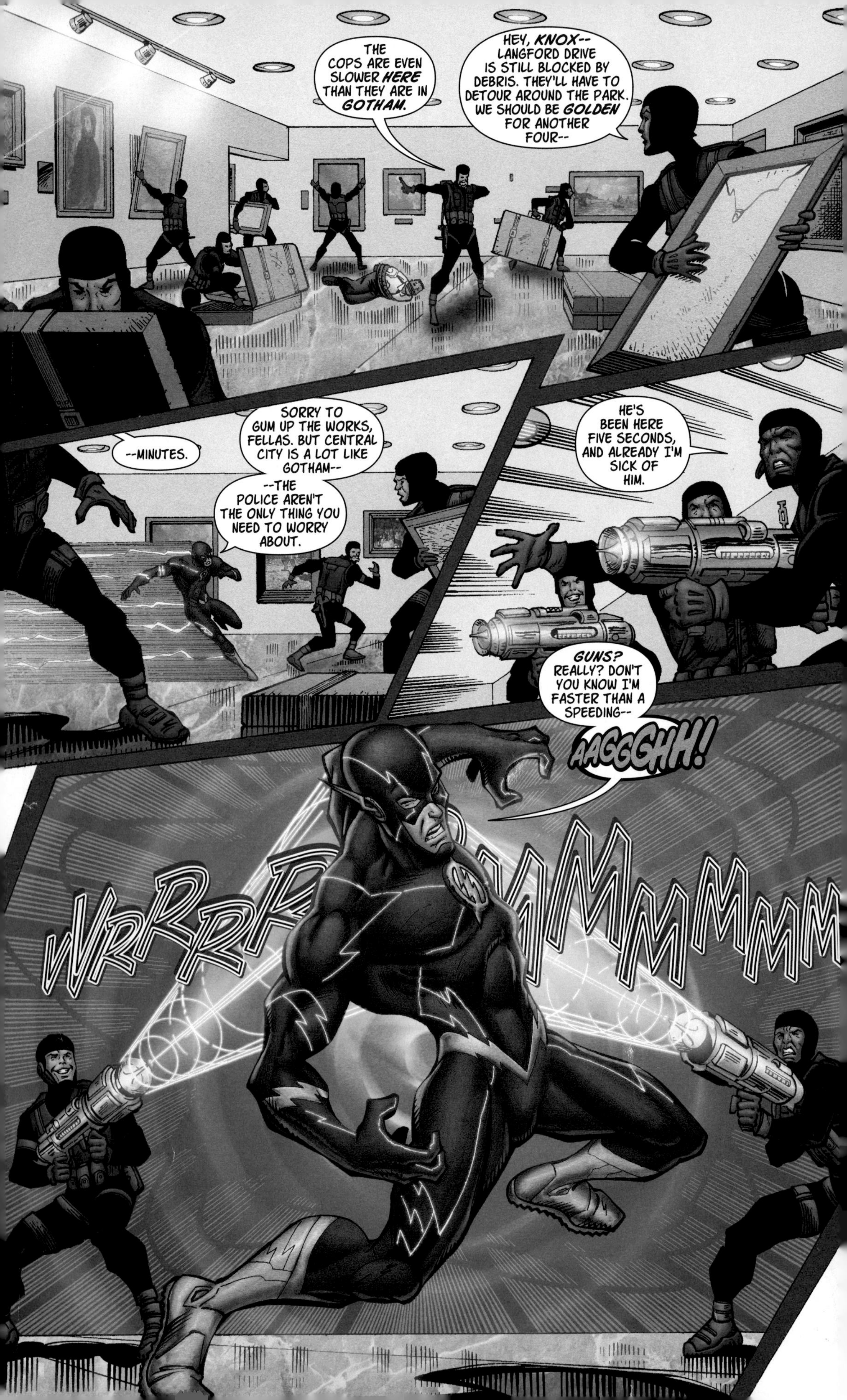
THE COPS ARE EVEN SLOWER HERE THAN THEY ARE IN GOTHAM.
HEY, KNOX-- LANGFORD DRIVE IS STILL BLOCKED BY DEBRIS. THEY'LL HAVE TO DETOUR AROUND THE PARK. WE SHOULD BE GOLDEN FOR ANOTHER FOUR--
--MINUTES.
SORRY TO GUM UP THE WORKS, FELLAS. BUT CENTRAL CITY IS A LOT LIKE GOTHAM--
--THE POLICE AREN'T THE ONLY THING YOU NEED TO WORRY ABOUT.
HE'S BEEN HERE FIVE SECONDS, AND ALREADY I'M SICK OF HIM.
GUNS? REALLY? DON'T YOU KNOW I'M FASTER THAN A SPEEDING--
AAGGGHH!
WRRRRMMMMMMMM

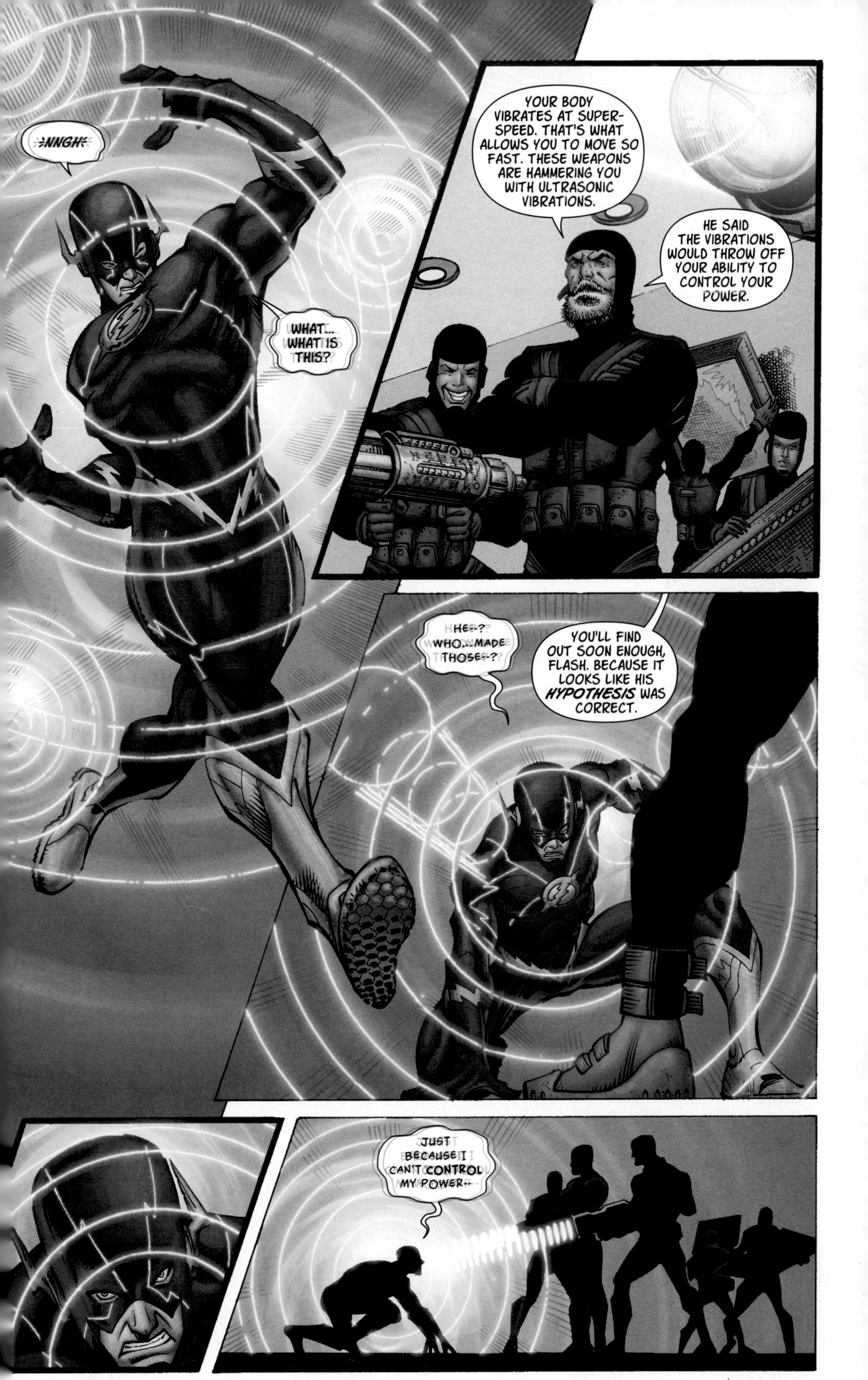
NNGH
WHAT... WHAT IS THIS?
YOUR BODY VIBRATES AT SUPER-SPEED. THAT'S WHAT ALLOWS YOU TO MOVE SO FAST. THESE WEAPONS ARE HAMMERING YOU WITH ULTRASONIC VIBRATIONS.
HE SAID THE VIBRATIONS WOULD THROW OFF YOUR ABILITY TO CONTROL YOUR POWER.
HE--? WHO... MADE THOSE--?
YOU'LL FIND OUT SOON ENOUGH, FLASH. BECAUSE IT LOOKS LIKE HIS HYPOTHESIS WAS CORRECT.
JUST BECAUSE I CAN'T CONTROL MY POWER--

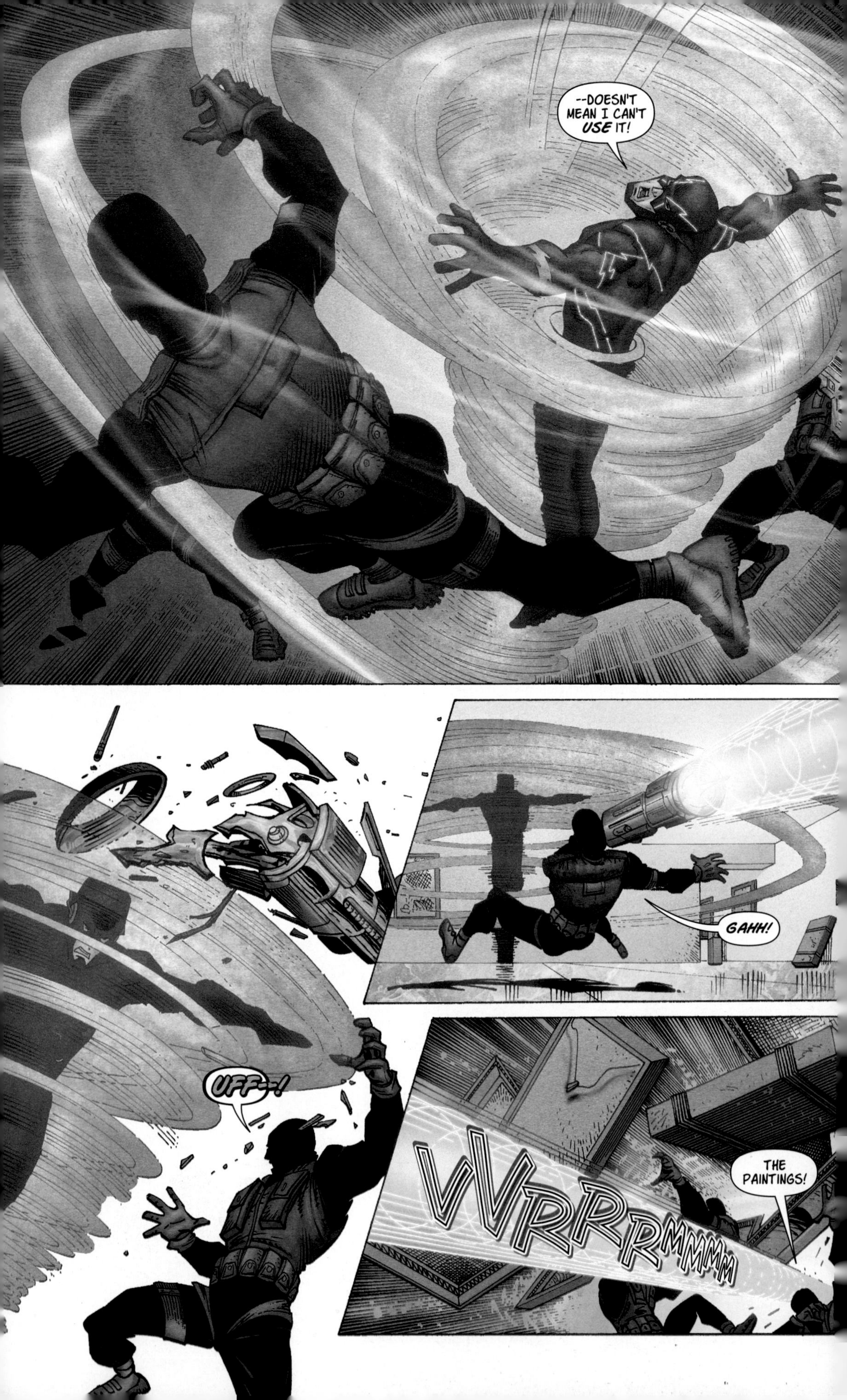
--DOESN'T MEAN I CAN'T USE IT!
GAHH!
UFF--!
VWRRRMMMMM
THE PAINTINGS!

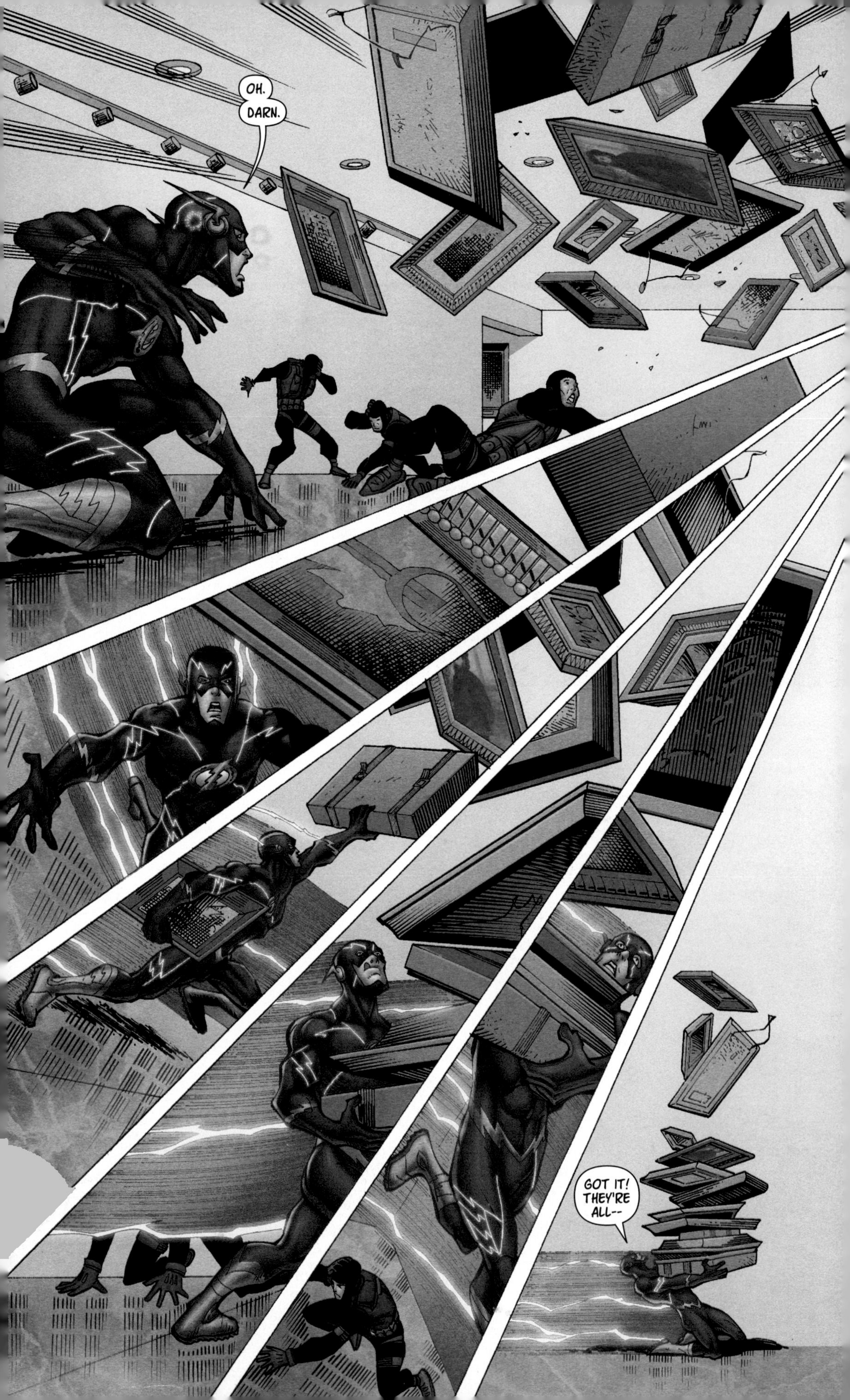
OH. DARN.
GOT IT! THEY'RE ALL--

--SAFE?

IMPRESSIVE, FLASH. BUT IT LOOKS LIKE IT WAS ALL FOR NOTHING.

aKkk

YOU CAN'T HIT ME WITHOUT *DESTROYING* THE PAINTINGS. YOU DESTROY THEM, AND THERE GOES YOUR *BIG SCORE.*

SO LET'S POIN THOSE WEAPON AWAY FROM T *PICASSO.*

TRUTH BE TOLD, I ALWAYS PREFERRED THE *RENAISSANCE.* BESIDES, THE PAINTINGS WERE NEVER OUR *ONLY* TARGET.

VREEE

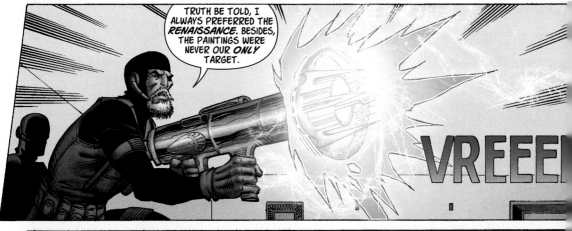

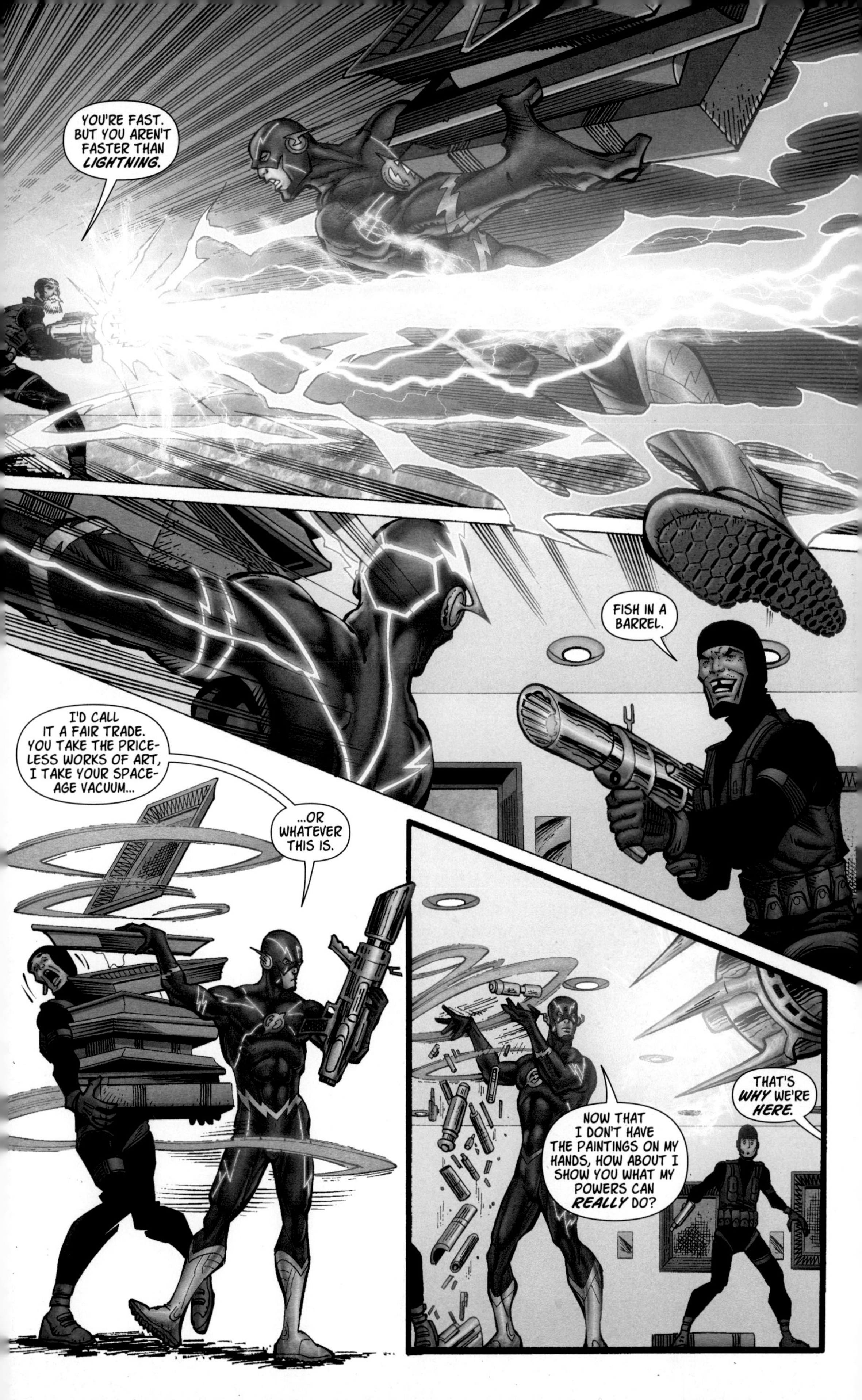

YOU'RE FAST. BUT YOU AREN'T FASTER THAN LIGHTNING.
FISH IN A BARREL.
I'D CALL IT A FAIR TRADE. YOU TAKE THE PRICE-LESS WORKS OF ART, I TAKE YOUR SPACE-AGE VACUUM...
...OR WHATEVER THIS IS.
NOW THAT I DON'T HAVE THE PAINTINGS ON MY HANDS, HOW ABOUT I SHOW YOU WHAT MY POWERS CAN REALLY DO?
THAT'S WHY WE'RE HERE.

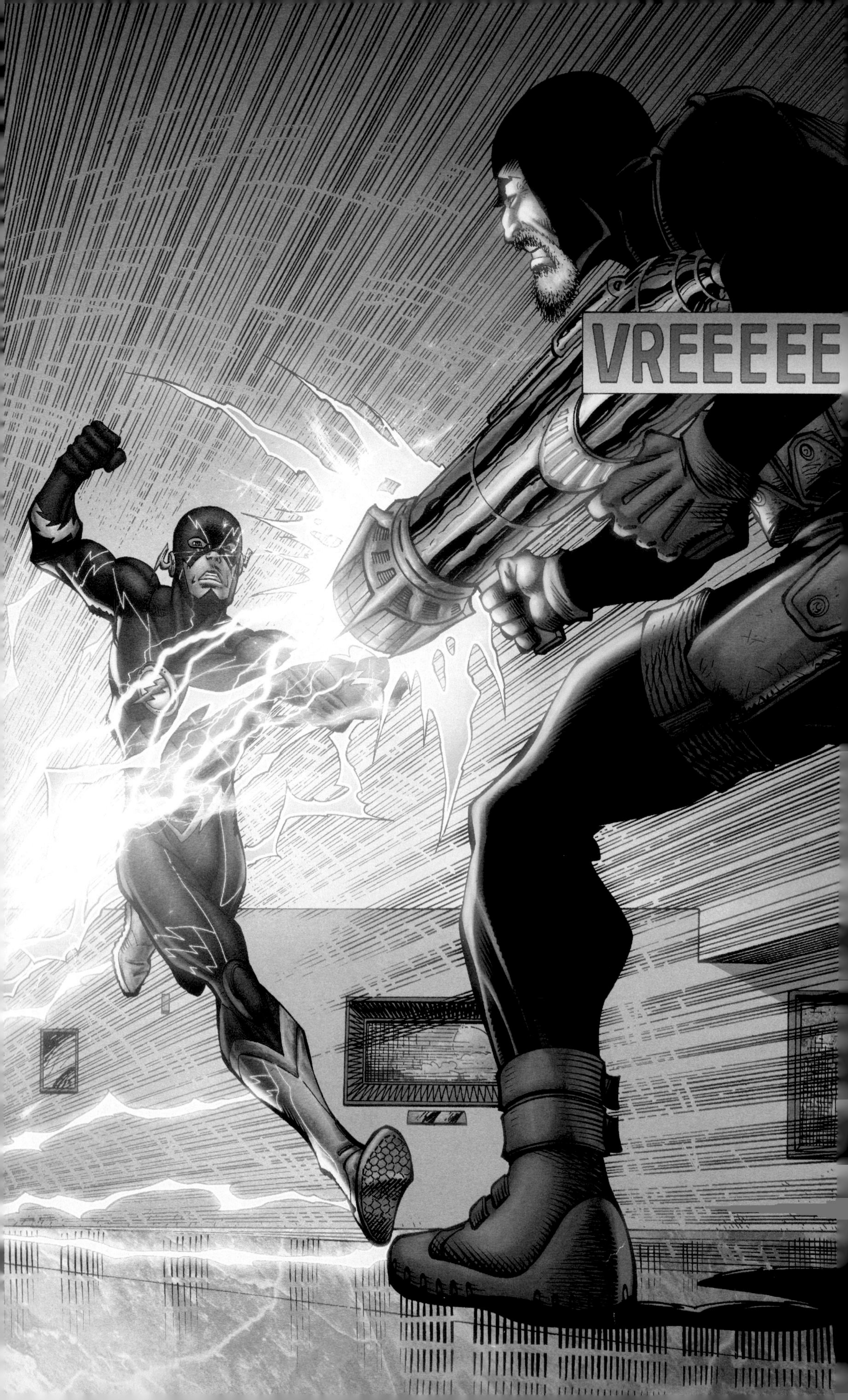
VREEEEE

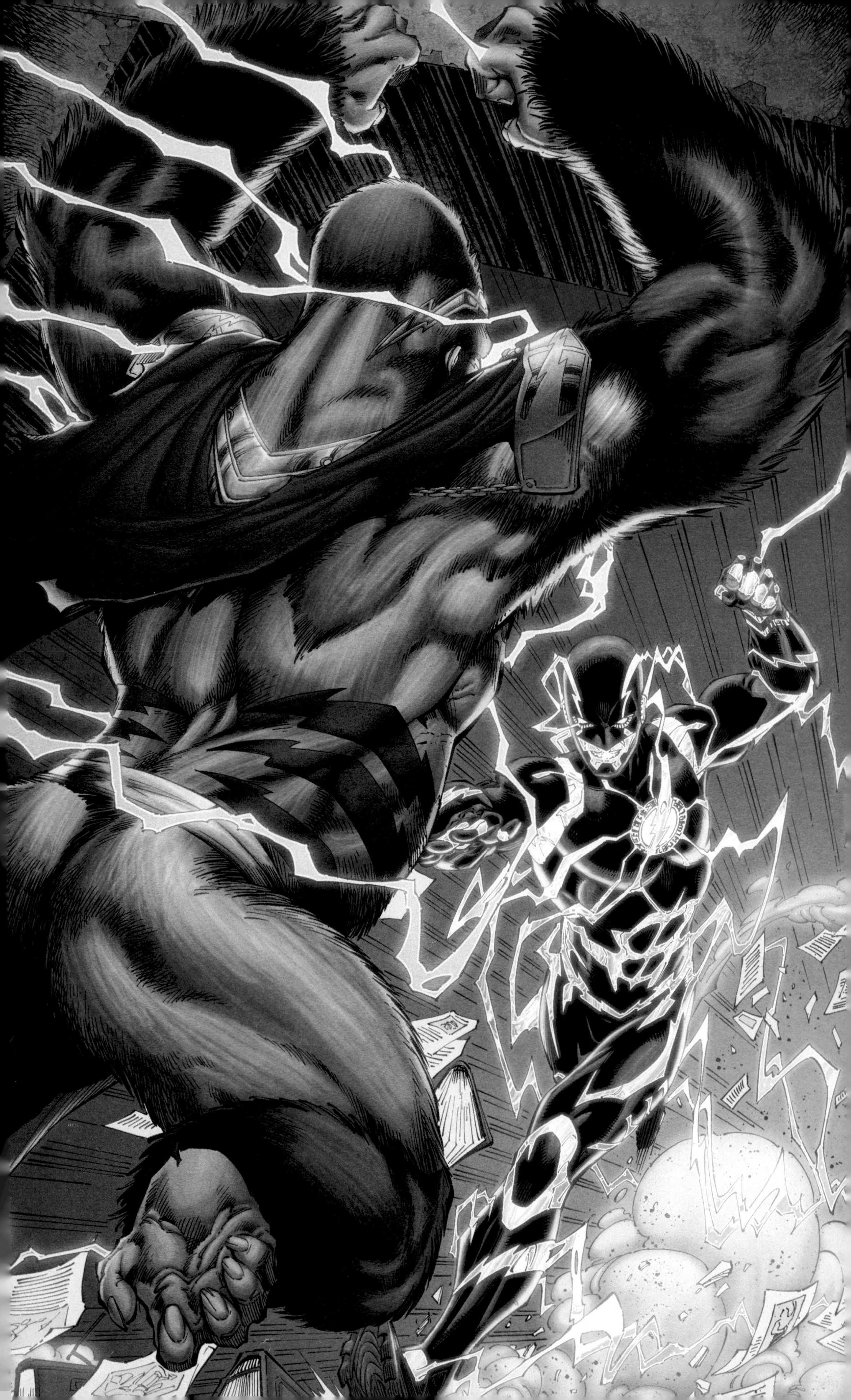

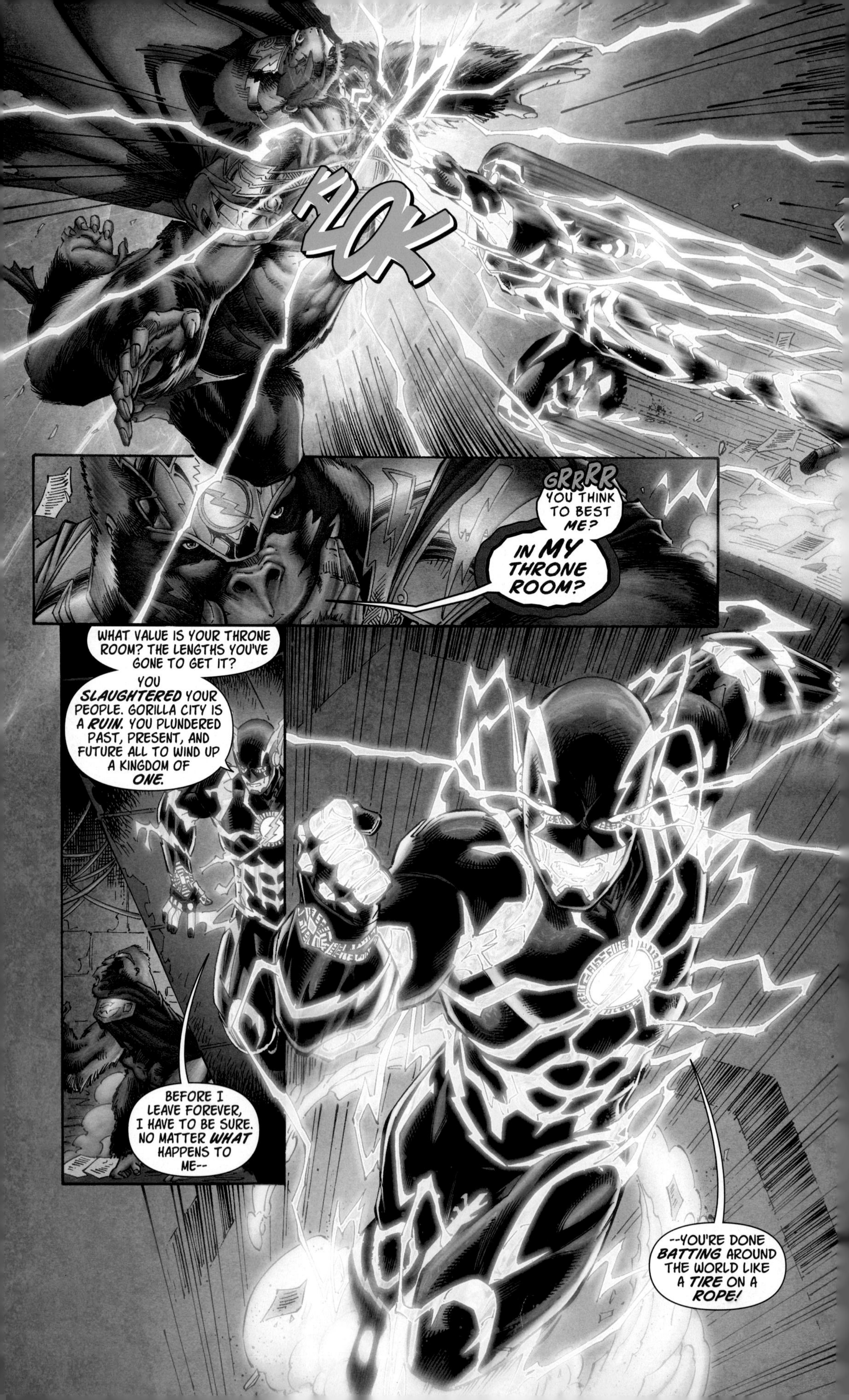
KLOK
GRRRR
YOU THINK TO BEST ME?
IN MY THRONE ROOM?
WHAT VALUE IS YOUR THRONE ROOM? THE LENGTHS YOU'VE GONE TO GET IT?
YOU SLAUGHTERED YOUR PEOPLE. GORILLA CITY IS A RUIN. YOU PLUNDERED PAST, PRESENT, AND FUTURE ALL TO WIND UP A KINGDOM OF ONE.
BEFORE I LEAVE FOREVER, I HAVE TO BE SURE. NO MATTER WHAT HAPPENS TO ME--
--YOU'RE DONE BATTING AROUND THE WORLD LIKE A TIRE ON A ROPE!

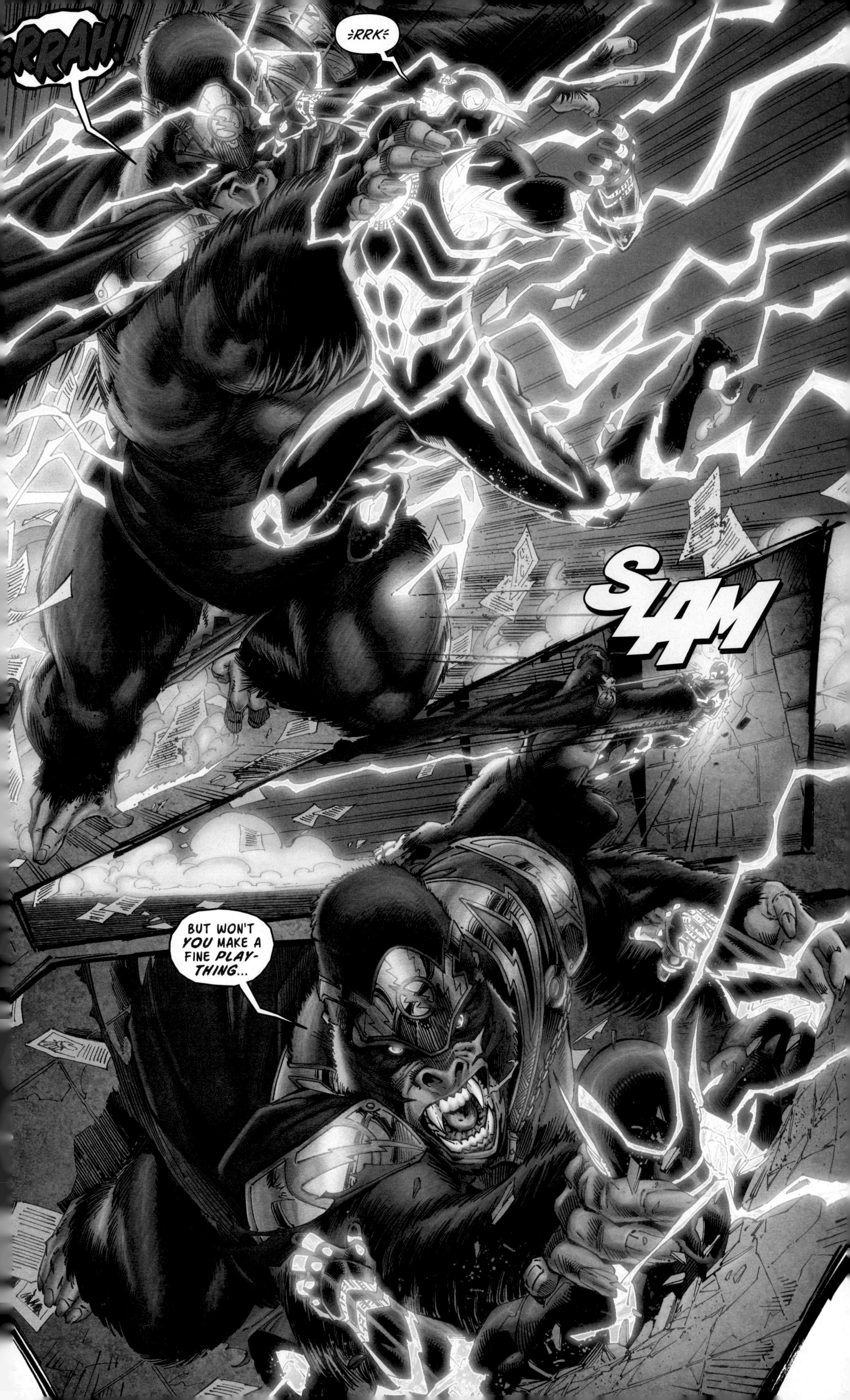

RRAH!
RRK
SLAM
BUT WON'T YOU MAKE A FINE PLAY-THING...

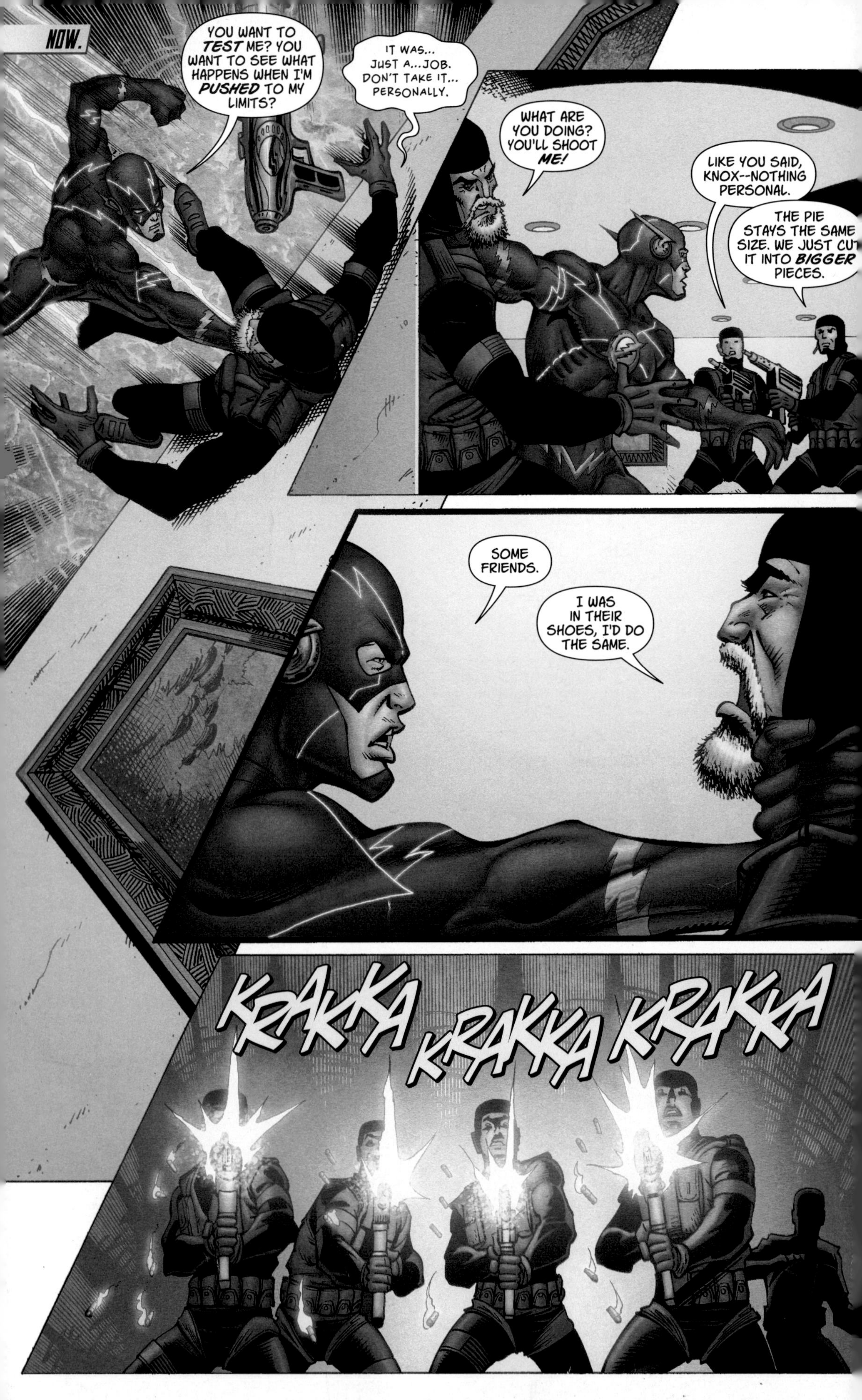
NOW.
YOU WANT TO TEST ME? YOU WANT TO SEE WHAT HAPPENS WHEN I'M PUSHED TO MY LIMITS?
IT WAS... JUST A...JOB. DON'T TAKE IT... PERSONALLY.
WHAT ARE YOU DOING? YOU'LL SHOOT ME!
LIKE YOU SAID, KNOX--NOTHING PERSONAL.
THE PIE STAYS THE SAME SIZE. WE JUST CUT IT INTO BIGGER PIECES.
SOME FRIENDS.
I WAS IN THEIR SHOES, I'D DO THE SAME.
KRAKKA KRAKKA KRAKKA

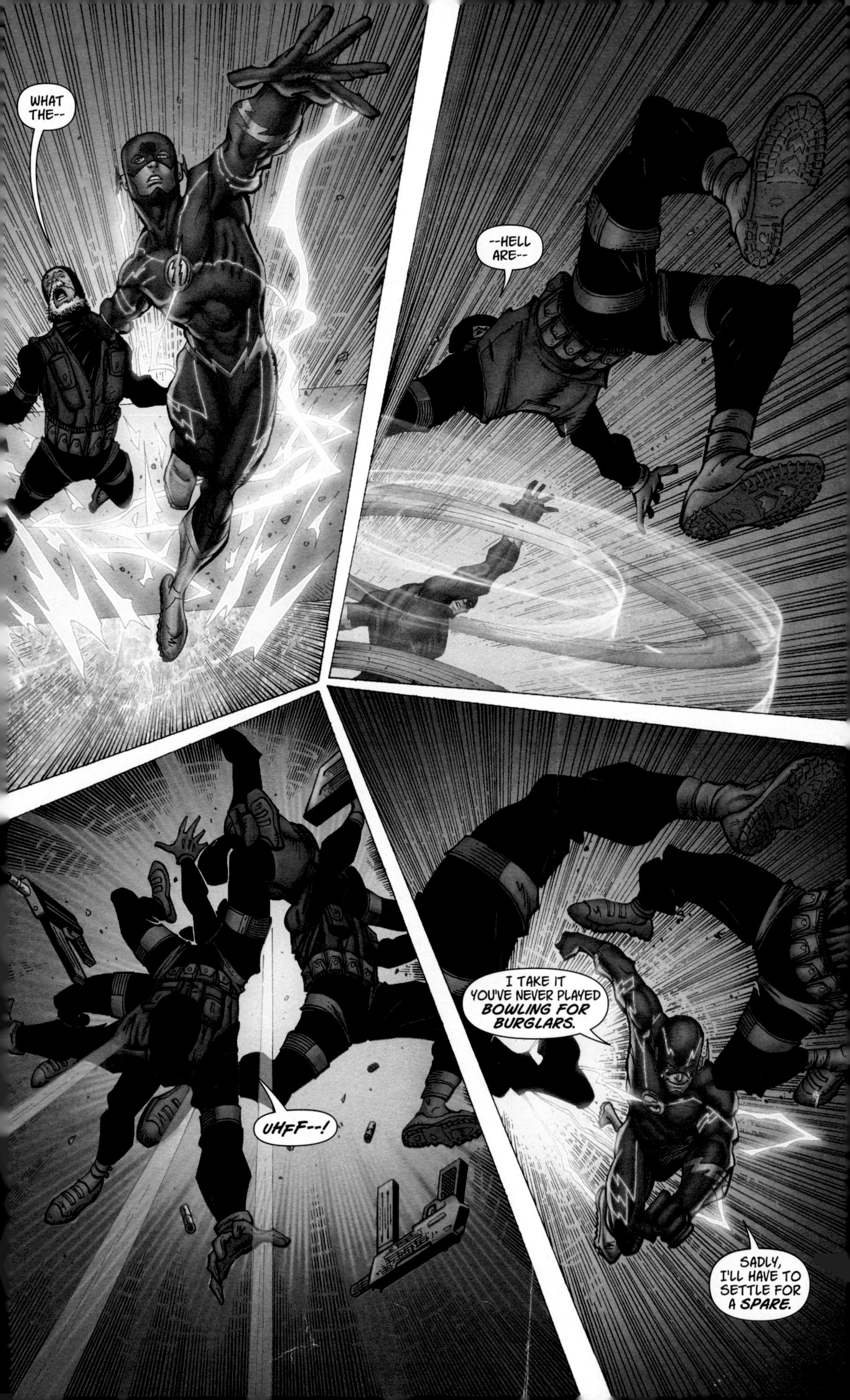
WHAT THE--
--HELL ARE--
UHFF--!
I TAKE IT YOU'VE NEVER PLAYED BOWLING FOR BURGLARS.
SADLY, I'LL HAVE TO SETTLE FOR A SPARE.

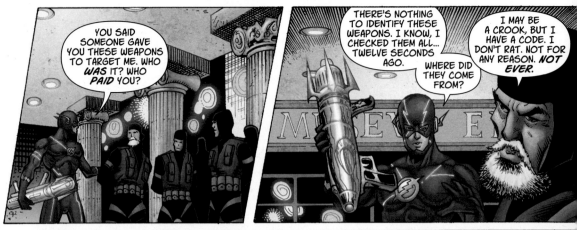

YOU SAID SOMEONE GAVE YOU THESE WEAPONS TO TARGET ME. WHO *WAS* IT? WHO *PAID* YOU?

THERE'S NOTHING TO IDENTIFY THESE WEAPONS. I KNOW, I CHECKED THEM ALL... TWELVE SECONDS AGO.

WHERE DID THEY COME FROM?

I MAY BE A CROOK, BUT I HAVE A CODE. I DON'T RAT. NOT FOR ANY REASON. *NOT EVER.*

I WANT TO KNOW *WHY.*

WHY WHAT?

IF I'D BEEN KILLED, IT WOULD'VE BEEN ON THEIR HEADS, NOT YOURS.

I HAD A CHANCE TO SAVE YOU, SO I HAD TO TRY. TO LET YOU DIE... IT'D BE NO DIFFERENT FROM KILLING YOU MYSELF.

I WON'T TAKE A LIFE. NOT FOR ANY REASON.

NOT *EVER.*

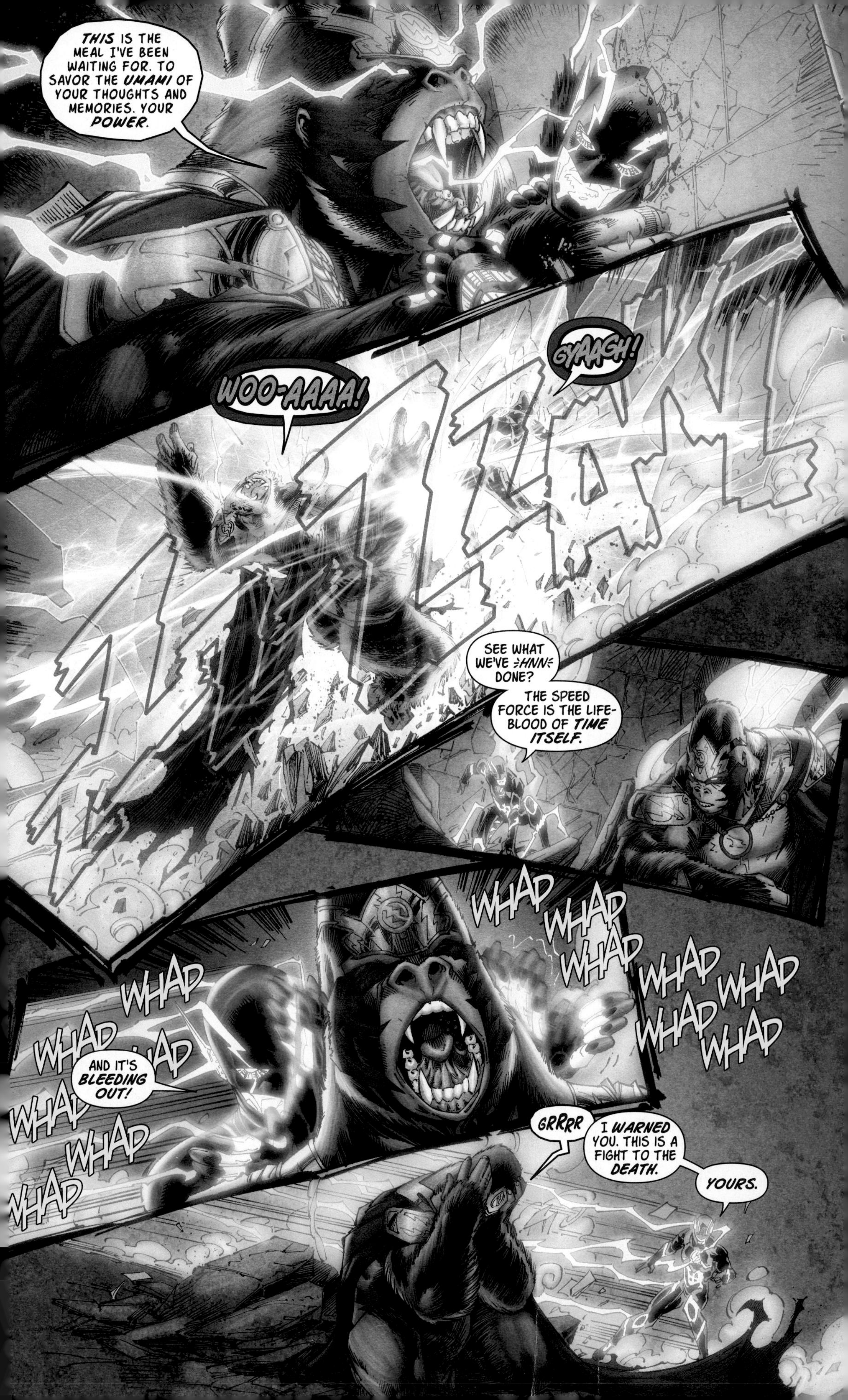
THIS IS THE MEAL I'VE BEEN WAITING FOR. TO SAVOR THE UMAMI OF YOUR THOUGHTS AND MEMORIES. YOUR POWER.
WOO-AAAA!
GYAAGH!
SEE WHAT WE'VE -HNN- DONE?
THE SPEED FORCE IS THE LIFE-BLOOD OF TIME ITSELF.
WHAP WHAP WHAP WHAP WHAP WHAP WHAP
WHAP WHAP WHAP WHAP WHAP WHAP
AND IT'S BLEEDING OUT!
GRRRR
I WARNED YOU. THIS IS A FIGHT TO THE DEATH.
YOURS.

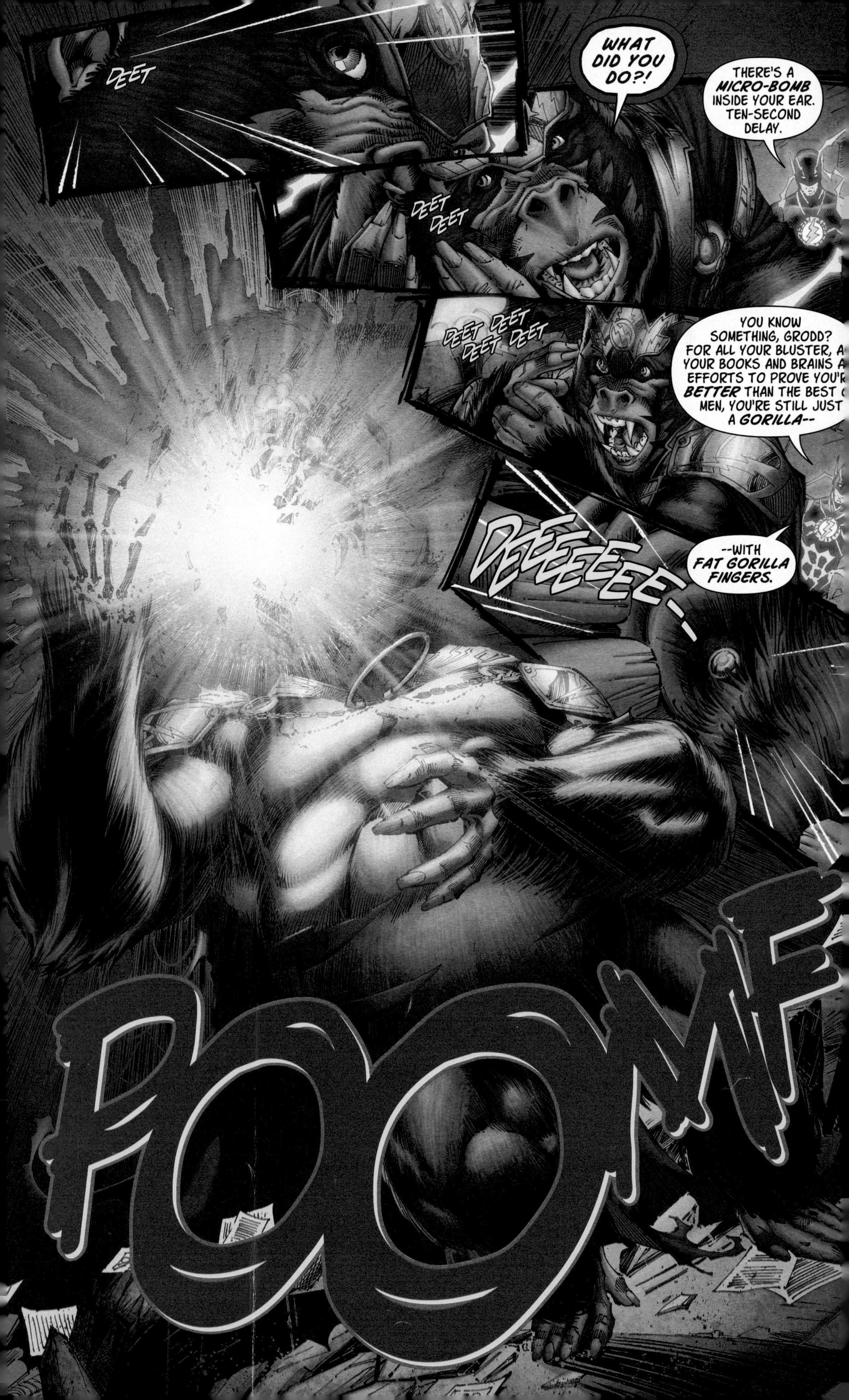
DEET
WHAT DID YOU DO?!
THERE'S A MICRO-BOMB INSIDE YOUR EAR. TEN-SECOND DELAY.
DEET DEET
DEET DEET DEET DEET
YOU KNOW SOMETHING, GRODD? FOR ALL YOUR BLUSTER, A YOUR BOOKS AND BRAINS A EFFORTS TO PROVE YOU'R BETTER THAN THE BEST MEN, YOU'RE STILL JUST A GORILLA--
DEEEEEEEE--
--WITH FAT GORILLA FINGERS.
FOOMF

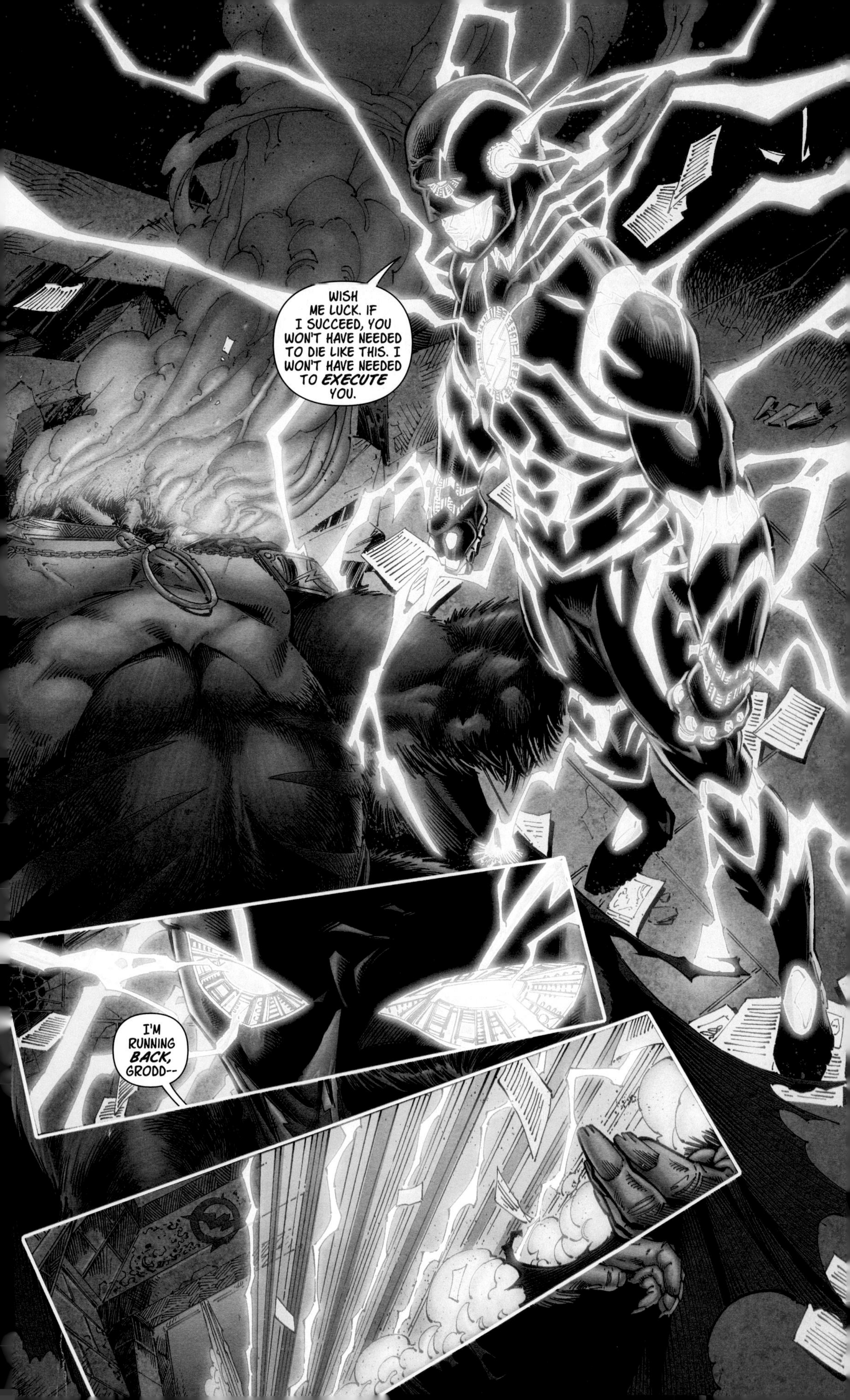
WISH ME LUCK. IF I SUCCEED, YOU WON'T HAVE NEEDED TO DIE LIKE THIS. I WON'T HAVE NEEDED TO *EXECUTE* YOU.
I'M RUNNING *BACK,* GRODD--

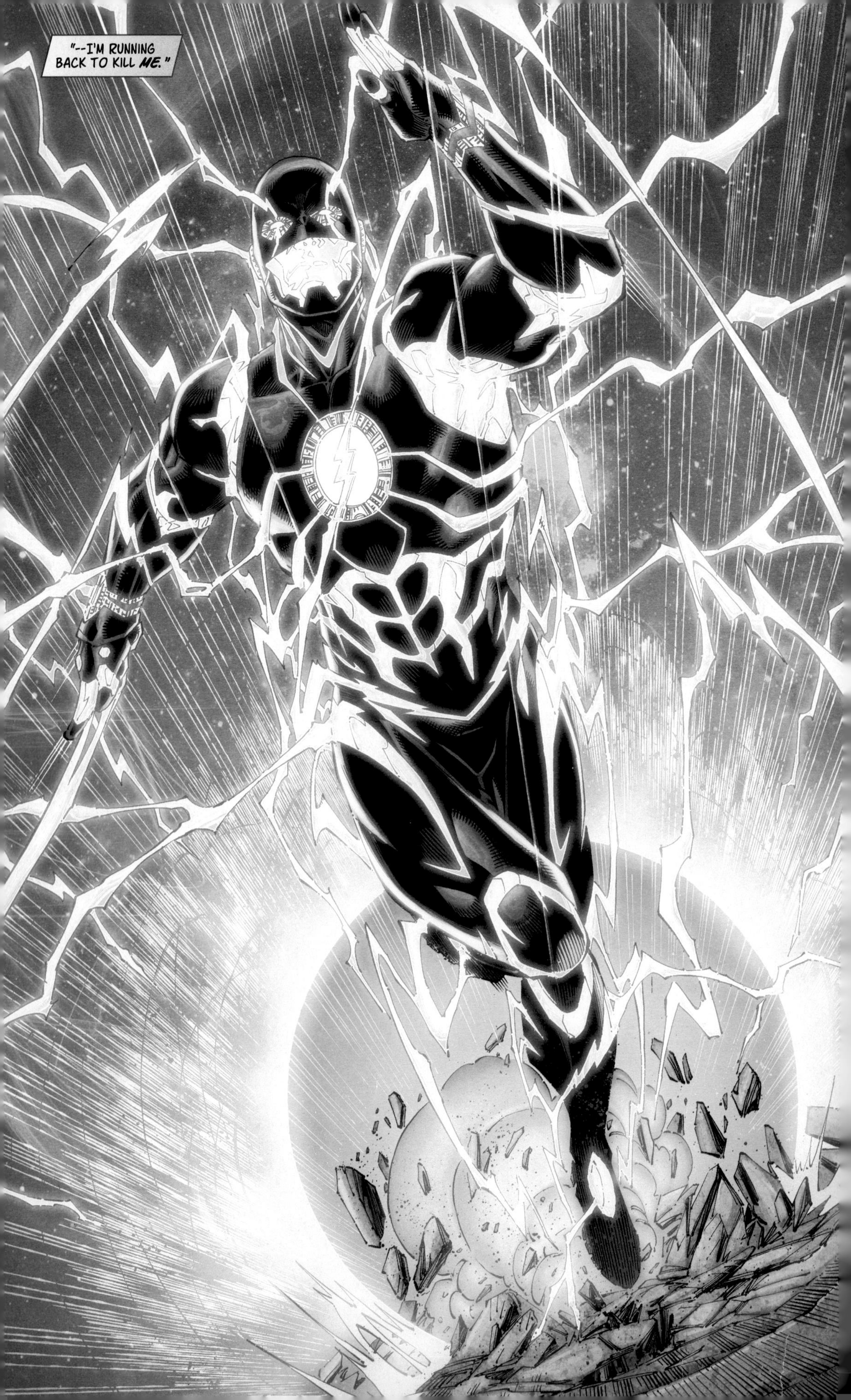
"--I'M RUNNING BACK TO KILL ME."

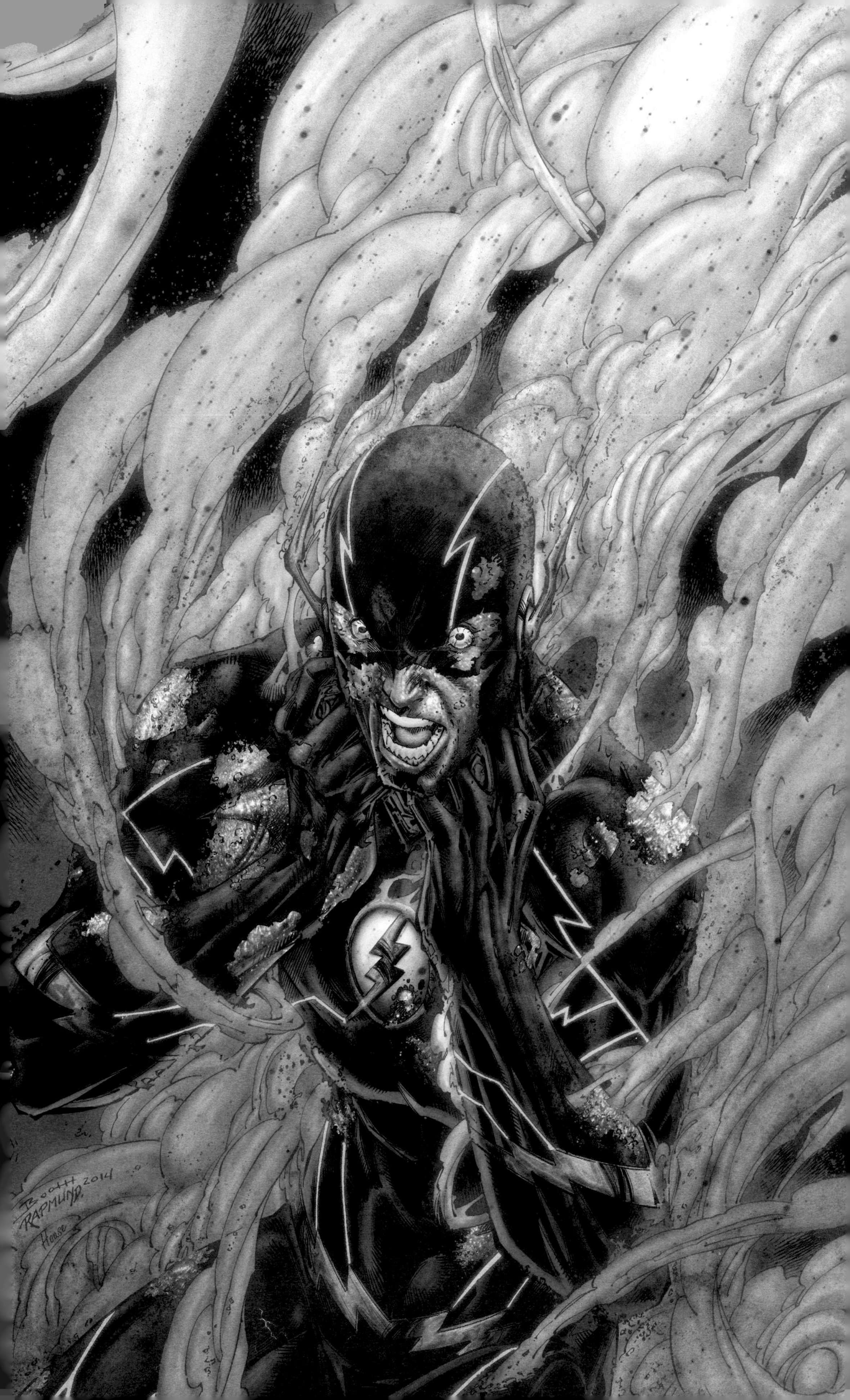
BOOTH 2014
RAPMUND

THROUGH A LOOKING GLASS DARKLY
ROBERT VENDITTI & VAN JENSEN writers **BRETT BOOTH** penciller **NORM RAPMUND** inker

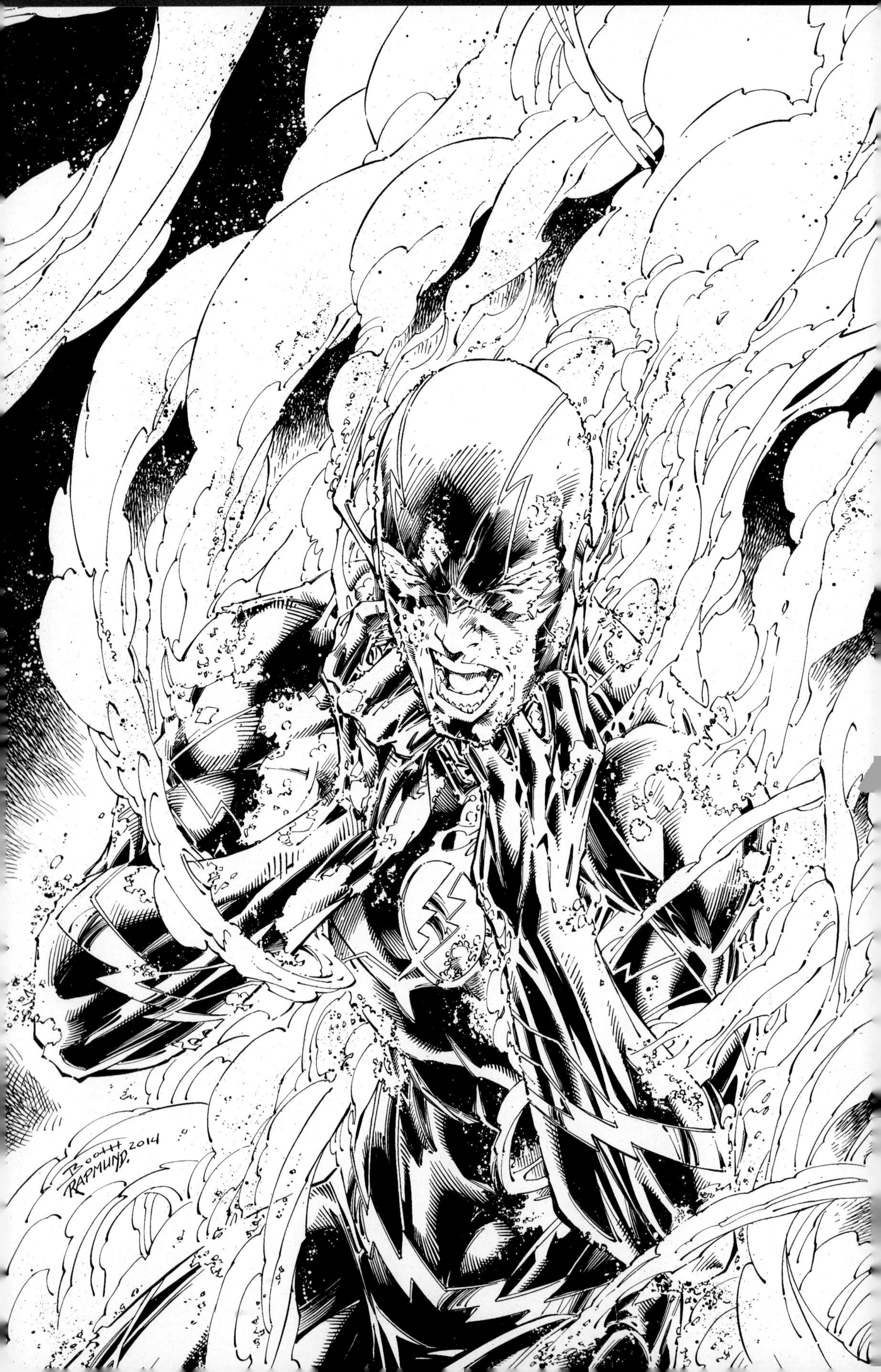
BOOTH 2014
RAPMUND.

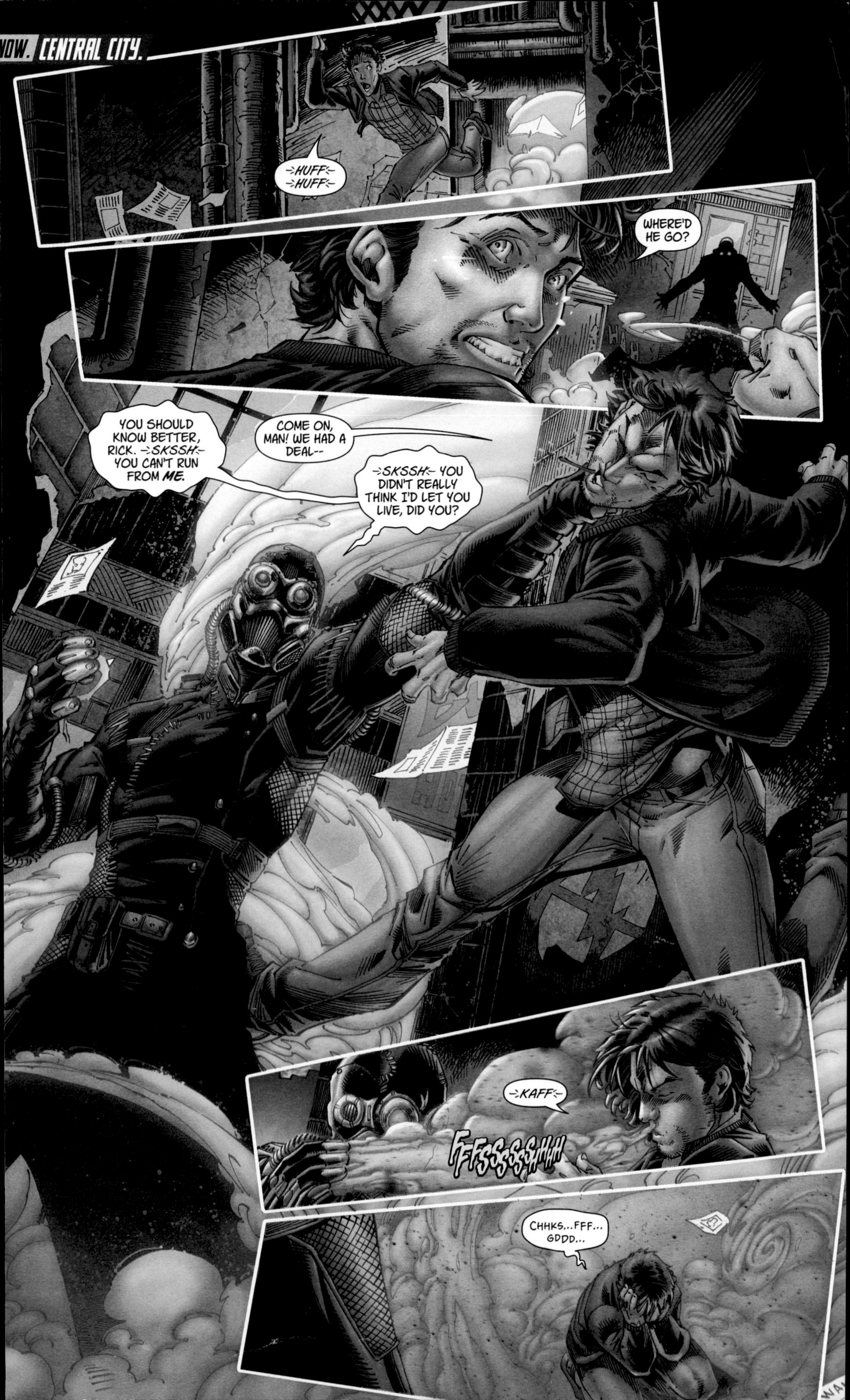
NOW. CENTRAL CITY.
-HUFF- -HUFF-
WHERE'D HE GO?
YOU SHOULD KNOW BETTER, RICK. -SKSSH- YOU CAN'T RUN FROM ME.
COME ON, MAN! WE HAD A DEAL--
-SKSSH- YOU DIDN'T REALLY THINK I'D LET YOU LIVE, DID YOU?
-KAFF-
FFFSSSSSSHHH
CHHKS...FFF... GDDD...

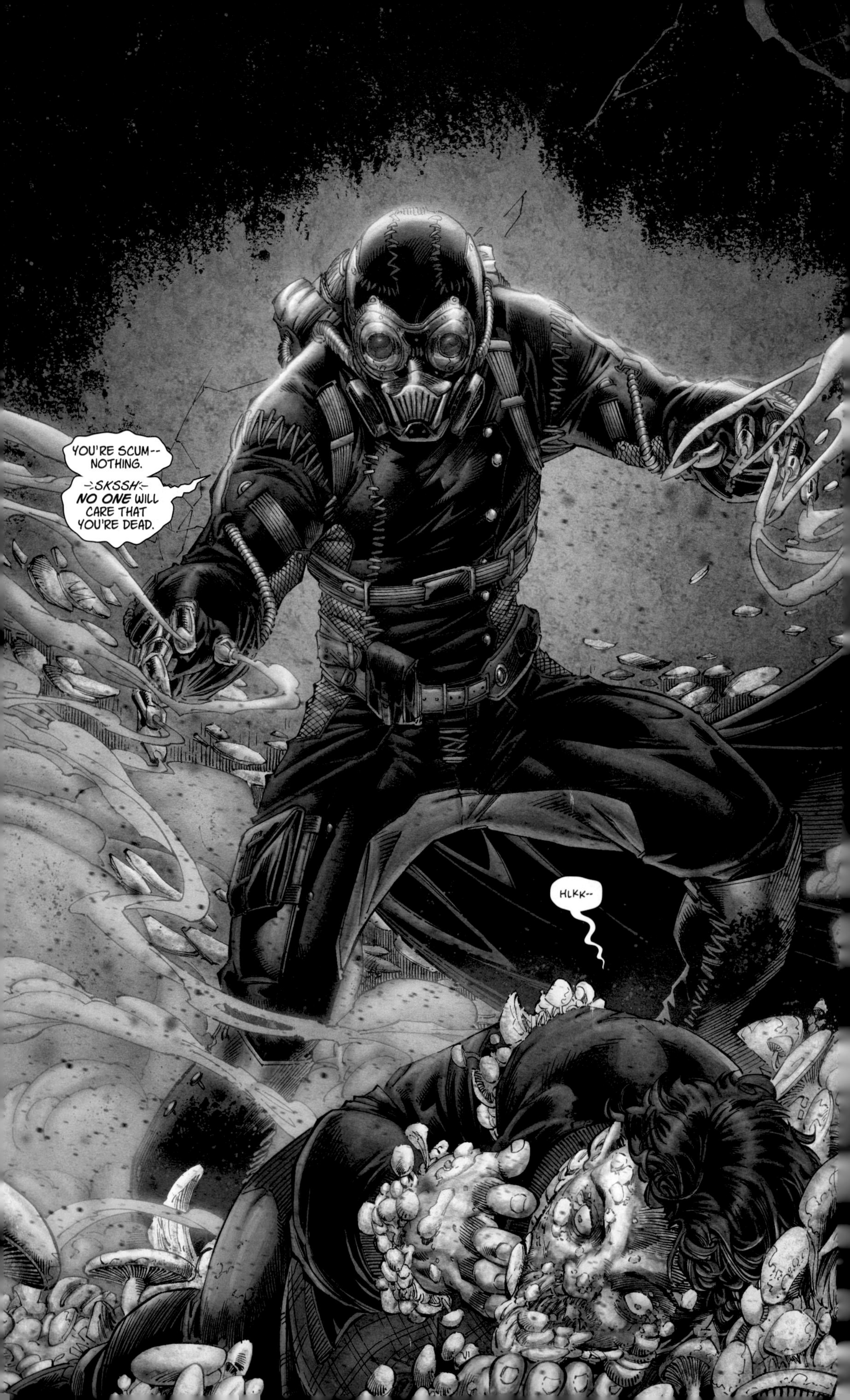
YOU'RE SCUM--
NOTHING.
-SKSSH- NO ONE WILL CARE THAT YOU'RE DEAD.
HLKK--

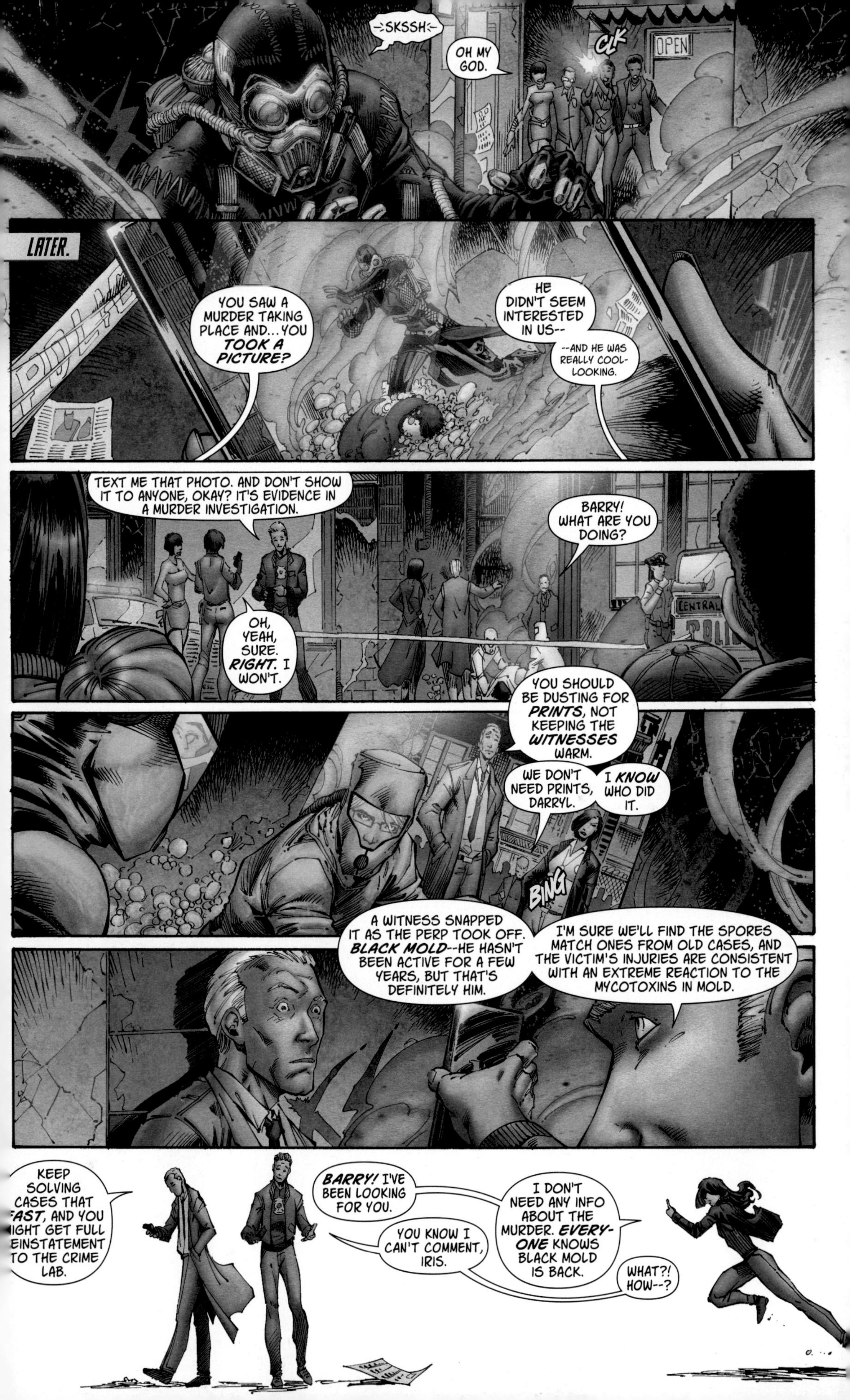
-SKSSH-
OH MY GOD.
CLK
OPEN
LATER.
YOU SAW A MURDER TAKING PLACE AND...YOU TOOK A PICTURE?
HE DIDN'T SEEM INTERESTED IN US--
--AND HE WAS REALLY COOL-LOOKING.
TEXT ME THAT PHOTO. AND DON'T SHOW IT TO ANYONE, OKAY? IT'S EVIDENCE IN A MURDER INVESTIGATION.
OH, YEAH, SURE. RIGHT. I WON'T.
BARRY! WHAT ARE YOU DOING?
CENTRAL
YOU SHOULD BE DUSTING FOR PRINTS, NOT KEEPING THE WITNESSES WARM.
WE DON'T NEED PRINTS, DARRYL.
I KNOW WHO DID IT.
BING
A WITNESS SNAPPED IT AS THE PERP TOOK OFF. BLACK MOLD--HE HASN'T BEEN ACTIVE FOR A FEW YEARS, BUT THAT'S DEFINITELY HIM.
I'M SURE WE'LL FIND THE SPORES MATCH ONES FROM OLD CASES, AND THE VICTIM'S INJURIES ARE CONSISTENT WITH AN EXTREME REACTION TO THE MYCOTOXINS IN MOLD.
KEEP SOLVING CASES THAT FAST, AND YOU MIGHT GET FULL REINSTATEMENT TO THE CRIME LAB.
BARRY! I'VE BEEN LOOKING FOR YOU.
YOU KNOW I CAN'T COMMENT, IRIS.
I DON'T NEED ANY INFO ABOUT THE MURDER. EVERY-ONE KNOWS BLACK MOLD IS BACK.
WHAT?! HOW--?

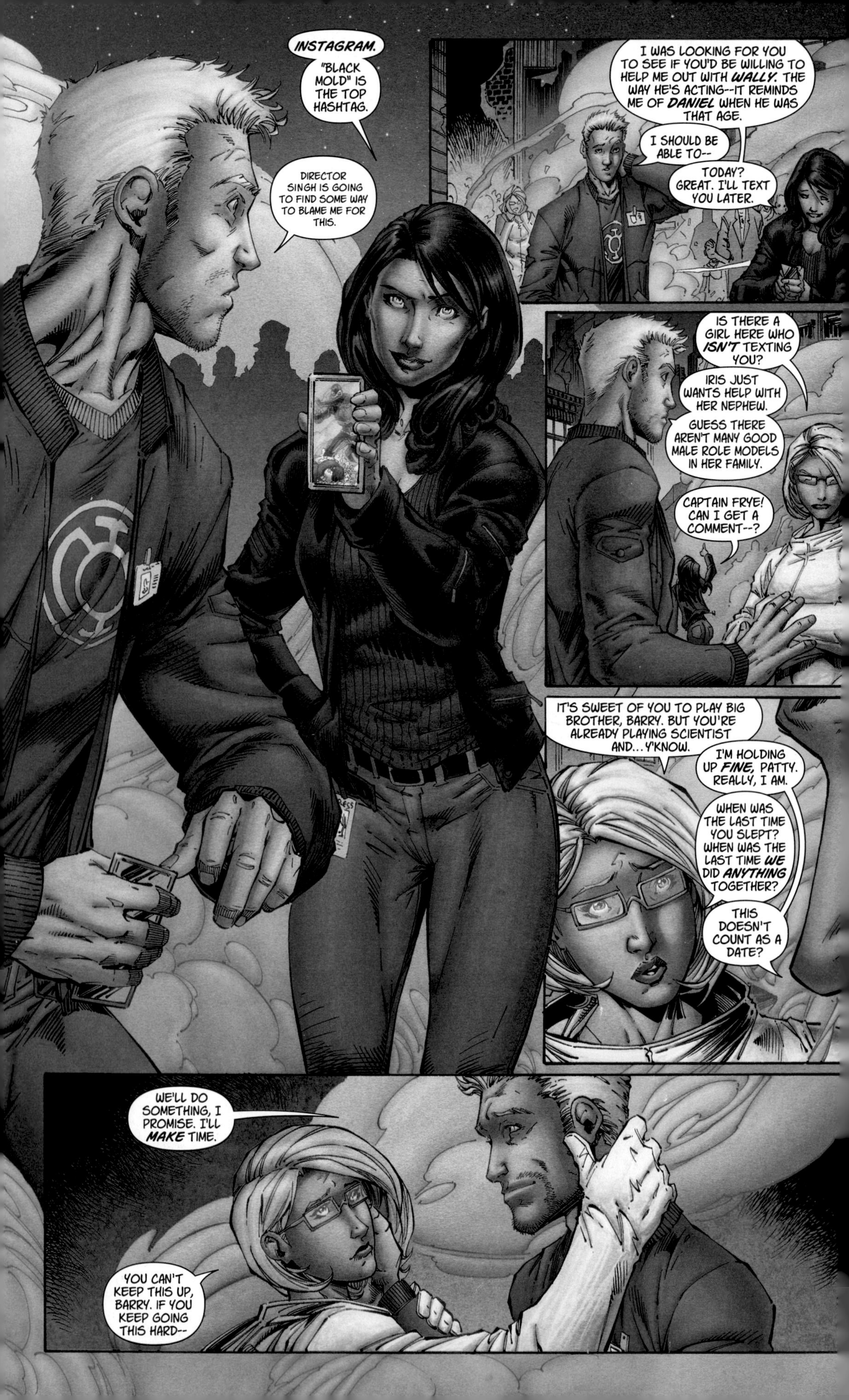

INSTAGRAM.
"BLACK MOLD" IS THE TOP HASHTAG.
DIRECTOR SINGH IS GOING TO FIND SOME WAY TO BLAME ME FOR THIS.
I WAS LOOKING FOR YOU TO SEE IF YOU'D BE WILLING TO HELP ME OUT WITH WALLY. THE WAY HE'S ACTING--IT REMINDS ME OF DANIEL WHEN HE WAS THAT AGE.
I SHOULD BE ABLE TO--
TODAY? GREAT. I'LL TEXT YOU LATER.
IS THERE A GIRL HERE WHO ISN'T TEXTING YOU?
IRIS JUST WANTS HELP WITH HER NEPHEW.
GUESS THERE AREN'T MANY GOOD MALE ROLE MODELS IN HER FAMILY.
CAPTAIN FRYE! CAN I GET A COMMENT--?
IT'S SWEET OF YOU TO PLAY BIG BROTHER, BARRY. BUT YOU'RE ALREADY PLAYING SCIENTIST AND... Y'KNOW.
I'M HOLDING UP FINE, PATTY. REALLY, I AM.
WHEN WAS THE LAST TIME YOU SLEPT? WHEN WAS THE LAST TIME WE DID ANYTHING TOGETHER?
THIS DOESN'T COUNT AS A DATE?
WE'LL DO SOMETHING, I PROMISE. I'LL MAKE TIME.
YOU CAN'T KEEP THIS UP, BARRY. IF YOU KEEP GOING THIS HARD--

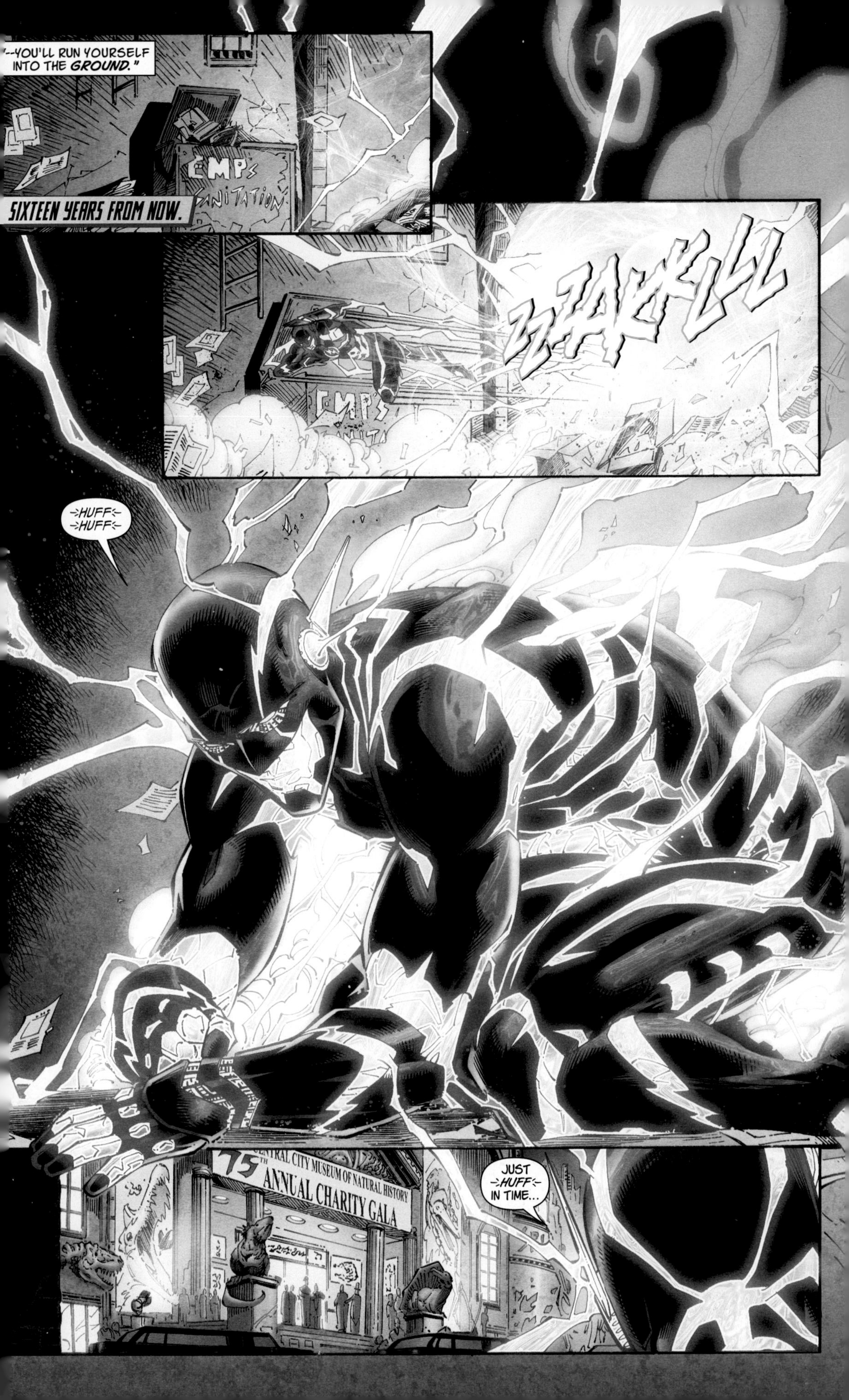
"--YOU'LL RUN YOURSELF INTO THE GROUND."
SIXTEEN YEARS FROM NOW.
CMP'S SANITATION
ZZZAKKLLL
-HUFF- -HUFF-
75TH ANNUAL CHARITY GALA
CENTRAL CITY MUSEUM OF NATURAL HISTORY
JUST -HUFF- IN TIME...

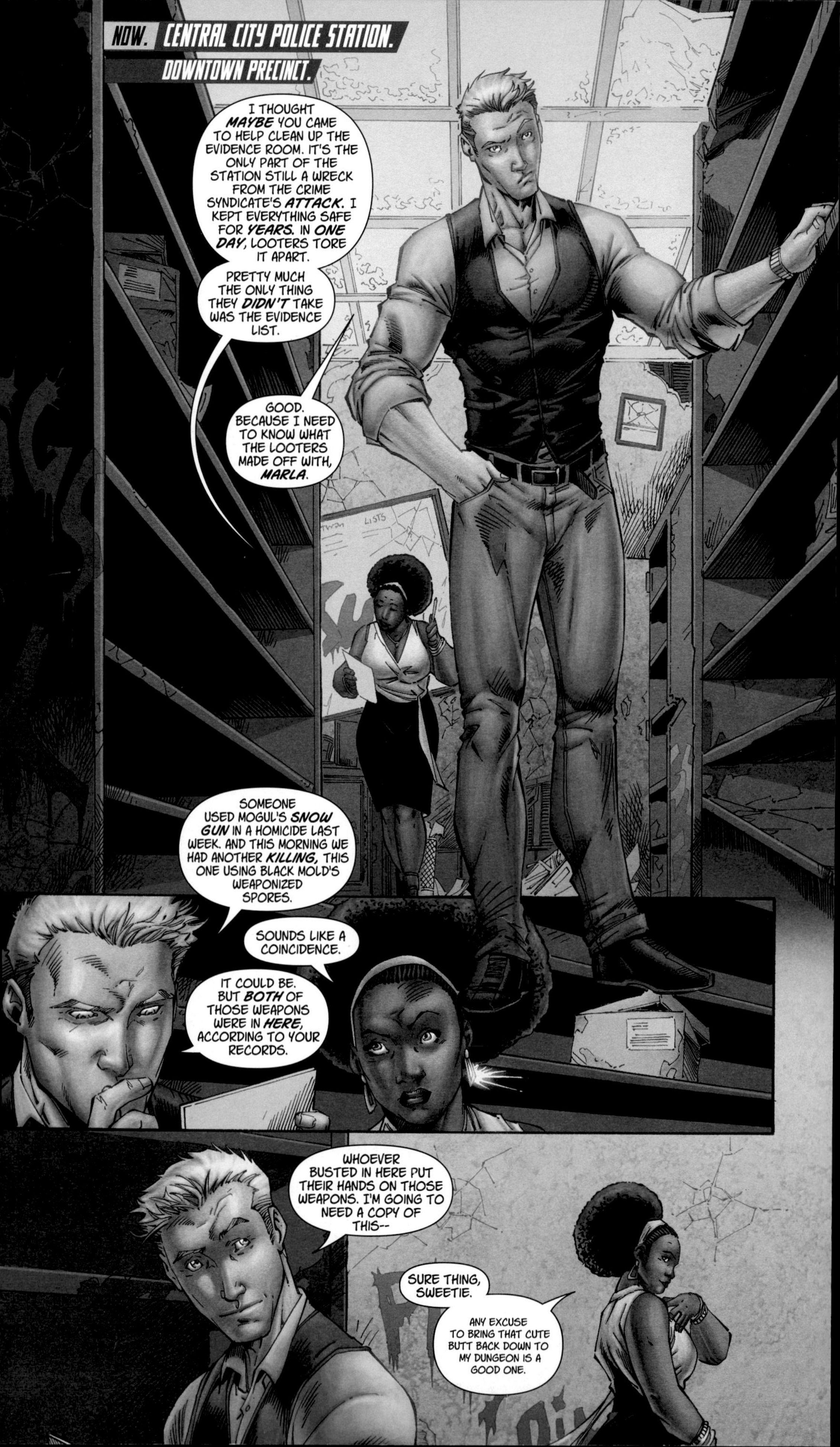
NOW. CENTRAL CITY POLICE STATION.
DOWNTOWN PRECINCT.
I THOUGHT MAYBE YOU CAME TO HELP CLEAN UP THE EVIDENCE ROOM. IT'S THE ONLY PART OF THE STATION STILL A WRECK FROM THE CRIME SYNDICATE'S ATTACK. I KEPT EVERYTHING SAFE FOR YEARS. IN ONE DAY, LOOTERS TORE IT APART.
PRETTY MUCH THE ONLY THING THEY DIDN'T TAKE WAS THE EVIDENCE LIST.
GOOD. BECAUSE I NEED TO KNOW WHAT THE LOOTERS MADE OFF WITH, MARLA.
SOMEONE USED MOGUL'S SNOW GUN IN A HOMICIDE LAST WEEK. AND THIS MORNING WE HAD ANOTHER KILLING, THIS ONE USING BLACK MOLD'S WEAPONIZED SPORES.
SOUNDS LIKE A COINCIDENCE.
IT COULD BE. BUT BOTH OF THOSE WEAPONS WERE IN HERE, ACCORDING TO YOUR RECORDS.
WHOEVER BUSTED IN HERE PUT THEIR HANDS ON THOSE WEAPONS. I'M GOING TO NEED A COPY OF THIS--
SURE THING, SWEETIE.
ANY EXCUSE TO BRING THAT CUTE BUTT BACK DOWN TO MY DUNGEON IS A GOOD ONE.

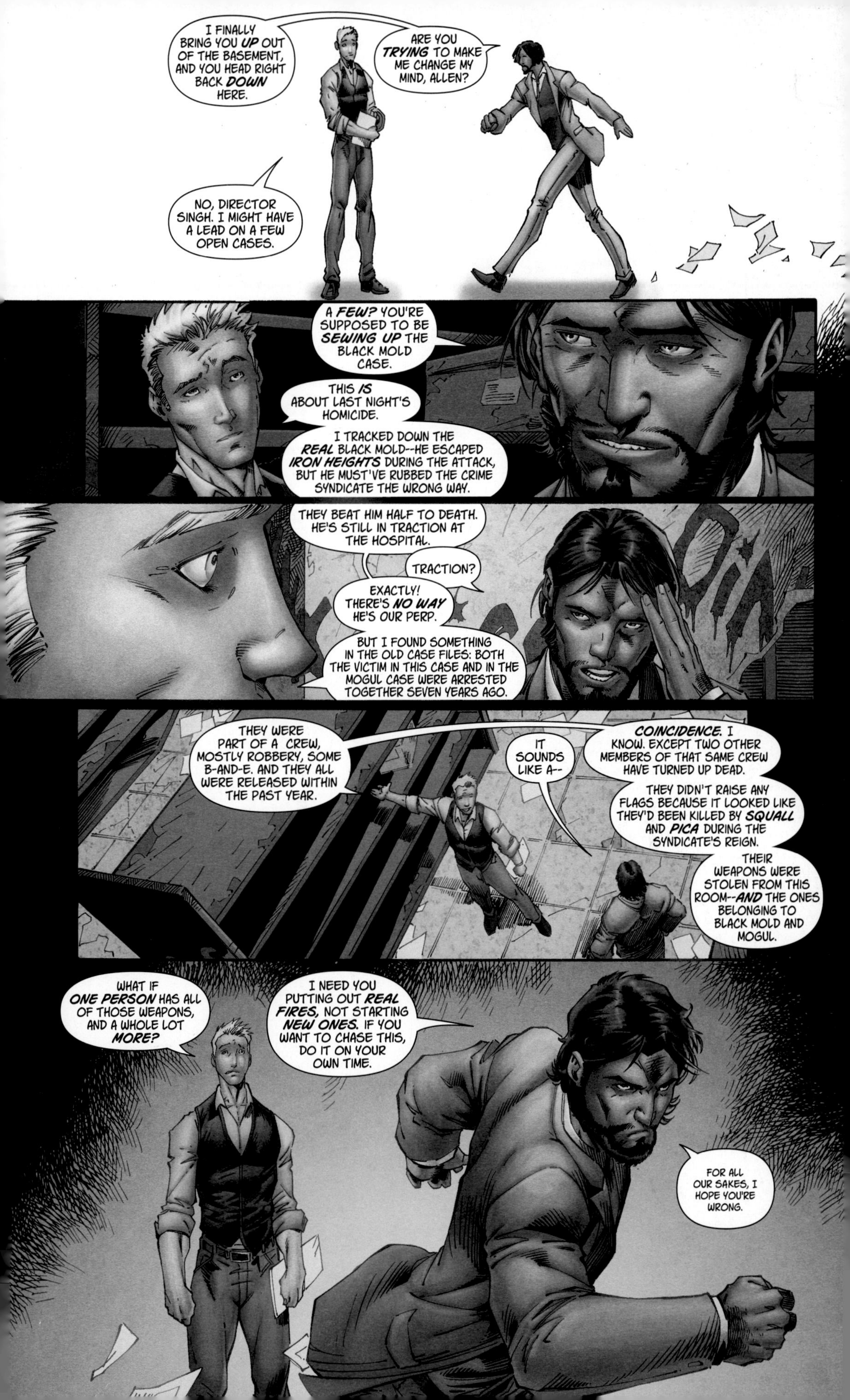

I FINALLY BRING YOU *UP* OUT OF THE BASEMENT, AND YOU HEAD RIGHT BACK *DOWN* HERE.
ARE YOU *TRYING* TO MAKE ME CHANGE MY MIND, ALLEN?
NO, DIRECTOR SINGH. I MIGHT HAVE A LEAD ON A FEW OPEN CASES.
A *FEW?* YOU'RE SUPPOSED TO BE *SEWING UP* THE BLACK MOLD CASE.
THIS *IS* ABOUT LAST NIGHT'S HOMICIDE.
I TRACKED DOWN THE *REAL* BLACK MOLD--HE ESCAPED *IRON HEIGHTS* DURING THE ATTACK, BUT HE MUST'VE RUBBED THE CRIME SYNDICATE THE WRONG WAY.
THEY BEAT HIM HALF TO DEATH. HE'S STILL IN TRACTION AT THE HOSPITAL.
TRACTION?
EXACTLY! THERE'S *NO WAY* HE'S OUR PERP.
BUT I FOUND SOMETHING IN THE OLD CASE FILES: BOTH THE VICTIM IN THIS CASE AND IN THE MOGUL CASE WERE ARRESTED TOGETHER SEVEN YEARS AGO.
THEY WERE PART OF A CREW, MOSTLY ROBBERY, SOME B-AND-E. AND THEY ALL WERE RELEASED WITHIN THE PAST YEAR.
IT SOUNDS LIKE A--
COINCIDENCE. I KNOW. EXCEPT TWO OTHER MEMBERS OF THAT SAME CREW HAVE TURNED UP DEAD.
THEY DIDN'T RAISE ANY FLAGS BECAUSE IT LOOKED LIKE THEY'D BEEN KILLED BY *SQUALL* AND *PICA* DURING THE SYNDICATE'S REIGN.
THEIR WEAPONS WERE STOLEN FROM THIS ROOM--*AND* THE ONES BELONGING TO BLACK MOLD AND MOGUL.
WHAT IF *ONE PERSON* HAS ALL OF THOSE WEAPONS, AND A WHOLE LOT *MORE?*
I NEED YOU PUTTING OUT *REAL FIRES,* NOT STARTING *NEW ONES.* IF YOU WANT TO CHASE THIS, DO IT ON YOUR OWN TIME.
FOR ALL OUR SAKES, I HOPE YOU'RE WRONG.

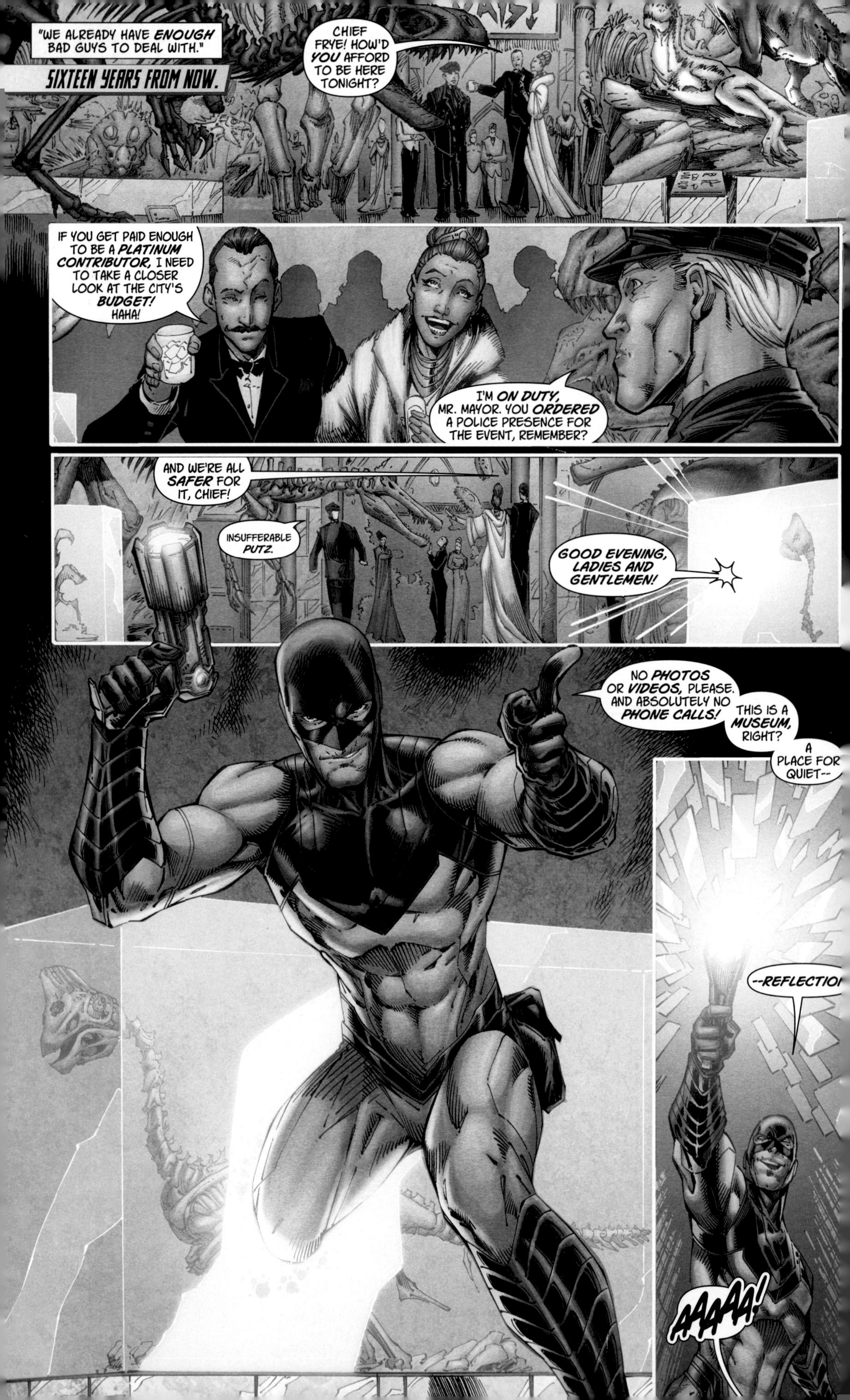
"WE ALREADY HAVE ENOUGH BAD GUYS TO DEAL WITH."
SIXTEEN YEARS FROM NOW.
CHIEF FRYE! HOW'D YOU AFFORD TO BE HERE TONIGHT?
IF YOU GET PAID ENOUGH TO BE A PLATINUM CONTRIBUTOR, I NEED TO TAKE A CLOSER LOOK AT THE CITY'S BUDGET! HAHA!
I'M ON DUTY, MR. MAYOR. YOU ORDERED A POLICE PRESENCE FOR THE EVENT, REMEMBER?
AND WE'RE ALL SAFER FOR IT, CHIEF!
INSUFFERABLE PUTZ.
GOOD EVENING, LADIES AND GENTLEMEN!
NO PHOTOS OR VIDEOS, PLEASE. AND ABSOLUTELY NO PHONE CALLS!
THIS IS A MUSEUM, RIGHT?
A PLACE FOR QUIET--
--REFLECTION
AAAAA!

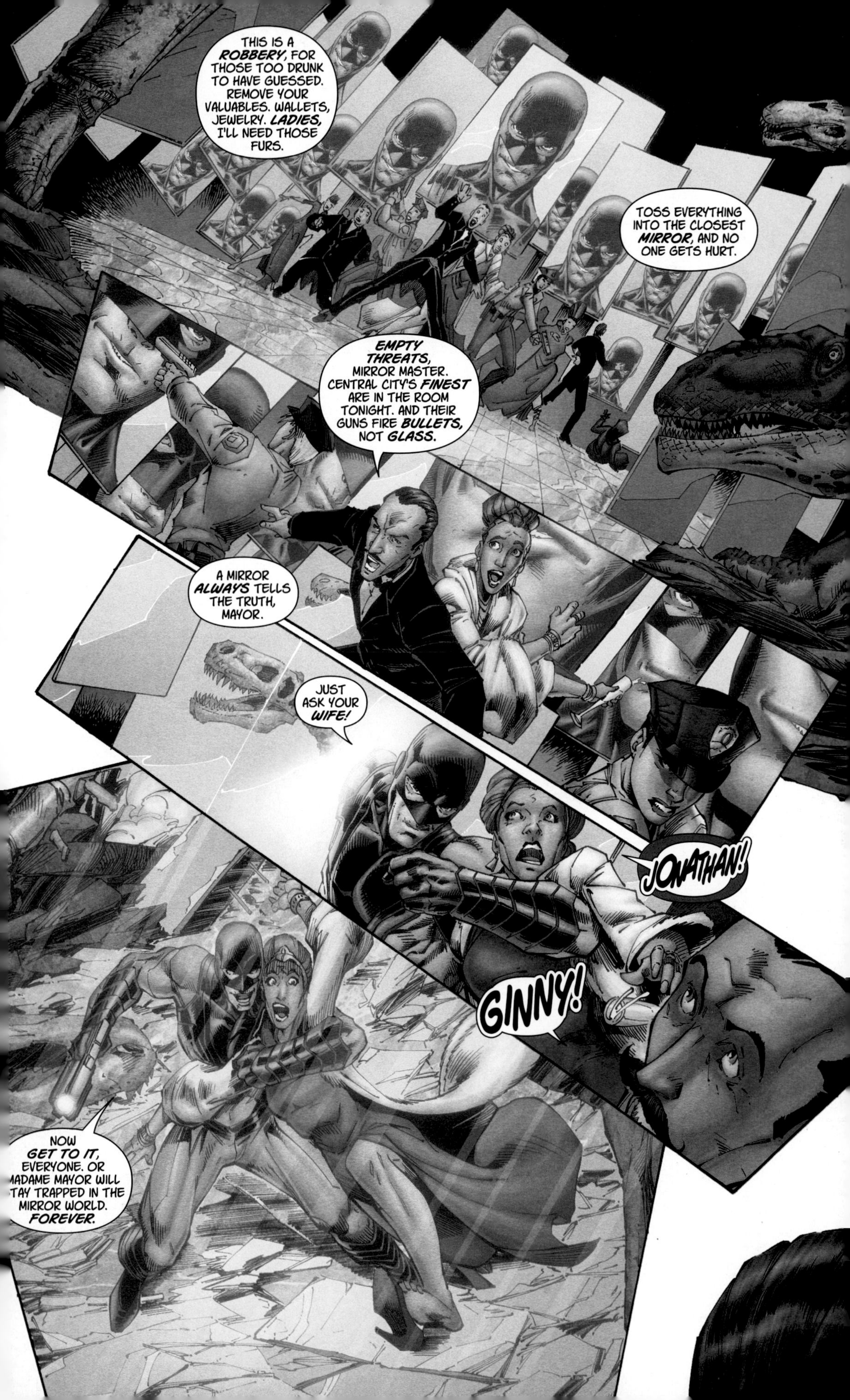
THIS IS A ROBBERY, FOR THOSE TOO DRUNK TO HAVE GUESSED. REMOVE YOUR VALUABLES. WALLETS, JEWELRY. LADIES, I'LL NEED THOSE FURS.
TOSS EVERYTHING INTO THE CLOSEST MIRROR, AND NO ONE GETS HURT.
EMPTY THREATS, MIRROR MASTER. CENTRAL CITY'S FINEST ARE IN THE ROOM TONIGHT. AND THEIR GUNS FIRE BULLETS, NOT GLASS.
A MIRROR ALWAYS TELLS THE TRUTH, MAYOR.
JUST ASK YOUR WIFE!
JONATHAN!
GINNY!
NOW GET TO IT, EVERYONE. OR ADAME MAYOR WILL TAY TRAPPED IN THE MIRROR WORLD. FOREVER.

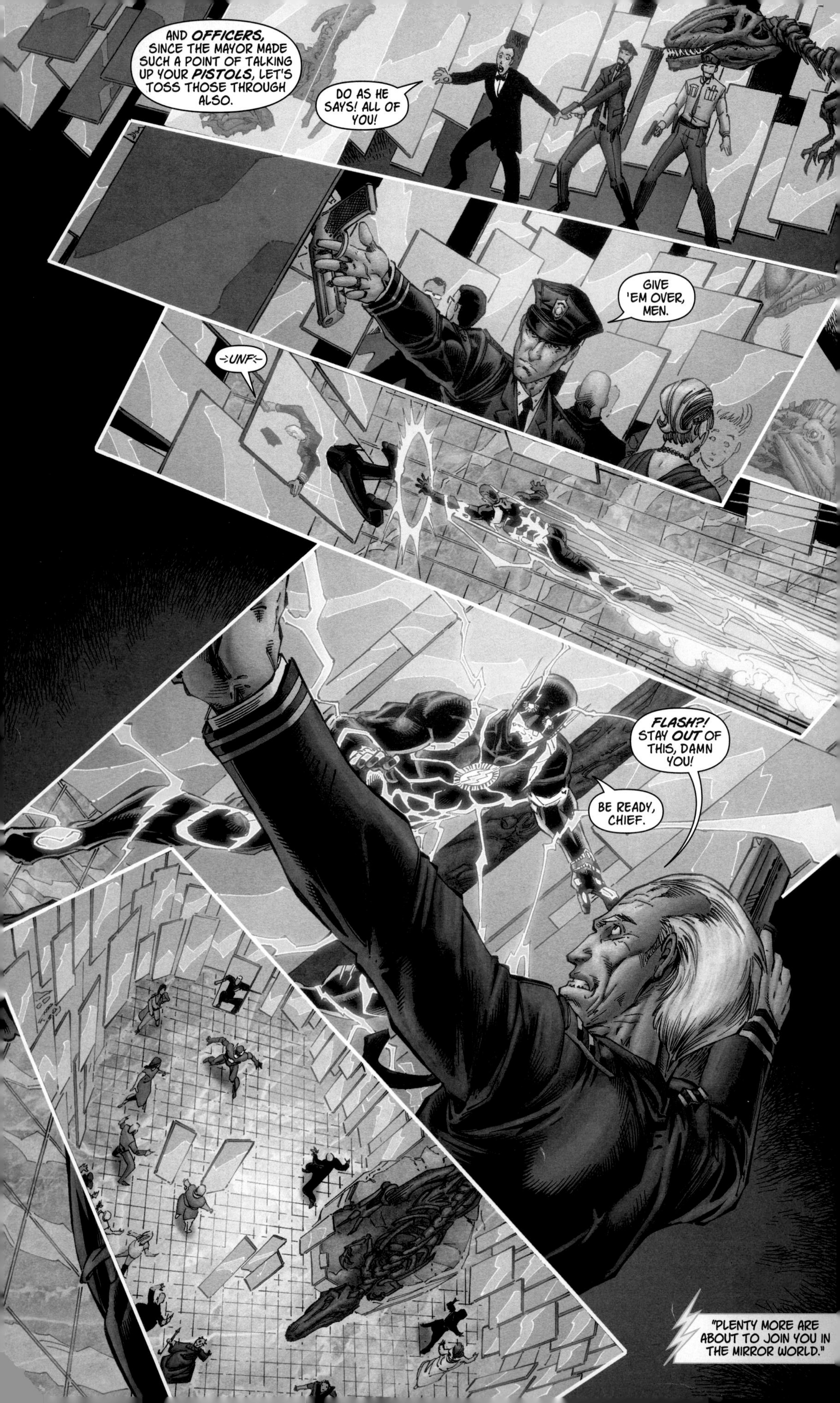
AND OFFICERS, SINCE THE MAYOR MADE SUCH A POINT OF TALKING UP YOUR PISTOLS, LET'S TOSS THOSE THROUGH ALSO.
DO AS HE SAYS! ALL OF YOU!
GIVE 'EM OVER, MEN.
UNF
FLASH?! STAY OUT OF THIS, DAMN YOU!
BE READY, CHIEF.
"PLENTY MORE ARE ABOUT TO JOIN YOU IN THE MIRROR WORLD."

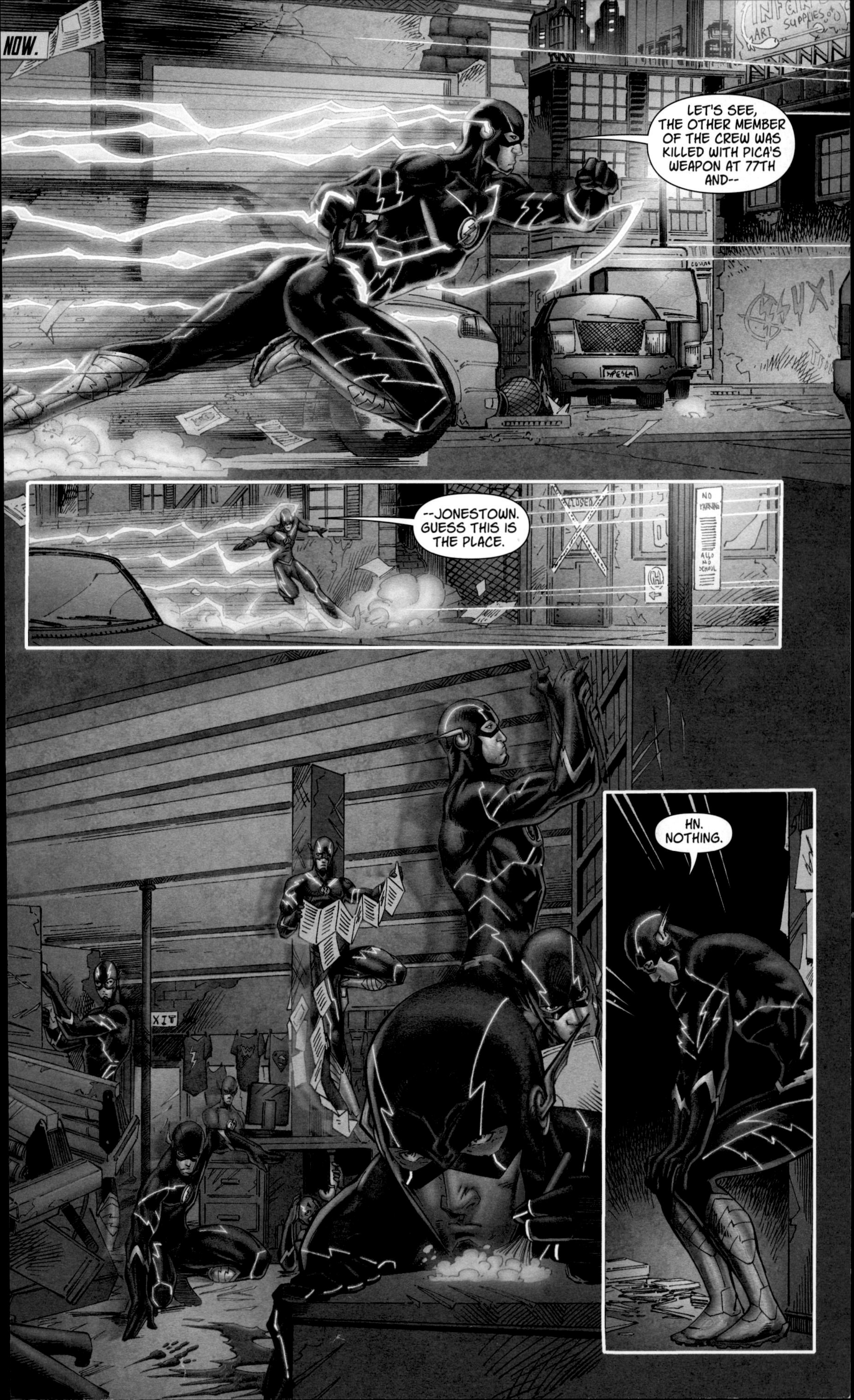
NOW.
LET'S SEE, THE OTHER MEMBER OF THE CREW WAS KILLED WITH PICA'S WEAPON AT 77TH AND--
--JONESTOWN. GUESS THIS IS THE PLACE.
HN. NOTHING.

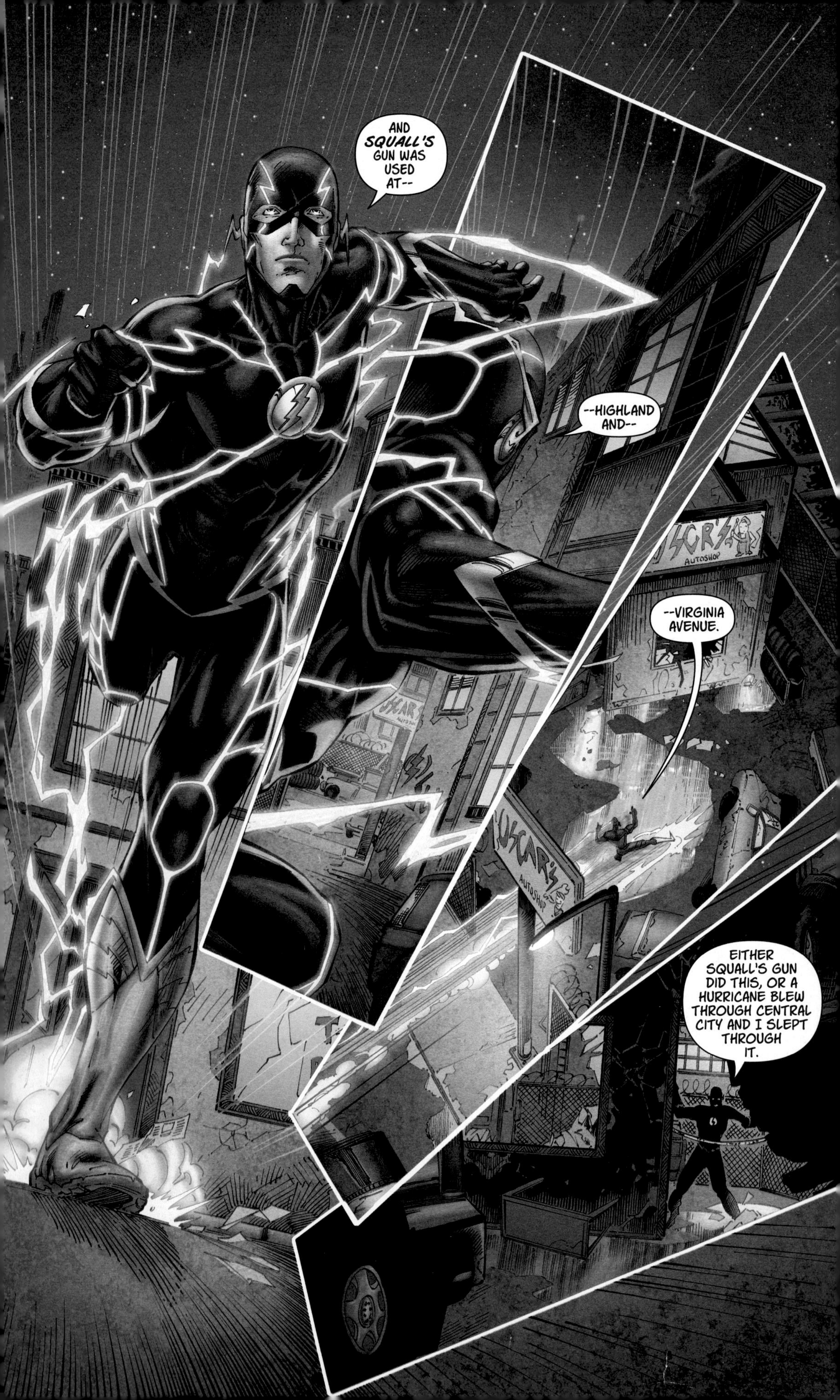
AND SQUALL'S GUN WAS USED AT--
--HIGHLAND AND--
--VIRGINIA AVENUE.
EITHER SQUALL'S GUN DID THIS, OR A HURRICANE BLEW THROUGH CENTRAL CITY AND I SLEPT THROUGH IT.

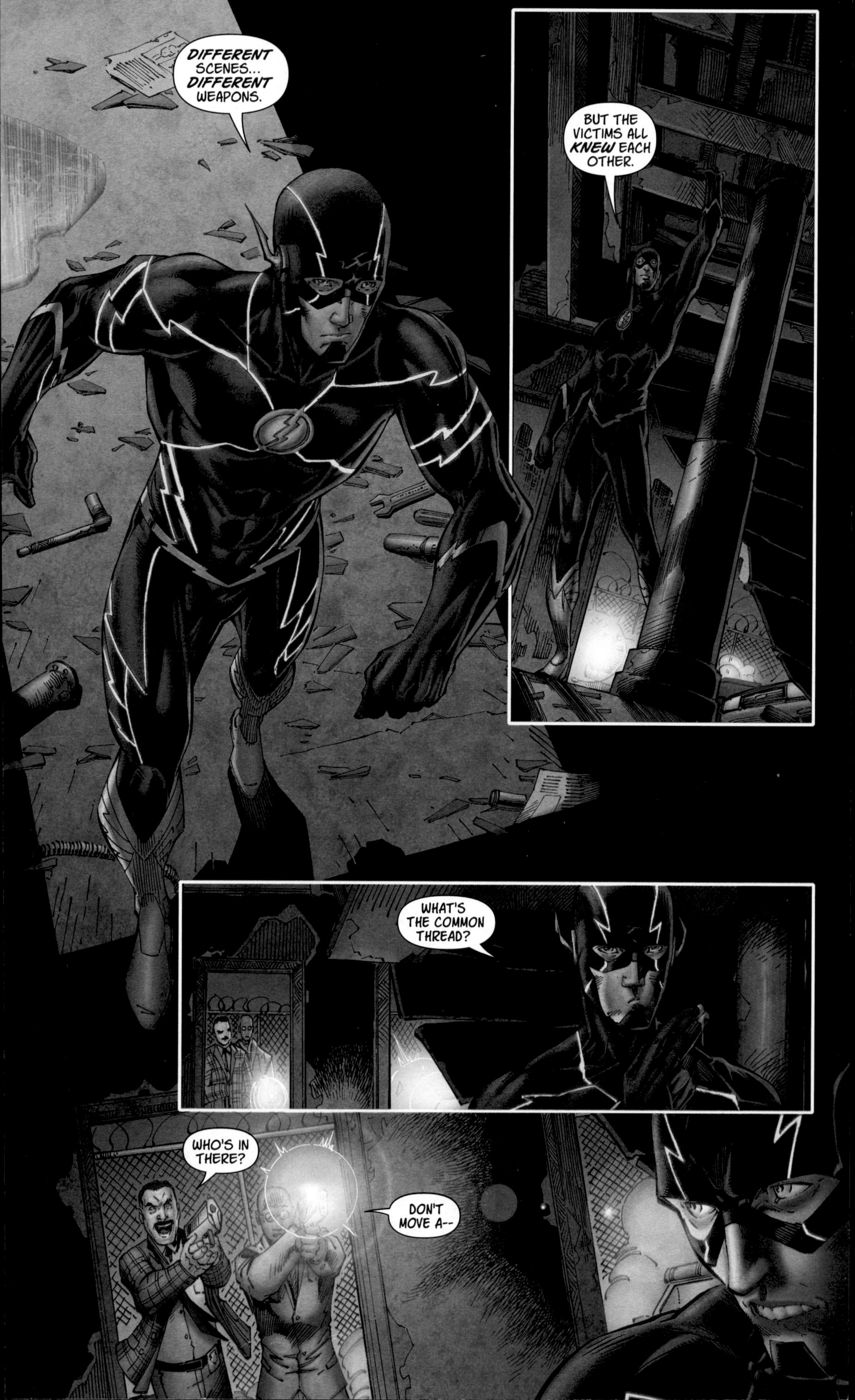
DIFFERENT SCENES... DIFFERENT WEAPONS.
BUT THE VICTIMS ALL KNEW EACH OTHER.
WHAT'S THE COMMON THREAD?
WHO'S IN THERE?
DON'T MOVE A--

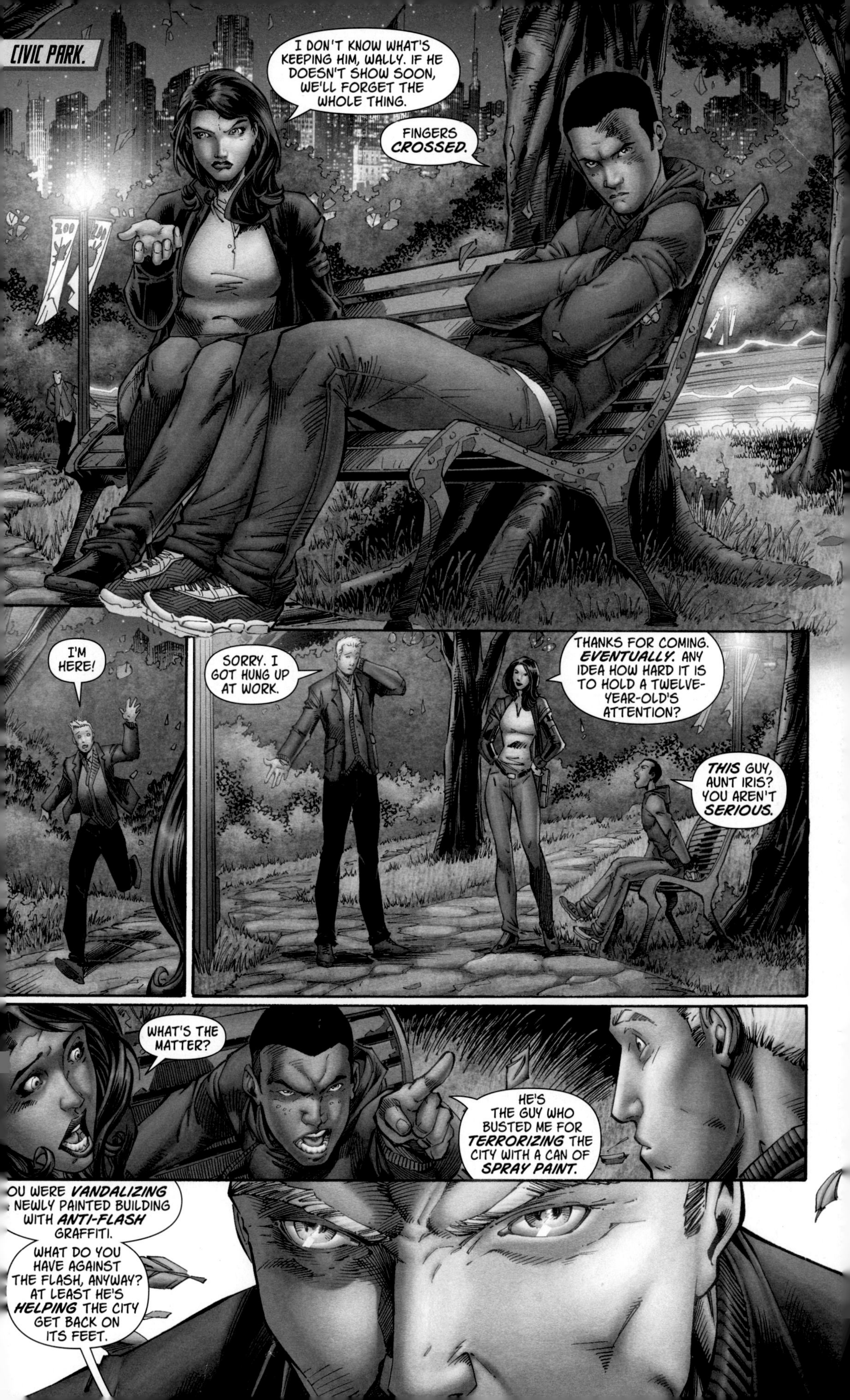
CIVIC PARK.
I DON'T KNOW WHAT'S KEEPING HIM, WALLY. IF HE DOESN'T SHOW SOON, WE'LL FORGET THE WHOLE THING.
FINGERS CROSSED.
ZOO
I'M HERE!
SORRY. I GOT HUNG UP AT WORK.
THANKS FOR COMING. EVENTUALLY. ANY IDEA HOW HARD IT IS TO HOLD A TWELVE-YEAR-OLD'S ATTENTION?
THIS GUY, AUNT IRIS? YOU AREN'T SERIOUS.
WHAT'S THE MATTER?
HE'S THE GUY WHO BUSTED ME FOR TERRORIZING THE CITY WITH A CAN OF SPRAY PAINT.
OU WERE VANDALIZING NEWLY PAINTED BUILDING WITH ANTI-FLASH GRAFFITI.
WHAT DO YOU HAVE AGAINST THE FLASH, ANYWAY? AT LEAST HE'S HELPING THE CITY GET BACK ON ITS FEET.

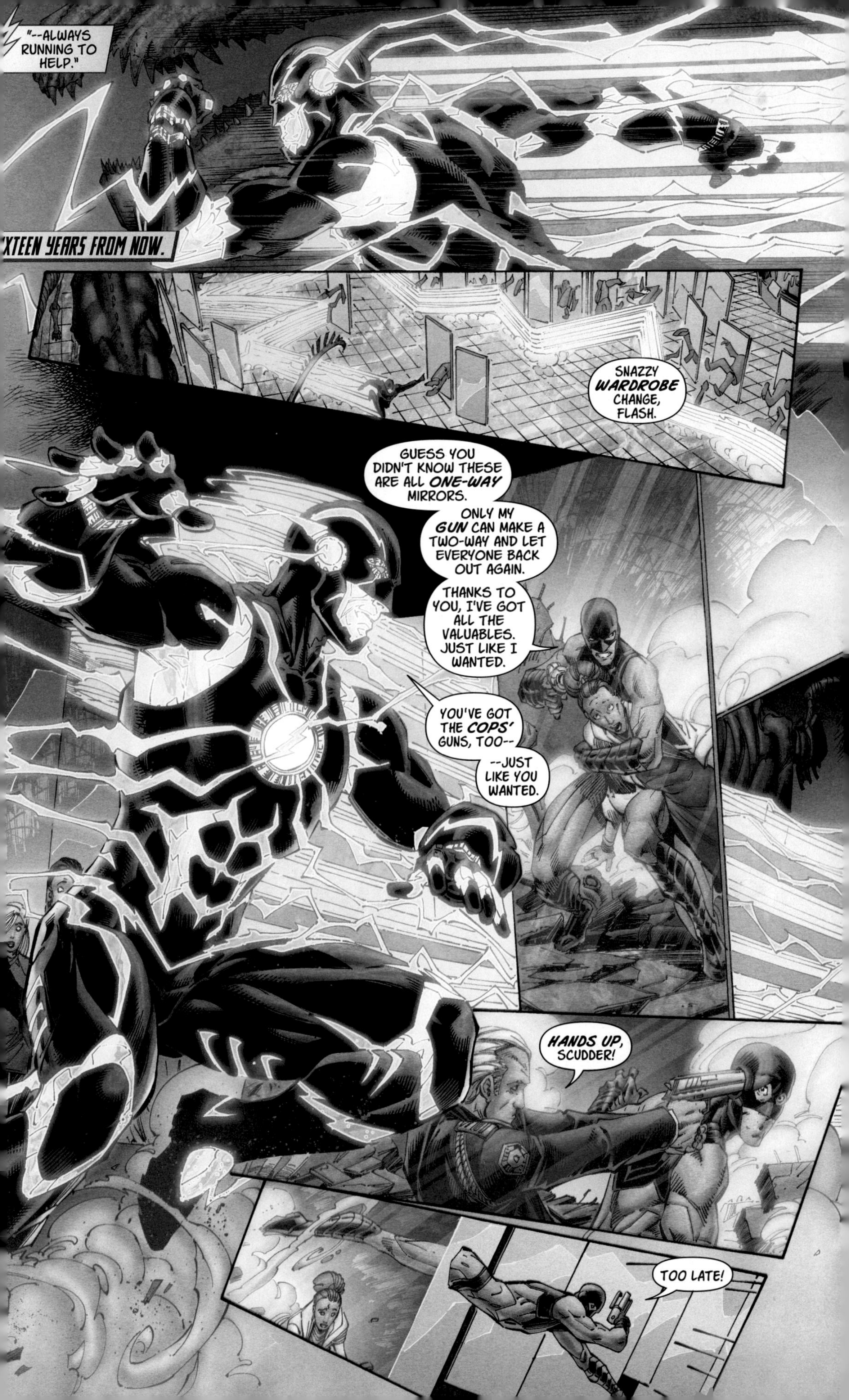

"--ALWAYS RUNNING TO HELP."
XTEEN YEARS FROM NOW.
SNAZZY WARDROBE CHANGE, FLASH.
GUESS YOU DIDN'T KNOW THESE ARE ALL ONE-WAY MIRRORS.
ONLY MY GUN CAN MAKE A TWO-WAY AND LET EVERYONE BACK OUT AGAIN.
THANKS TO YOU, I'VE GOT ALL THE VALUABLES. JUST LIKE I WANTED.
YOU'VE GOT THE COPS' GUNS, TOO--
--JUST LIKE YOU WANTED.
HANDS UP, SCUDDER!
TOO LATE!

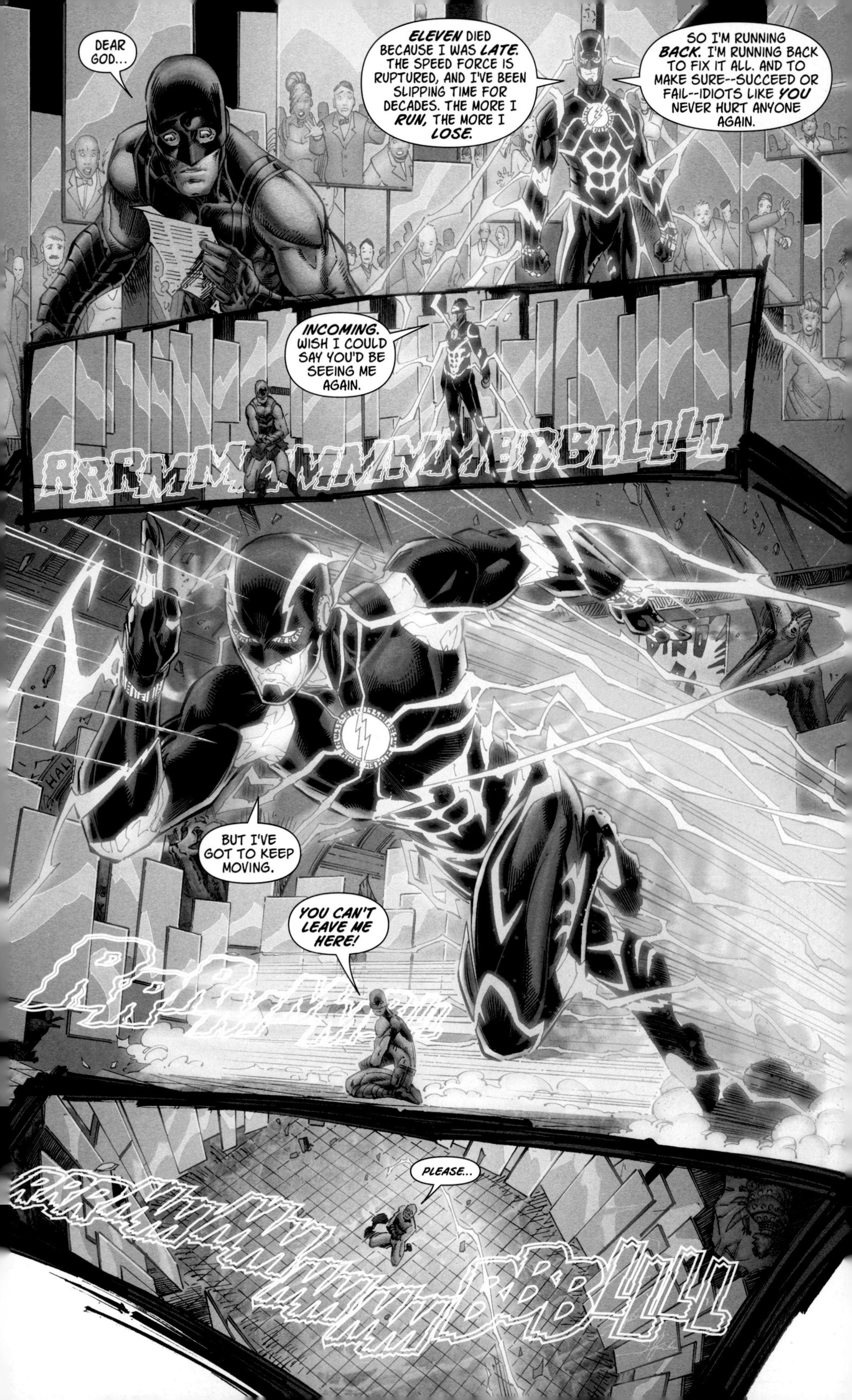
DEAR GOD...
ELEVEN DIED BECAUSE I WAS LATE. THE SPEED FORCE IS RUPTURED, AND I'VE BEEN SLIPPING TIME FOR DECADES. THE MORE I RUN, THE MORE I LOSE.
SO I'M RUNNING BACK. I'M RUNNING BACK TO FIX IT ALL. AND TO MAKE SURE--SUCCEED OR FAIL--IDIOTS LIKE YOU NEVER HURT ANYONE AGAIN.
INCOMING. WISH I COULD SAY YOU'D BE SEEING ME AGAIN.
RRRMMMMMMMMBBLLLL
BUT I'VE GOT TO KEEP MOVING.
YOU CAN'T LEAVE ME HERE!
PLEASE...
BLLLL

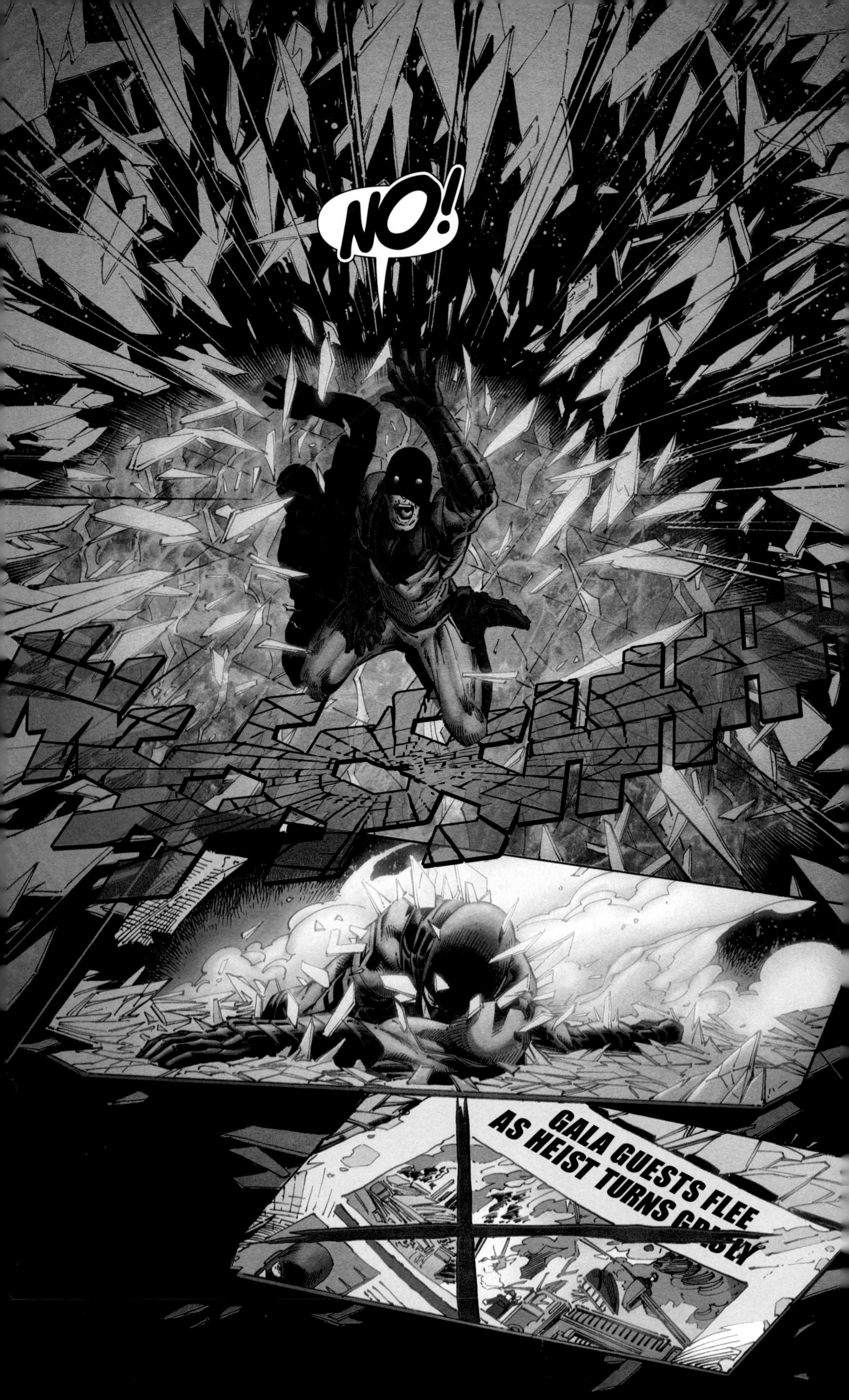
NO!
GALA GUESTS FLEE
AS HEIST TURNS

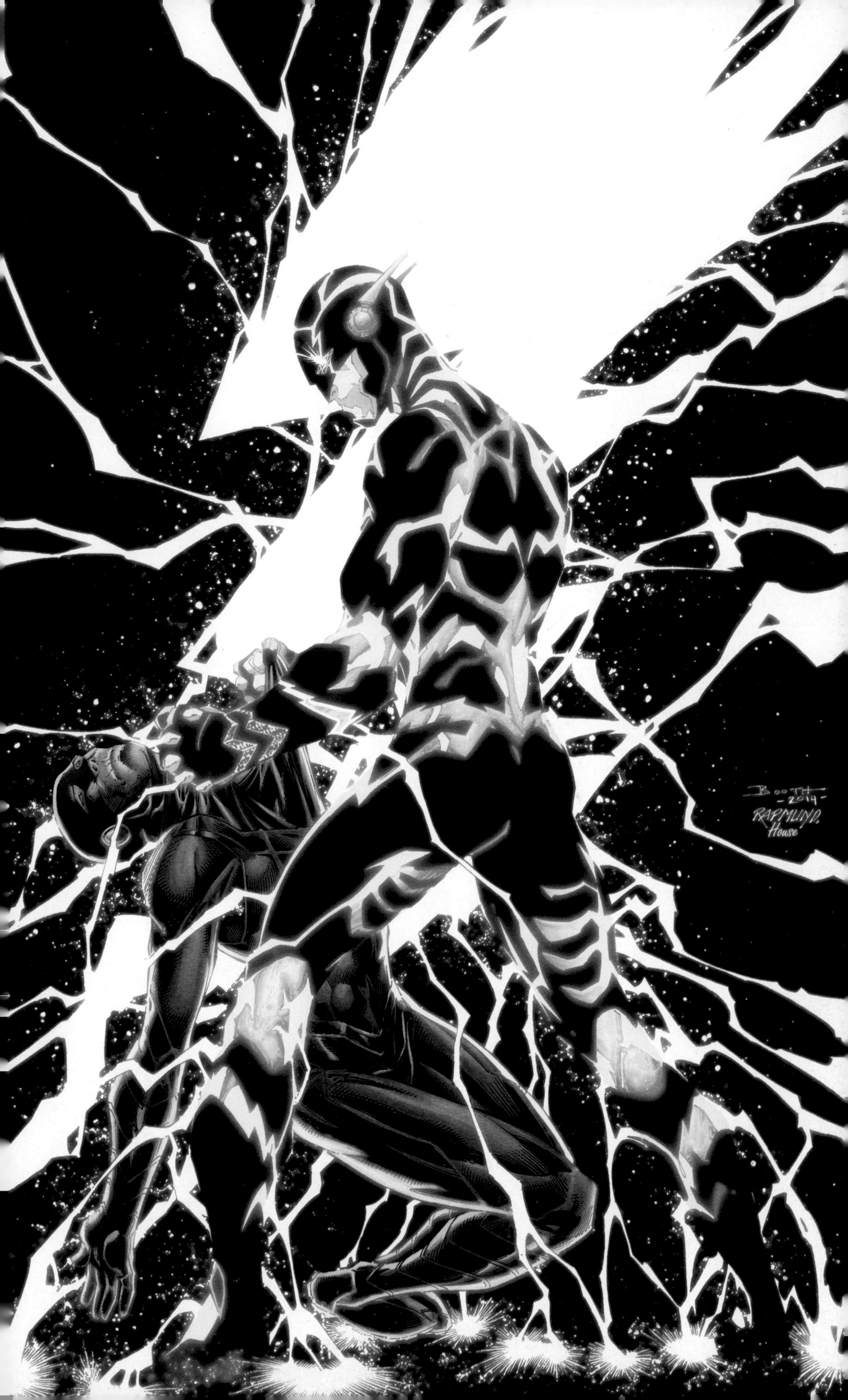
BOOTH
-2014-
House

COLD CALL

ROBERT VENDITTI & VAN JENSEN writers **BRETT BOOTH** penciller **NORM RAPMUND** inker

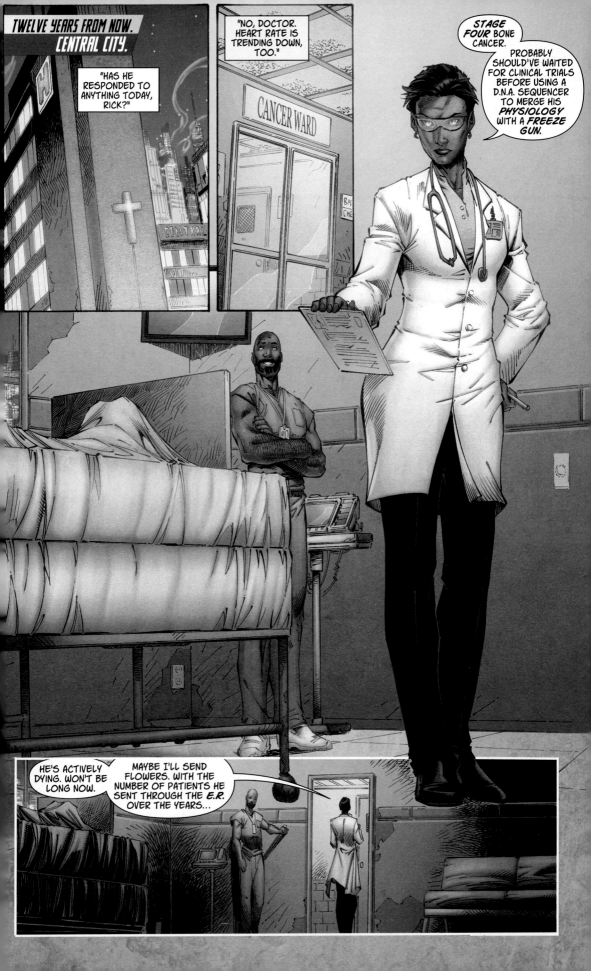

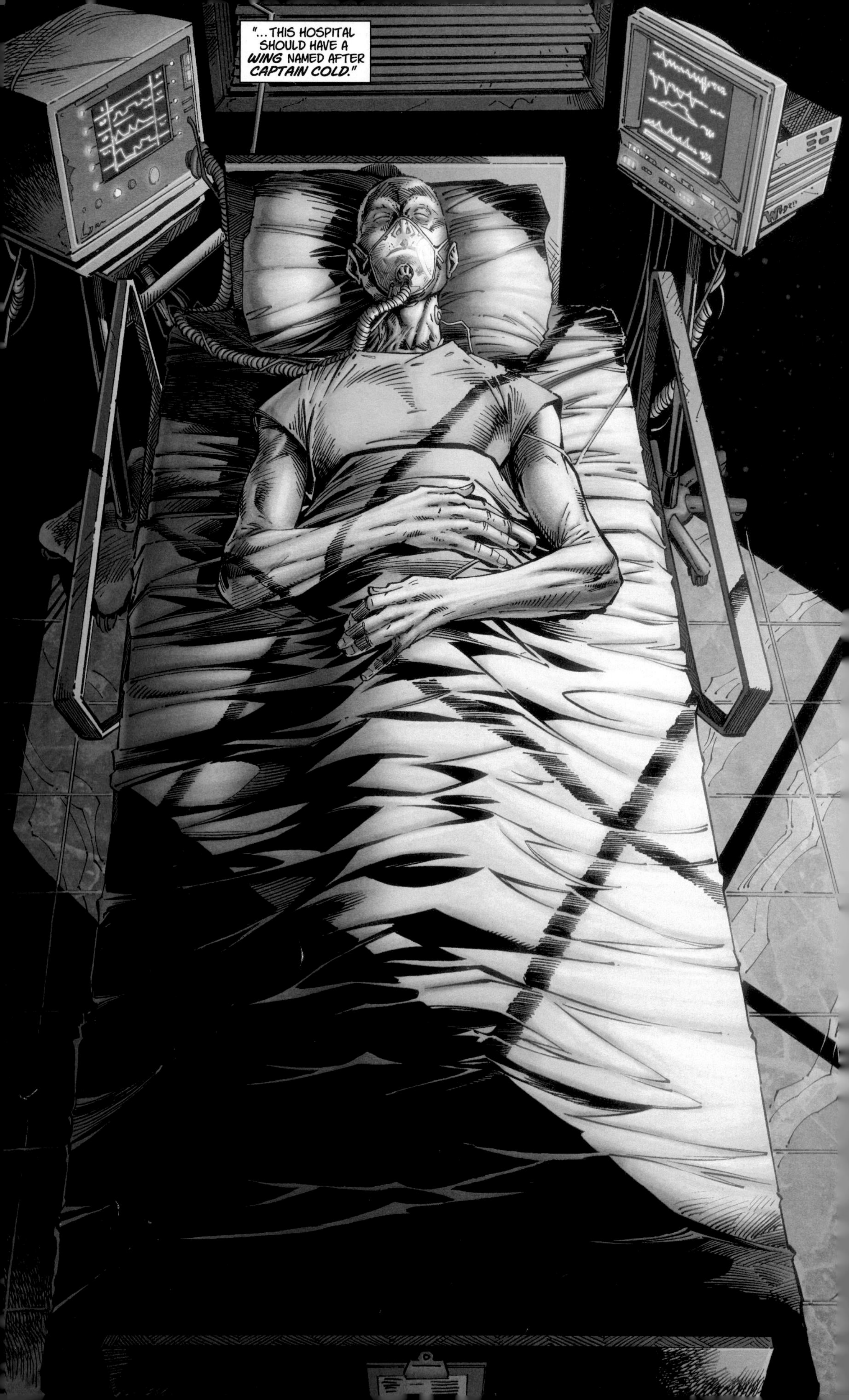
"...THIS HOSPITAL SHOULD HAVE A *WING* NAMED AFTER *CAPTAIN COLD*."

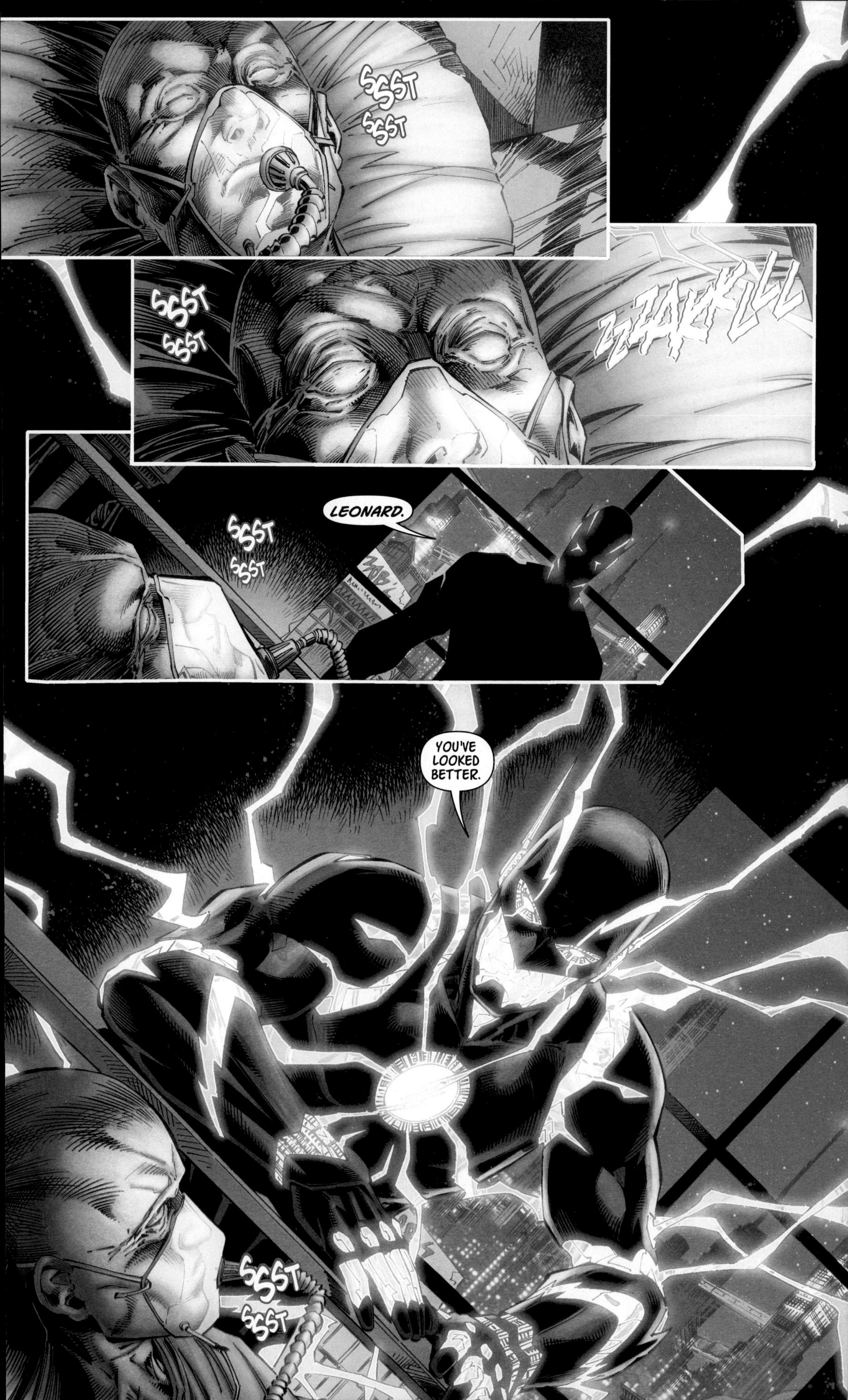
SSST
SSST
SSST
SSST
ZZZAKKLLL
SSST
SSST
LEONARD.
YOU'VE LOOKED BETTER.
SSST
SSST

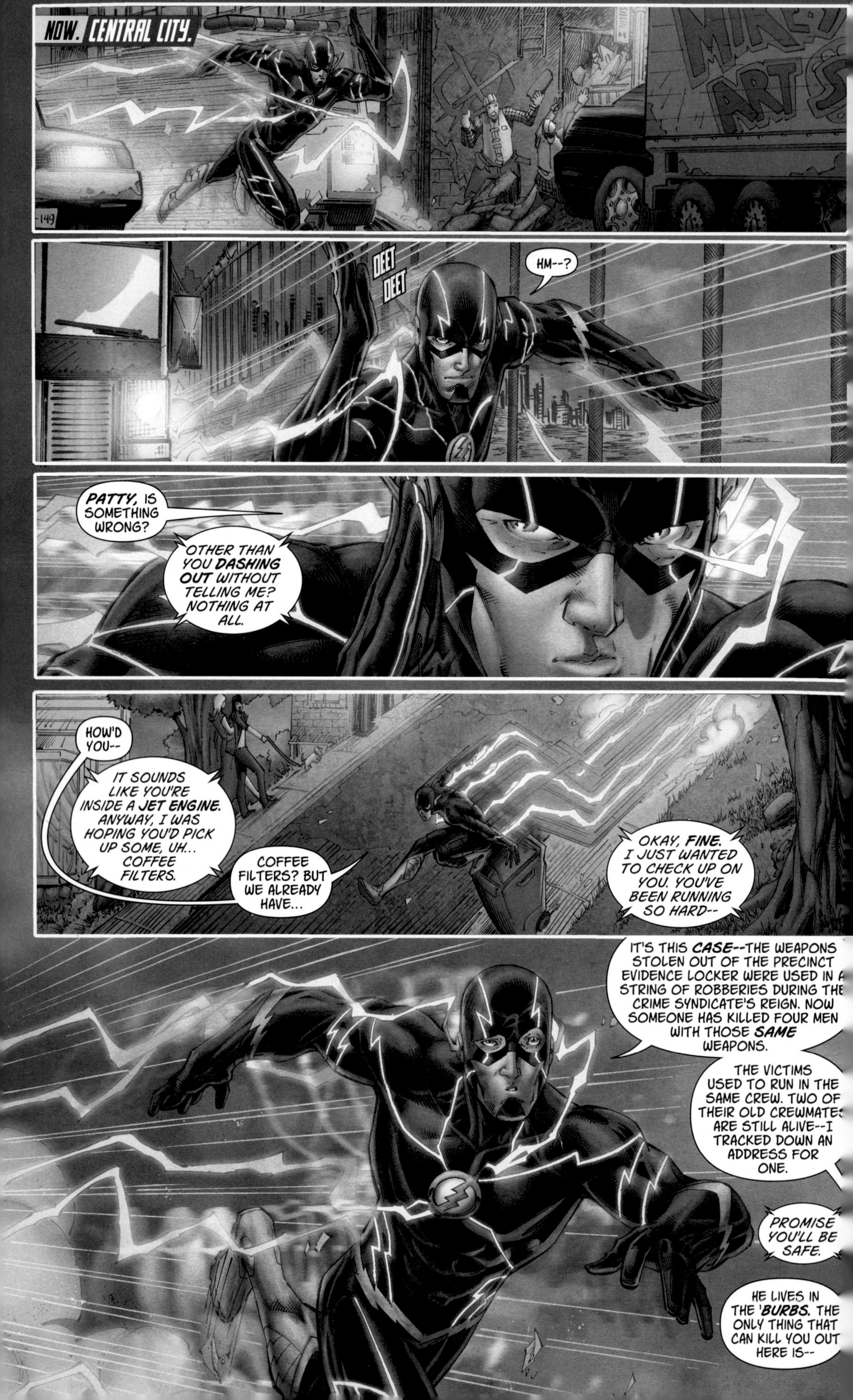
NOW. CENTRAL CITY.
149
DEET DEET
HM--?
PATTY, IS SOMETHING WRONG?
OTHER THAN YOU DASHING OUT WITHOUT TELLING ME? NOTHING AT ALL.
HOW'D YOU--
IT SOUNDS LIKE YOU'RE INSIDE A JET ENGINE. ANYWAY, I WAS HOPING YOU'D PICK UP SOME, UH... COFFEE FILTERS.
COFFEE FILTERS? BUT WE ALREADY HAVE...
OKAY, FINE. I JUST WANTED TO CHECK UP ON YOU. YOU'VE BEEN RUNNING SO HARD--
IT'S THIS CASE--THE WEAPONS STOLEN OUT OF THE PRECINCT EVIDENCE LOCKER WERE USED IN A STRING OF ROBBERIES DURING THE CRIME SYNDICATE'S REIGN. NOW SOMEONE HAS KILLED FOUR MEN WITH THOSE SAME WEAPONS.
THE VICTIMS USED TO RUN IN THE SAME CREW. TWO OF THEIR OLD CREWMATES ARE STILL ALIVE--I TRACKED DOWN AN ADDRESS FOR ONE.
PROMISE YOU'LL BE SAFE.
HE LIVES IN THE 'BURBS. THE ONLY THING THAT CAN KILL YOU OUT HERE IS--

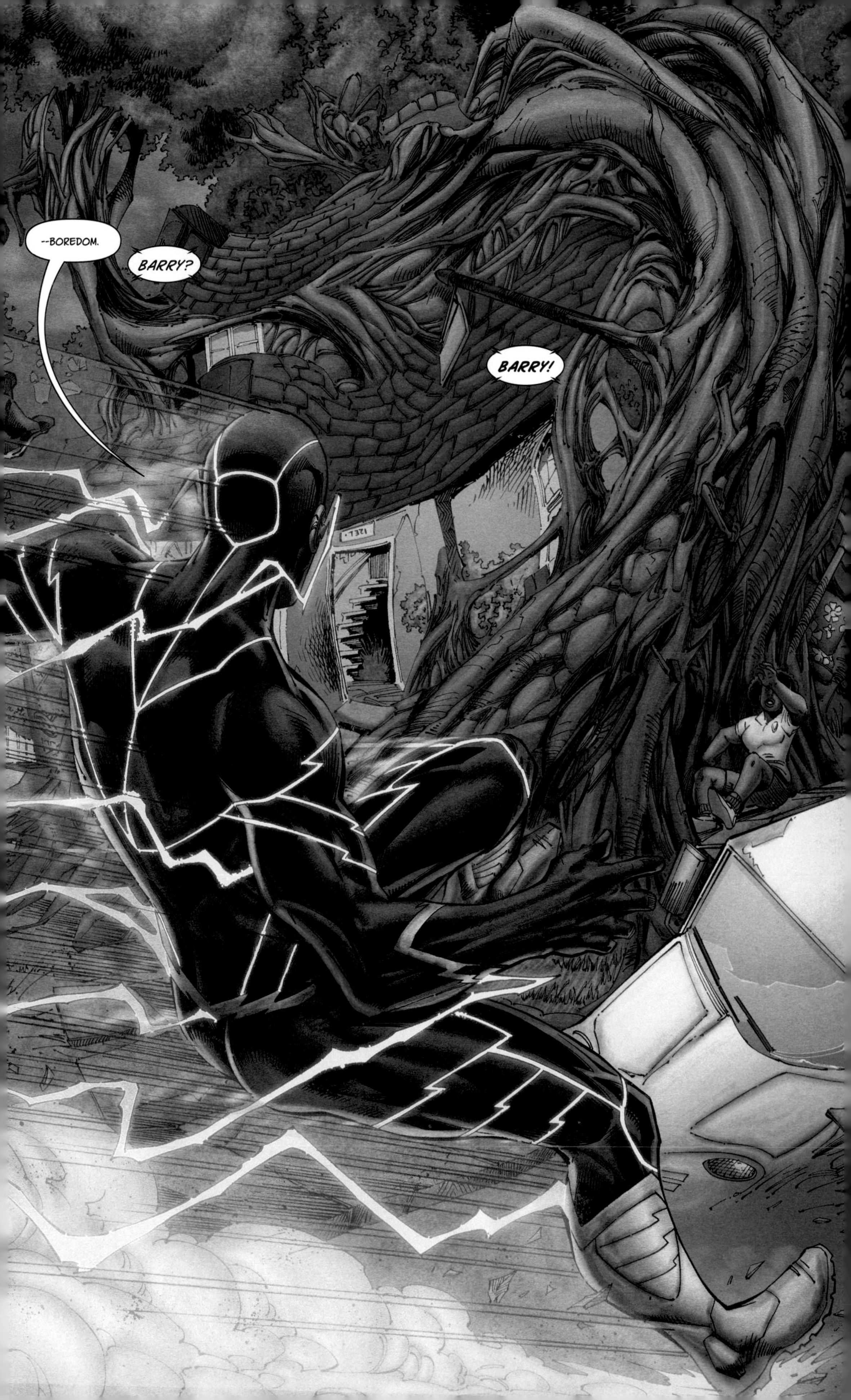
--BOREDOM.
BARRY?
BARRY!

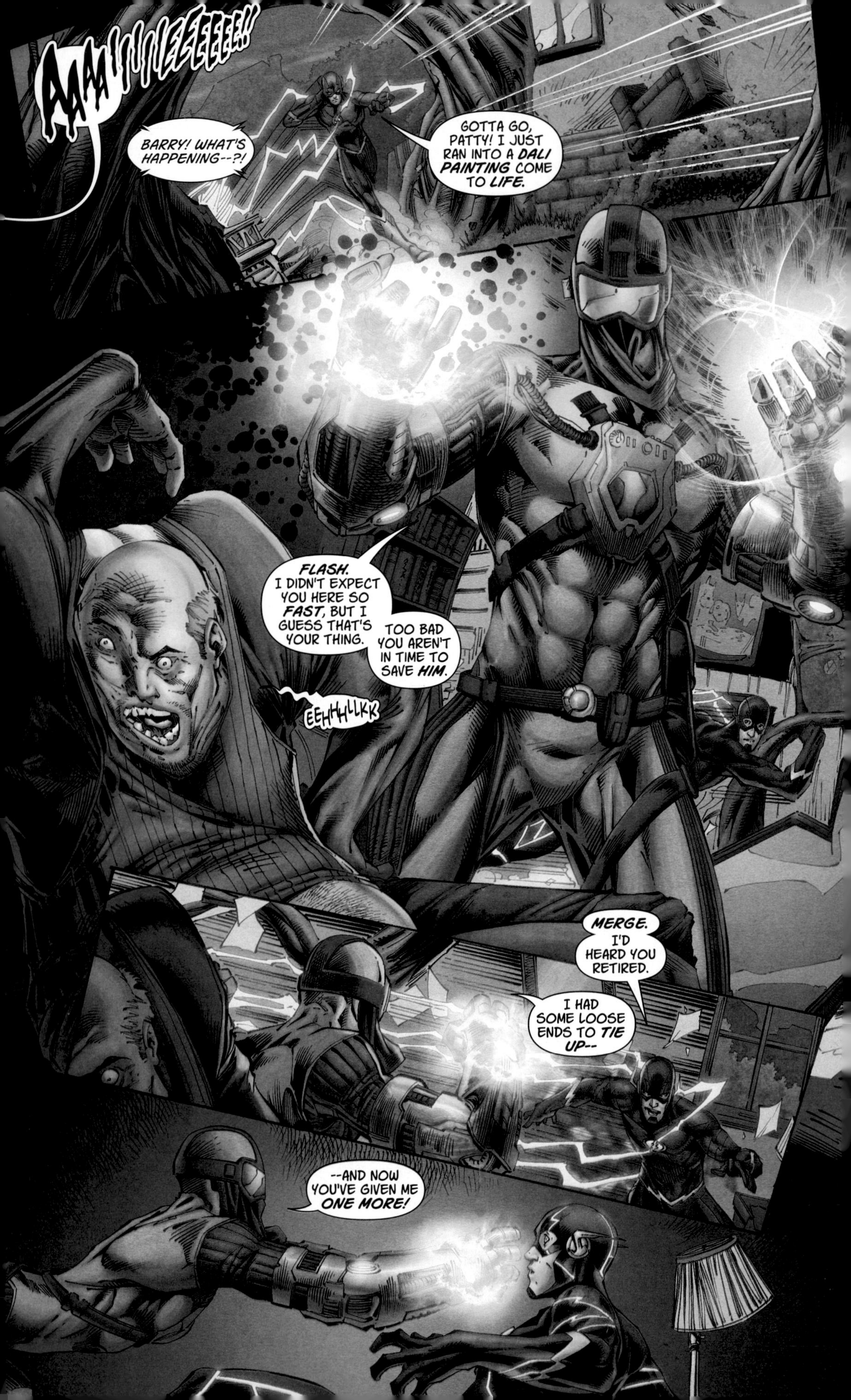
AAAIIIIIEEEEEE!!
BARRY! WHAT'S HAPPENING--?!
GOTTA GO, PATTY! I JUST RAN INTO A DALI PAINTING COME TO LIFE.
FLASH. I DIDN'T EXPECT YOU HERE SO FAST, BUT I GUESS THAT'S YOUR THING.
TOO BAD YOU AREN'T IN TIME TO SAVE HIM.
EEHHHLLKK
MERGE. I'D HEARD YOU RETIRED.
I HAD SOME LOOSE ENDS TO TIE UP--
--AND NOW YOU'VE GIVEN ME ONE MORE!

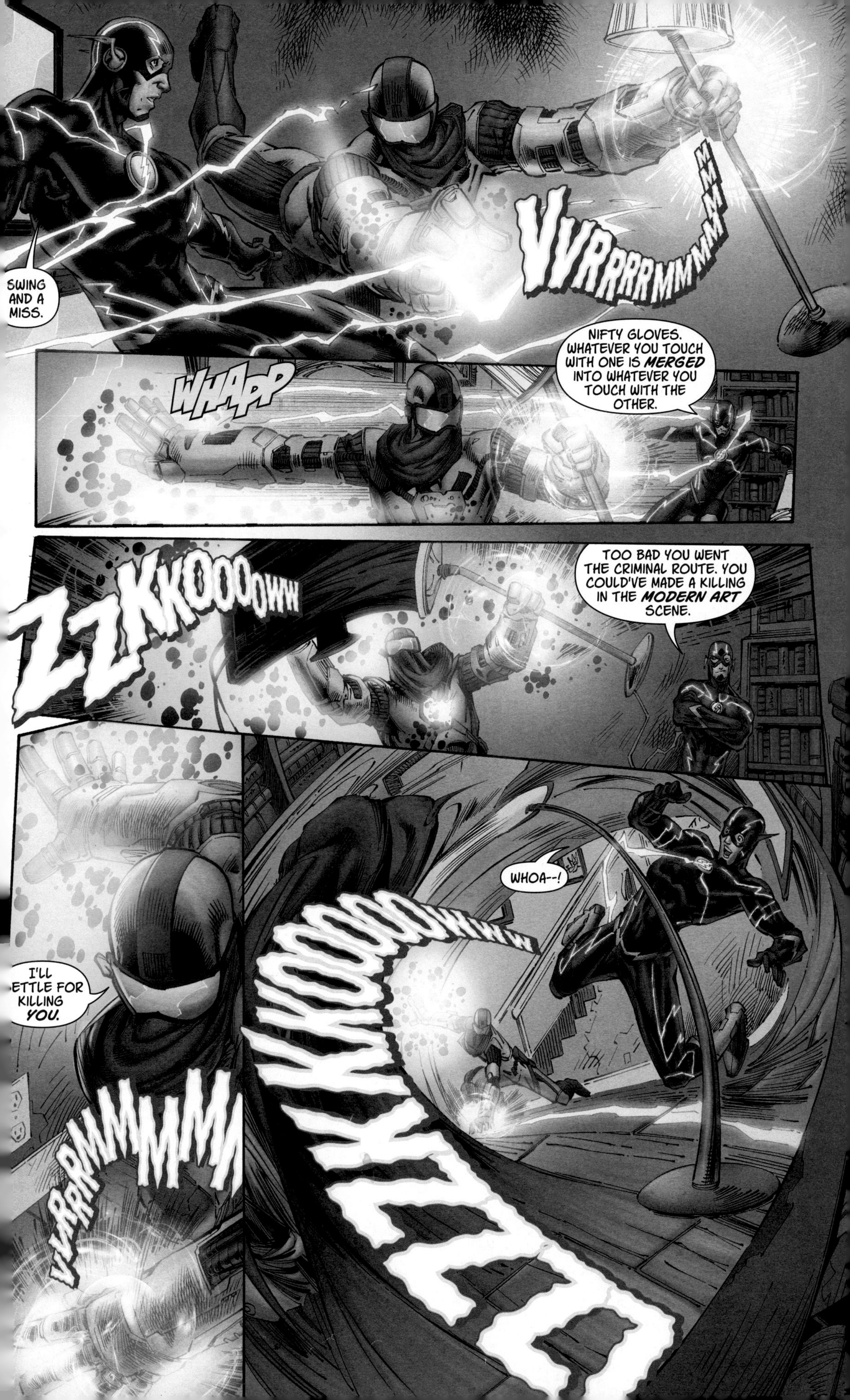
VVRRRRMMMMMMMMMM
SWING AND A MISS.
WHAPP
NIFTY GLOVES. WHATEVER YOU TOUCH WITH ONE IS *MERGED* INTO WHATEVER YOU TOUCH WITH THE OTHER.
ZZKKOOOOWW
TOO BAD YOU WENT THE CRIMINAL ROUTE. YOU COULD'VE MADE A KILLING IN THE *MODERN ART* SCENE.
I'LL ETTLE FOR KILLING *YOU.*
VVRRRMMMMMM
WHOA--!
ZZKKKKOOOOOOWWW

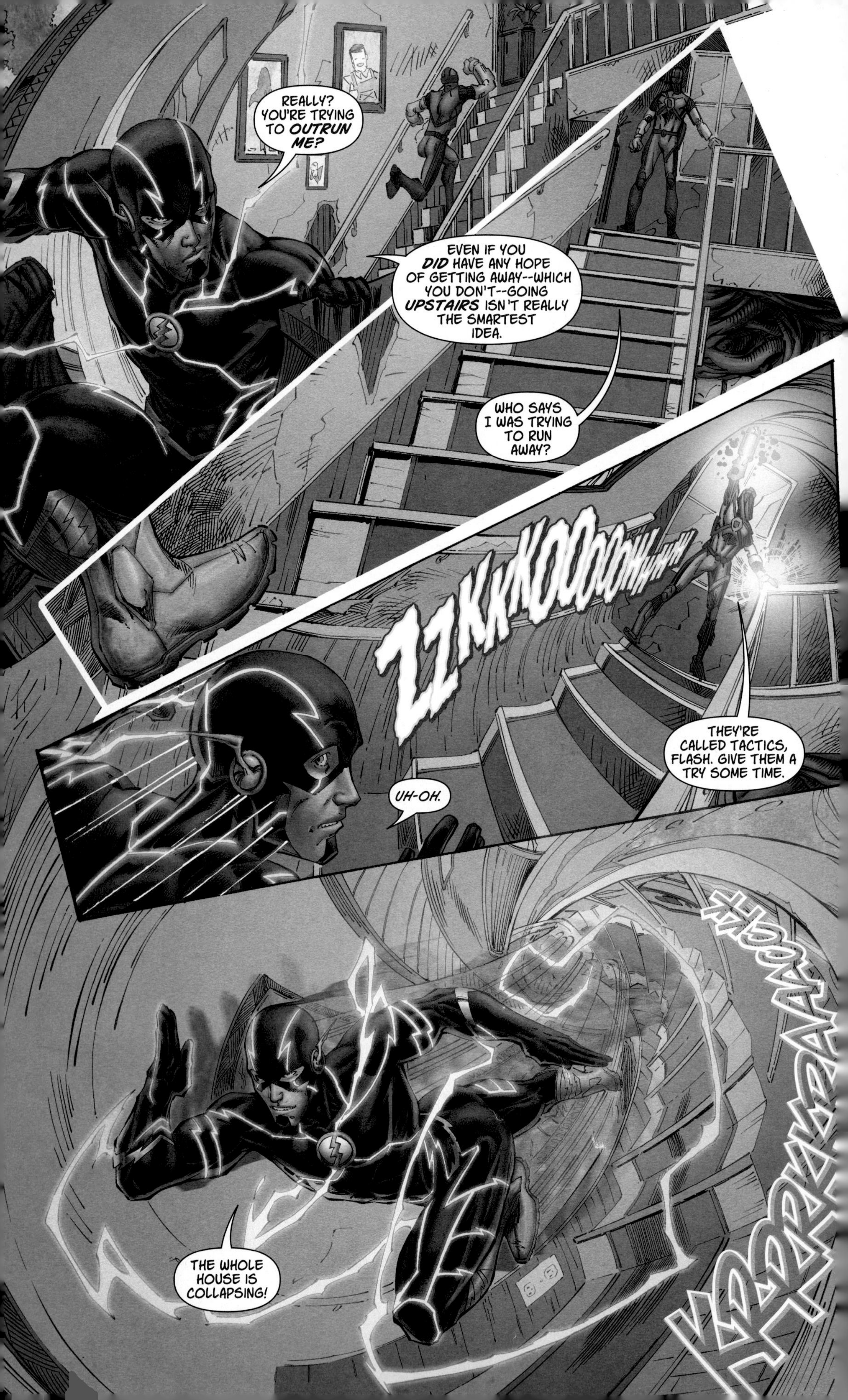
REALLY? YOU'RE TRYING TO OUTRUN ME?
EVEN IF YOU DID HAVE ANY HOPE OF GETTING AWAY--WHICH YOU DON'T--GOING UPSTAIRS ISN'T REALLY THE SMARTEST IDEA.
WHO SAYS I WAS TRYING TO RUN AWAY?
ZZKKKOOOOOHHHHH
THEY'RE CALLED TACTICS, FLASH. GIVE THEM A TRY SOME TIME.
UH-OH.
KRRRRKDAAAAOOOGHH
THE WHOLE HOUSE IS COLLAPSING!

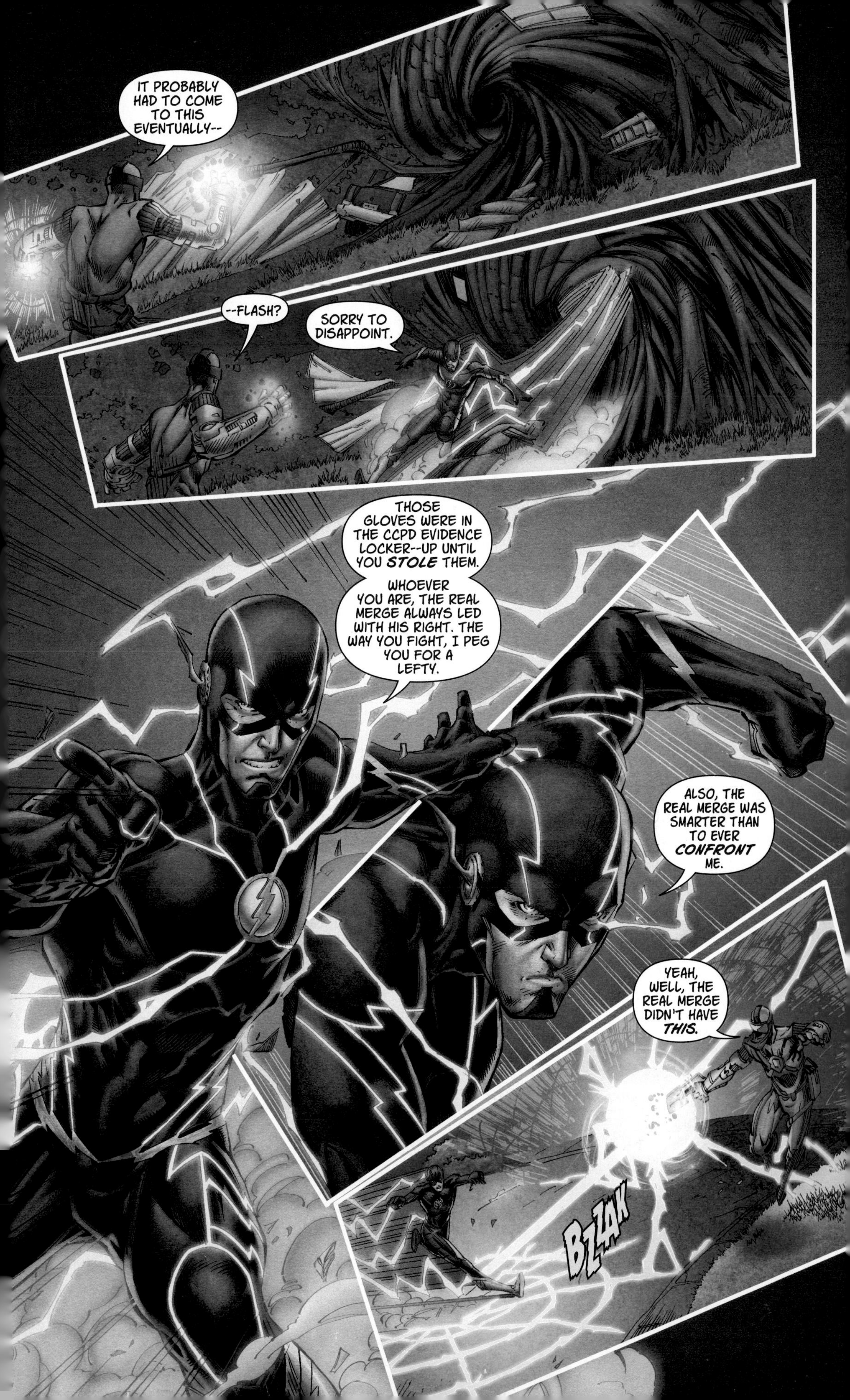
IT PROBABLY HAD TO COME TO THIS EVENTUALLY--
--FLASH?
SORRY TO DISAPPOINT.
THOSE GLOVES WERE IN THE CCPD EVIDENCE LOCKER--UP UNTIL YOU *STOLE* THEM.
WHOEVER YOU ARE, THE REAL MERGE ALWAYS LED WITH HIS RIGHT. THE WAY YOU FIGHT, I PEG YOU FOR A LEFTY.
ALSO, THE REAL MERGE WAS SMARTER THAN TO EVER *CONFRONT* ME.
YEAH, WELL, THE REAL MERGE DIDN'T HAVE *THIS*.
BZZAK

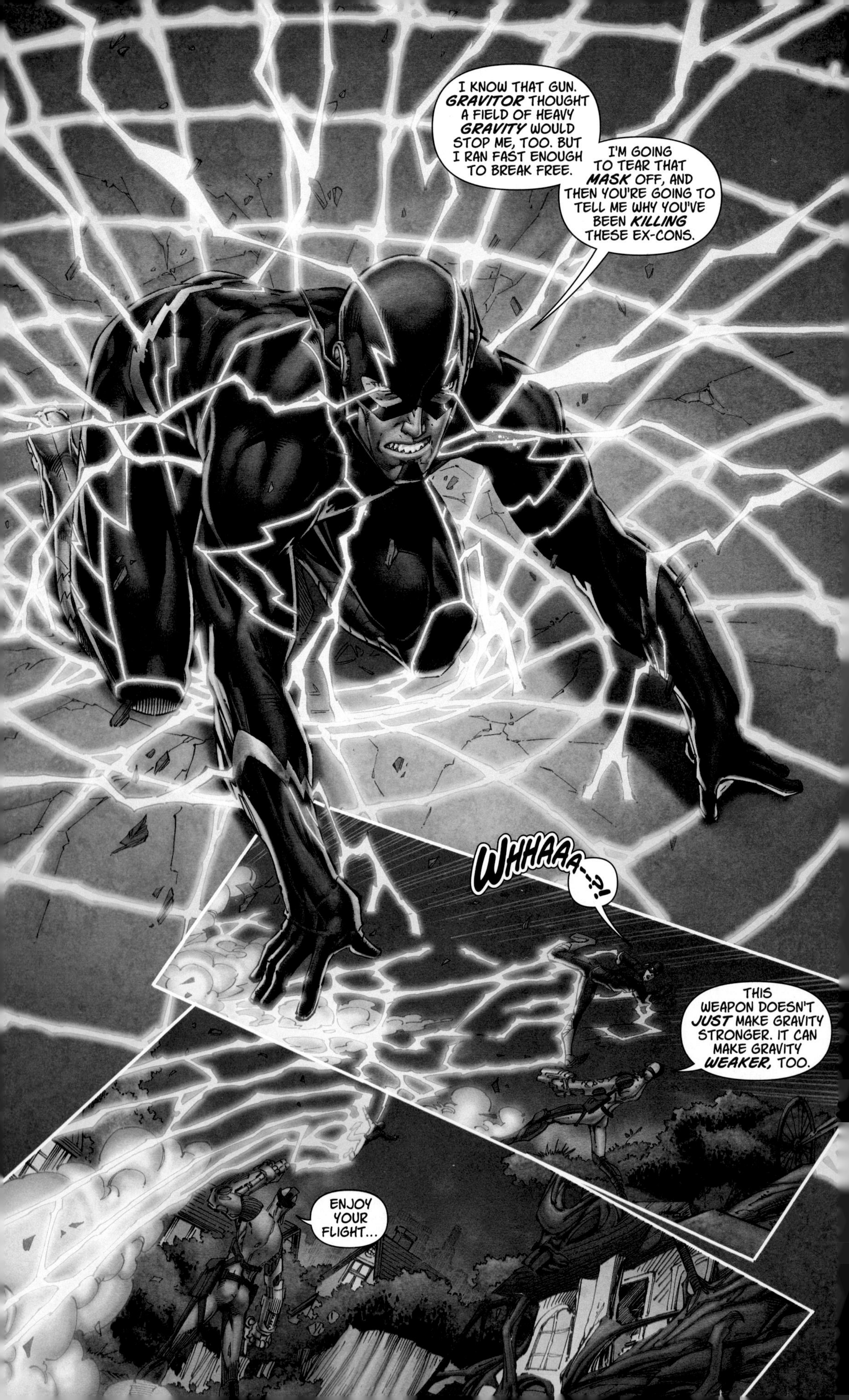
I KNOW THAT GUN. GRAVITOR THOUGHT A FIELD OF HEAVY GRAVITY WOULD STOP ME, TOO. BUT I RAN FAST ENOUGH TO BREAK FREE.
I'M GOING TO TEAR THAT MASK OFF, AND THEN YOU'RE GOING TO TELL ME WHY YOU'VE BEEN KILLING THESE EX-CONS.
WHHAAA--?!
THIS WEAPON DOESN'T JUST MAKE GRAVITY STRONGER. IT CAN MAKE GRAVITY WEAKER, TOO.
ENJOY YOUR FLIGHT...

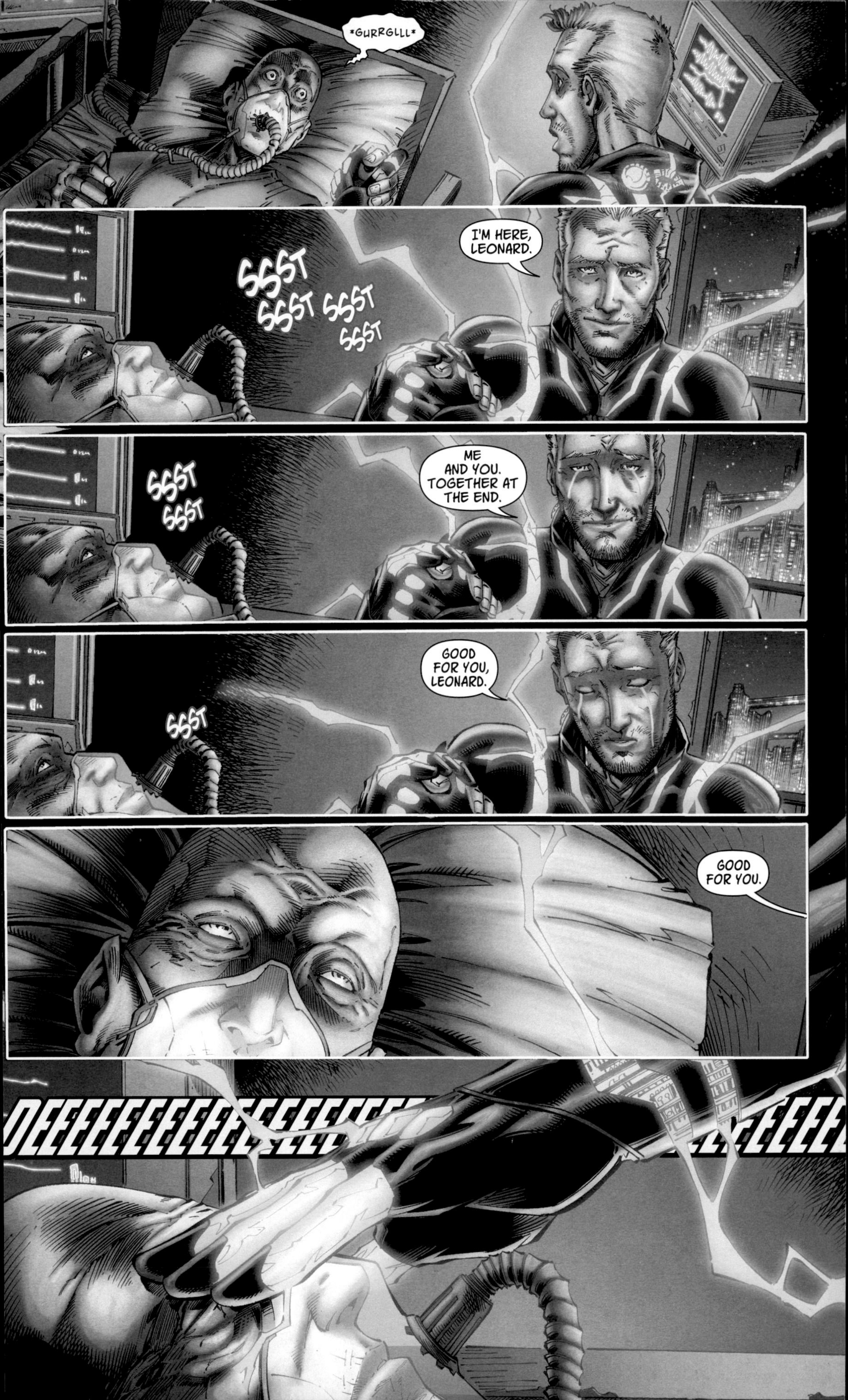
GURRGLLL
I'M HERE, LEONARD.
SSST SSST SSST SSST
ME AND YOU. TOGETHER AT THE END.
SSST SSST
GOOD FOR YOU, LEONARD.
SSST
GOOD FOR YOU.
DEEEEEEEEEEEEEEEEEEEEEEEEEEEEEEEEEEEEE

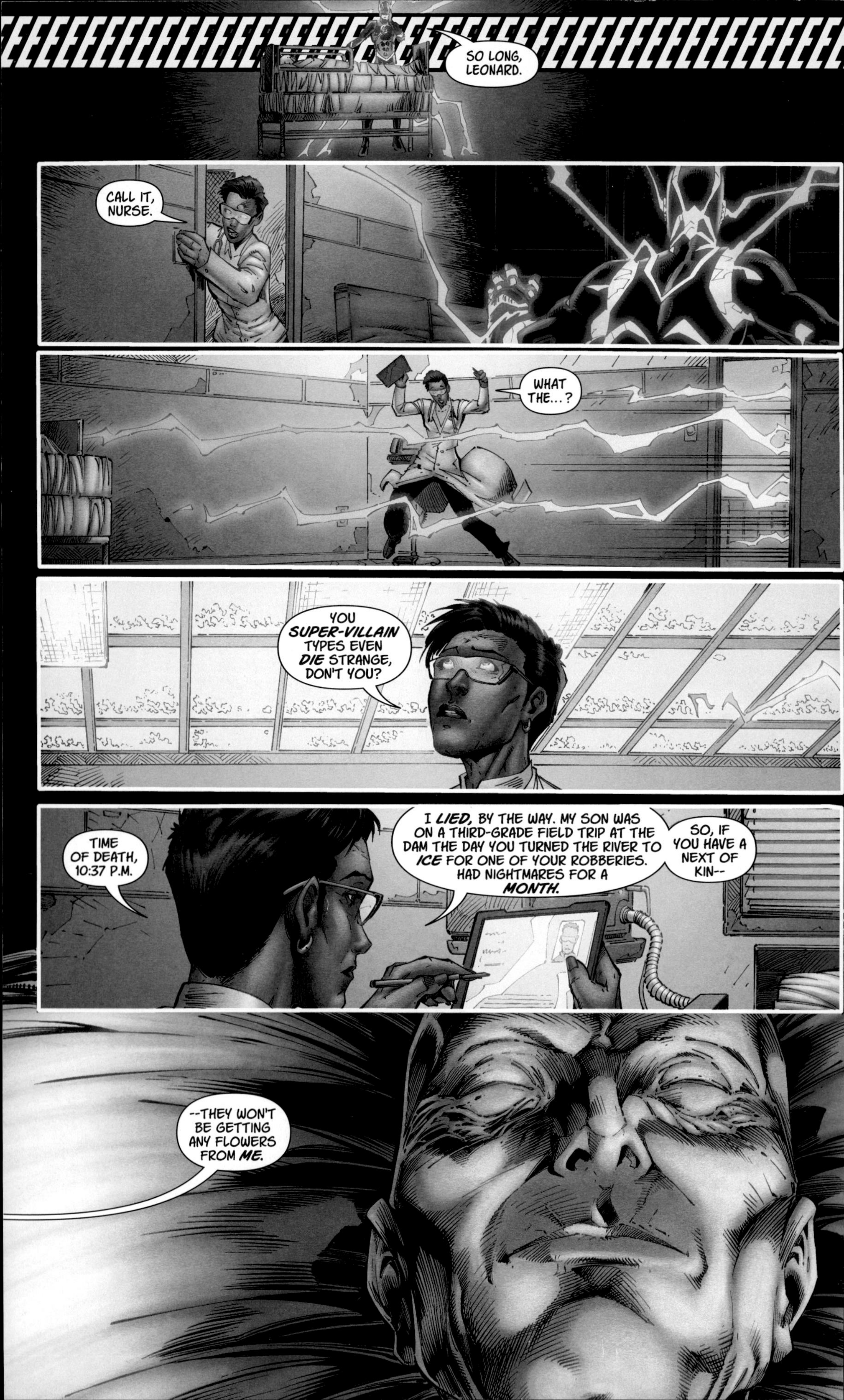
EEEEEEEEEEEEEEEEEEEEEEEEEEEEEEEEEEEE
SO LONG, LEONARD.
CALL IT, NURSE.
WHAT THE...?
YOU SUPER-VILLAIN TYPES EVEN DIE STRANGE, DON'T YOU?
TIME OF DEATH, 10:37 P.M.
I LIED, BY THE WAY. MY SON WAS ON A THIRD-GRADE FIELD TRIP AT THE DAM THE DAY YOU TURNED THE RIVER TO ICE FOR ONE OF YOUR ROBBERIES. HAD NIGHTMARES FOR A MONTH.
SO, IF YOU HAVE A NEXT OF KIN--
--THEY WON'T BE GETTING ANY FLOWERS FROM ME.

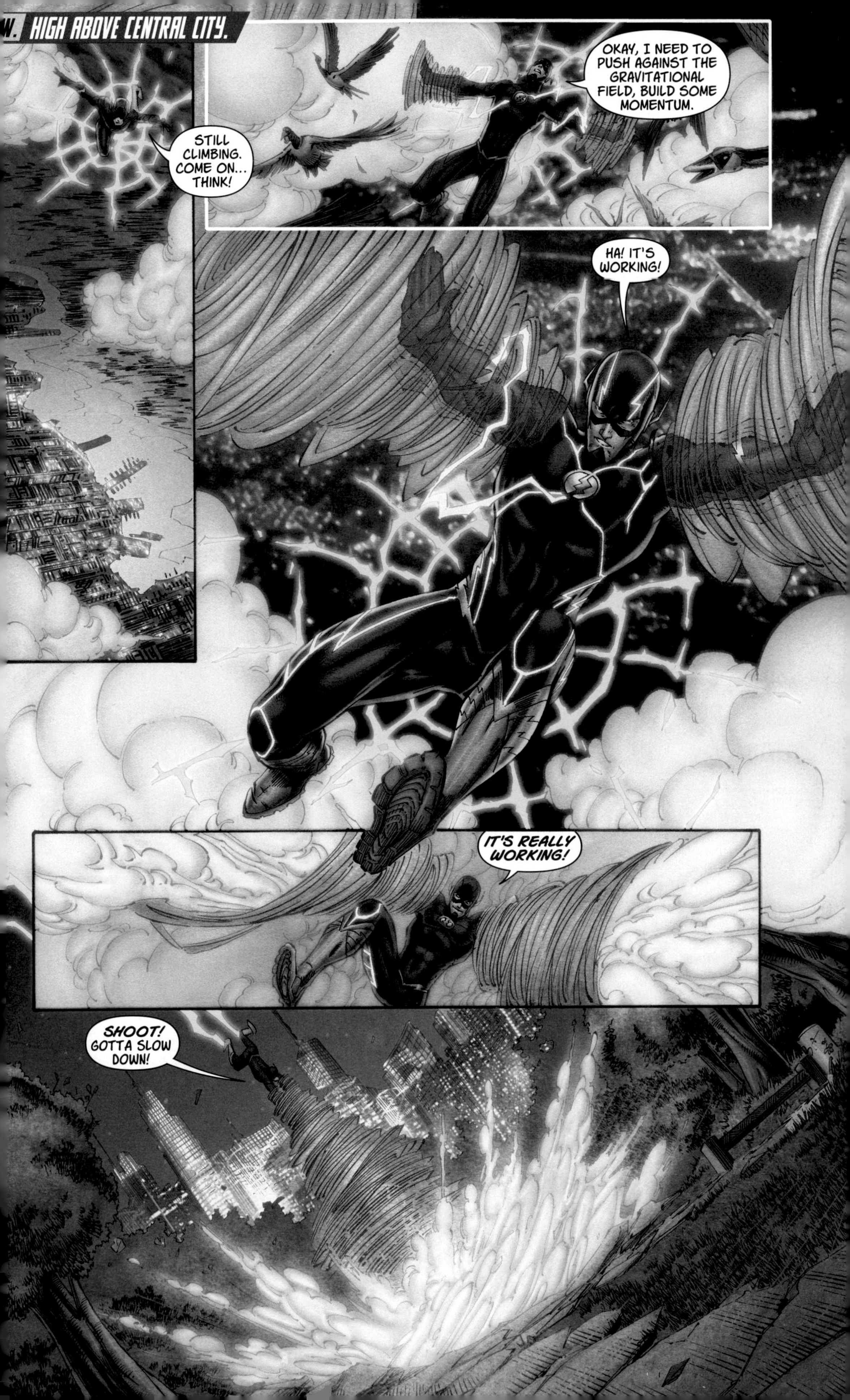
W. HIGH ABOVE CENTRAL CITY.
STILL CLIMBING. COME ON... THINK!
OKAY, I NEED TO PUSH AGAINST THE GRAVITATIONAL FIELD, BUILD SOME MOMENTUM.
HA! IT'S WORKING!
IT'S REALLY WORKING!
SHOOT! GOTTA SLOW DOWN!

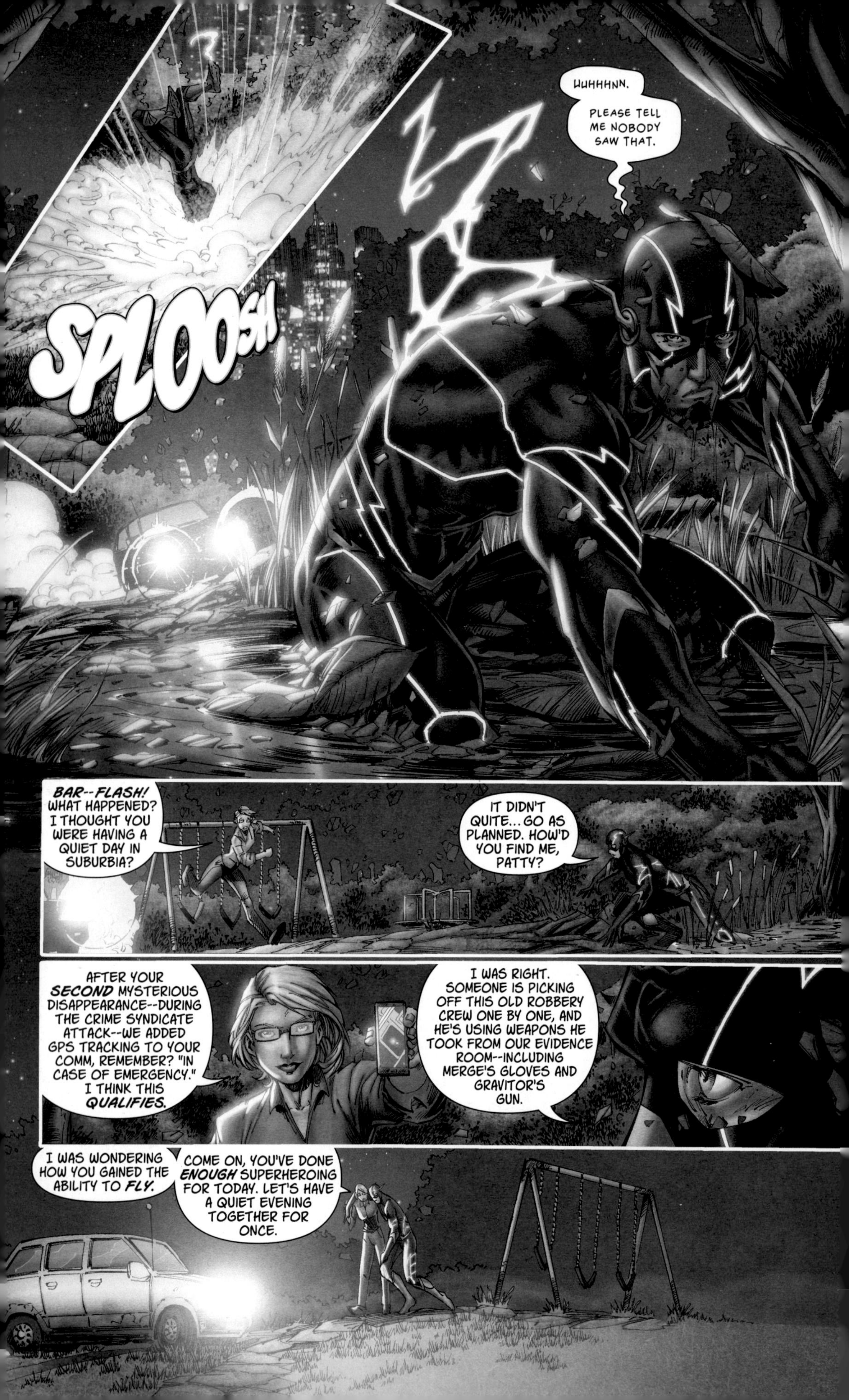

SPLOOSH
UHHHHNN.
PLEASE TELL ME NOBODY SAW THAT.
BAR--FLASH! WHAT HAPPENED? I THOUGHT YOU WERE HAVING A QUIET DAY IN SUBURBIA?
IT DIDN'T QUITE... GO AS PLANNED. HOW'D YOU FIND ME, PATTY?
AFTER YOUR SECOND MYSTERIOUS DISAPPEARANCE--DURING THE CRIME SYNDICATE ATTACK--WE ADDED GPS TRACKING TO YOUR COMM, REMEMBER? "IN CASE OF EMERGENCY." I THINK THIS QUALIFIES.
I WAS RIGHT. SOMEONE IS PICKING OFF THIS OLD ROBBERY CREW ONE BY ONE, AND HE'S USING WEAPONS HE TOOK FROM OUR EVIDENCE ROOM--INCLUDING MERGE'S GLOVES AND GRAVITOR'S GUN.
I WAS WONDERING HOW YOU GAINED THE ABILITY TO FLY.
COME ON, YOU'VE DONE ENOUGH SUPERHEROING FOR TODAY. LET'S HAVE A QUIET EVENING TOGETHER FOR ONCE.

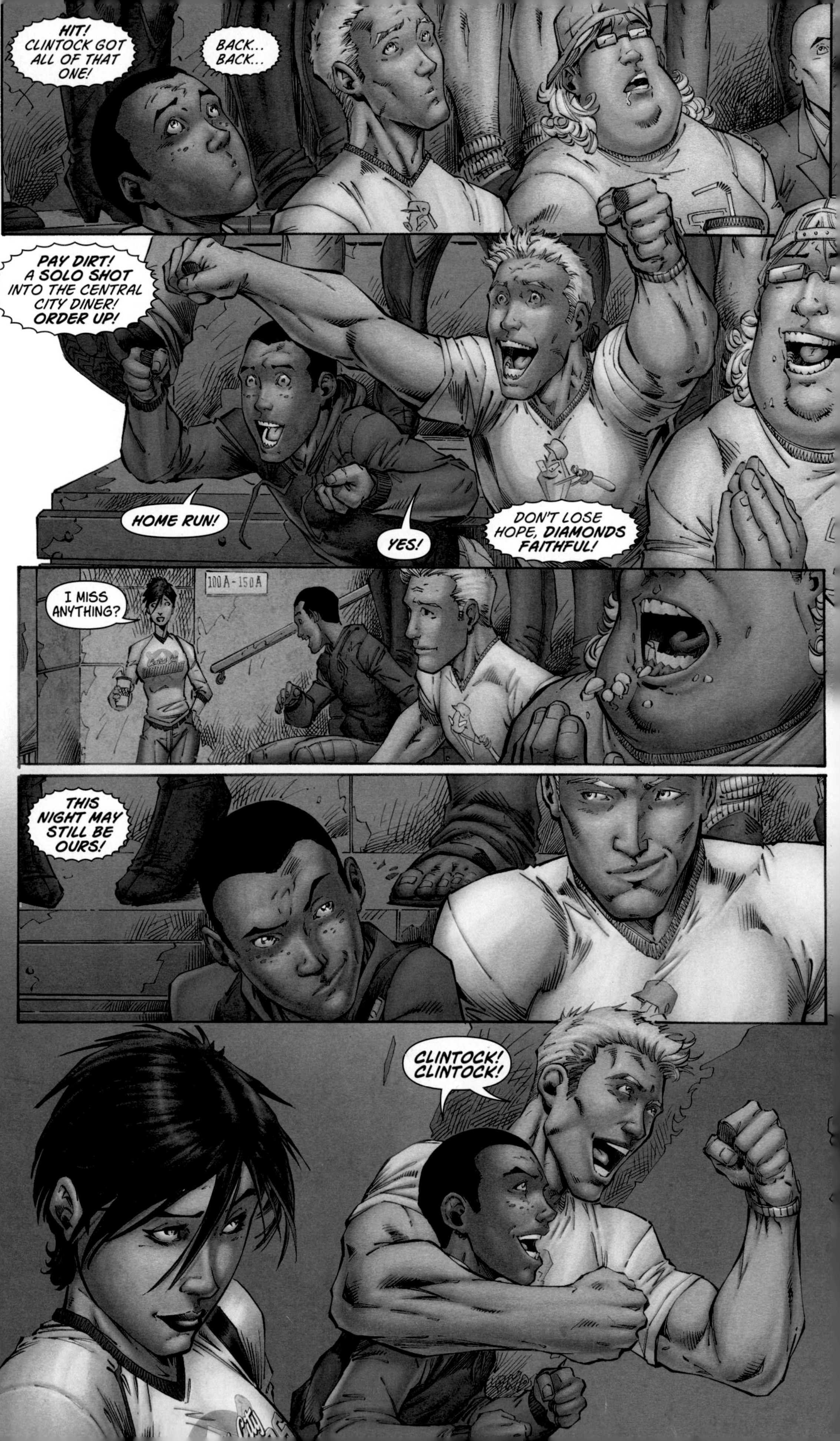
HIT! CLINTOCK GOT ALL OF THAT ONE!
BACK... BACK...
PAY DIRT! A SOLO SHOT INTO THE CENTRAL CITY DINER! ORDER UP!
HOME RUN!
YES!
DON'T LOSE HOPE, DIAMONDS FAITHFUL!
100A-150A
I MISS ANYTHING?
THIS NIGHT MAY STILL BE OURS!
CLINTOCK! CLINTOCK!

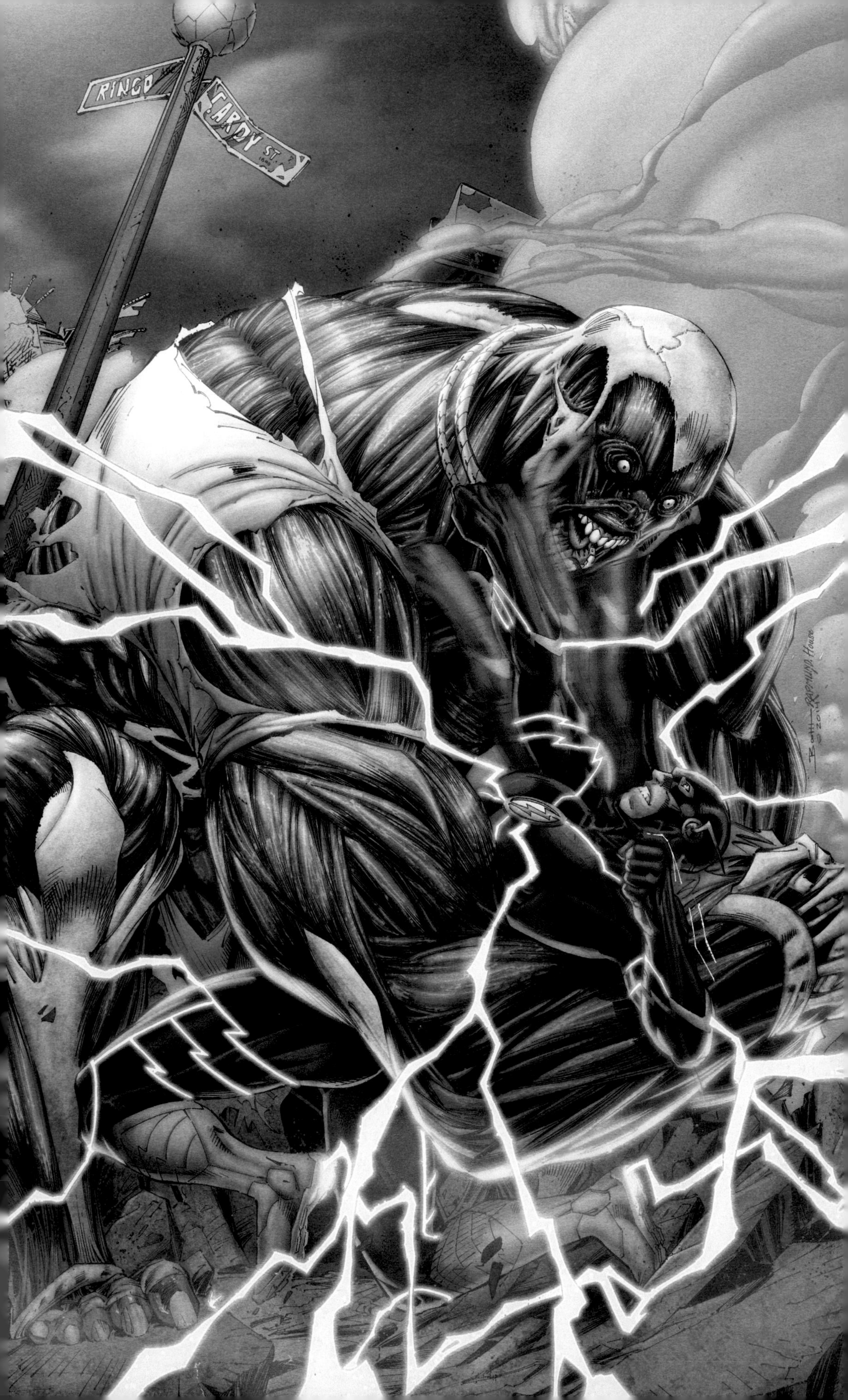
RINGO
ST.

A STEP BEHIND
ROBERT VENDITTI & VAN JENSEN writers **BRETT BOOTH** penciller **NORM RAPMUND** inker

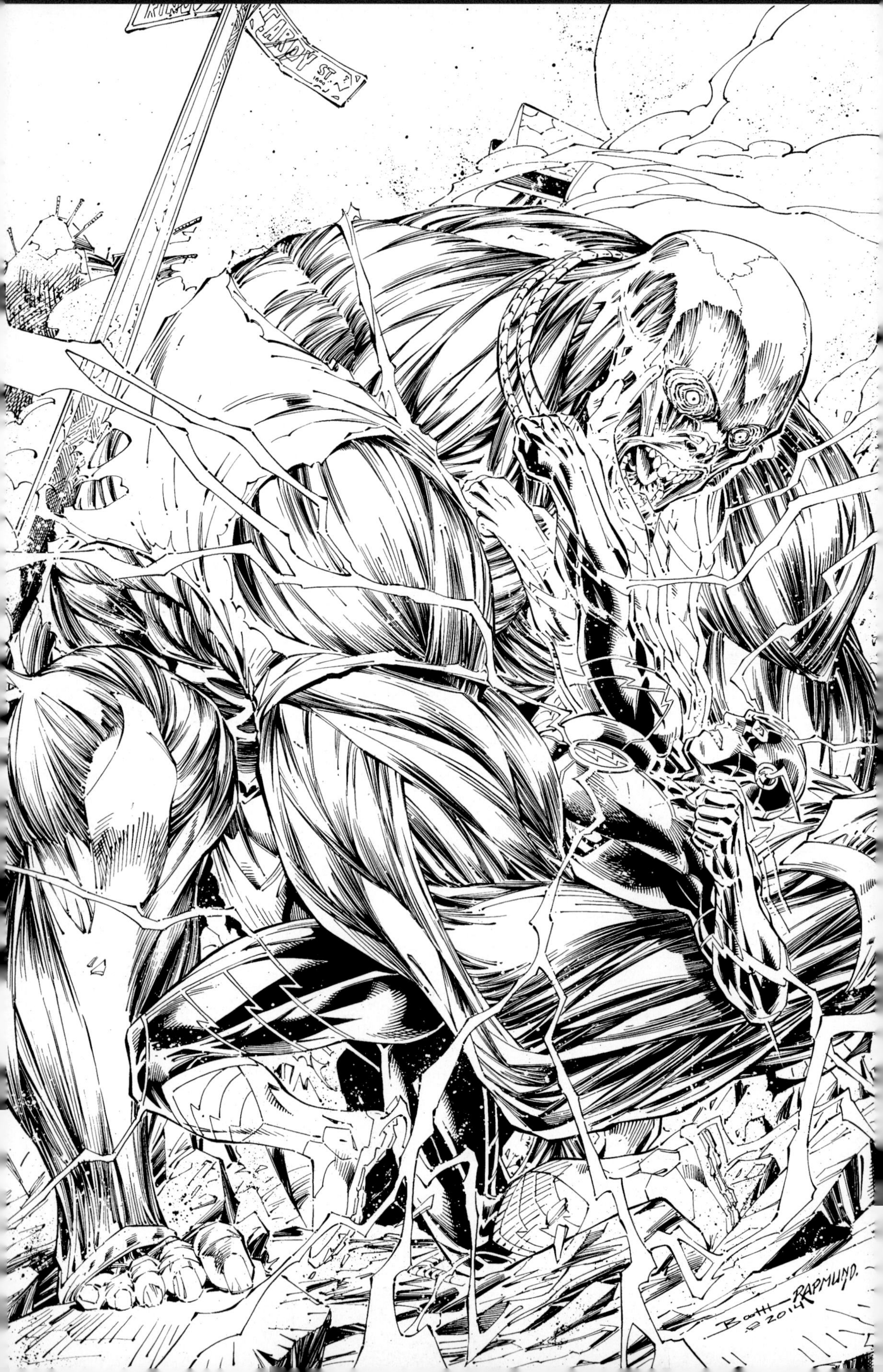

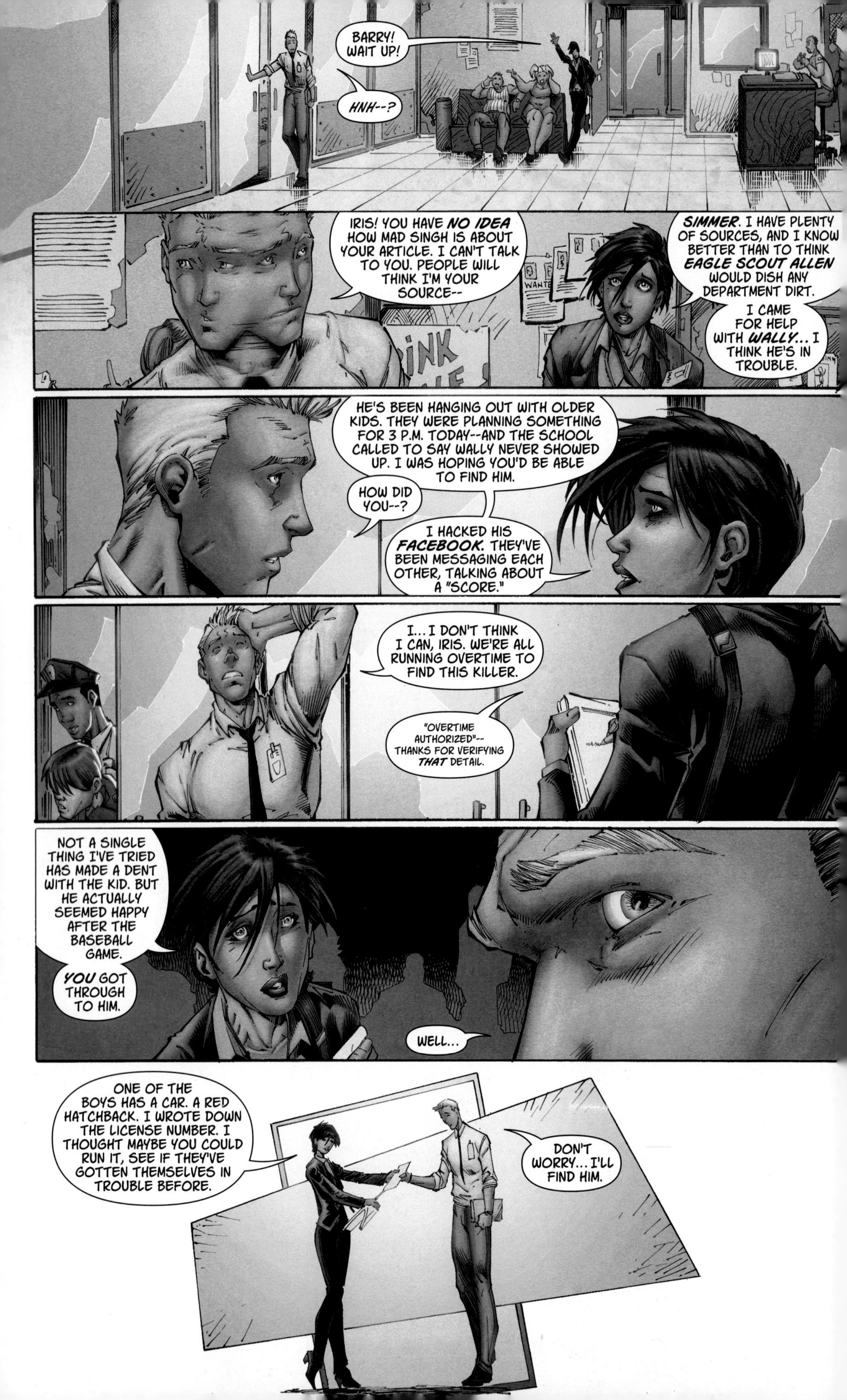

BARRY! WAIT UP!
HNH--?
IRIS! YOU HAVE NO IDEA HOW MAD SINGH IS ABOUT YOUR ARTICLE. I CAN'T TALK TO YOU. PEOPLE WILL THINK I'M YOUR SOURCE--
SIMMER. I HAVE PLENTY OF SOURCES, AND I KNOW BETTER THAN TO THINK EAGLE SCOUT ALLEN WOULD DISH ANY DEPARTMENT DIRT.
I CAME FOR HELP WITH WALLY... I THINK HE'S IN TROUBLE.
HE'S BEEN HANGING OUT WITH OLDER KIDS. THEY WERE PLANNING SOMETHING FOR 3 P.M. TODAY--AND THE SCHOOL CALLED TO SAY WALLY NEVER SHOWED UP. I WAS HOPING YOU'D BE ABLE TO FIND HIM.
HOW DID YOU--?
I HACKED HIS FACEBOOK. THEY'VE BEEN MESSAGING EACH OTHER, TALKING ABOUT A "SCORE."
I... I DON'T THINK I CAN, IRIS. WE'RE ALL RUNNING OVERTIME TO FIND THIS KILLER.
"OVERTIME AUTHORIZED"-- THANKS FOR VERIFYING THAT DETAIL.
NOT A SINGLE THING I'VE TRIED HAS MADE A DENT WITH THE KID. BUT HE ACTUALLY SEEMED HAPPY AFTER THE BASEBALL GAME.
YOU GOT THROUGH TO HIM.
WELL...
ONE OF THE BOYS HAS A CAR. A RED HATCHBACK. I WROTE DOWN THE LICENSE NUMBER. I THOUGHT MAYBE YOU COULD RUN IT, SEE IF THEY'VE GOTTEN THEMSELVES IN TROUBLE BEFORE.
DON'T WORRY... I'LL FIND HIM.

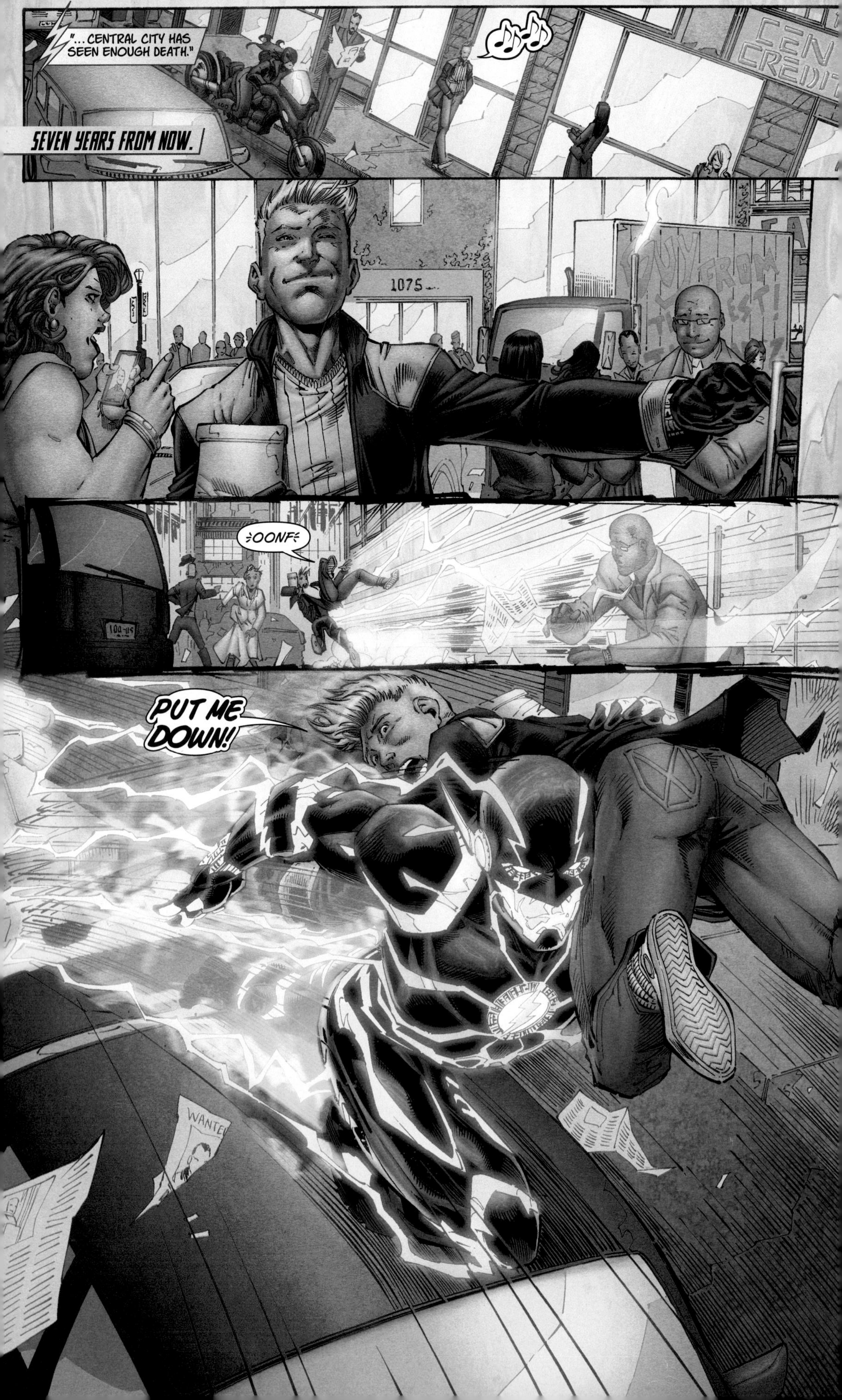

"...CENTRAL CITY HAS SEEN ENOUGH DEATH."
SEVEN YEARS FROM NOW.
1075
OONF
PUT ME DOWN!

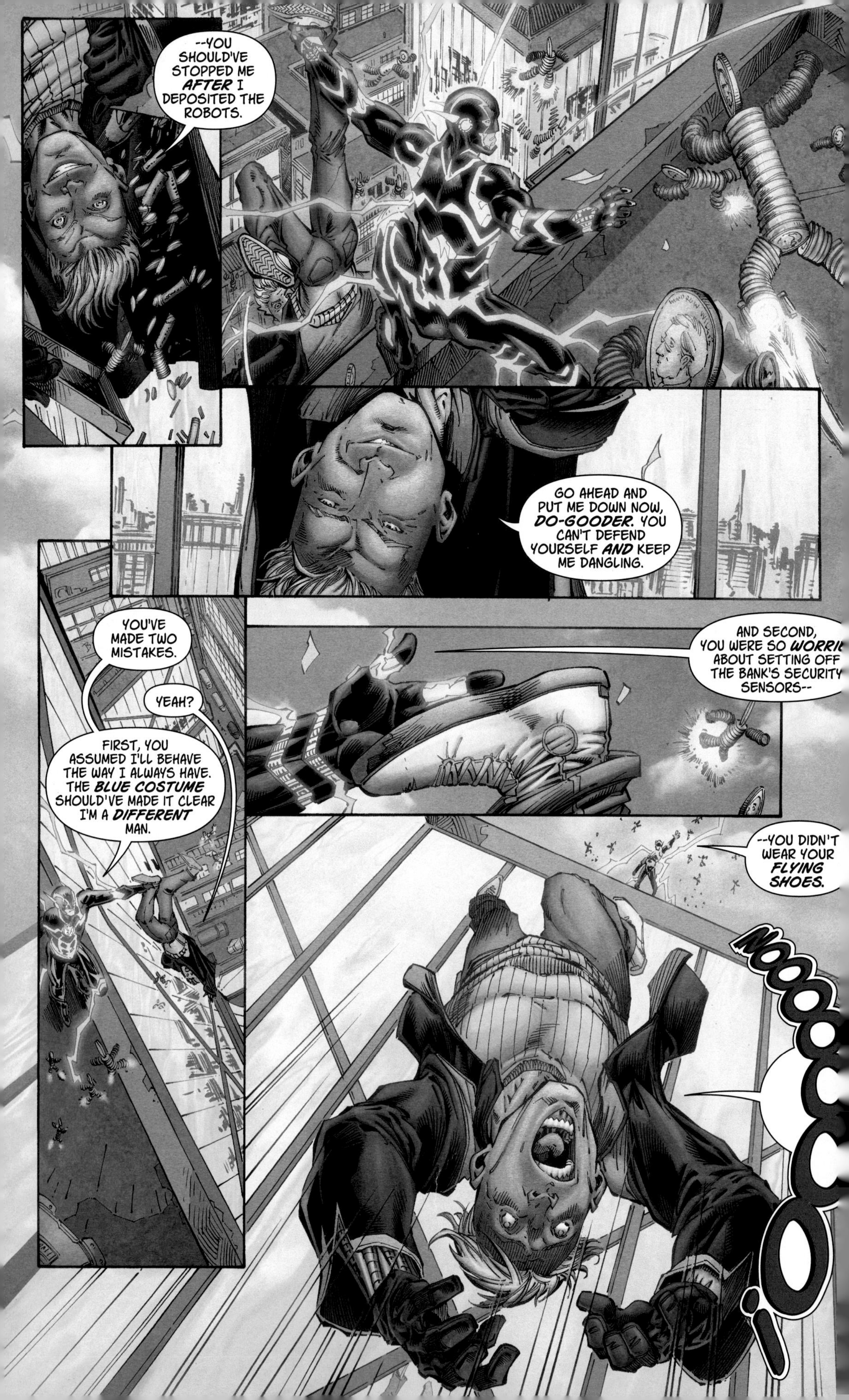
--YOU SHOULD'VE STOPPED ME *AFTER* I DEPOSITED THE ROBOTS.
GO AHEAD AND PUT ME DOWN NOW, *DO-GOODER*. YOU CAN'T DEFEND YOURSELF *AND* KEEP ME DANGLING.
YOU'VE MADE TWO MISTAKES.
YEAH?
FIRST, YOU ASSUMED I'LL BEHAVE THE WAY I ALWAYS HAVE. THE *BLUE COSTUME* SHOULD'VE MADE IT CLEAR I'M A *DIFFERENT* MAN.
AND SECOND, YOU WERE SO *WORRI* ABOUT SETTING OFF THE BANK'S SECURITY SENSORS--
--YOU DIDN'T WEAR YOUR *FLYING SHOES*.
NOOOOOOO!

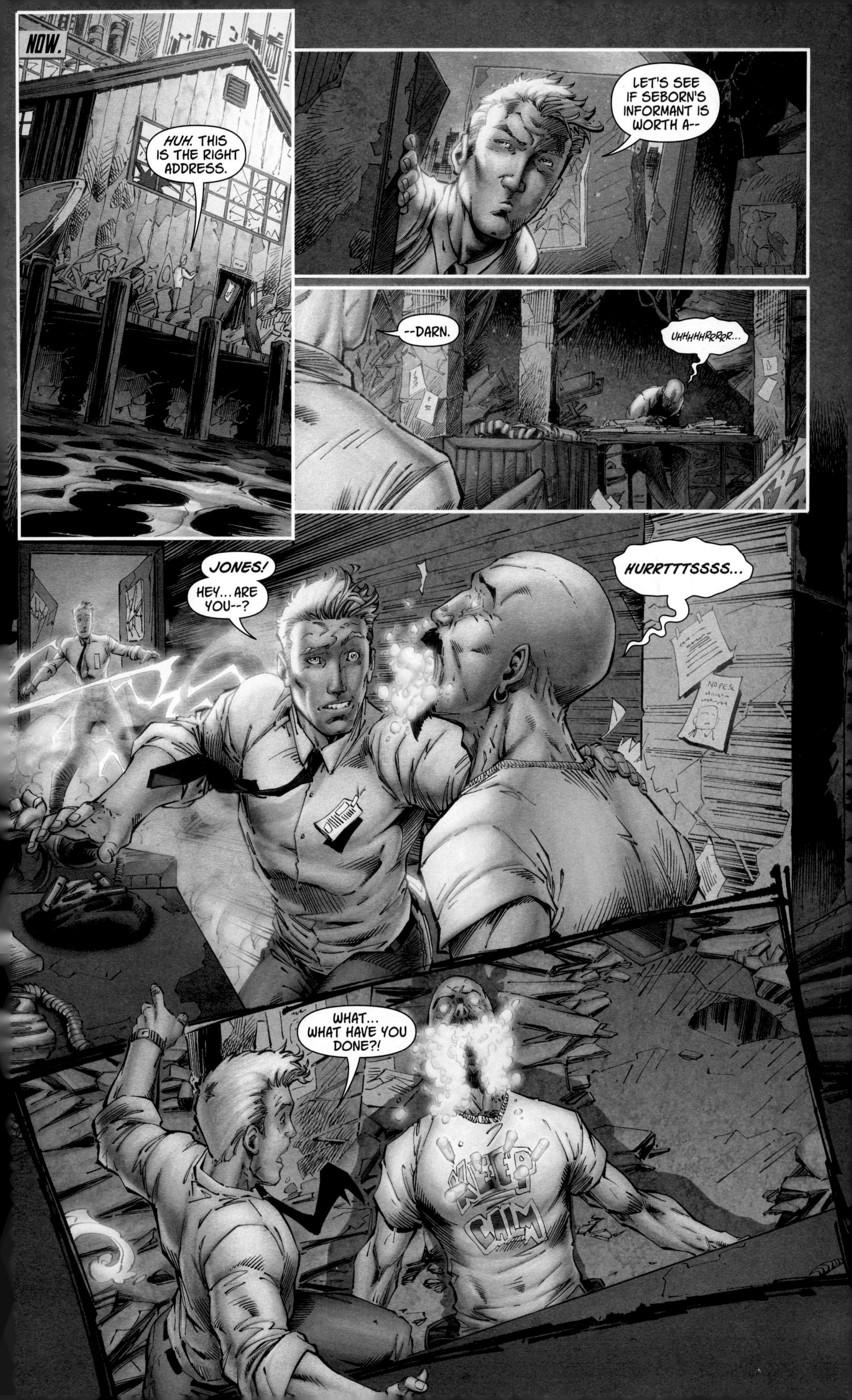
NOW.
HUH. THIS IS THE RIGHT ADDRESS.
LET'S SEE IF SEBORN'S INFORMANT IS WORTH A--
--DARN.
UHHHHHRRRRR...
JONES!
HEY... ARE YOU--?
HURRTTTSSSS...
WHAT... WHAT HAVE YOU DONE?!

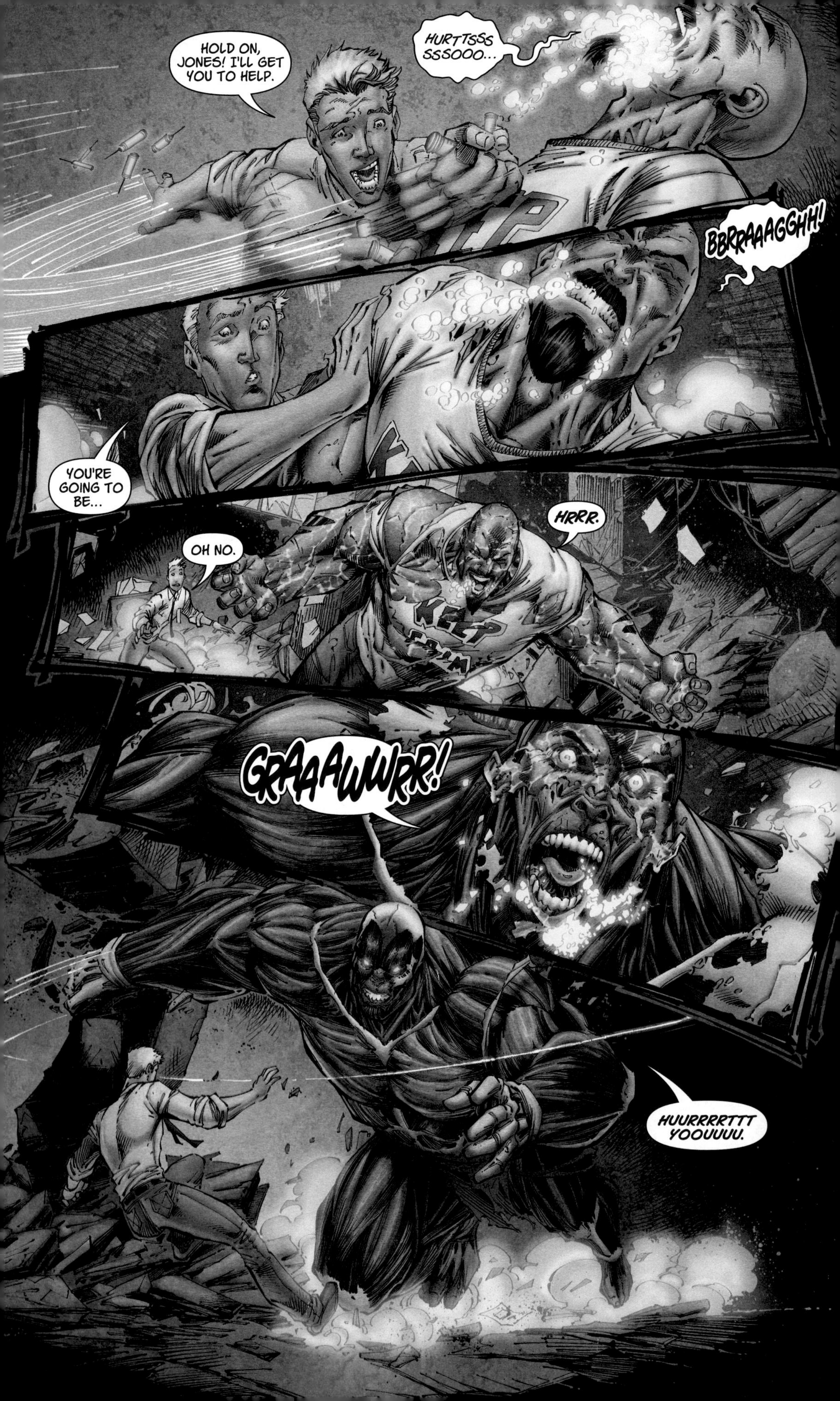
HOLD ON, JONES! I'LL GET YOU TO HELP.
HURTTSSS SSSOOO...
BBRRAAAGGHH!
YOU'RE GOING TO BE...
OH NO.
HRRR.
GRAAAWWRR!
HUURRRRTTT YOOUUUU.

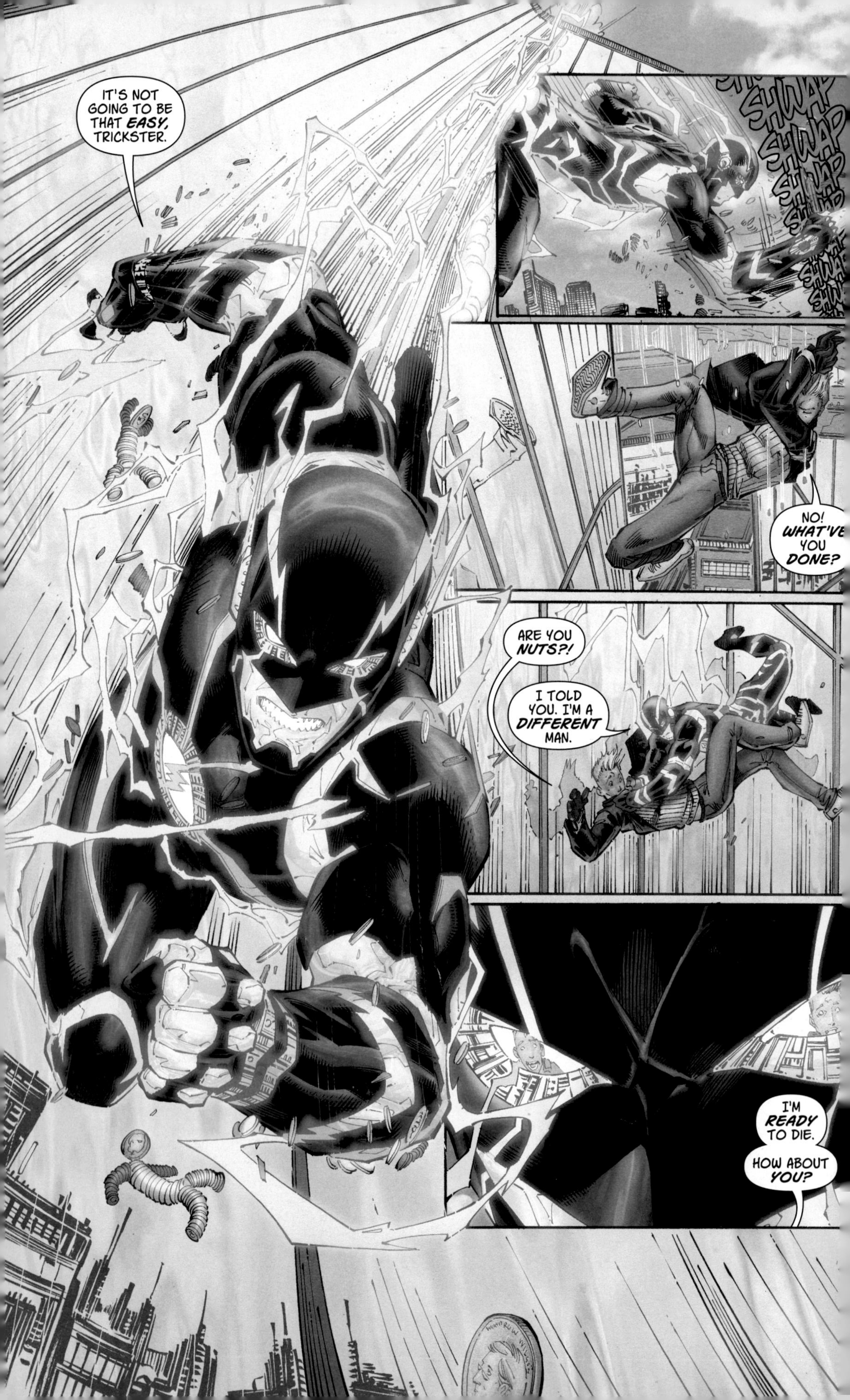
IT'S NOT GOING TO BE THAT *EASY,* TRICKSTER.
SHWAP SHWAP SHWAP
NO! *WHAT'VE* YOU *DONE?*
ARE YOU *NUTS?!*
I TOLD YOU. I'M A *DIFFERENT* MAN.
I'M *READY* TO DIE.
HOW ABOUT *YOU?*

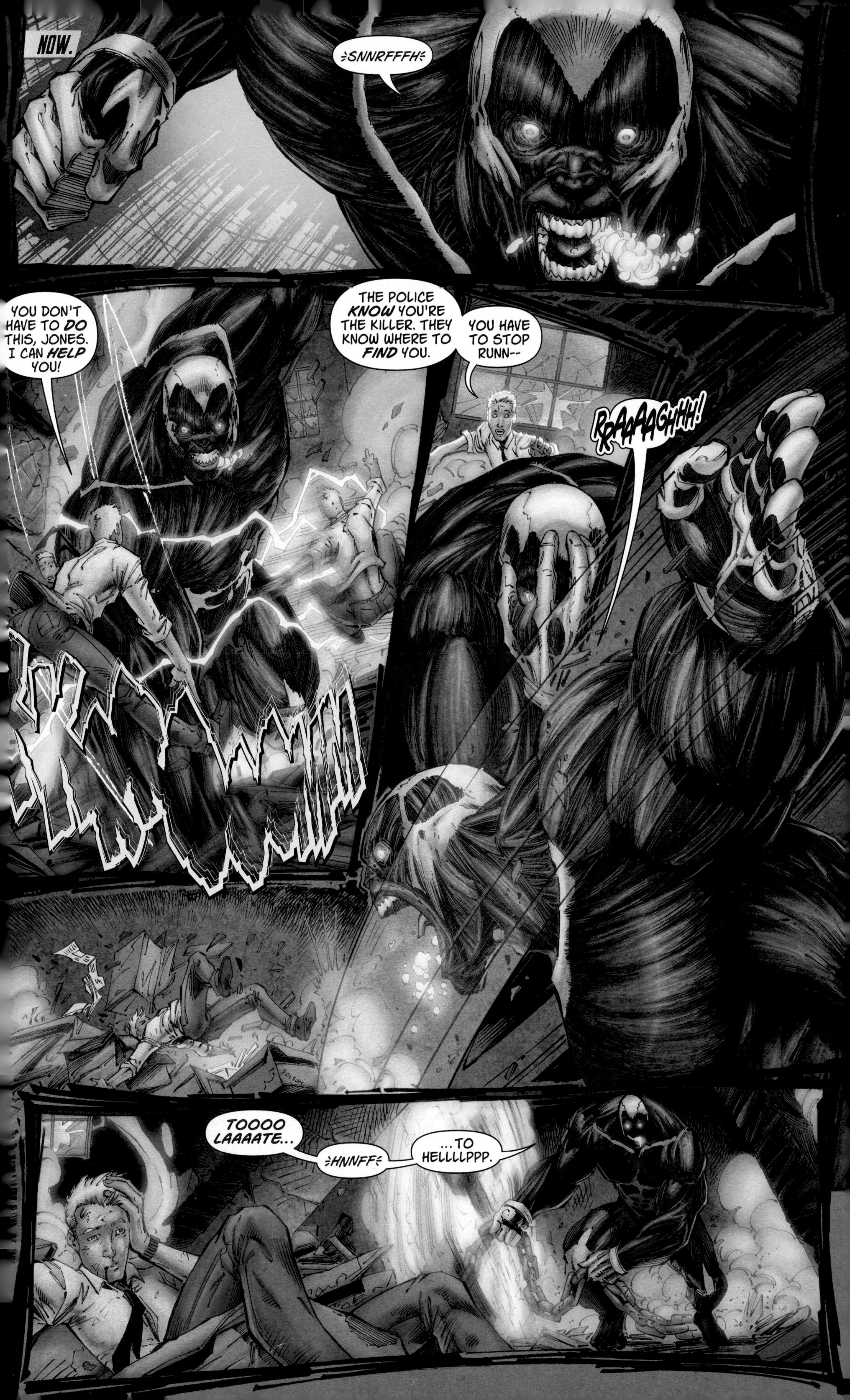
NOW.
SNNRFFFH
YOU DON'T HAVE TO DO THIS, JONES. I CAN HELP YOU!
THE POLICE KNOW YOU'RE THE KILLER. THEY KNOW WHERE TO FIND YOU.
YOU HAVE TO STOP RUNN--
RRAAAAGHHH!
TOOOO LAAAATE...
HNNFF
...TO HELLLLLPPP.

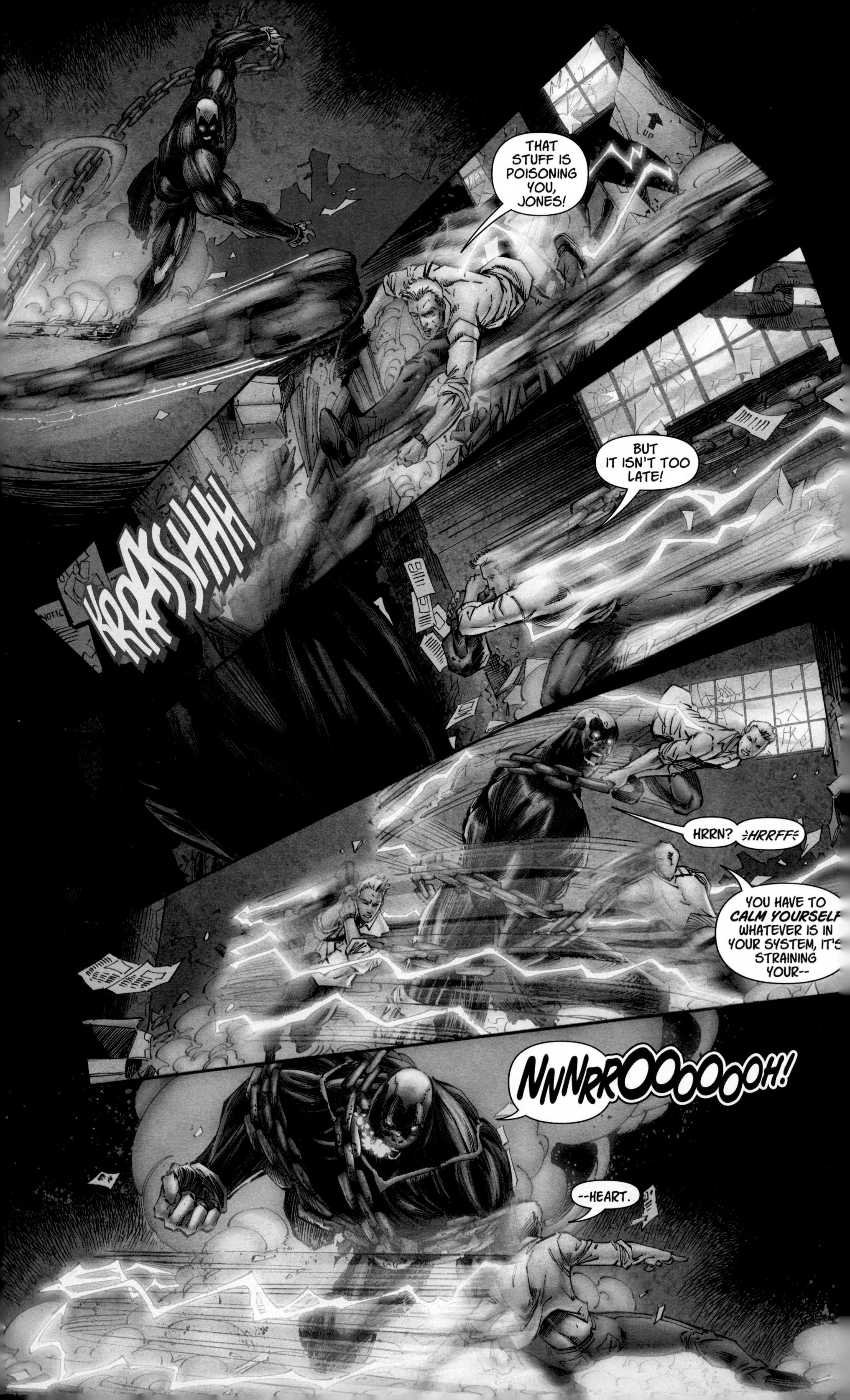
THAT STUFF IS POISONING YOU, JONES!
BUT IT ISN'T TOO LATE!
KRRASHHH
HRRN? HRRFF
YOU HAVE TO CALM YOURSELF WHATEVER IS IN YOUR SYSTEM, IT'S STRAINING YOUR--
NNNRROOOOOOOH!
--HEART.

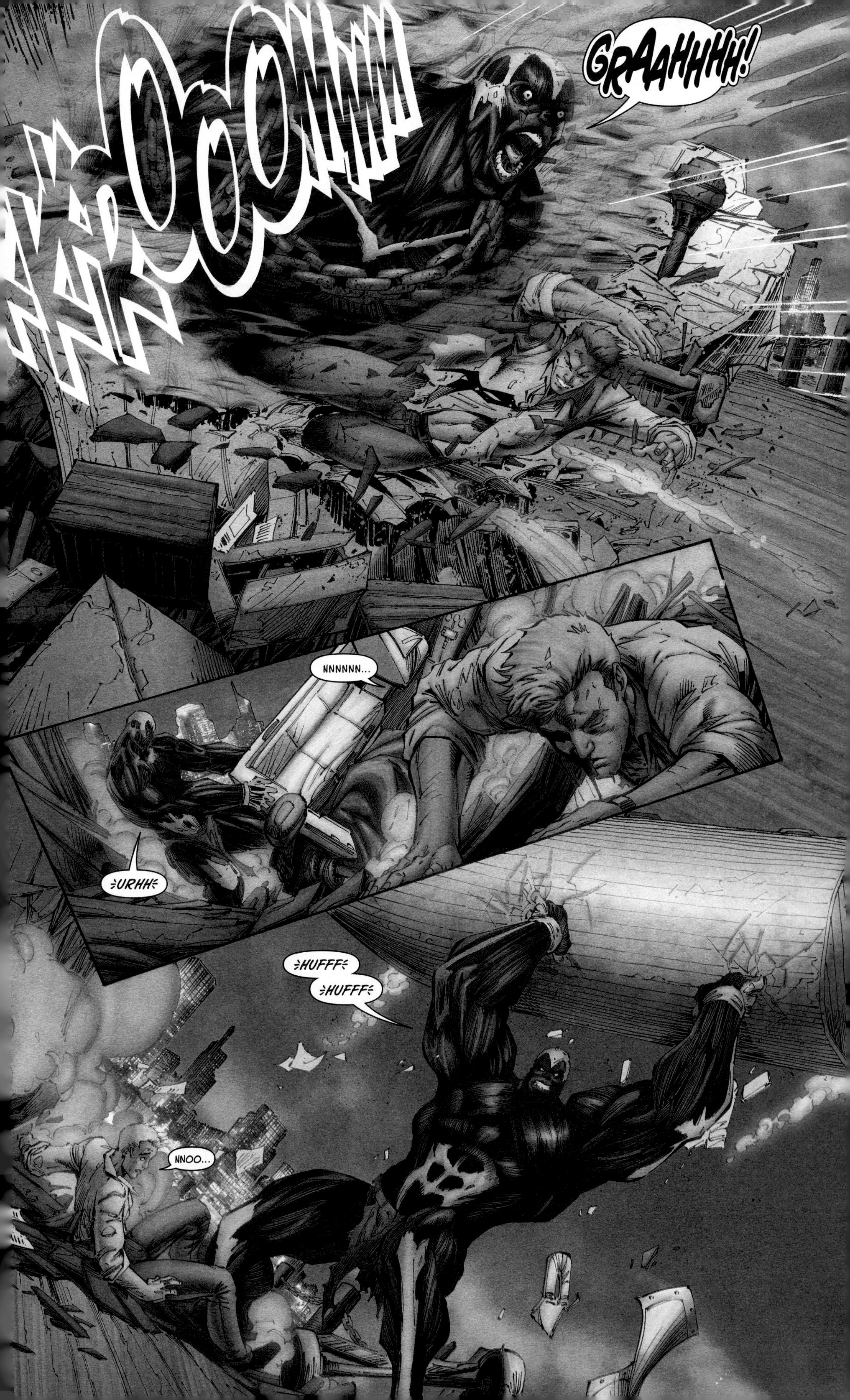
GRAAHHHH!
NNNNNN...
URHH
HUFFF
HUFFF
NNOO...

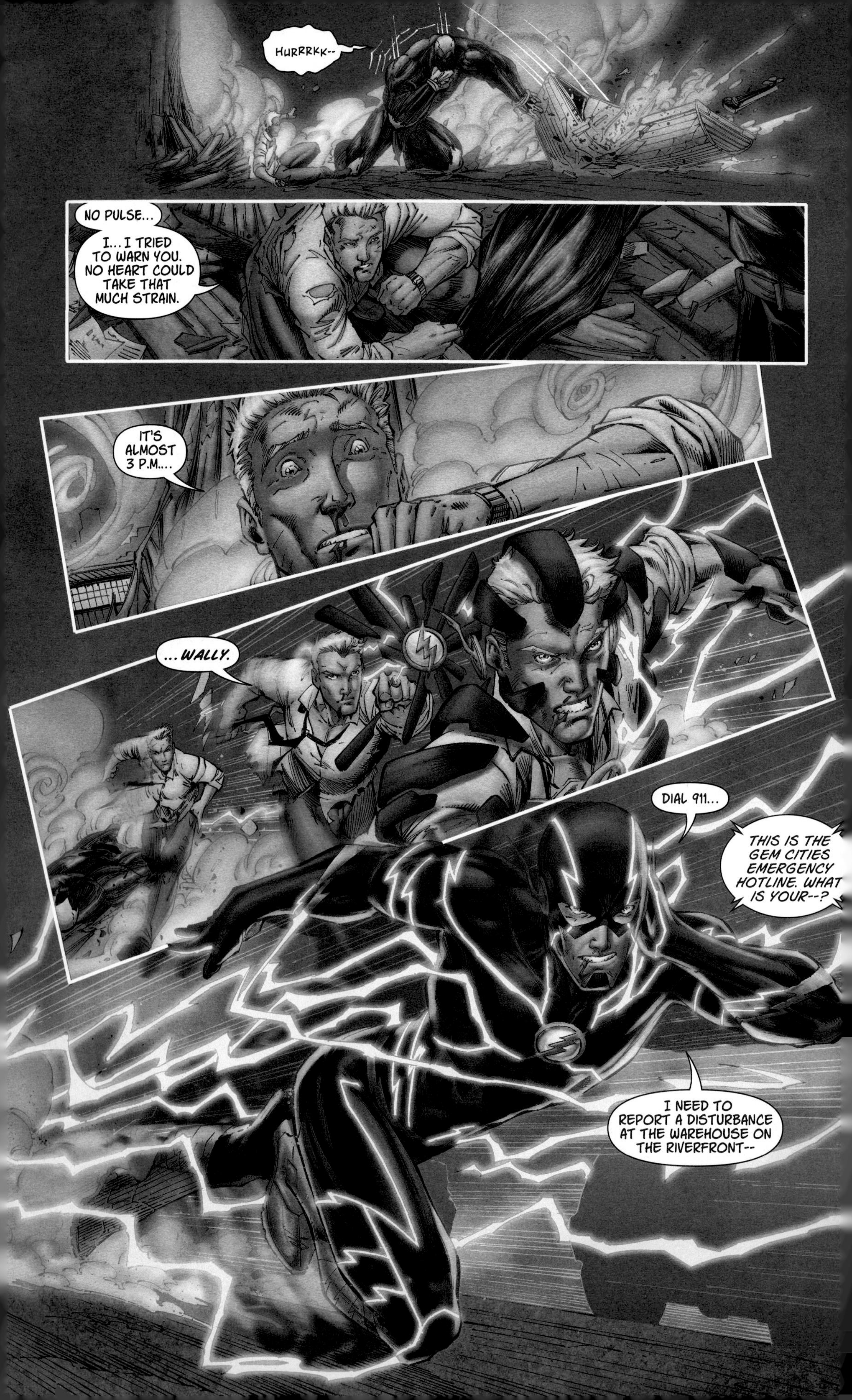
HURRRKK--
NO PULSE...
I... I TRIED TO WARN YOU. NO HEART COULD TAKE THAT MUCH STRAIN.
IT'S ALMOST 3 P.M....
...WALLY.
DIAL 911...
THIS IS THE GEM CITIES EMERGENCY HOTLINE. WHAT IS YOUR--?
I NEED TO REPORT A DISTURBANCE AT THE WAREHOUSE ON THE RIVERFRONT--

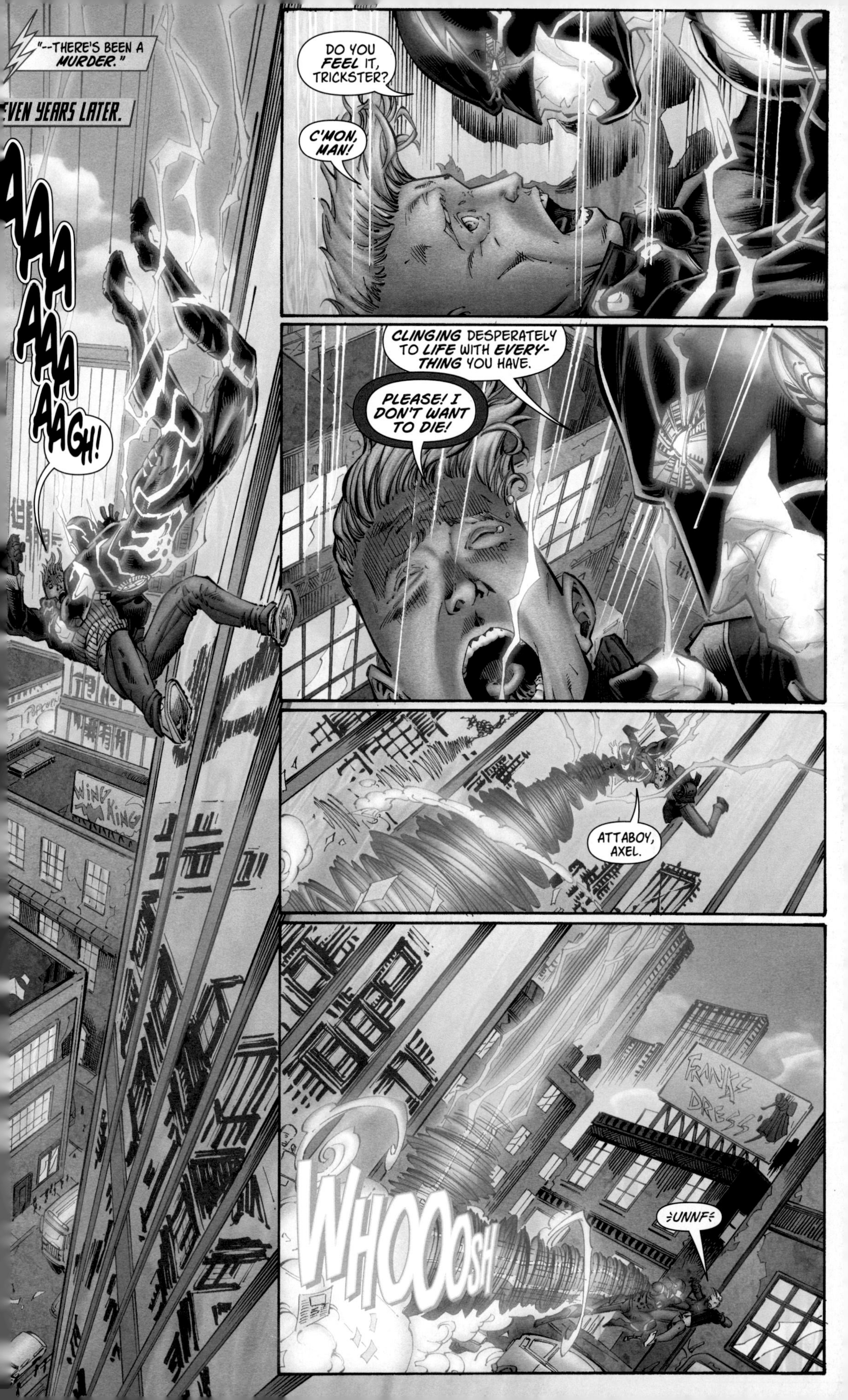
"--THERE'S BEEN A MURDER."
EVEN YEARS LATER.
AAAAAAAAAAAGH!
DO YOU FEEL IT, TRICKSTER?
C'MON, MAN!
CLINGING DESPERATELY TO LIFE WITH EVERY-THING YOU HAVE.
PLEASE! I DON'T WANT TO DIE!
ATTABOY, AXEL.
WHOOOSH
UNNF

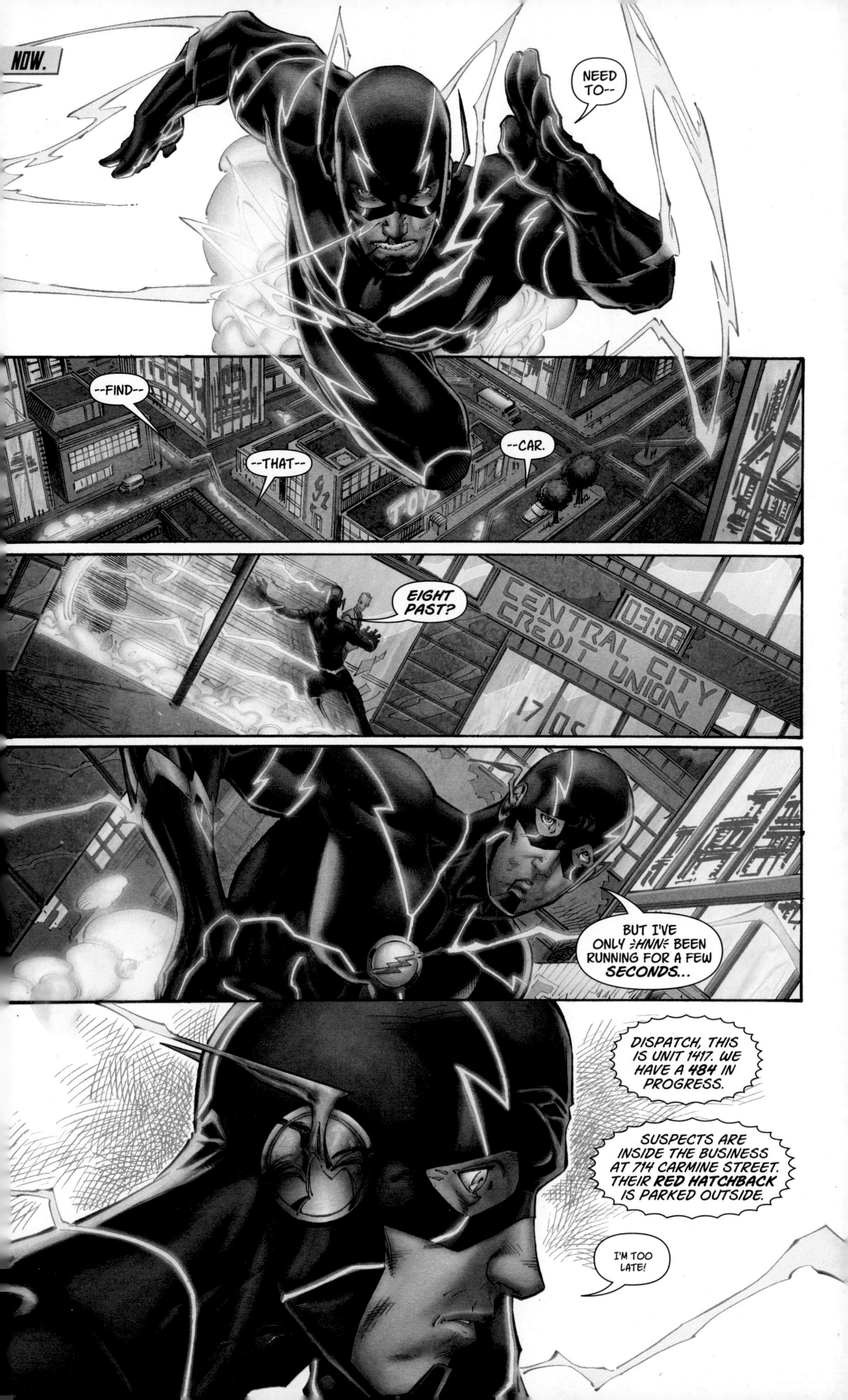
NOW.
NEED TO--
--FIND--
--THAT--
--CAR.
EIGHT PAST?
CENTRAL CITY CREDIT UNION
03:08
BUT I'VE ONLY ≠HNN≠ BEEN RUNNING FOR A FEW SECONDS...
DISPATCH, THIS IS UNIT 1417. WE HAVE A 484 IN PROGRESS.
SUSPECTS ARE INSIDE THE BUSINESS AT 714 CARMINE STREET. THEIR RED HATCHBACK IS PARKED OUTSIDE.
I'M TOO LATE!

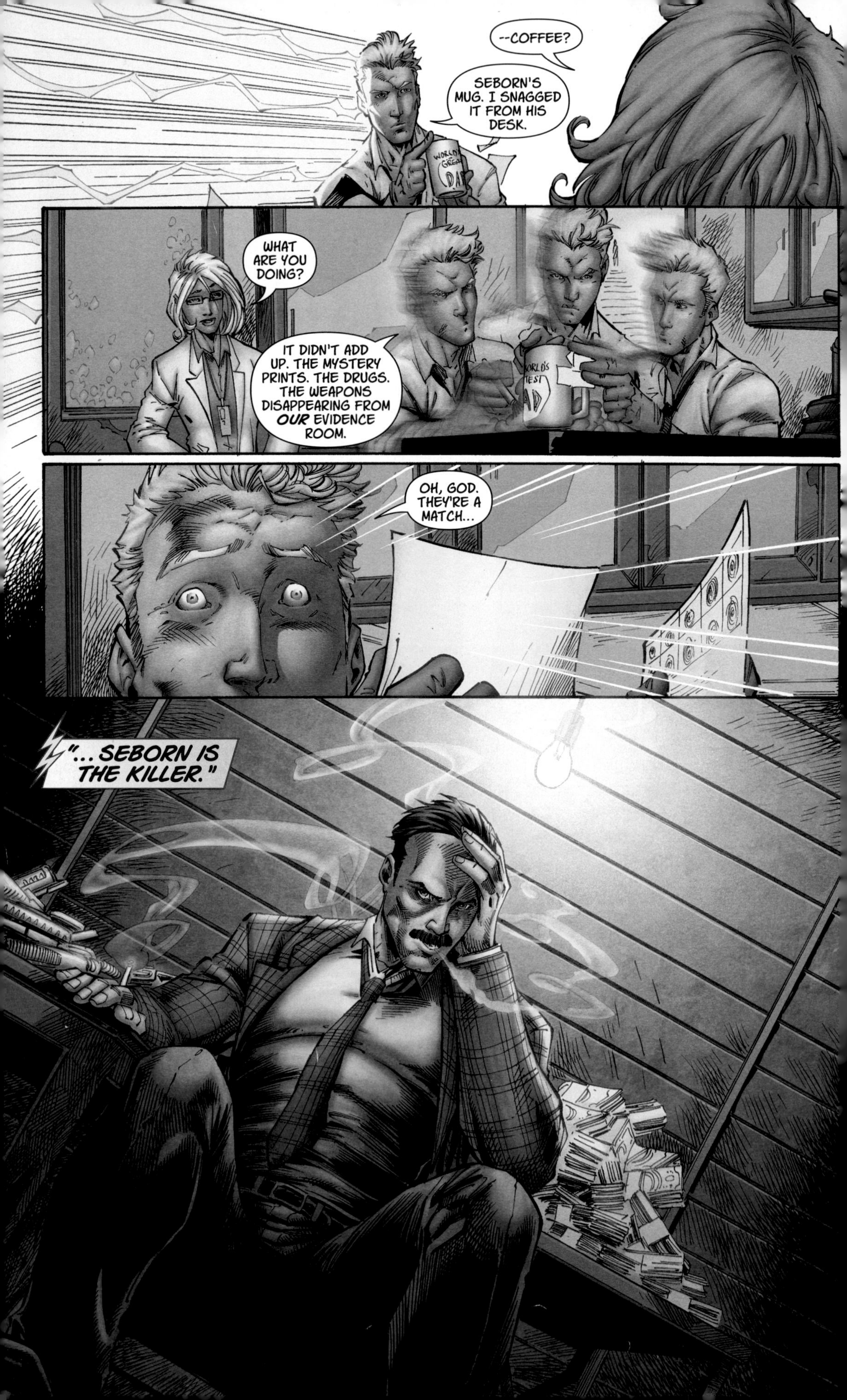
--COFFEE?
SEBORN'S MUG. I SNAGGED IT FROM HIS DESK.
WHAT ARE YOU DOING?
IT DIDN'T ADD UP. THE MYSTERY PRINTS. THE DRUGS. THE WEAPONS DISAPPEARING FROM OUR EVIDENCE ROOM.
OH, GOD. THEY'RE A MATCH...
"...SEBORN IS THE KILLER."

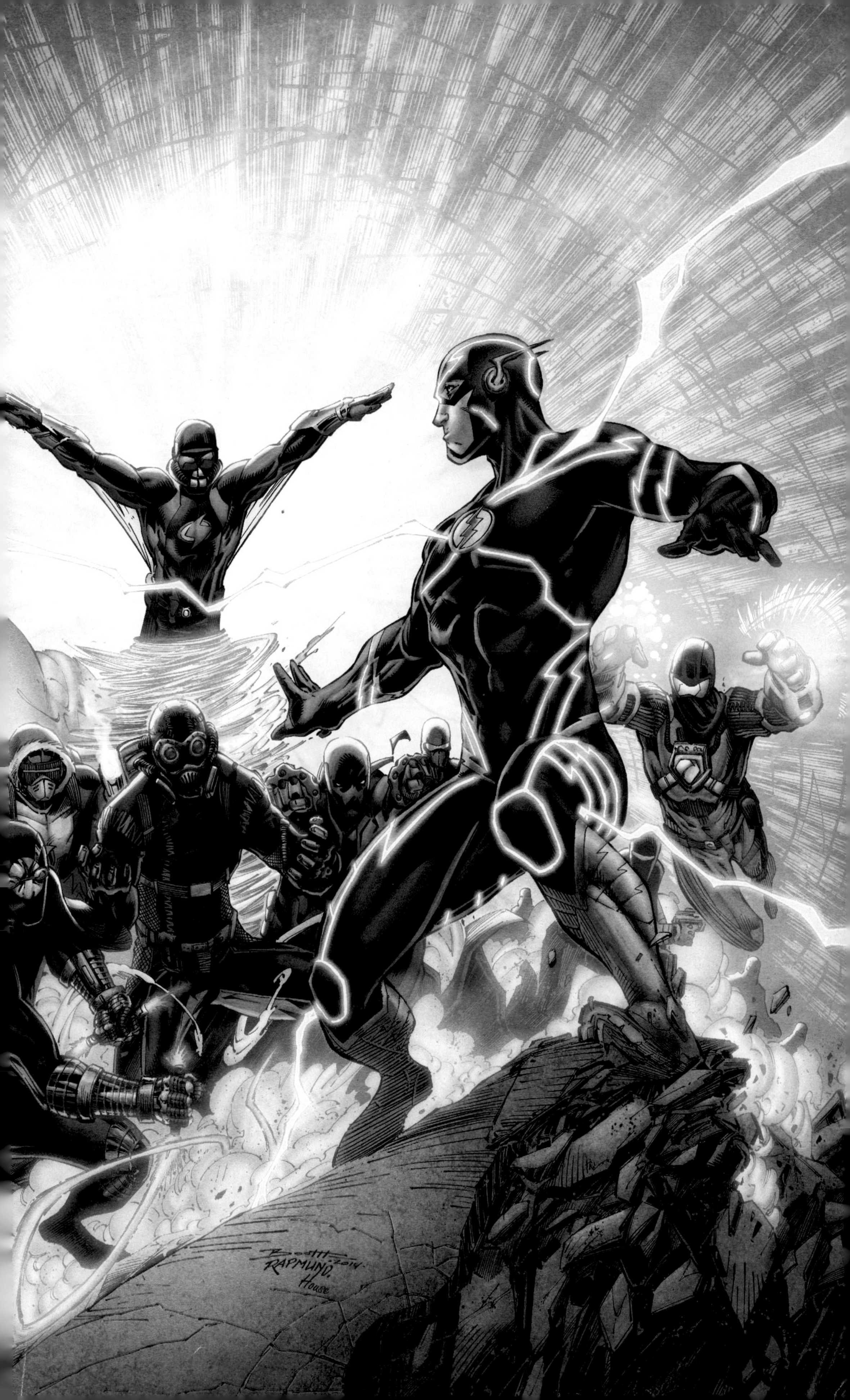
Booth 2014
RAPMUND.
House

COLLISION COURSE
ROBERT VENDITTI & VAN JENSEN writers **BRETT BOOTH** penciller **NORM RAPMUND** inker

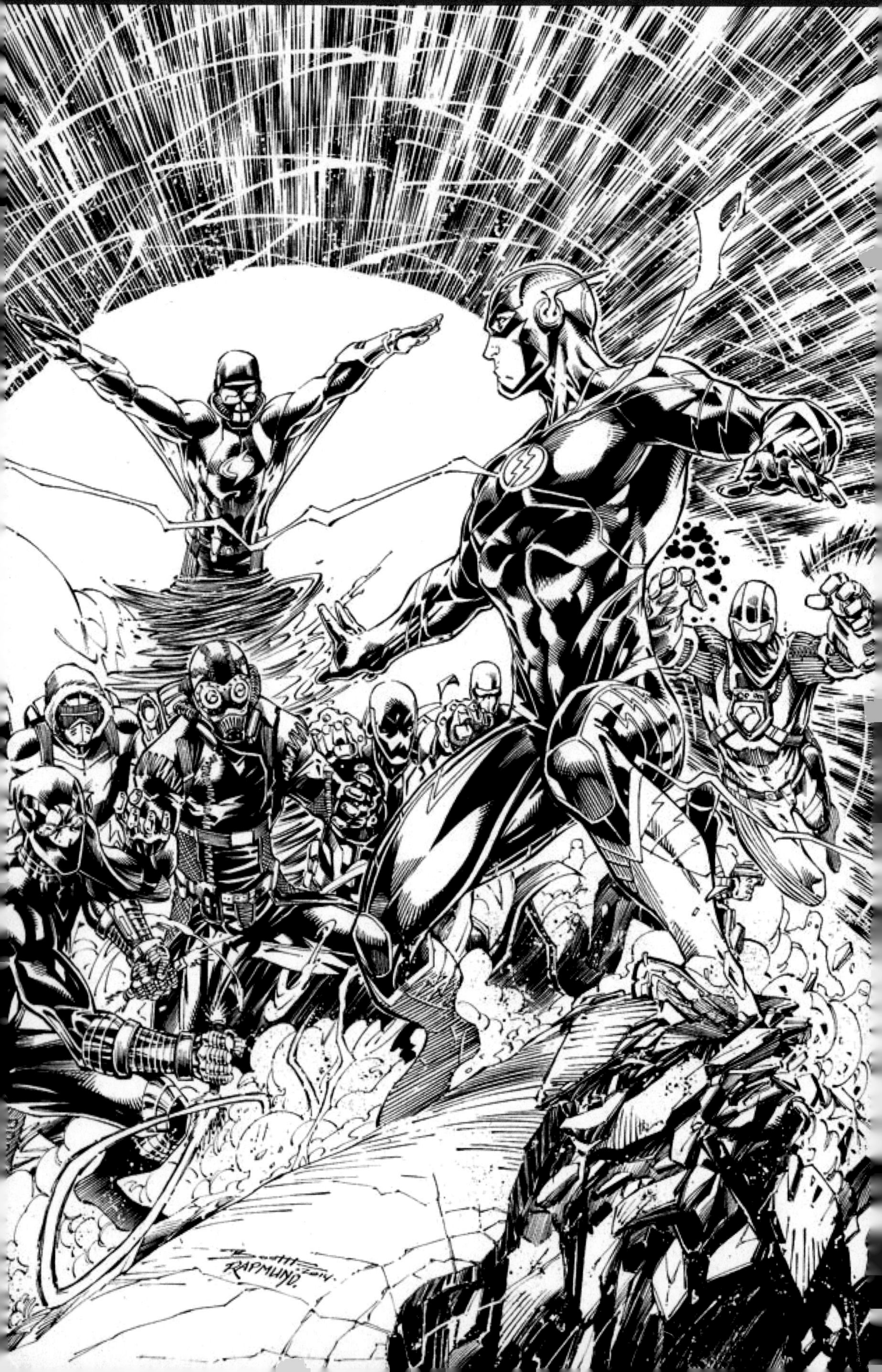

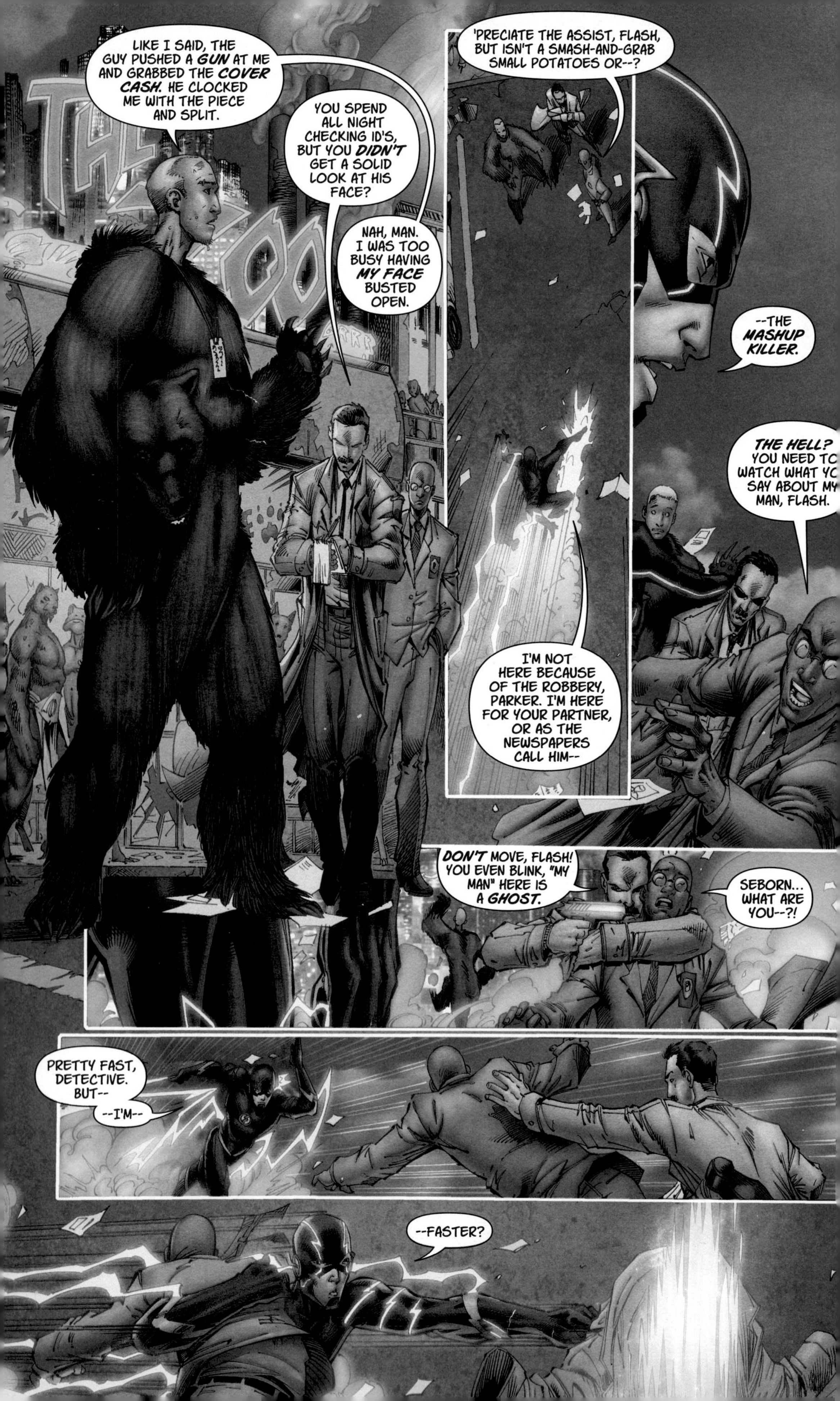

LIKE I SAID, THE GUY PUSHED A GUN AT ME AND GRABBED THE COVER CASH. HE CLOCKED ME WITH THE PIECE AND SPLIT.
YOU SPEND ALL NIGHT CHECKING ID'S, BUT YOU DIDN'T GET A SOLID LOOK AT HIS FACE?
NAH, MAN. I WAS TOO BUSY HAVING MY FACE BUSTED OPEN.
'PRECIATE THE ASSIST, FLASH, BUT ISN'T A SMASH-AND-GRAB SMALL POTATOES OR--?
I'M NOT HERE BECAUSE OF THE ROBBERY, PARKER. I'M HERE FOR YOUR PARTNER, OR AS THE NEWSPAPERS CALL HIM--
--THE MASHUP KILLER.
THE HELL? YOU NEED TO WATCH WHAT YO SAY ABOUT MY MAN, FLASH.
DON'T MOVE, FLASH! YOU EVEN BLINK, "MY MAN" HERE IS A GHOST.
SEBORN... WHAT ARE YOU--?!
PRETTY FAST, DETECTIVE. BUT--
--I'M--
--FASTER?

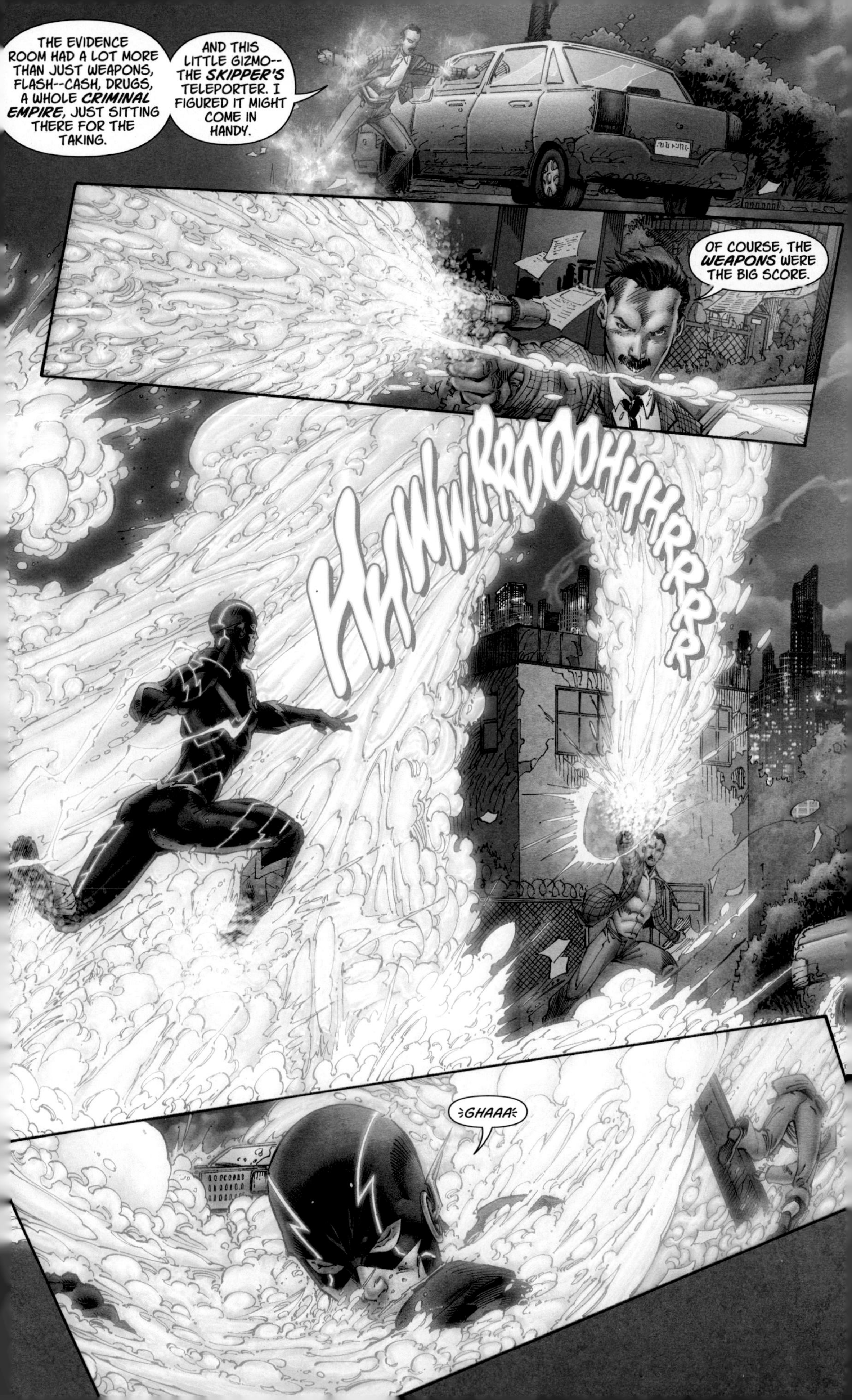
THE EVIDENCE ROOM HAD A LOT MORE THAN JUST WEAPONS, FLASH--CASH, DRUGS, A WHOLE CRIMINAL EMPIRE, JUST SITTING THERE FOR THE TAKING.
AND THIS LITTLE GIZMO--THE SKIPPER'S TELEPORTER. I FIGURED IT MIGHT COME IN HANDY.
OF COURSE, THE WEAPONS WERE THE BIG SCORE.
HHWWRROOOHHHRRRR
GHAAA

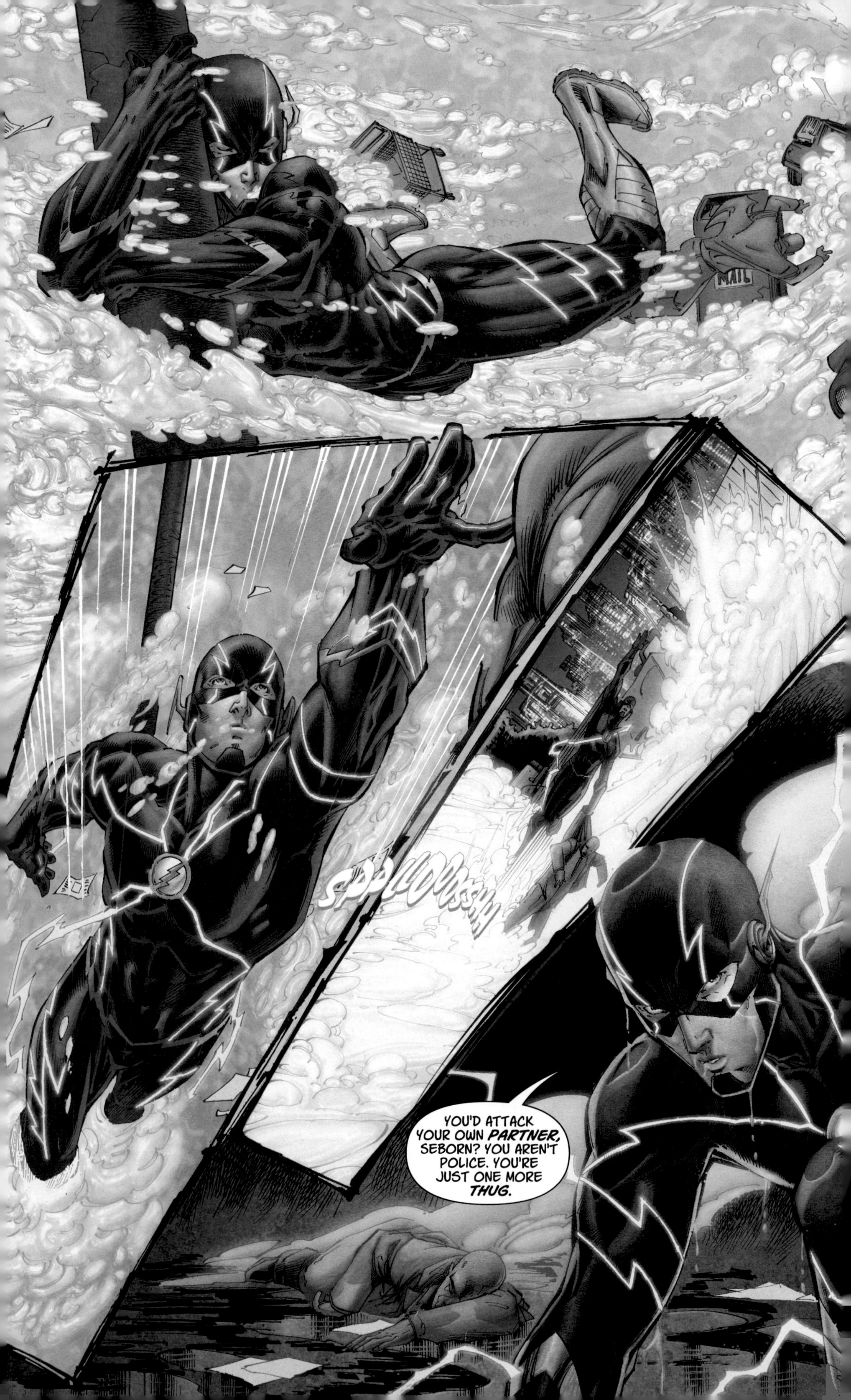
SPPLLOOSSH!
YOU'D ATTACK YOUR OWN *PARTNER,* SEBORN? YOU AREN'T POLICE. YOU'RE JUST ONE MORE *THUG.*

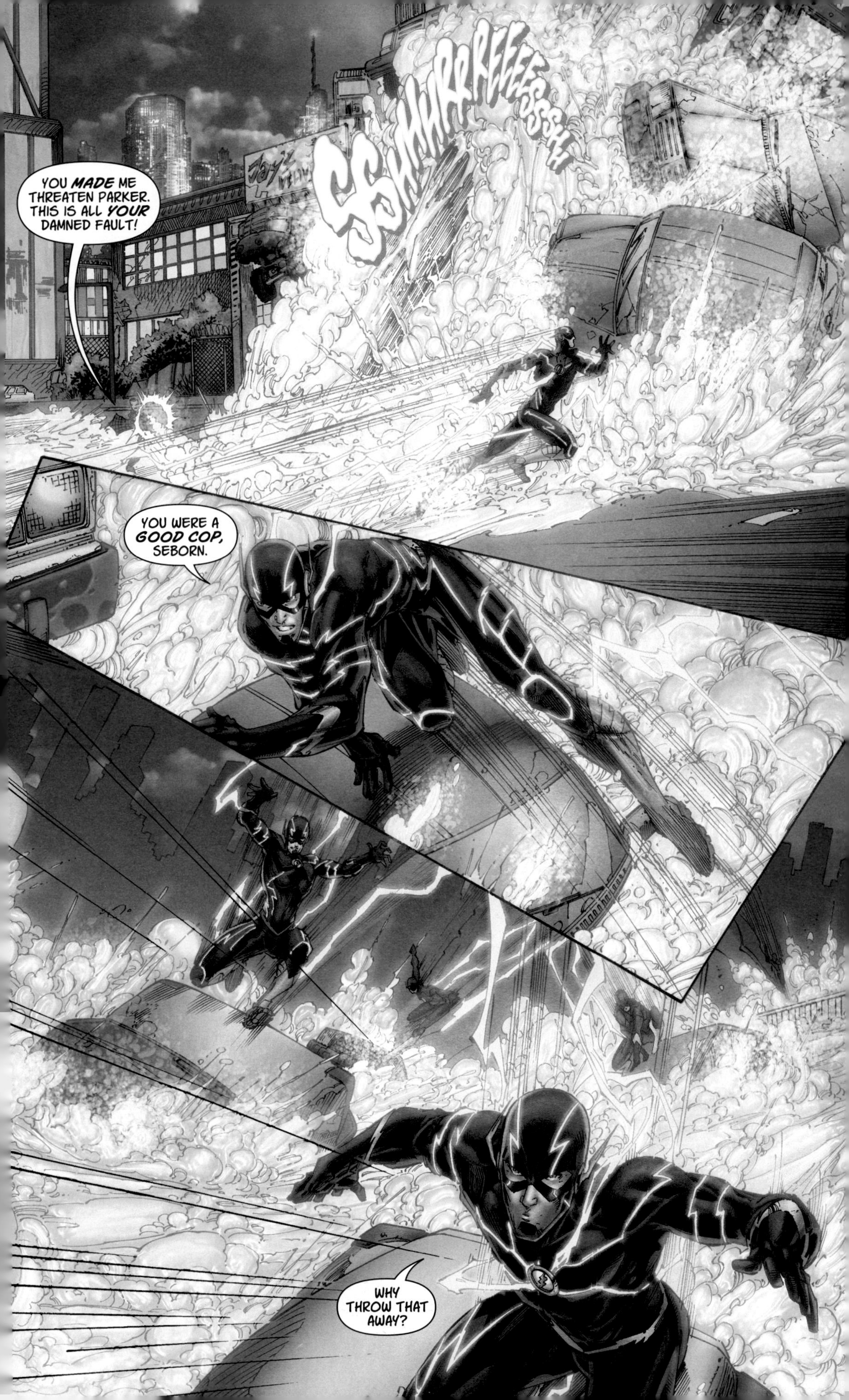

SSHHRRREEEESSSH
Jay's
YOU MADE ME THREATEN PARKER. THIS IS ALL YOUR DAMNED FAULT!
YOU WERE A GOOD COP, SEBORN.
WHY THROW THAT AWAY?

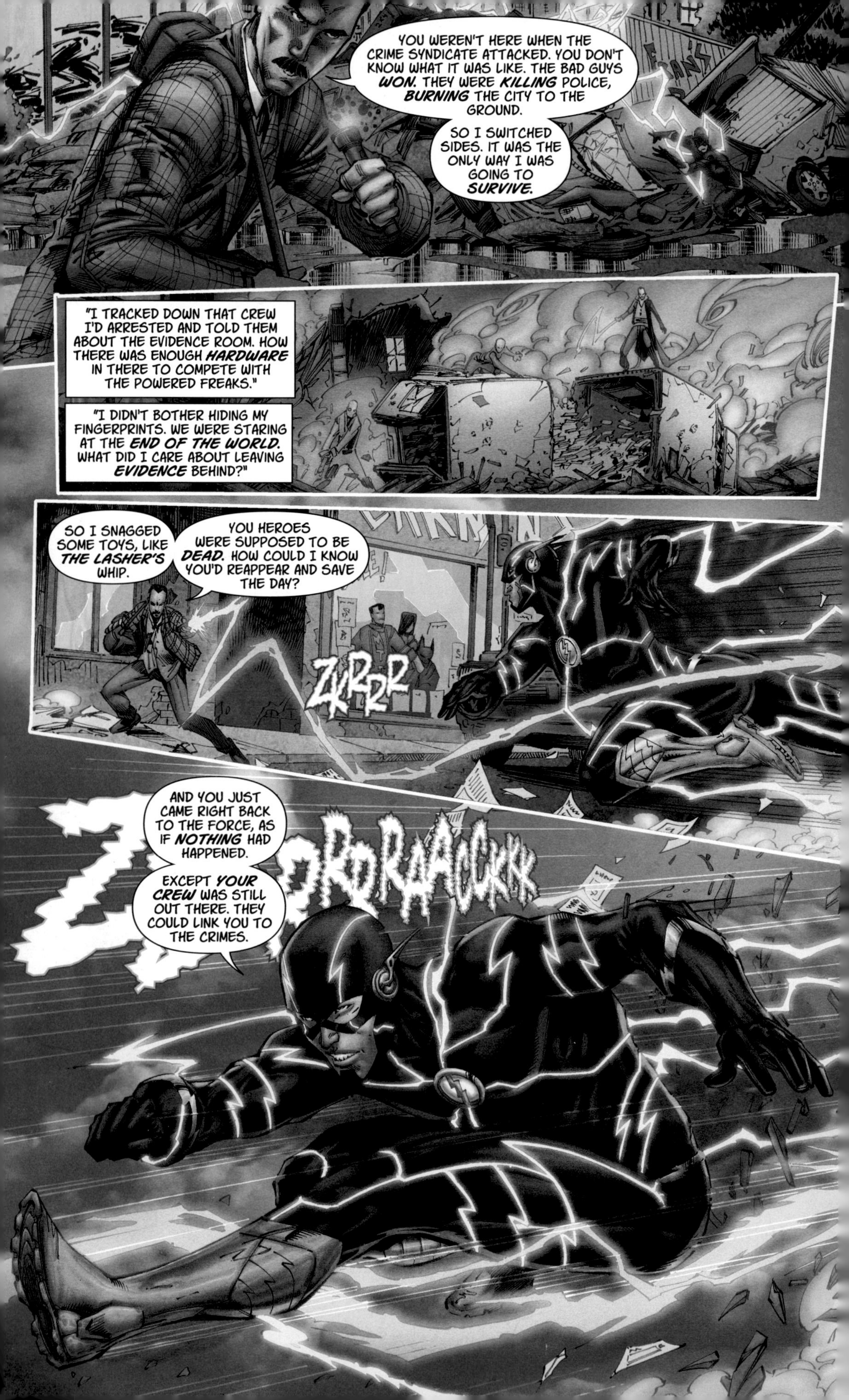

YOU WEREN'T HERE WHEN THE CRIME SYNDICATE ATTACKED. YOU DON'T KNOW WHAT IT WAS LIKE. THE BAD GUYS **WON.** THEY WERE **KILLING** POLICE, **BURNING** THE CITY TO THE GROUND.
SO I SWITCHED SIDES. IT WAS THE ONLY WAY I WAS GOING TO **SURVIVE.**
"I TRACKED DOWN THAT CREW I'D ARRESTED AND TOLD THEM ABOUT THE EVIDENCE ROOM. HOW THERE WAS ENOUGH **HARDWARE** IN THERE TO COMPETE WITH THE POWERED FREAKS."
"I DIDN'T BOTHER HIDING MY FINGERPRINTS. WE WERE STARING AT THE **END OF THE WORLD.** WHAT DID I CARE ABOUT LEAVING **EVIDENCE** BEHIND?"
SO I SNAGGED SOME TOYS, LIKE **THE LASHER'S** WHIP.
YOU HEROES WERE SUPPOSED TO BE **DEAD.** HOW COULD I KNOW YOU'D REAPPEAR AND SAVE THE DAY?
ZKRRR
AND YOU JUST CAME RIGHT BACK TO THE FORCE, AS IF **NOTHING** HAD HAPPENED.
EXCEPT **YOUR CREW** WAS STILL OUT THERE. THEY COULD LINK YOU TO THE CRIMES.
ZDRDRAACCKKK

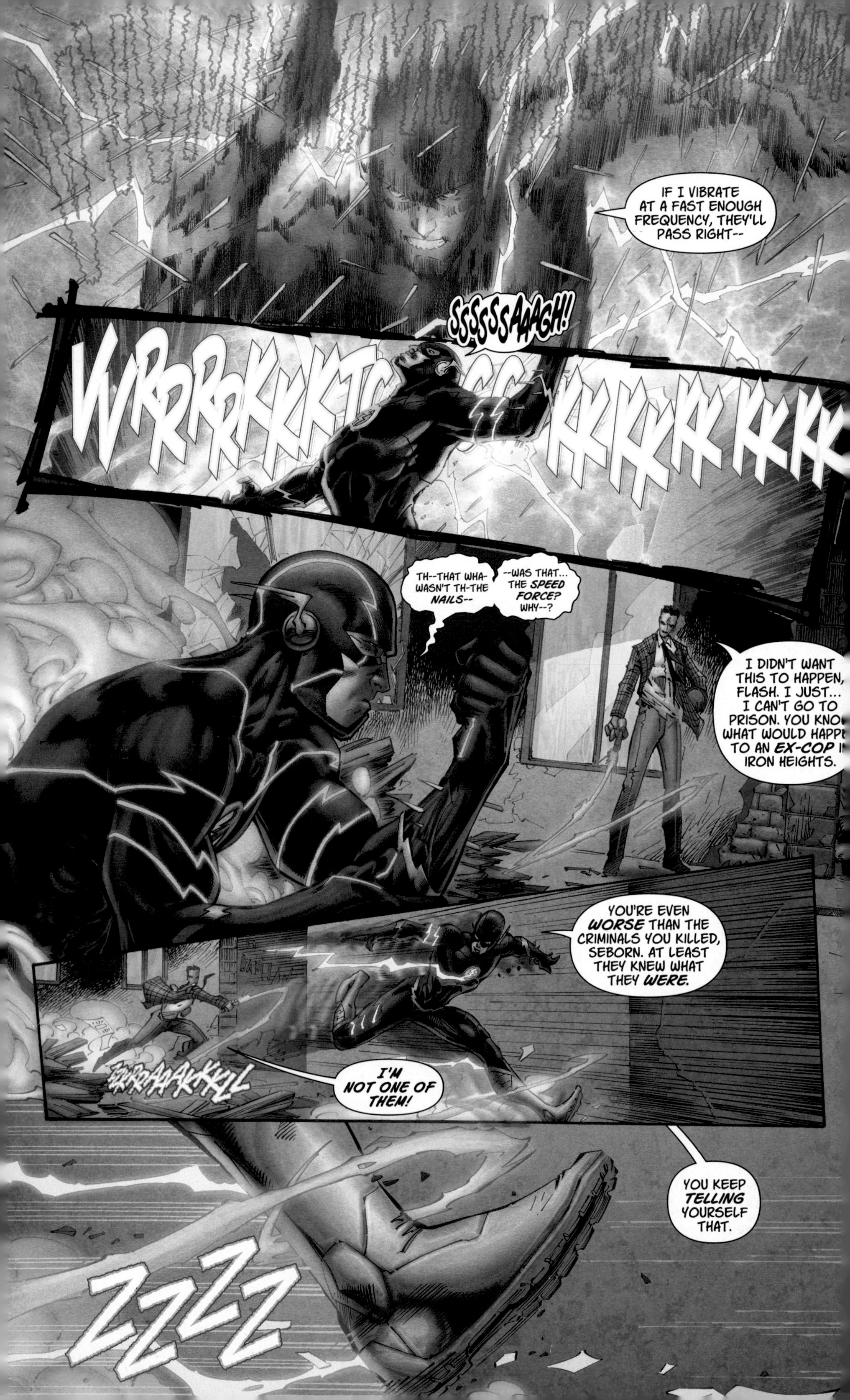
IF I VIBRATE AT A FAST ENOUGH FREQUENCY, THEY'LL PASS RIGHT--
SSSSSAAAGH!
VVRRRKKKTC
KKKKKKKKK
TH--THAT WHA- WASN'T TH-THE NAILS--
--WAS THAT... THE SPEED FORCE? WHY--?
I DIDN'T WANT THIS TO HAPPEN, FLASH. I JUST... I CAN'T GO TO PRISON. YOU KNO WHAT WOULD HAPP TO AN EX-COP I IRON HEIGHTS.
YOU'RE EVEN WORSE THAN THE CRIMINALS YOU KILLED, SEBORN. AT LEAST THEY KNEW WHAT THEY WERE.
ZZRRRAAAKKKLL
I'M NOT ONE OF THEM!
YOU KEEP TELLING YOURSELF THAT.
ZZZZ

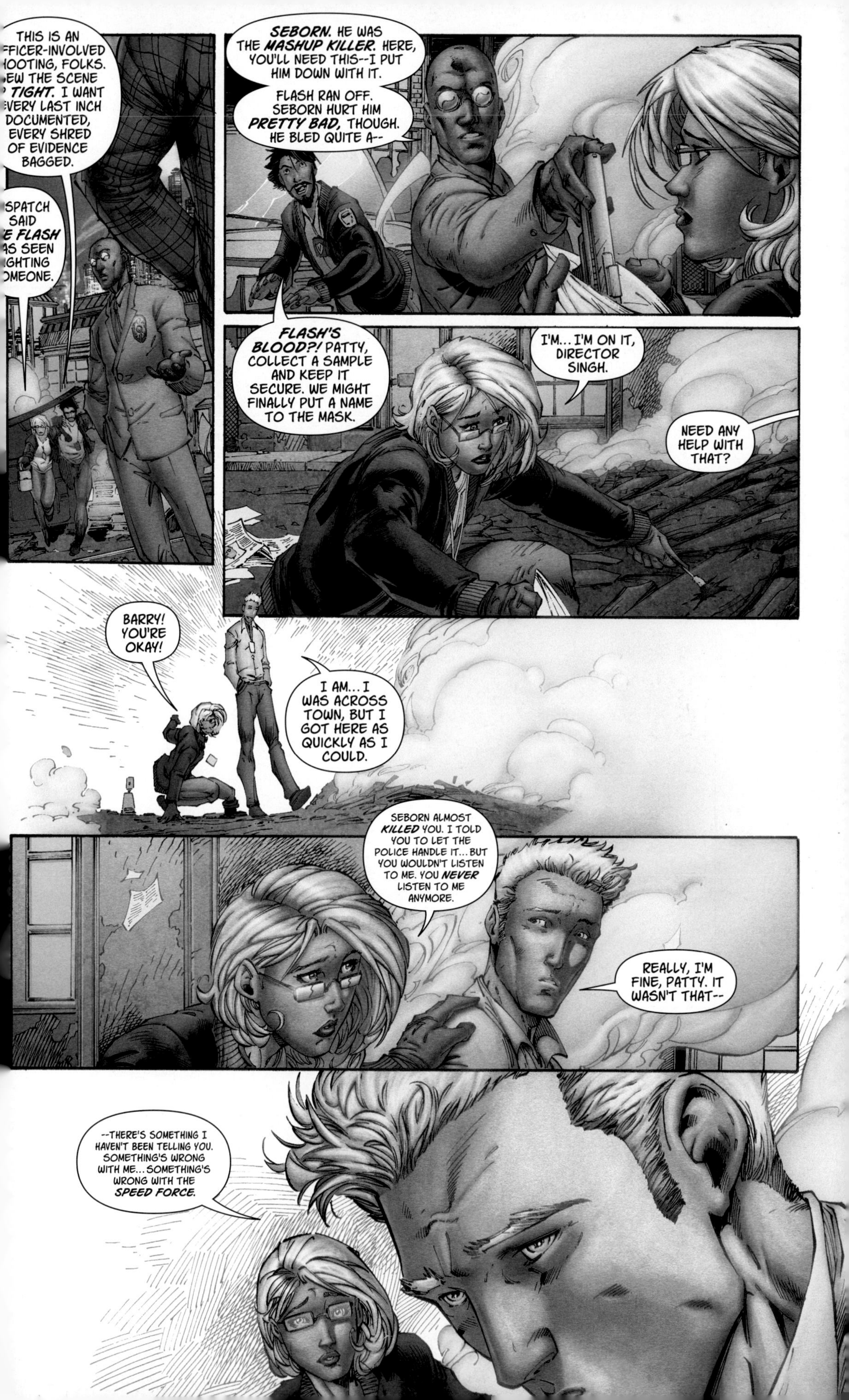
THIS IS AN
FFICER-INVOLVED
HOOTING, FOLKS.
EW THE SCENE
TIGHT. I WANT
VERY LAST INCH
DOCUMENTED,
EVERY SHRED
OF EVIDENCE
BAGGED.
SPATCH
SAID
FLASH
AS SEEN
GHTING
OMEONE.
SEBORN. HE WAS THE MASHUP KILLER. HERE, YOU'LL NEED THIS--I PUT HIM DOWN WITH IT.
FLASH RAN OFF. SEBORN HURT HIM PRETTY BAD, THOUGH. HE BLED QUITE A--
FLASH'S BLOOD?! PATTY, COLLECT A SAMPLE AND KEEP IT SECURE. WE MIGHT FINALLY PUT A NAME TO THE MASK.
I'M... I'M ON IT, DIRECTOR SINGH.
NEED ANY HELP WITH THAT?
BARRY! YOU'RE OKAY!
I AM... I WAS ACROSS TOWN, BUT I GOT HERE AS QUICKLY AS I COULD.
SEBORN ALMOST KILLED YOU. I TOLD YOU TO LET THE POLICE HANDLE IT... BUT YOU WOULDN'T LISTEN TO ME. YOU NEVER LISTEN TO ME ANYMORE.
REALLY, I'M FINE, PATTY. IT WASN'T THAT--
--THERE'S SOMETHING I HAVEN'T BEEN TELLING YOU. SOMETHING'S WRONG WITH ME... SOMETHING'S WRONG WITH THE SPEED FORCE.

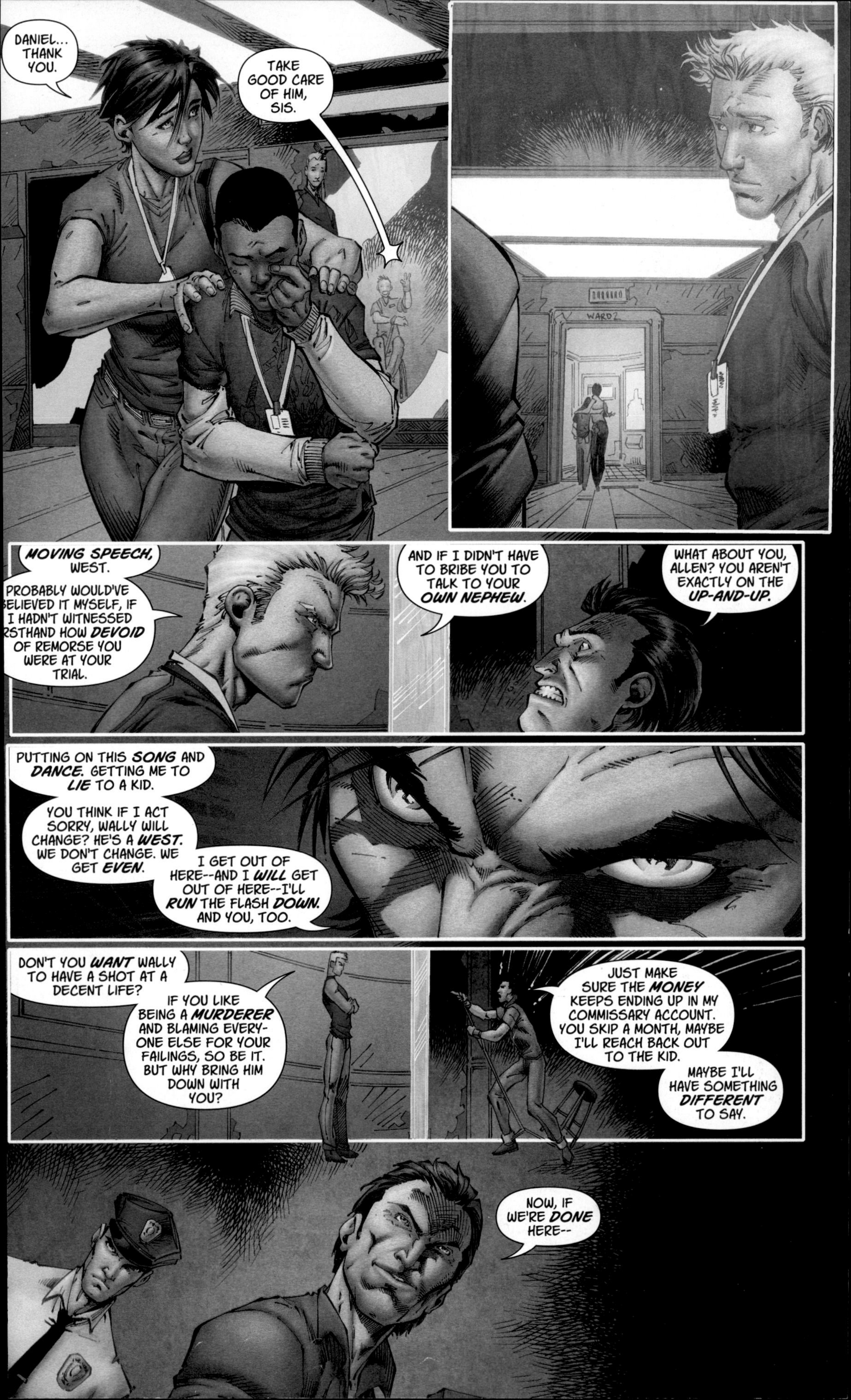

DANIEL... THANK YOU.
TAKE GOOD CARE OF HIM, SIS.
MOVING SPEECH, WEST.
PROBABLY WOULD'VE BELIEVED IT MYSELF, IF I HADN'T WITNESSED FIRSTHAND HOW DEVOID OF REMORSE YOU WERE AT YOUR TRIAL.
AND IF I DIDN'T HAVE TO BRIBE YOU TO TALK TO YOUR OWN NEPHEW.
WHAT ABOUT YOU, ALLEN? YOU AREN'T EXACTLY ON THE UP-AND-UP.
PUTTING ON THIS SONG AND DANCE. GETTING ME TO LIE TO A KID.
YOU THINK IF I ACT SORRY, WALLY WILL CHANGE? HE'S A WEST. WE DON'T CHANGE. WE GET EVEN.
I GET OUT OF HERE--AND I WILL GET OUT OF HERE--I'LL RUN THE FLASH DOWN. AND YOU, TOO.
DON'T YOU WANT WALLY TO HAVE A SHOT AT A DECENT LIFE?
IF YOU LIKE BEING A MURDERER AND BLAMING EVERY-ONE ELSE FOR YOUR FAILINGS, SO BE IT. BUT WHY BRING HIM DOWN WITH YOU?
JUST MAKE SURE THE MONEY KEEPS ENDING UP IN MY COMMISSARY ACCOUNT. YOU SKIP A MONTH, MAYBE I'LL REACH BACK OUT TO THE KID.
MAYBE I'LL HAVE SOMETHING DIFFERENT TO SAY.
NOW, IF WE'RE DONE HERE--

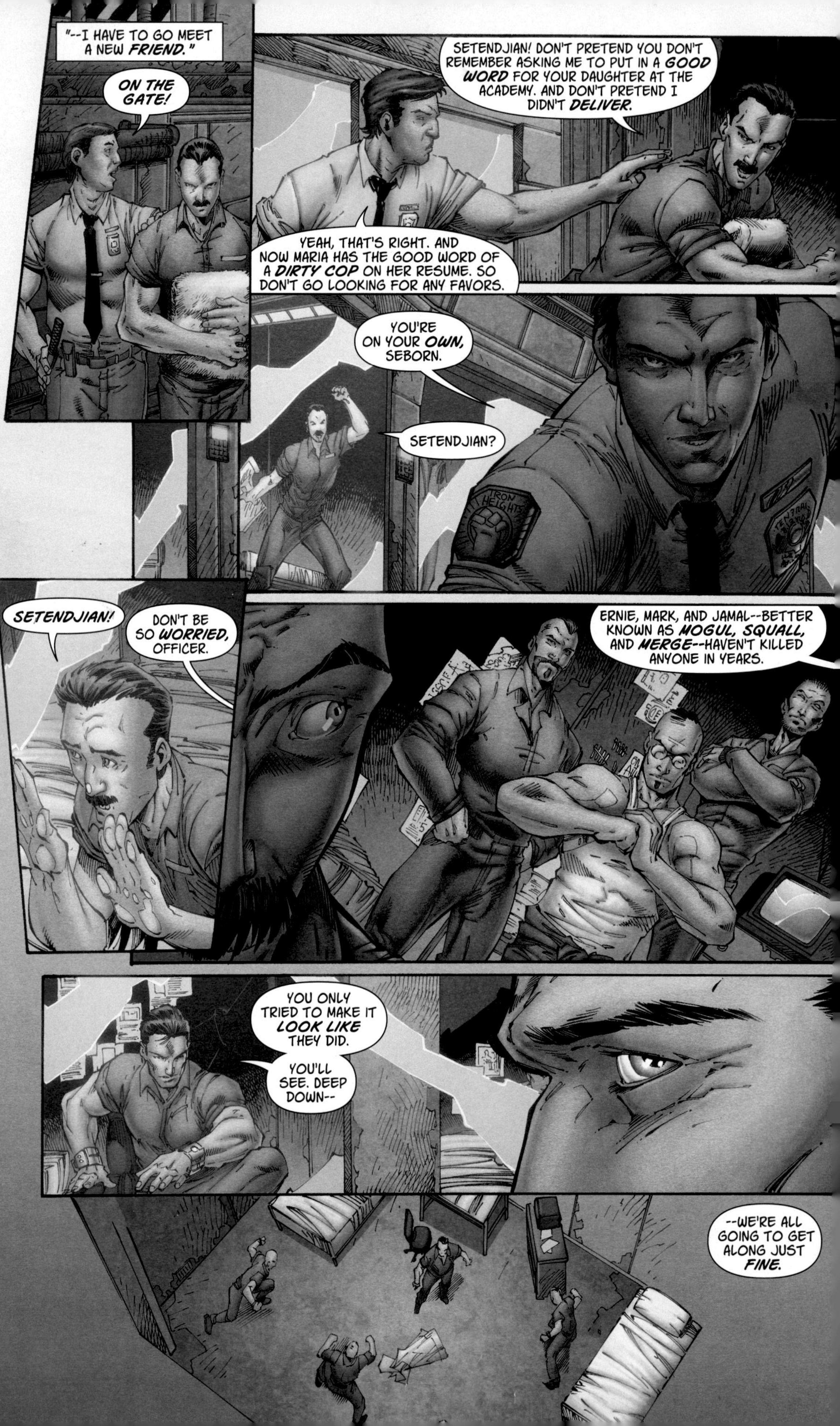
"--I HAVE TO GO MEET A NEW FRIEND."
ON THE GATE!
SETENDJIAN! DON'T PRETEND YOU DON'T REMEMBER ASKING ME TO PUT IN A GOOD WORD FOR YOUR DAUGHTER AT THE ACADEMY. AND DON'T PRETEND I DIDN'T DELIVER.
YEAH, THAT'S RIGHT. AND NOW MARIA HAS THE GOOD WORD OF A DIRTY COP ON HER RESUME. SO DON'T GO LOOKING FOR ANY FAVORS.
YOU'RE ON YOUR OWN, SEBORN.
SETENDJIAN?
IRON HEIGHTS
SETENDJIAN!
DON'T BE SO WORRIED, OFFICER.
ERNIE, MARK, AND JAMAL--BETTER KNOWN AS MOGUL, SQUALL, AND MERGE--HAVEN'T KILLED ANYONE IN YEARS.
YOU ONLY TRIED TO MAKE IT LOOK LIKE THEY DID.
YOU'LL SEE. DEEP DOWN--
--WE'RE ALL GOING TO GET ALONG JUST FINE.

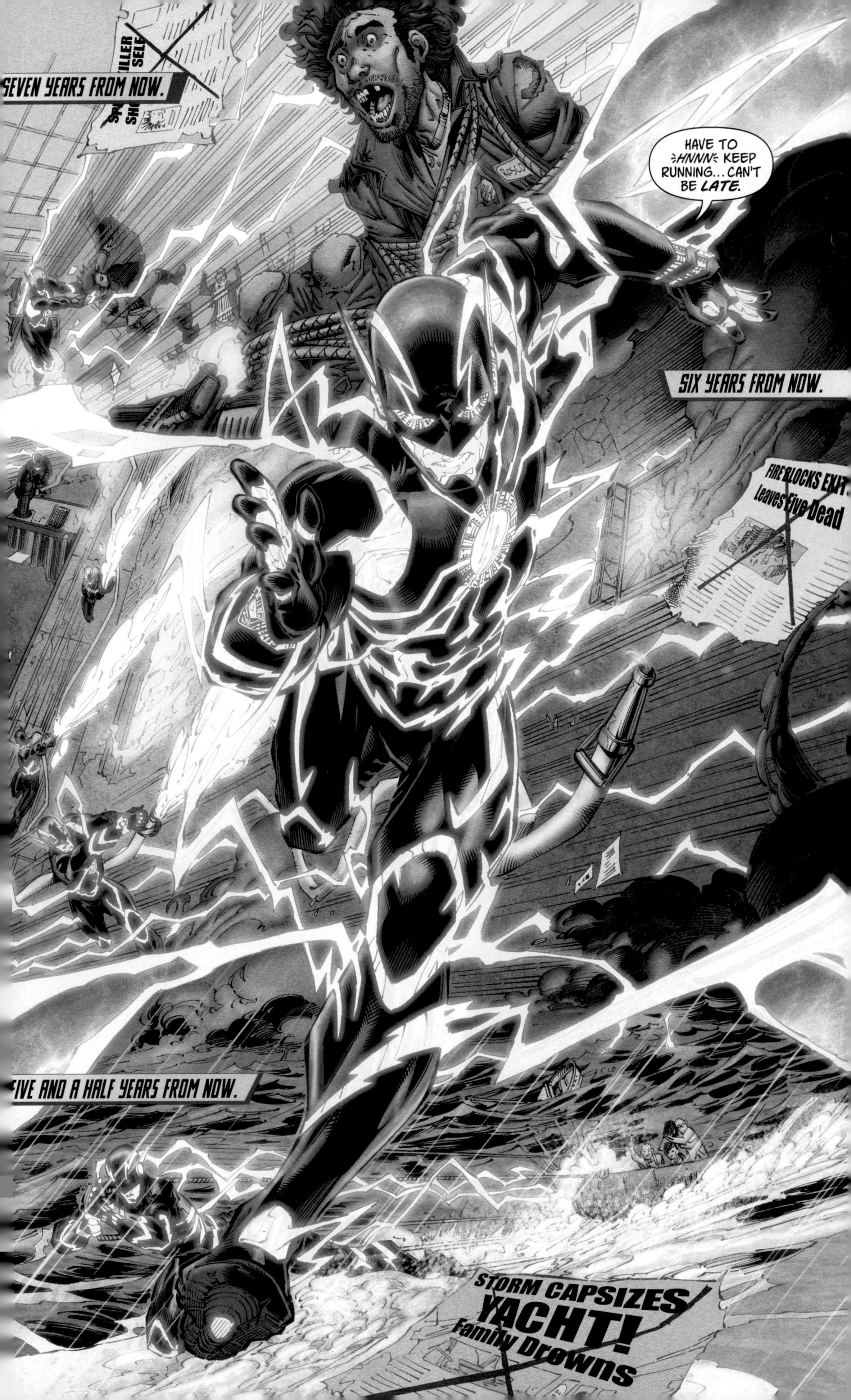
SEVEN YEARS FROM NOW.
HAVE TO
HNNN KEEP
RUNNING... CAN'T
BE LATE.
SIX YEARS FROM NOW.
FIRE BLOCKS EXIT
Leaves Five Dead
FIVE AND A HALF YEARS FROM NOW.
STORM CAPSIZES
YACHT!
Family Drowns

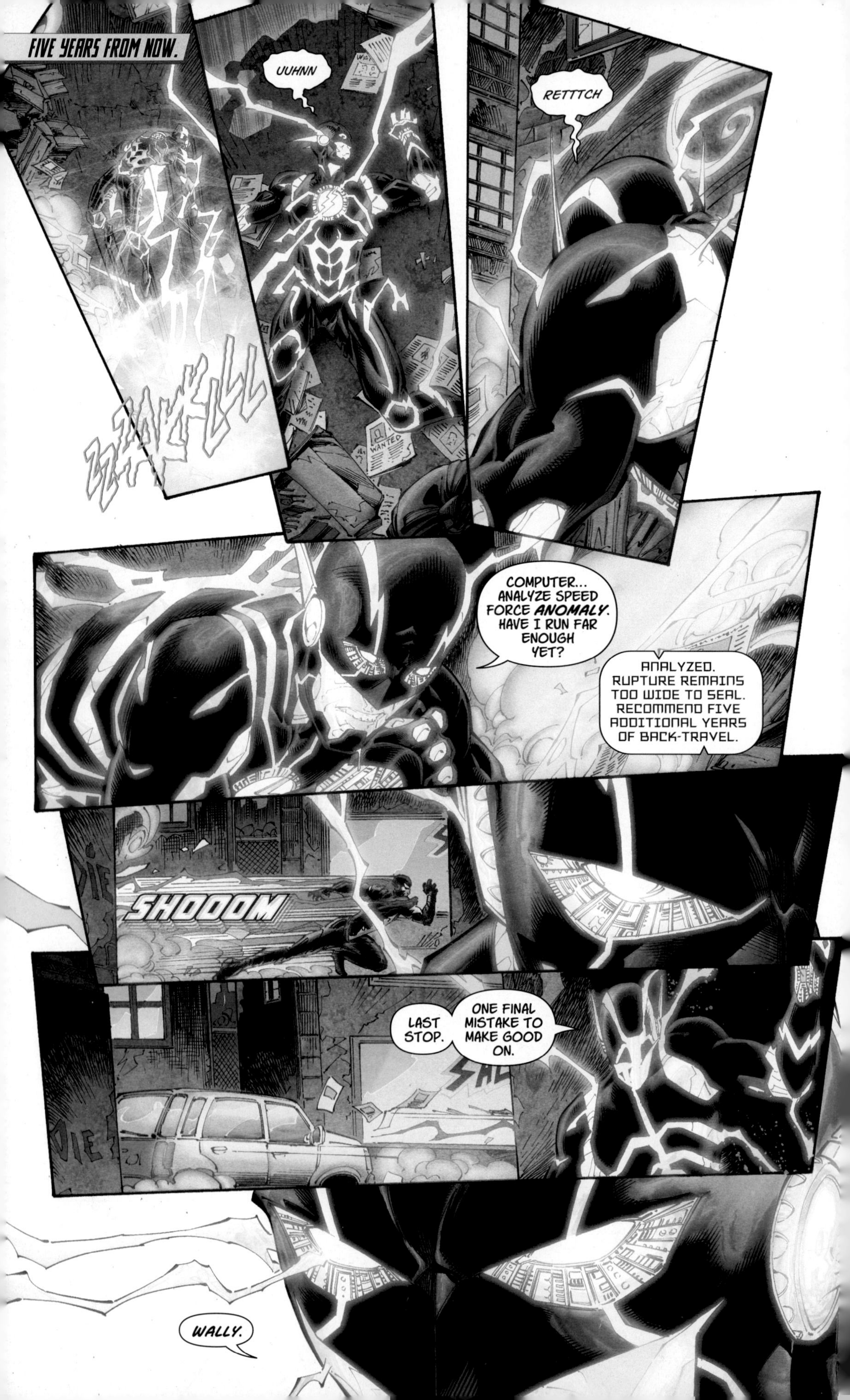
FIVE YEARS FROM NOW.
ZZZAKKKLLL
UUHNN
WANTED
RETTTCH
COMPUTER... ANALYZE SPEED FORCE ANOMALY. HAVE I RUN FAR ENOUGH YET?
ANALYZED. RUPTURE REMAINS TOO WIDE TO SEAL. RECOMMEND FIVE ADDITIONAL YEARS OF BACK-TRAVEL.
SHOOOM
LAST STOP.
ONE FINAL MISTAKE TO MAKE GOOD ON.
WALLY.

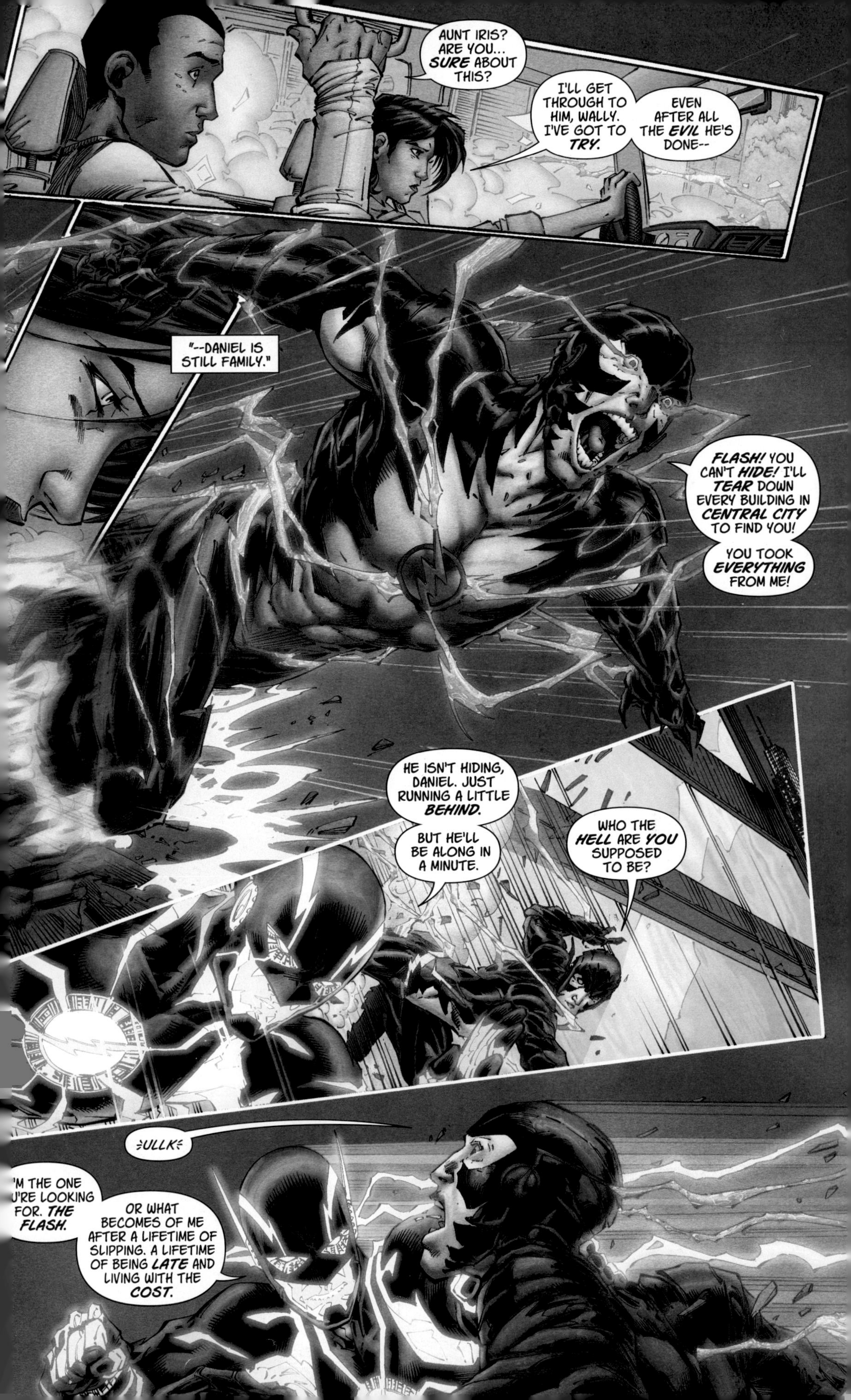

AUNT IRIS? ARE YOU... SURE ABOUT THIS?
I'LL GET THROUGH TO HIM, WALLY. I'VE GOT TO TRY.
EVEN AFTER ALL THE EVIL HE'S DONE--
"--DANIEL IS STILL FAMILY."
FLASH! YOU CAN'T HIDE! I'LL TEAR DOWN EVERY BUILDING IN CENTRAL CITY TO FIND YOU!
YOU TOOK EVERYTHING FROM ME!
HE ISN'T HIDING, DANIEL. JUST RUNNING A LITTLE BEHIND.
BUT HE'LL BE ALONG IN A MINUTE.
WHO THE HELL ARE YOU SUPPOSED TO BE?
ULLK
'M THE ONE 'U'RE LOOKING FOR. THE FLASH.
OR WHAT BECOMES OF ME AFTER A LIFETIME OF SLIPPING. A LIFETIME OF BEING LATE AND LIVING WITH THE COST.

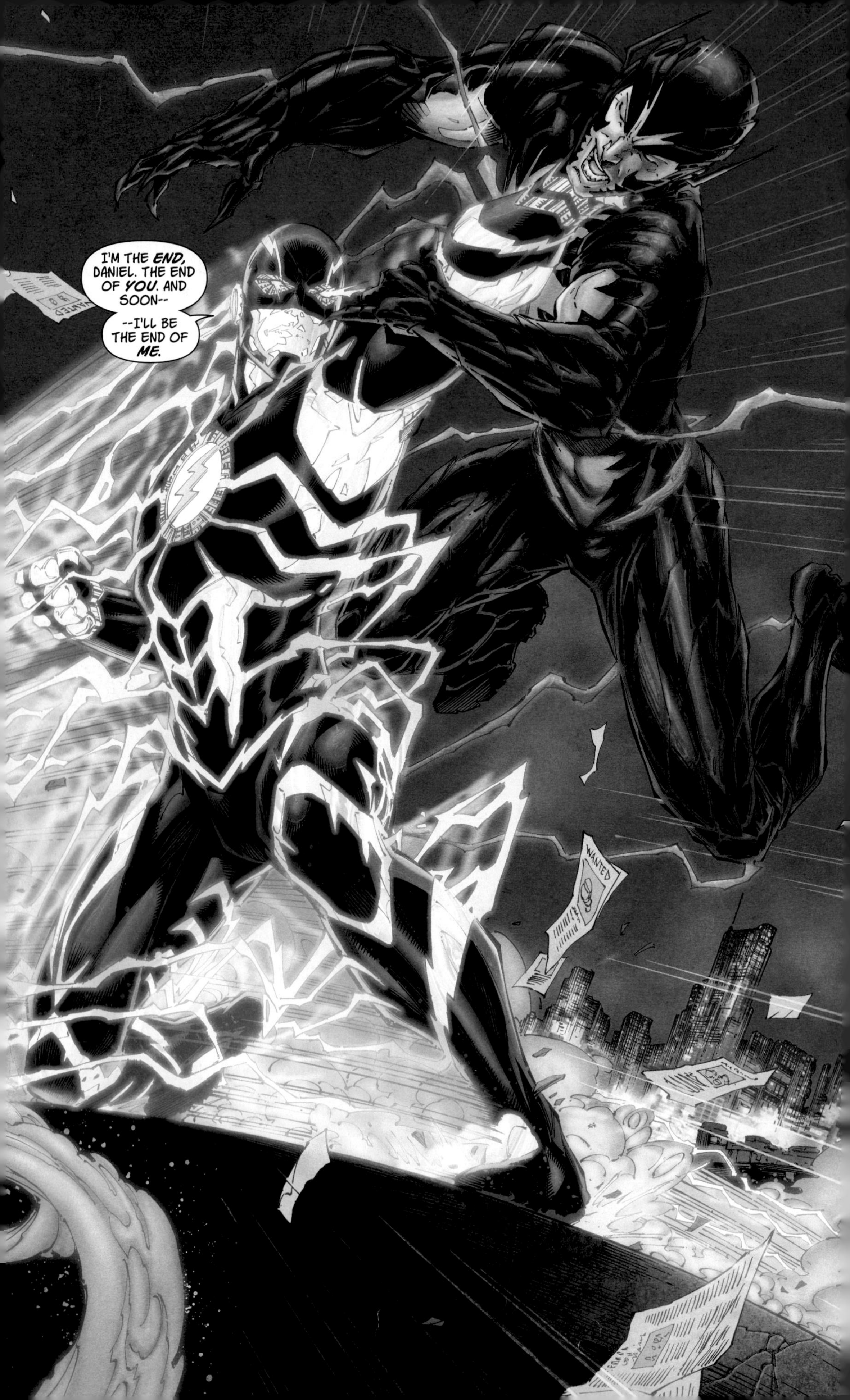
I'M THE END, DANIEL. THE END OF YOU. AND SOON--
--I'LL BE THE END OF ME.
WANTED

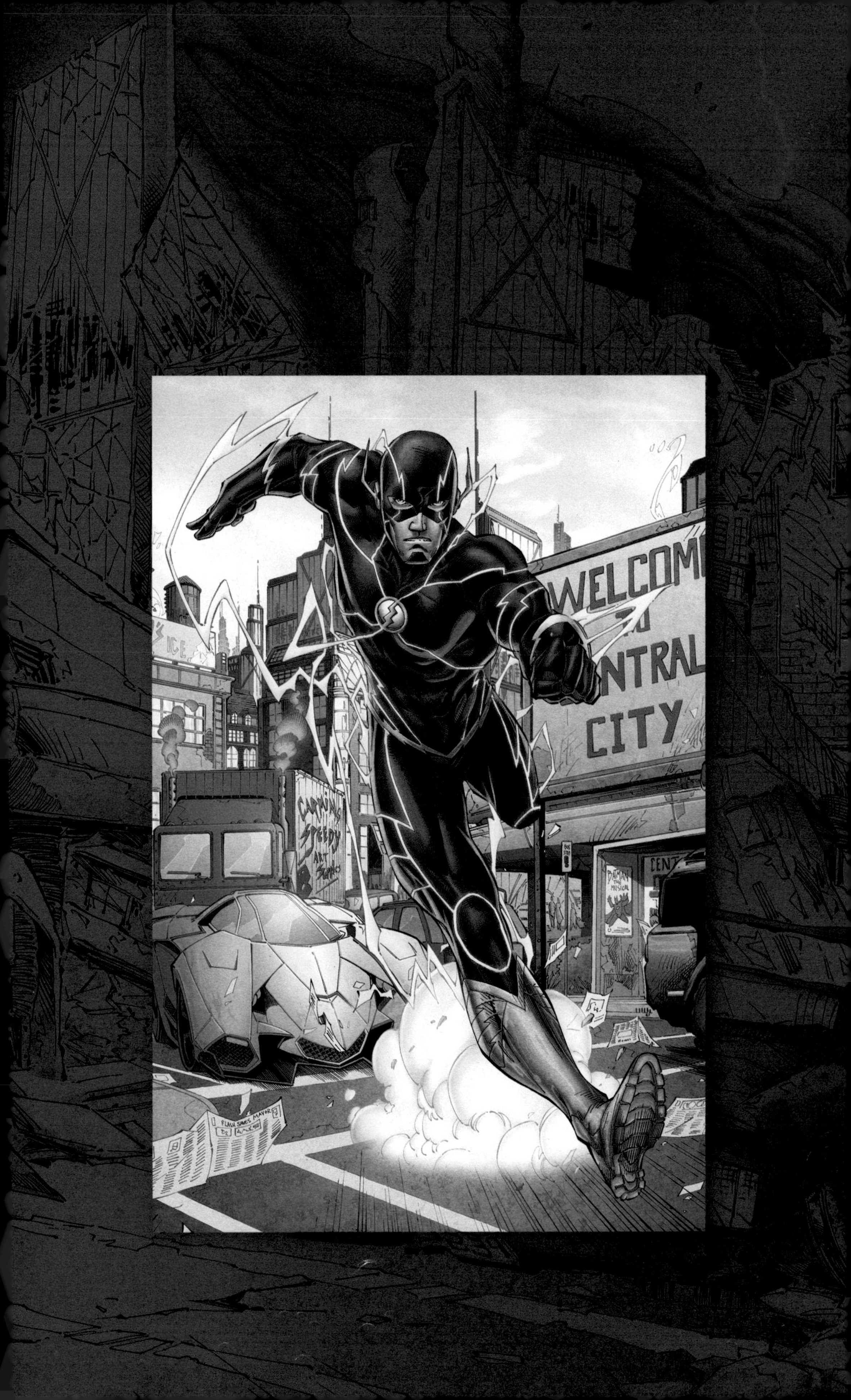
WELCOM
NTRAL
CITY
ICE
CARMINE'S SPEEDY ART SUPPLIES
BUS STOP
BATMAN THE MUSICAL
FLASH SAVES MAYOR

IMPACT VELOCITY

ROBERT VENDITTI & **VAN JENSEN** writers **BRETT BOOTH** penciller **NORM RAPMUND** inker

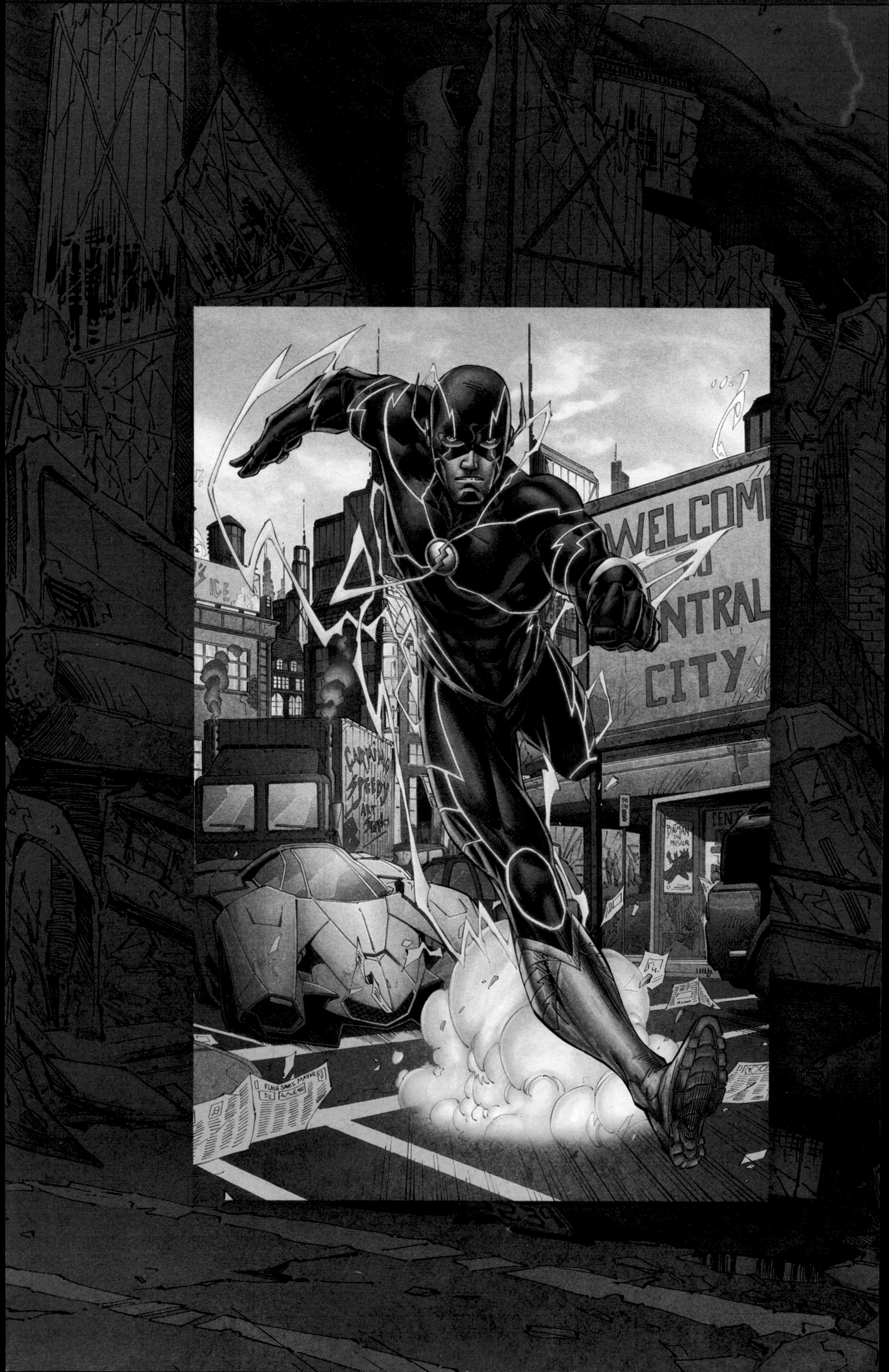

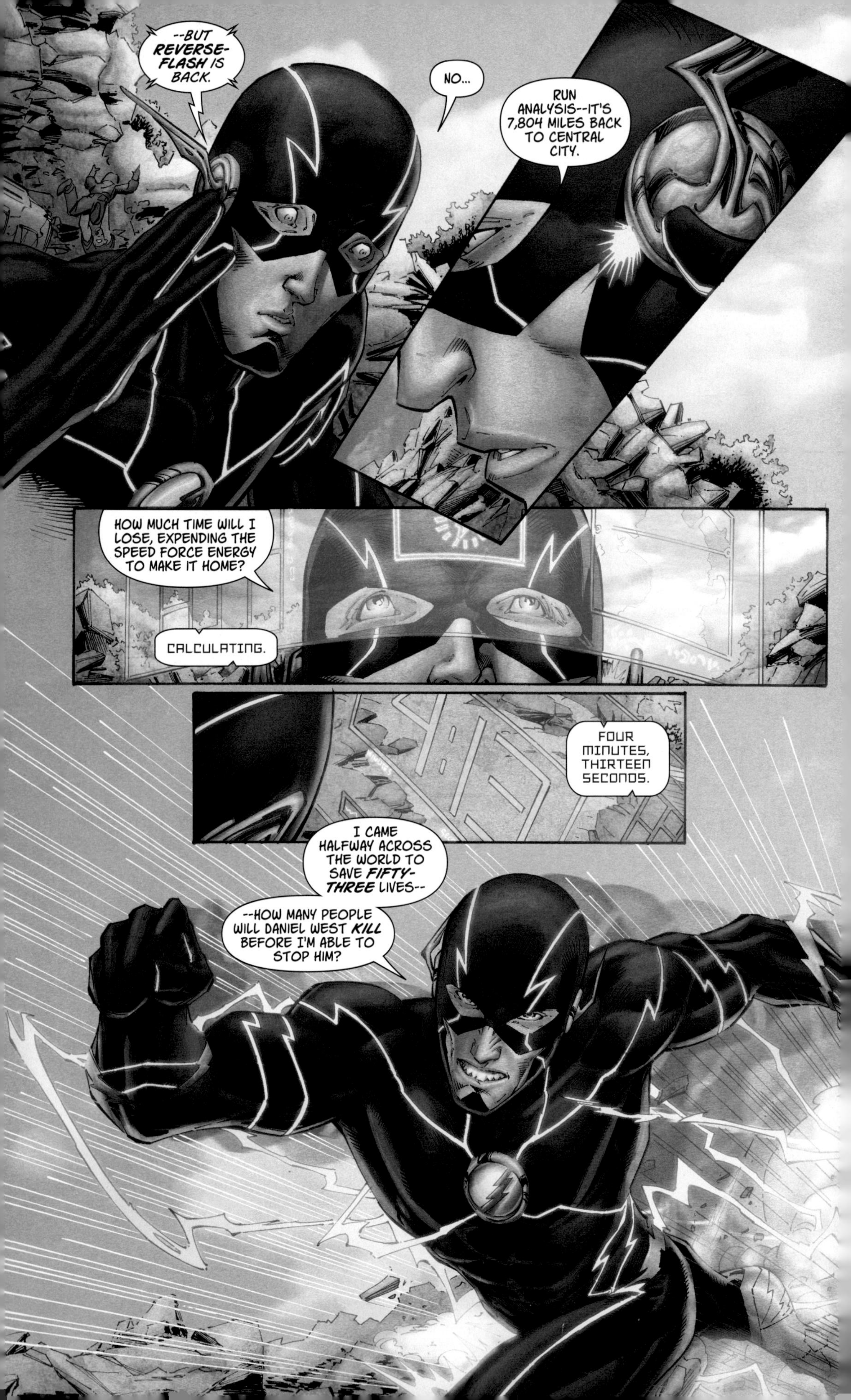
--BUT *REVERSE-FLASH* IS BACK.
NO...
RUN ANALYSIS--IT'S 7,804 MILES BACK TO CENTRAL CITY.
HOW MUCH TIME WILL I LOSE, EXPENDING THE SPEED FORCE ENERGY TO MAKE IT HOME?
CALCULATING.
FOUR MINUTES, THIRTEEN SECONDS.
I CAME HALFWAY ACROSS THE WORLD TO SAVE *FIFTY-THREE* LIVES--
--HOW MANY PEOPLE WILL DANIEL WEST *KILL* BEFORE I'M ABLE TO STOP HIM?

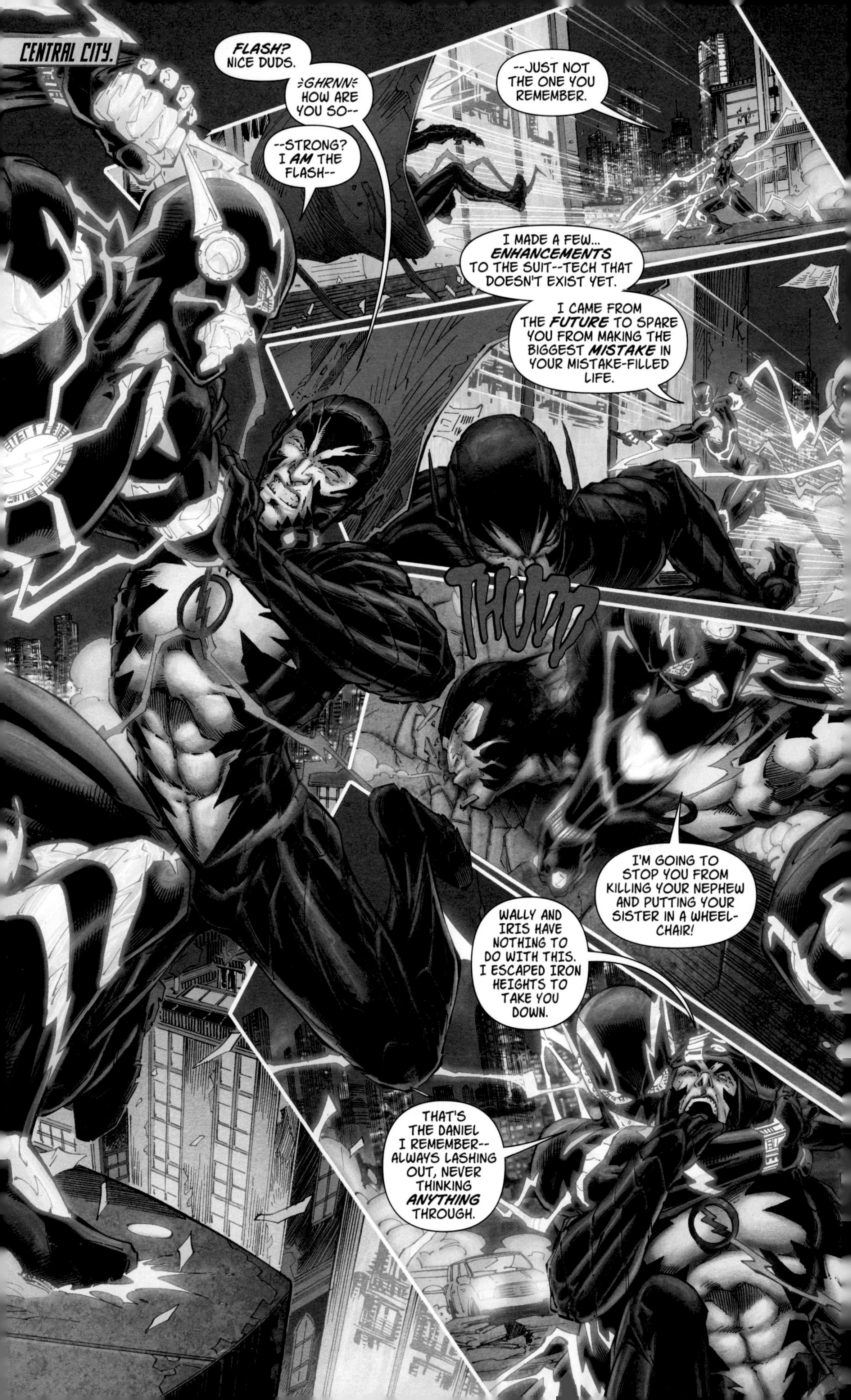
CENTRAL CITY.
FLASH? NICE DUDS.
GHRNN HOW ARE YOU SO--
--STRONG? I AM THE FLASH--
--JUST NOT THE ONE YOU REMEMBER.
I MADE A FEW... ENHANCEMENTS TO THE SUIT--TECH THAT DOESN'T EXIST YET.
I CAME FROM THE FUTURE TO SPARE YOU FROM MAKING THE BIGGEST MISTAKE IN YOUR MISTAKE-FILLED LIFE.
THUDD
I'M GOING TO STOP YOU FROM KILLING YOUR NEPHEW AND PUTTING YOUR SISTER IN A WHEEL-CHAIR!
WALLY AND IRIS HAVE NOTHING TO DO WITH THIS. I ESCAPED IRON HEIGHTS TO TAKE YOU DOWN.
THAT'S THE DANIEL I REMEMBER--ALWAYS LASHING OUT, NEVER THINKING ANYTHING THROUGH.

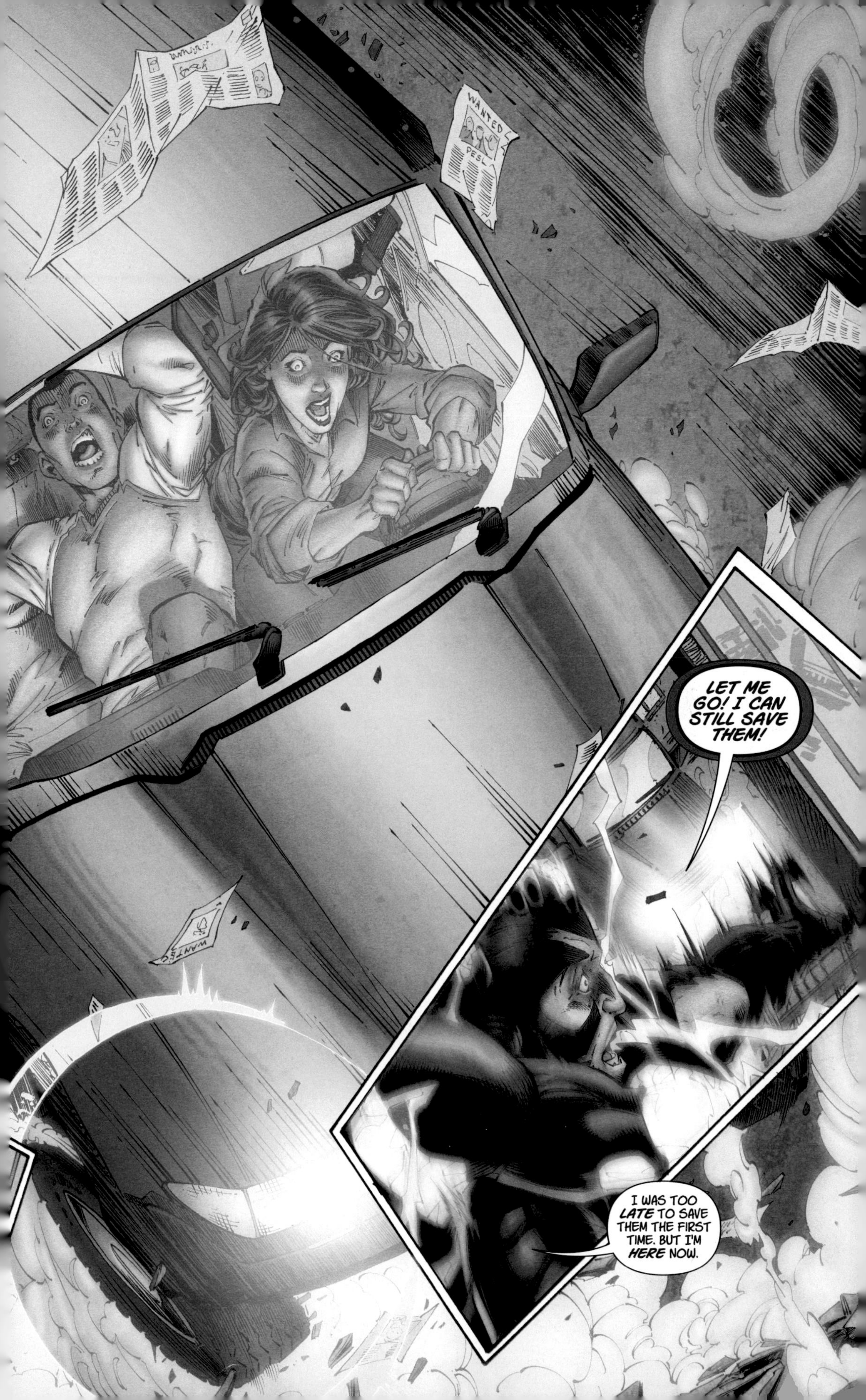
LET ME GO! I CAN STILL SAVE THEM!
I WAS TOO LATE TO SAVE THEM THE FIRST TIME. BUT I'M HERE NOW.

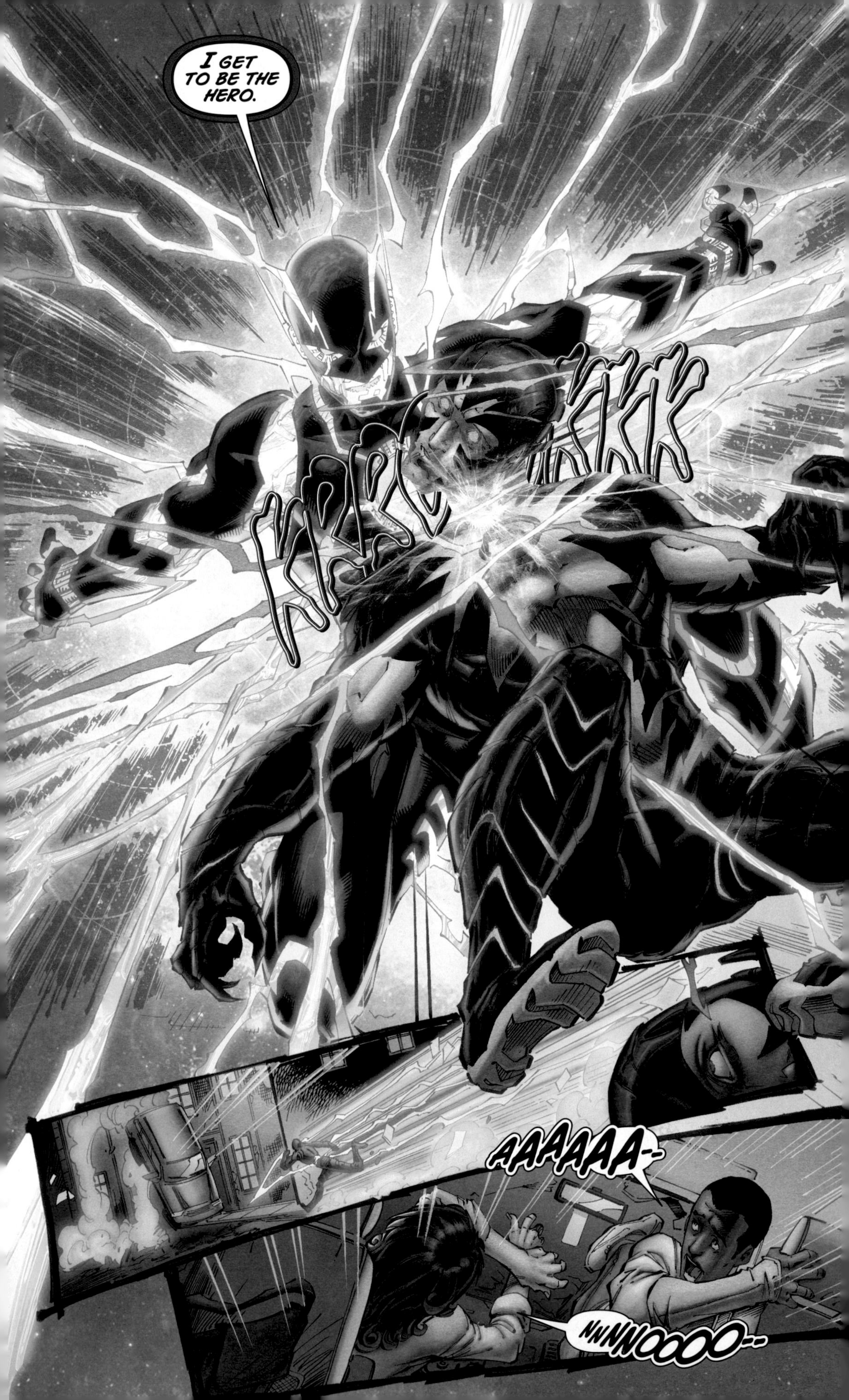
I GET TO BE THE HERO.
AAAAAA--
NNNNOOOO--

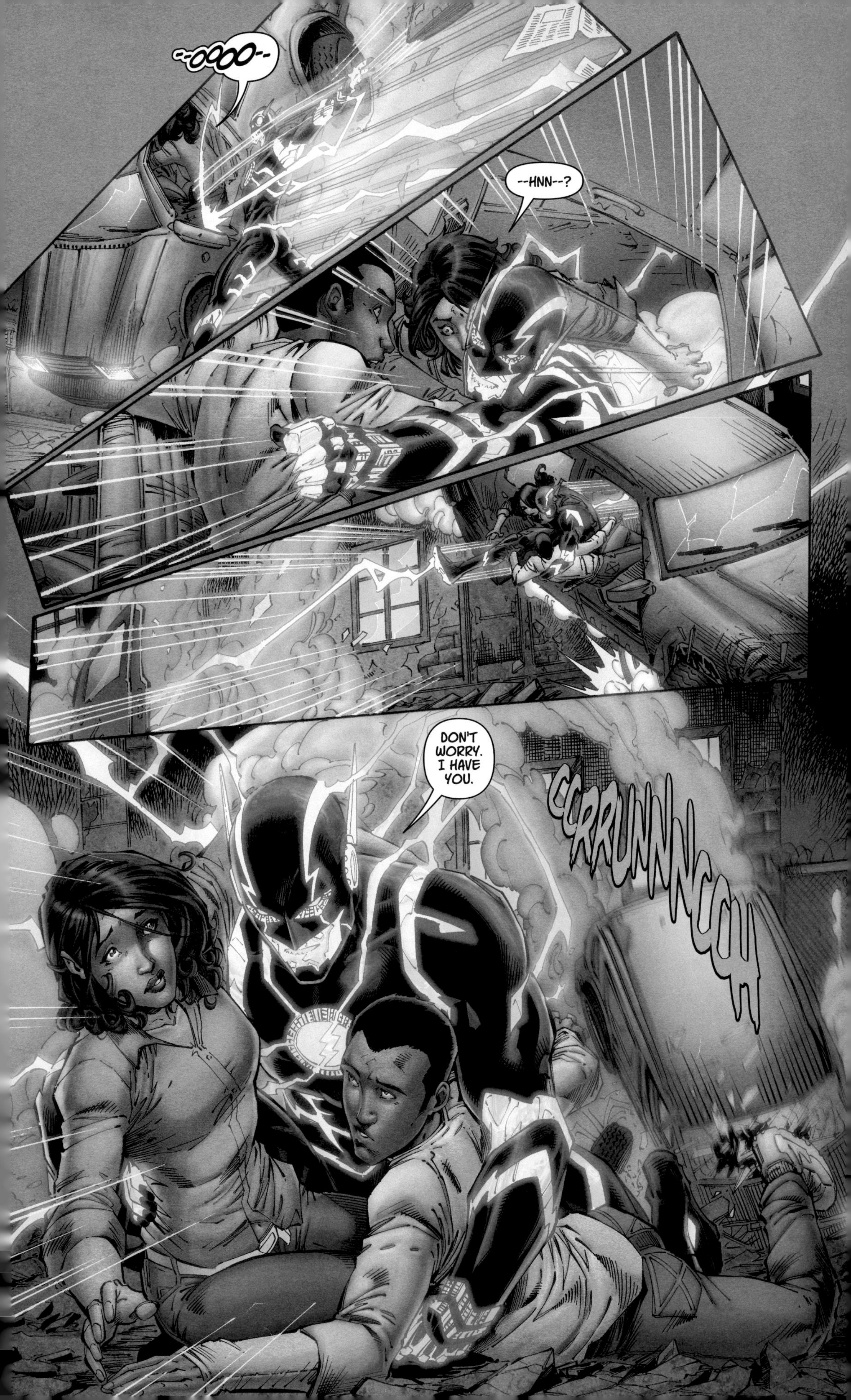
--OOOO--
--HNN--?
DON'T WORRY. I HAVE YOU.
CCRRUNNNCCCH

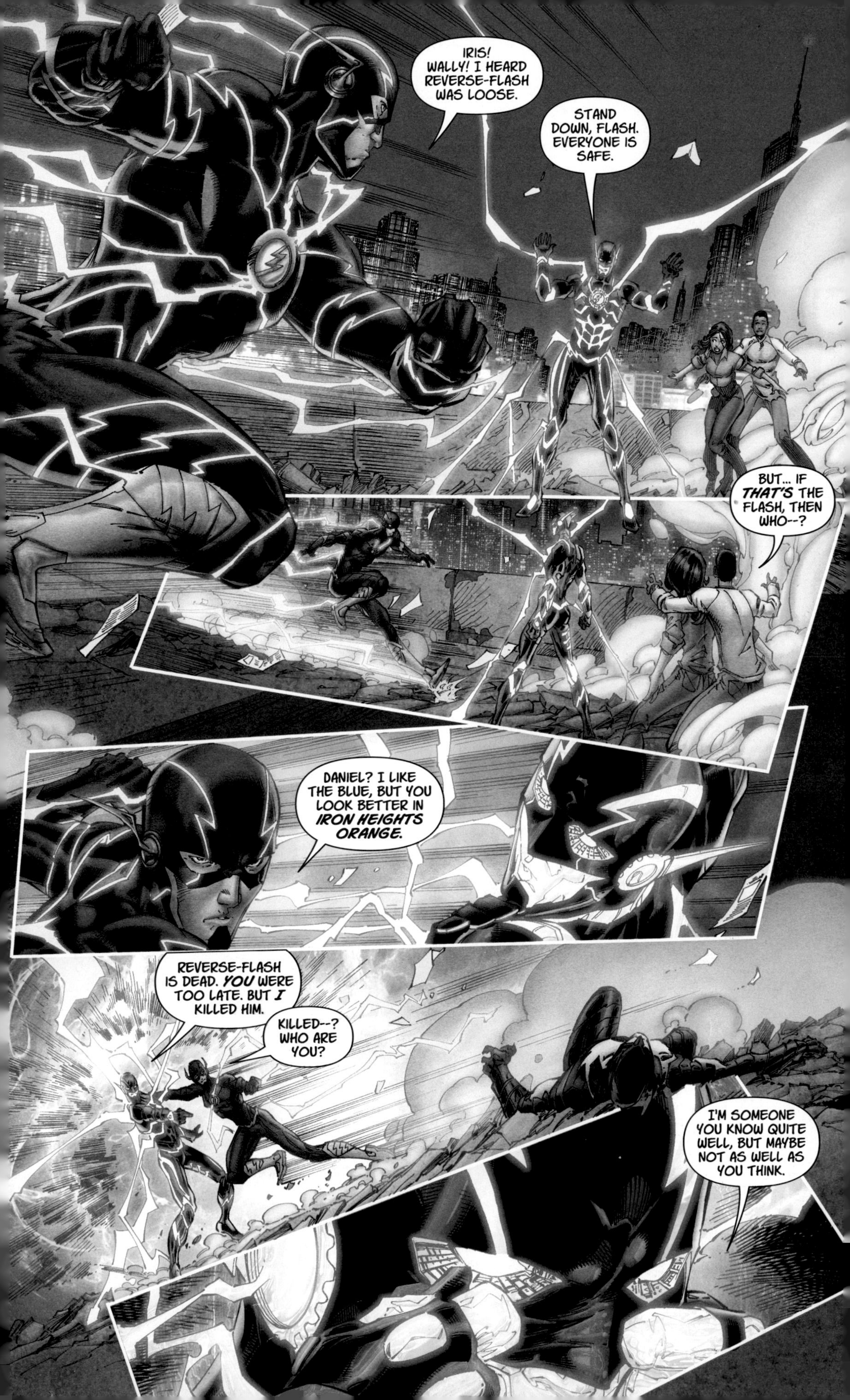
IRIS! WALLY! I HEARD REVERSE-FLASH WAS LOOSE.
STAND DOWN, FLASH. EVERYONE IS SAFE.
BUT... IF *THAT'S* THE FLASH, THEN WHO--?
DANIEL? I LIKE THE BLUE, BUT YOU LOOK BETTER IN ***IRON HEIGHTS ORANGE.***
REVERSE-FLASH IS DEAD. *YOU* WERE TOO LATE. BUT *I* KILLED HIM.
KILLED--? WHO ARE YOU?
I'M SOMEONE YOU KNOW QUITE WELL, BUT MAYBE NOT AS WELL AS YOU THINK.

LOOK AT ME. YOU KNOW MY FACE...

...ALTHOUGH IT SHOWS A FEW MORE MILES.

IT...IT CAN'T BE...

YOU'RE... *ME?*

HOW...HOW IS THIS POSSIBLE?

THE SPEED FORCE IS *BROKEN.* YOU'VE FIGURED THAT MUCH OUT BY NOW. EVERY TIME YOU RUN, YOU LOSE MORE TIME. TODAY, YOU WOULD HAVE MISSED SOMETHING TERRIBLE. IRIS'S CAR CRASHED. SHE WAS *PARALYZED.* WALLY *DIED.*

I'VE LIVED WITH THAT GUILT FOR *FIFTEEN* YEARS. BUT I CAME BACK. I *SAVED* THEM.

BARRY?! YOU'RE THE FLASH? WHY DIDN'T YOU--?

I DON'T HAVE TIME TO EXPLAIN, WALLY. I'M SORRY. I DIDN'T JUST COME BACK TO SAVE YOU.

THE SPEED FORCE IS DAMAGED BECAUSE OF *ME.* I LET TOO MANY OTHERS CLAIM THE POWER-- EVEN YOU, IRIS.

BUT DANIEL AND GRODD ABUSED IT, TRAVELING THROUGH TIME TO PLUNDER THE PAST AND THE FUTURE.

THERE HAS TO BE A WAY TO FIX IT.

I FIGURED OUT ONE SOLUTION. THAT'S WHY I'M TRAVELING BACK, EVEN THOUGH I KNOW I'M CAUSING MORE DAMAGE. I HAVE ONE MORE STOP TO MAKE.

I'M GOING BACK TO A POINT WHEN THE RIFT IS STILL SMALL ENOUGH TO HEAL. BUT TO ACCOMPLISH THAT--

THERE'S A WOUND IN THE SPEED FORCE. AND EVERY TIME THEY TRAVELED THROUGH TIME, THEY TORE IT EVEN WIDER.

THAT'S WHAT'S CAUSING US TO LOSE TIME. THAT'S WHY YOU WOULDN'T HAVE BEEN ABLE TO SAVE WALLY... OR SO MANY OTHERS. I'VE FIXED THE WORST MISTAKES, BUT WE HAVE TO REPAIR THE SPEED FORCE BEFORE IT UNRAVELS THE VERY FABRIC OF TIME AND SPACE.

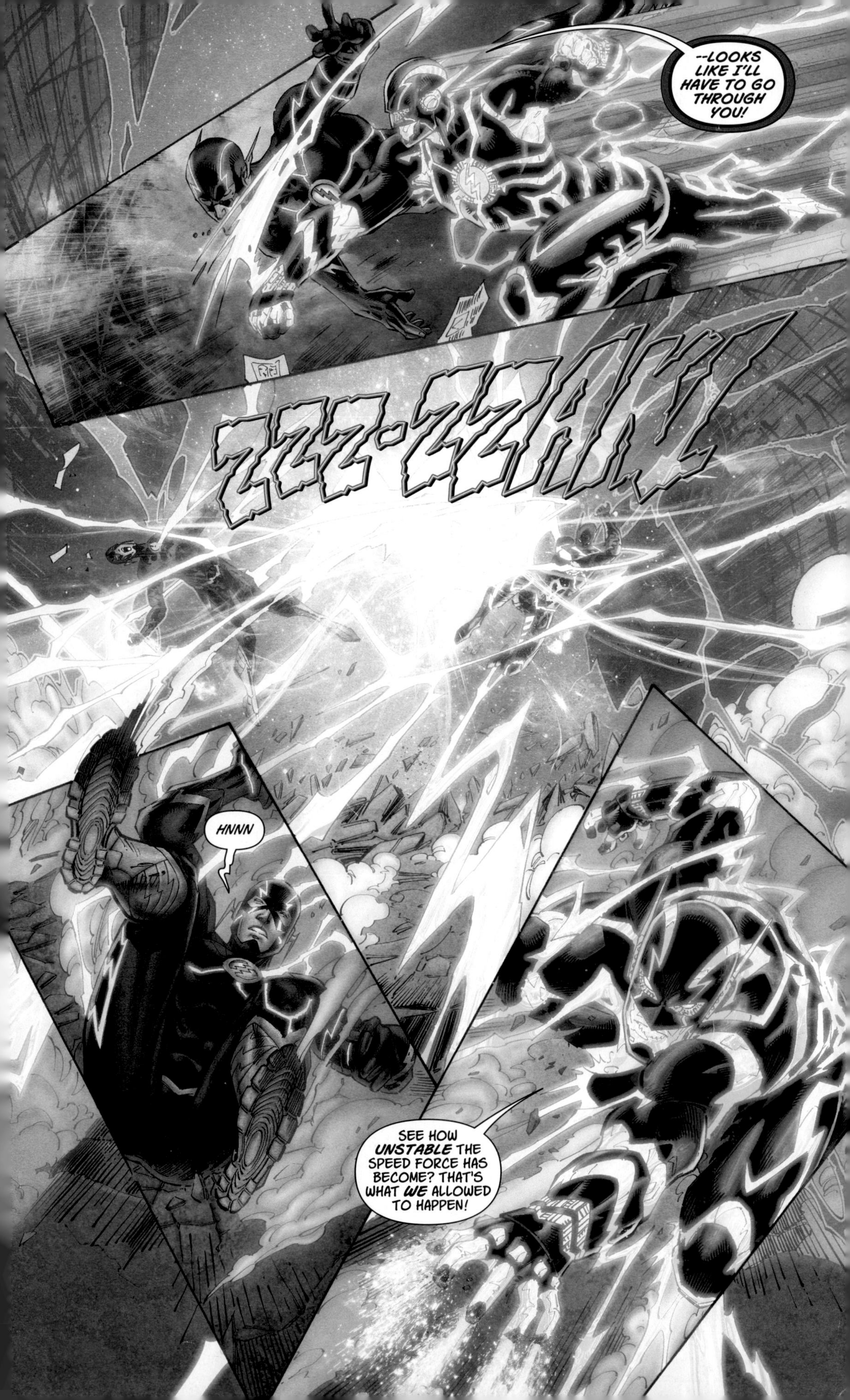
--LOOKS LIKE I'LL HAVE TO GO THROUGH YOU!
ZZZ-ZZZAKK
HNNN
SEE HOW UNSTABLE THE SPEED FORCE HAS BECOME? THAT'S WHAT WE ALLOWED TO HAPPEN!

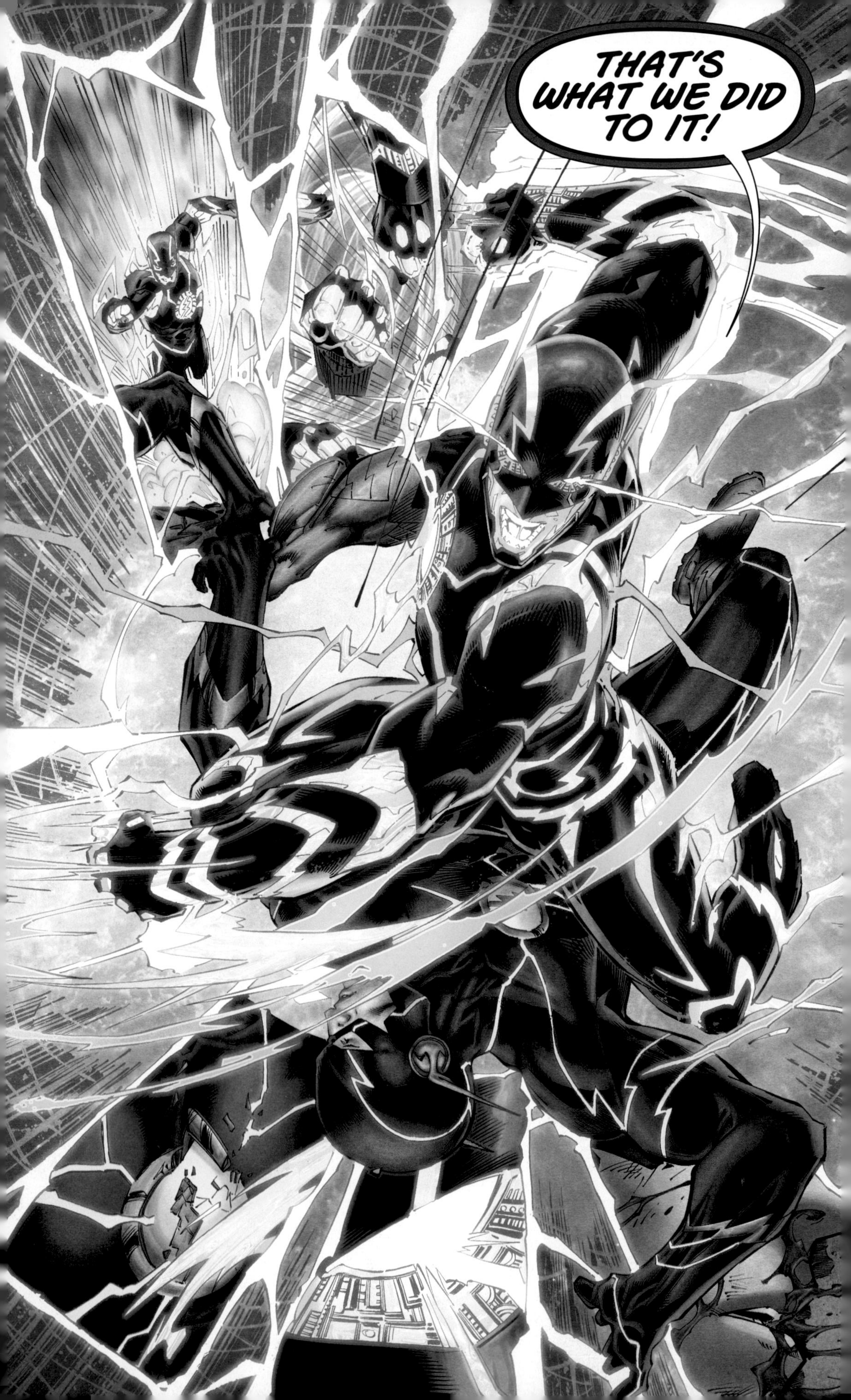
THAT'S WHAT WE DID TO IT!

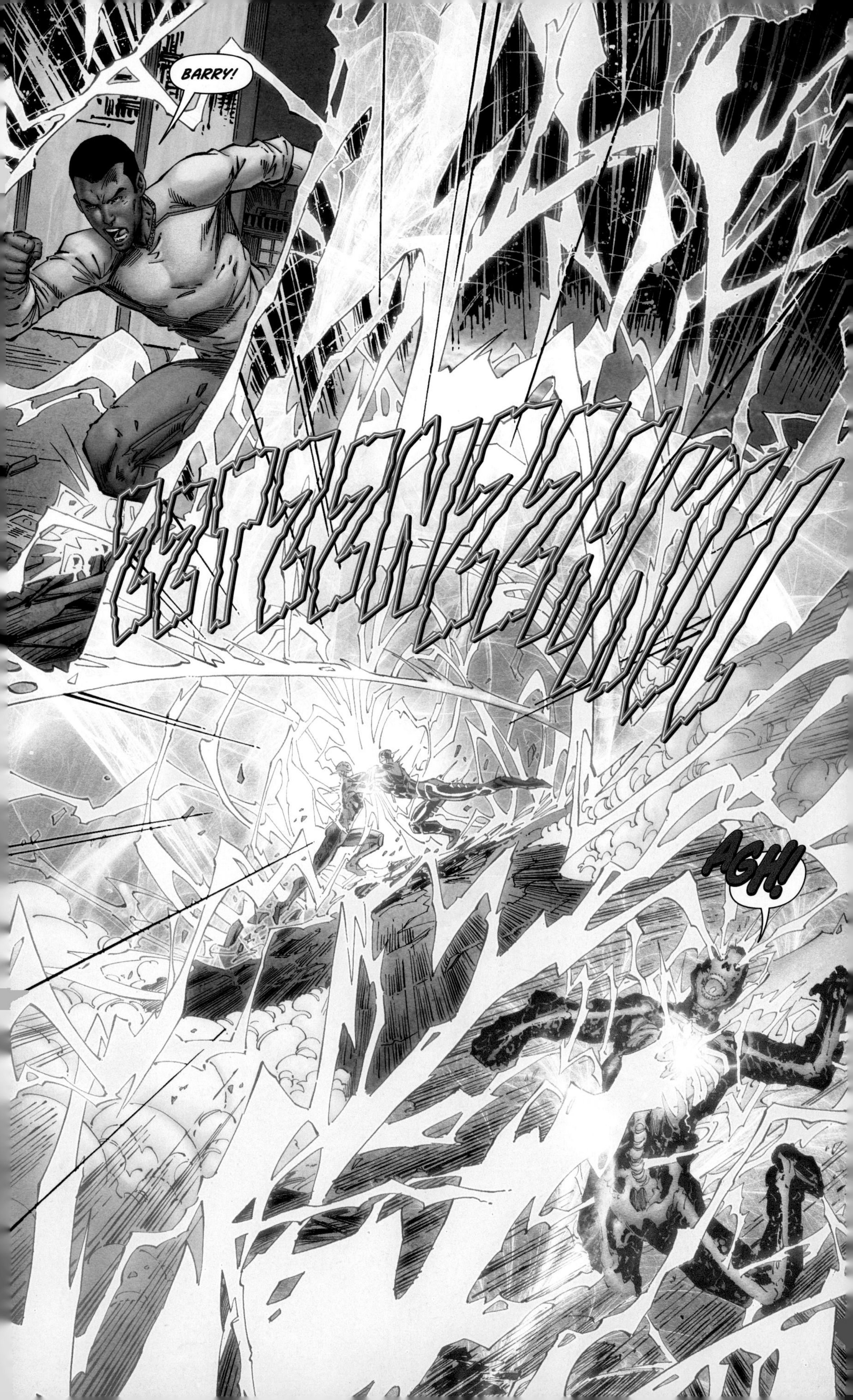
BARRY!
AGH!

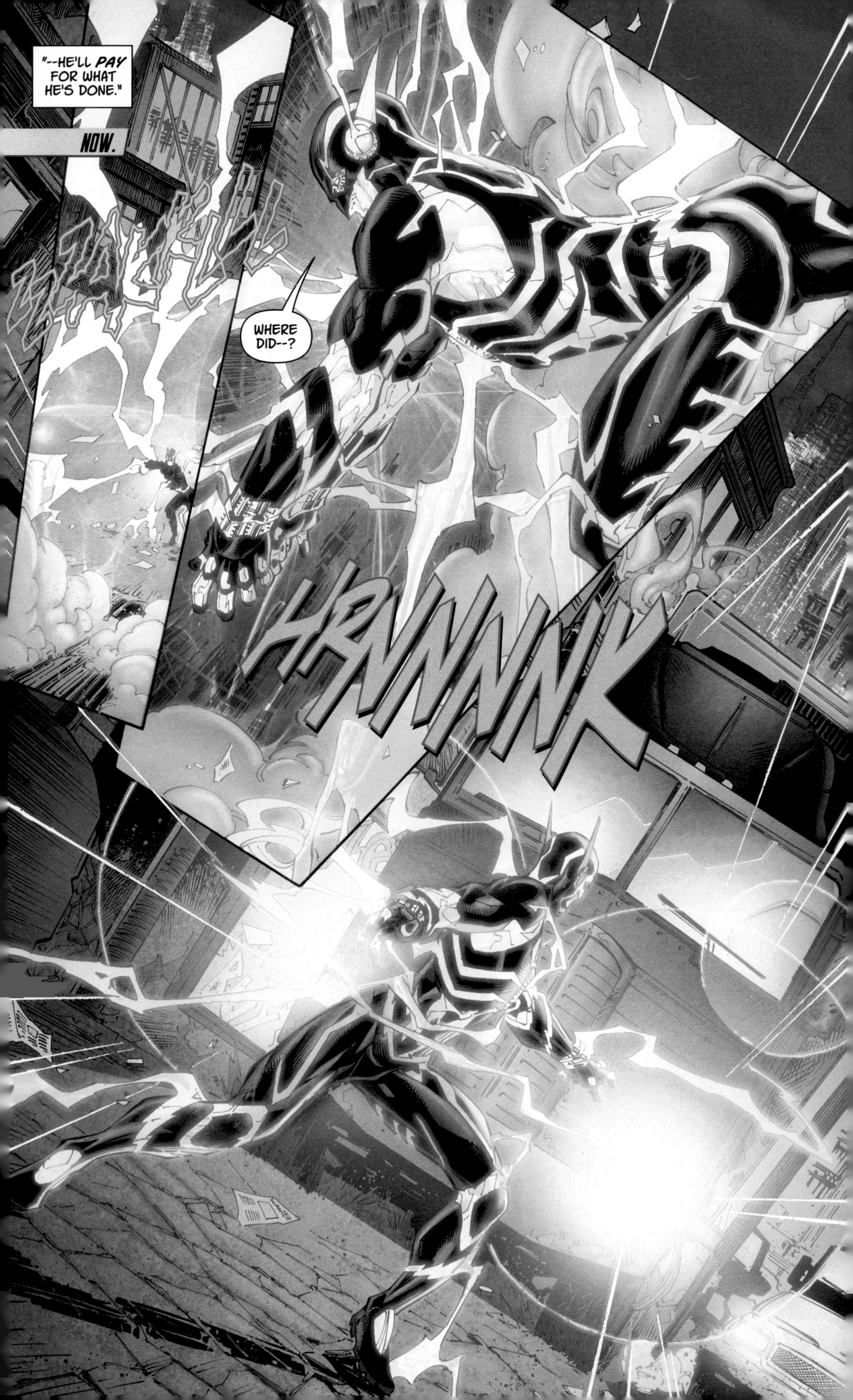
"--HE'LL PAY FOR WHAT HE'S DONE."
NOW.
ZZZAKKKKK
WHERE DID--?
HRNNNNK

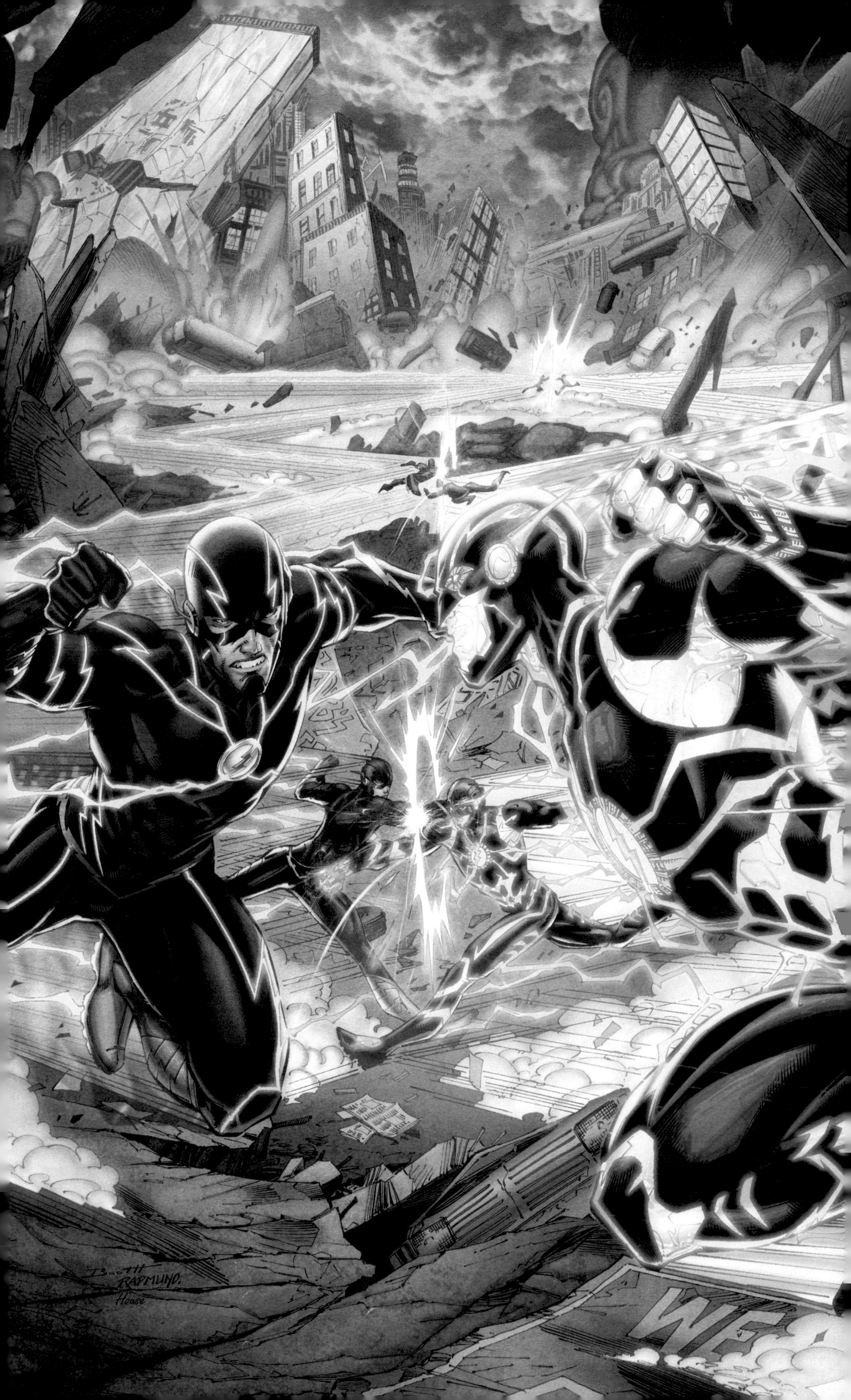

OUT OF TIME

ROBERT VENDITTI & VAN JENSEN writers BRETT BOOTH penciller NORM RAPMUND inker

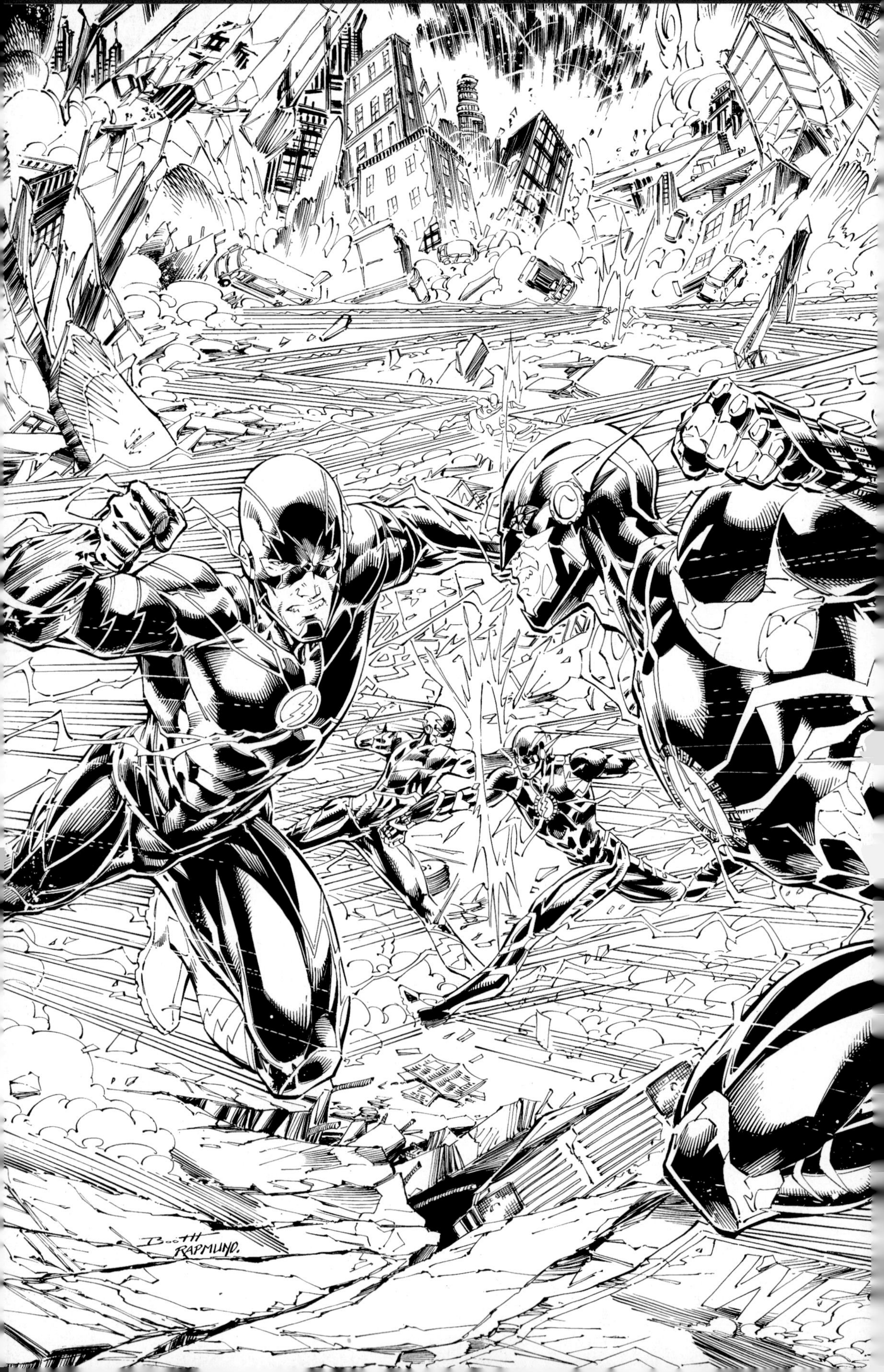

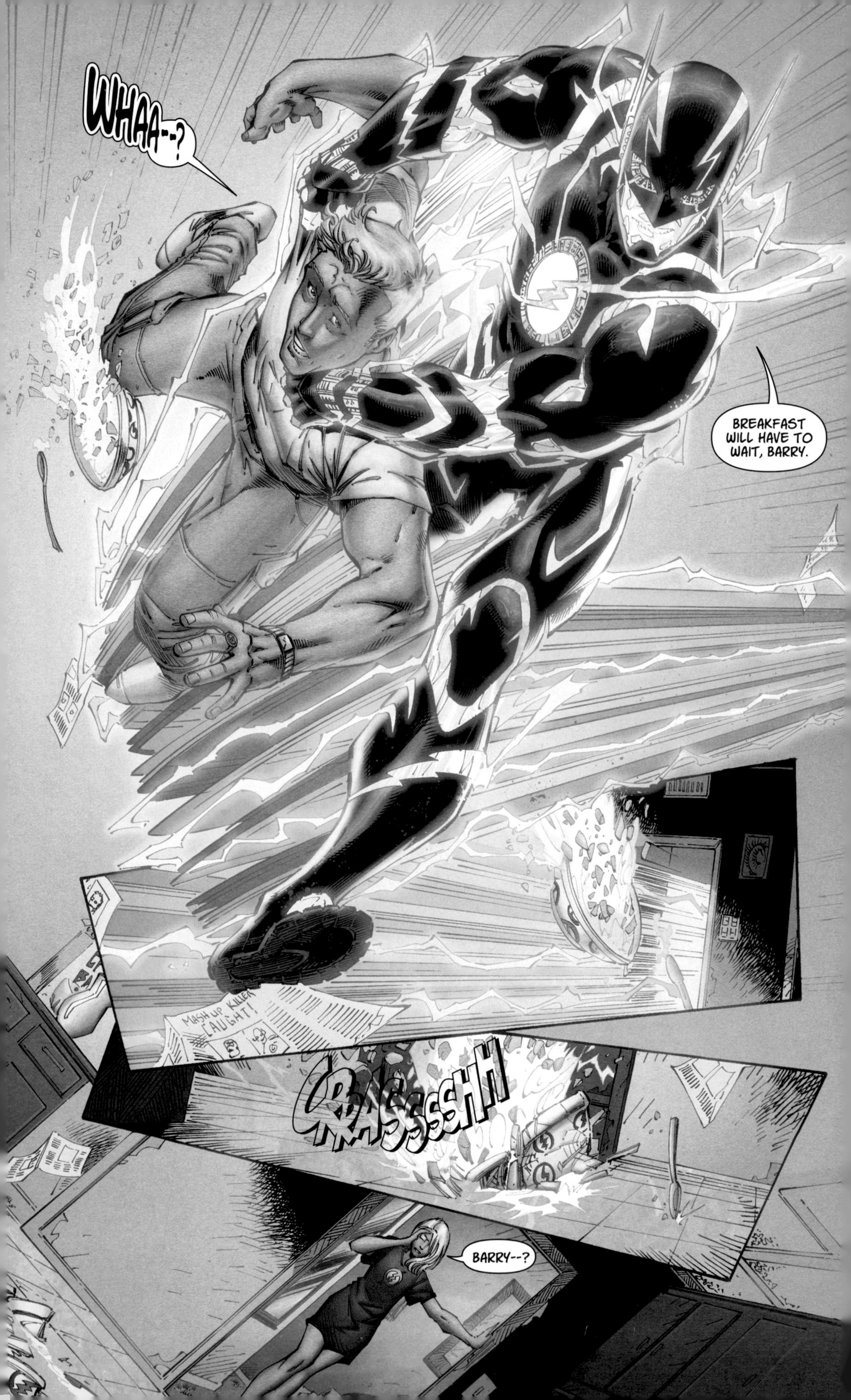
WHAA--?
BREAKFAST WILL HAVE TO WAIT, BARRY.
MASH UP KILLER CAUGHT!
CRASSSSHH
BARRY--?

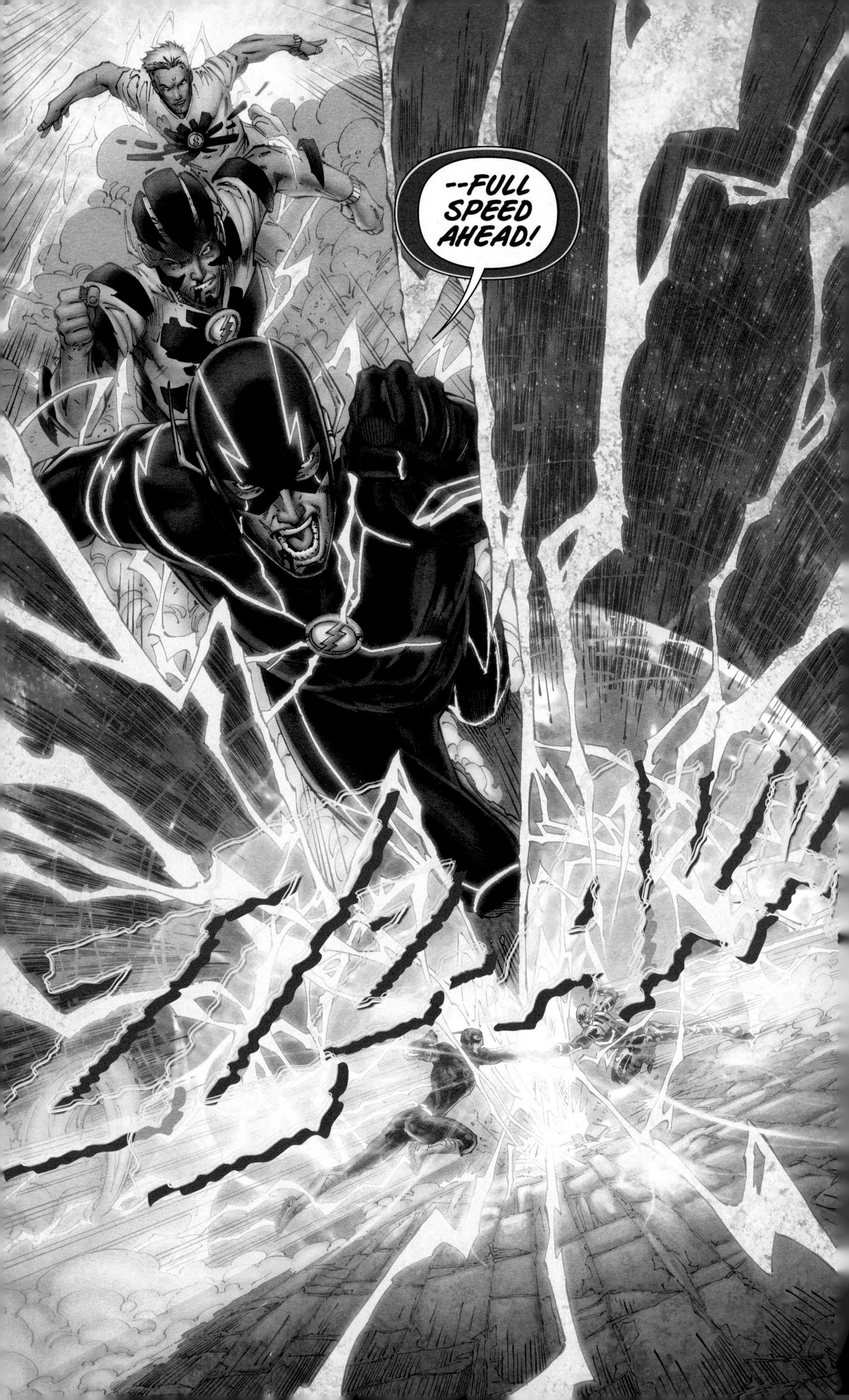
--FULL SPEED AHEAD!

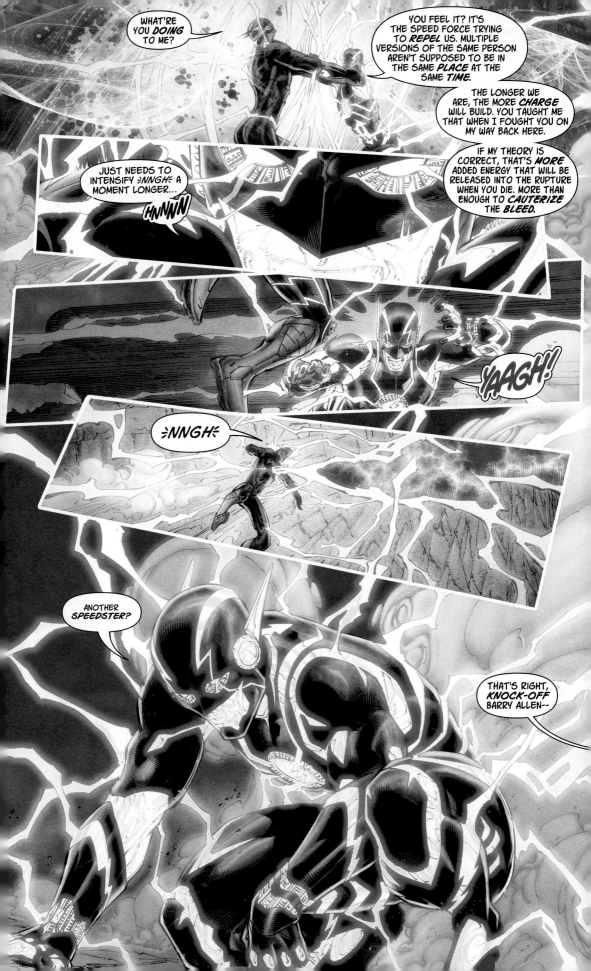

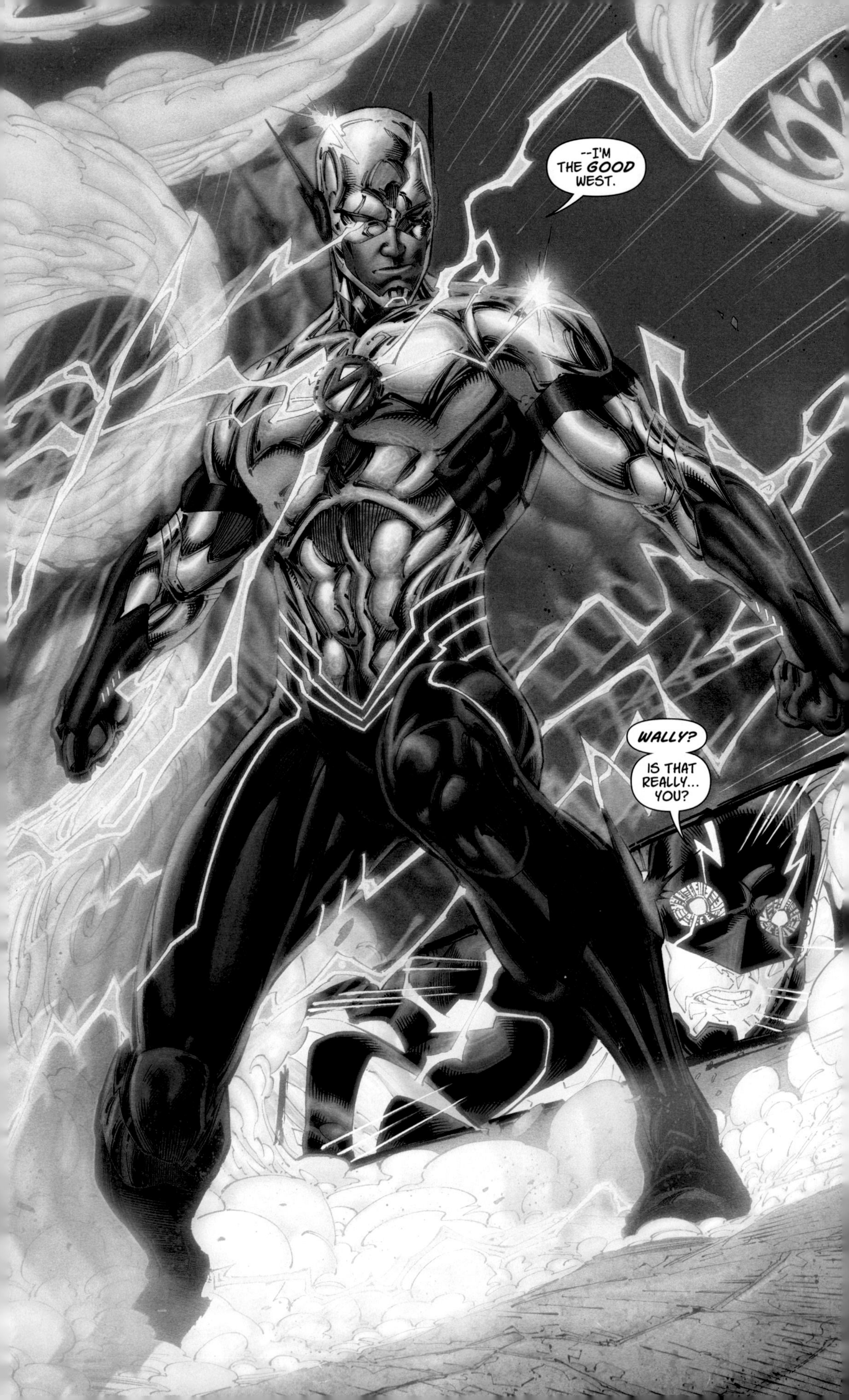
--I'M THE GOOD WEST.
WALLY?
IS THAT REALLY... YOU?

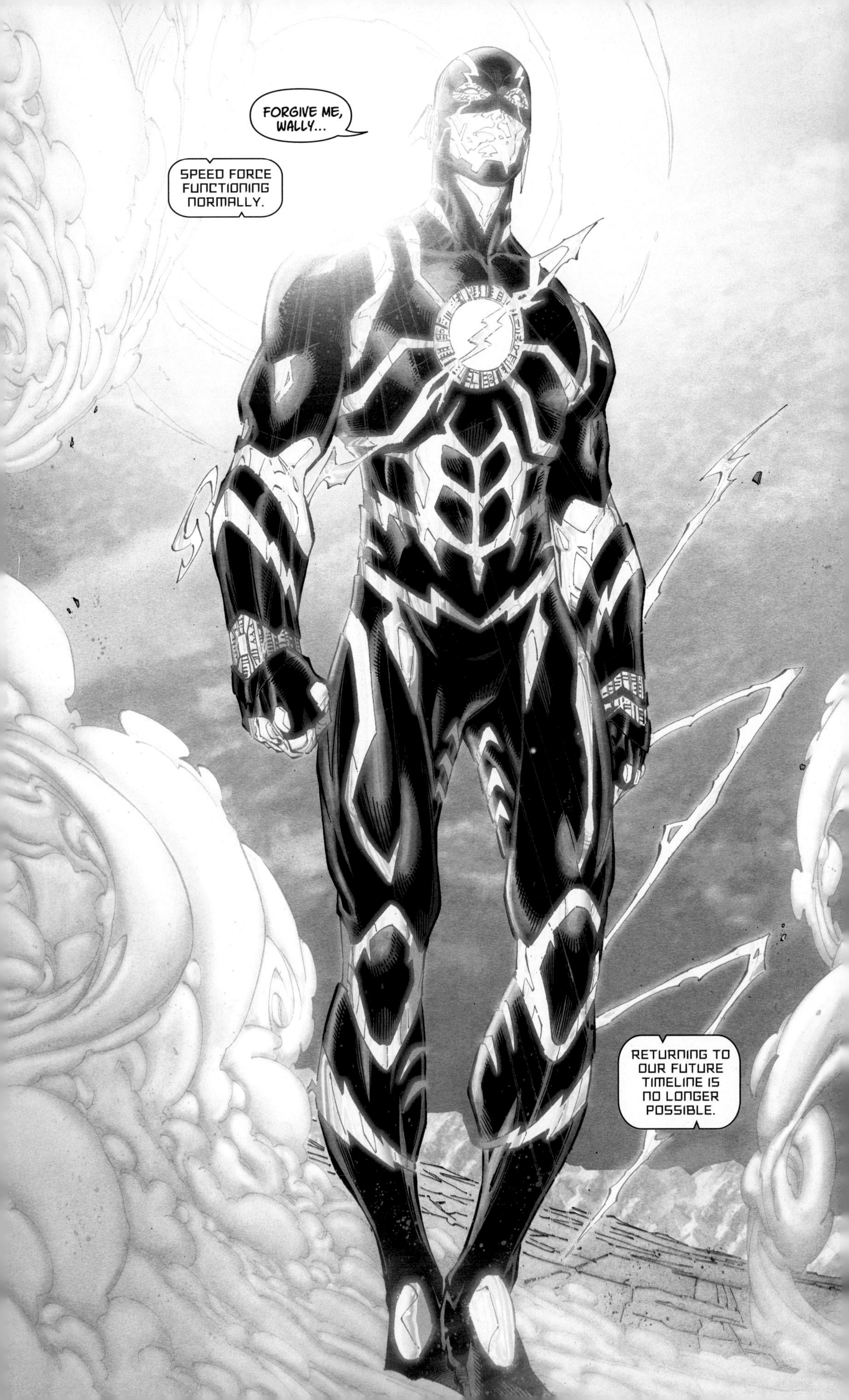
FORGIVE ME, WALLY...
SPEED FORCE FUNCTIONING NORMALLY.
RETURNING TO OUR FUTURE TIMELINE IS NO LONGER POSSIBLE.

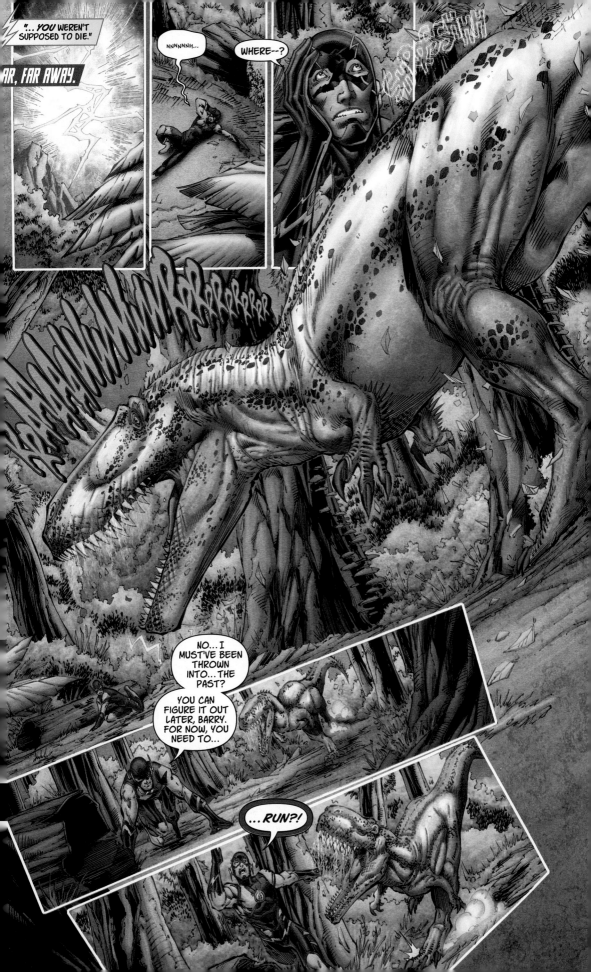

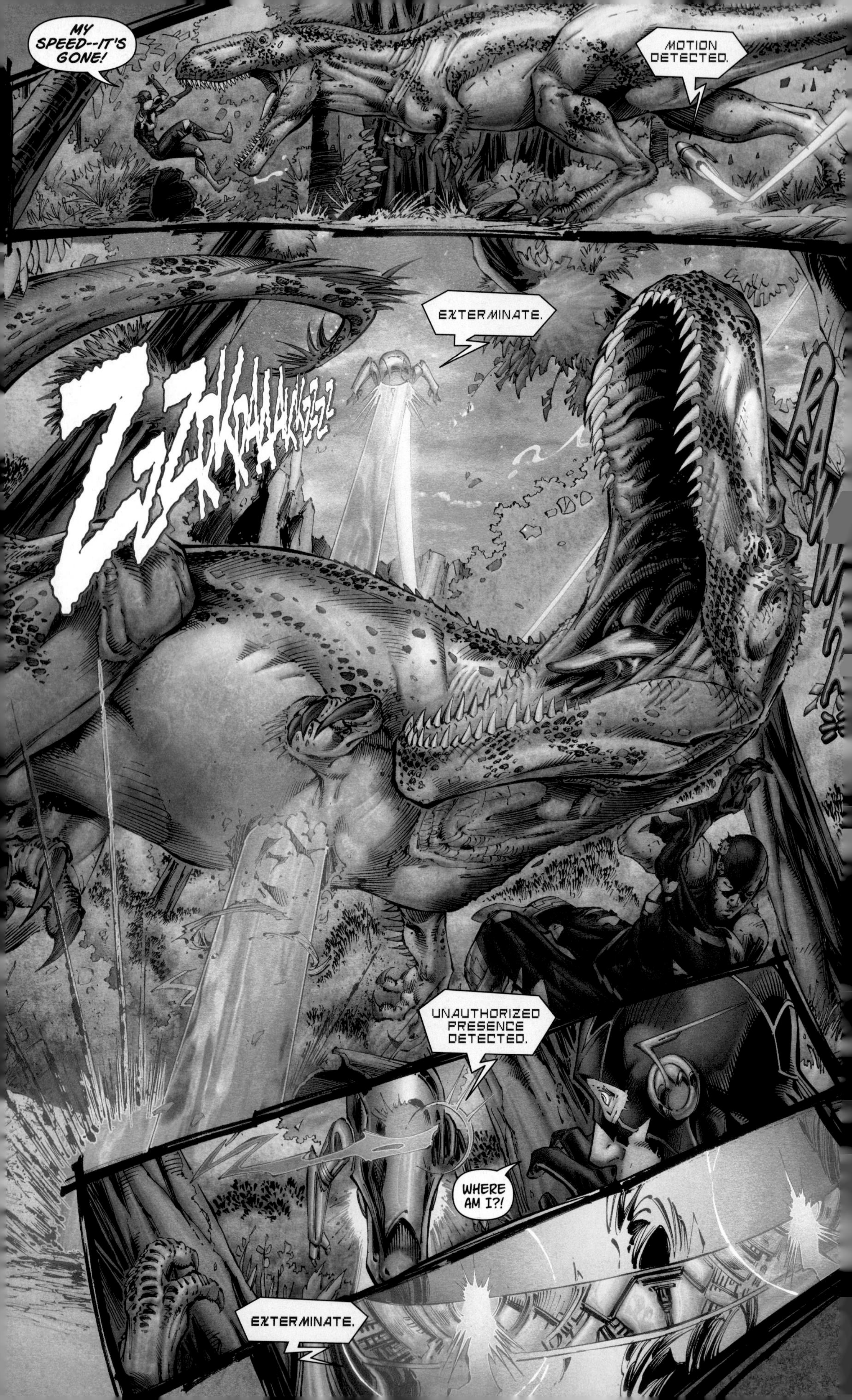
MY SPEED--IT'S GONE!
MOTION DETECTED.
EXTERMINATE.
UNAUTHORIZED PRESENCE DETECTED.
WHERE AM I?!
EXTERMINATE.

VARIANT COVER GALLERY

FLASH #30
MAD variant cover by Anton Emoin

FLASH #31
Batman '66 Variant cover by Mike and Laura Allred

FLASH #32
Bombshell variant cover by Ant Lucia

FLASH #33
Batman 75th Anniversary variant cover by Kim Jung Gi

FLASH #34
Selfie variant cover by Eddy Barrows, Eber Ferreira and HI-FI

FLASH: FUTURES END #1
Brett Booth, Norm Rapmund and Andrew Dalhouse

FLASH #35
Monsters of the Month variant cover by Ryan Ottley and FCO Plascencia

FLASH #30
MAD variant cover by Anton Emoin

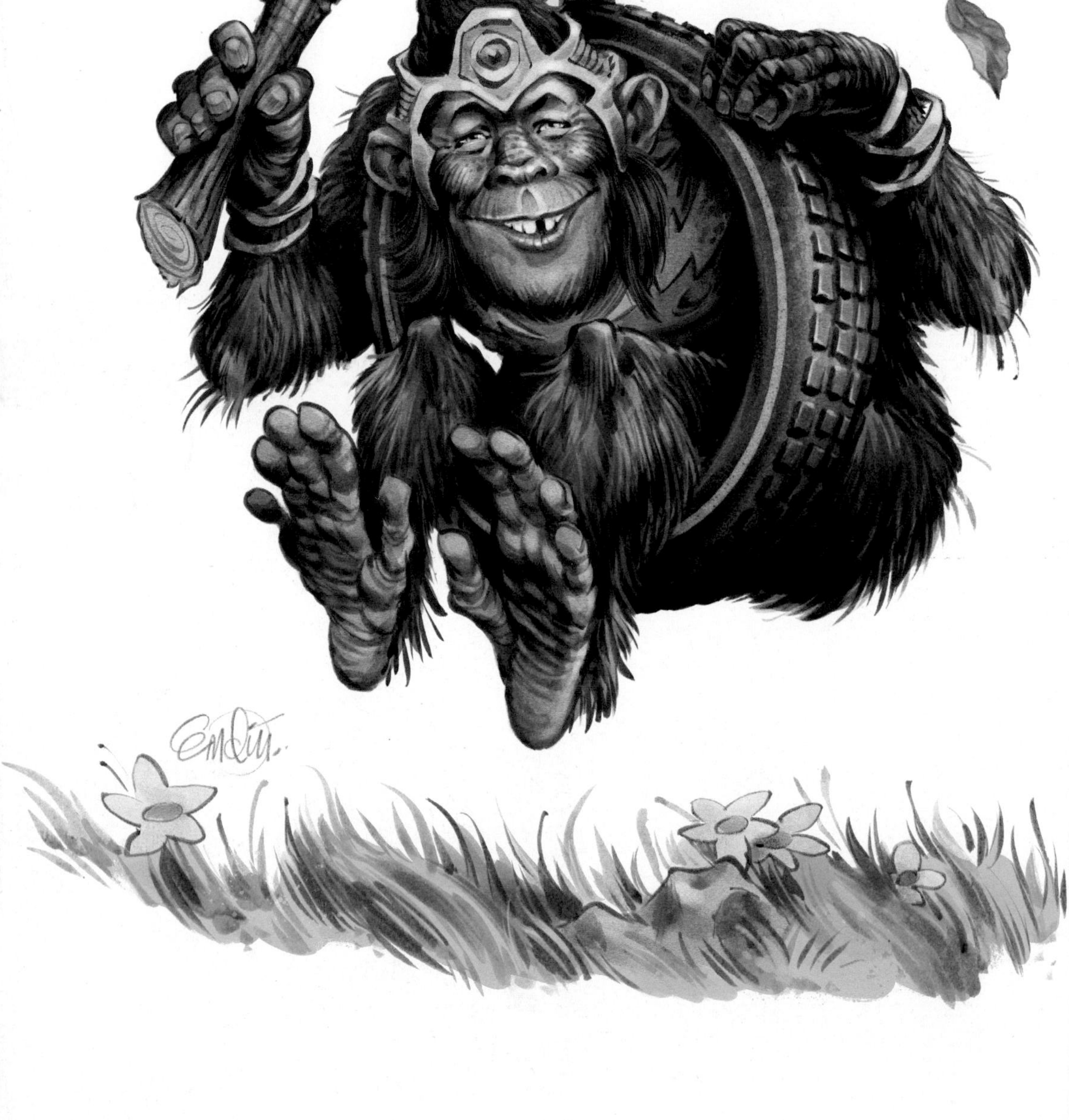

FLASH #31
Batman 66 Variant cover by Mike and Laura Allred

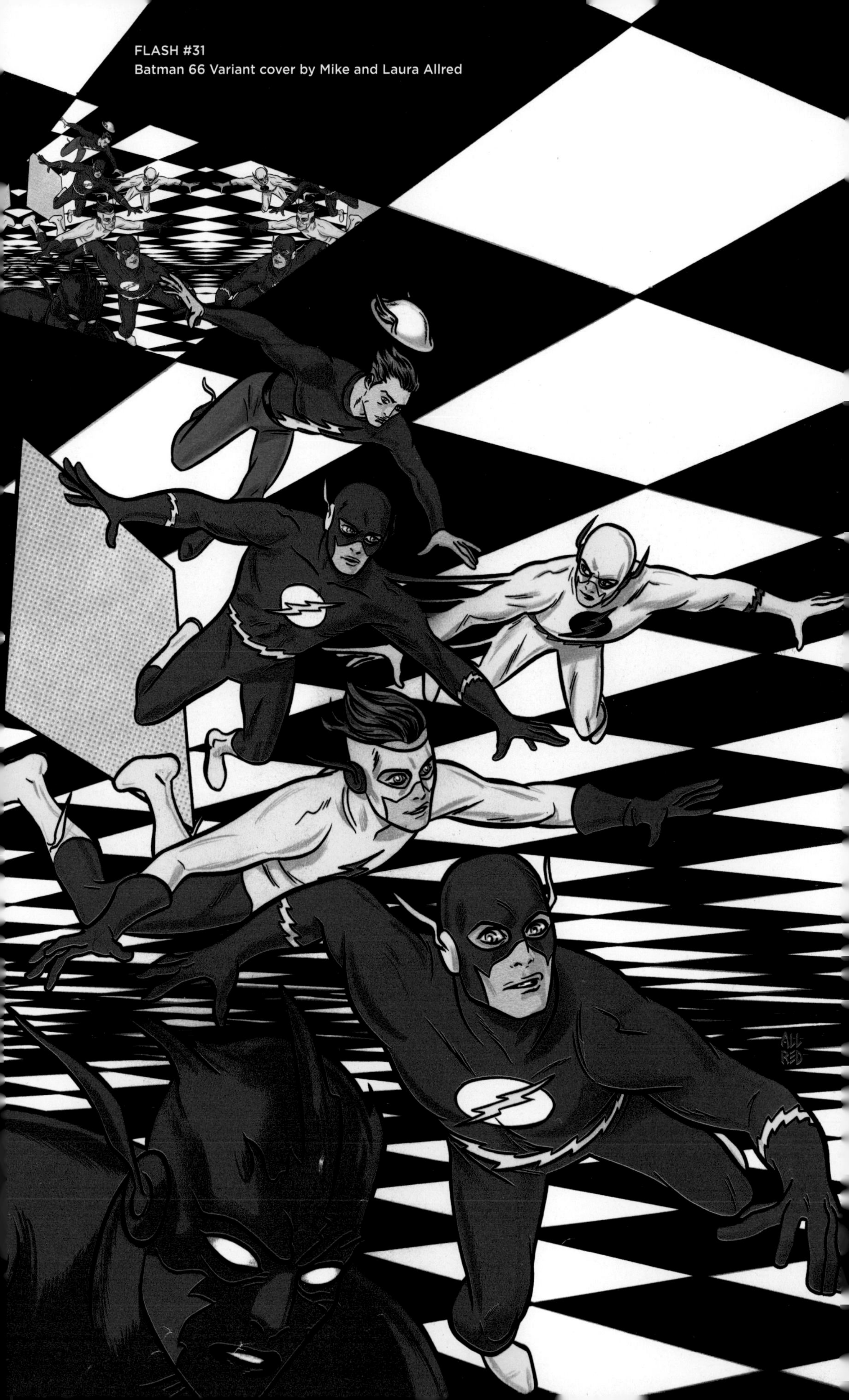
ALL RED

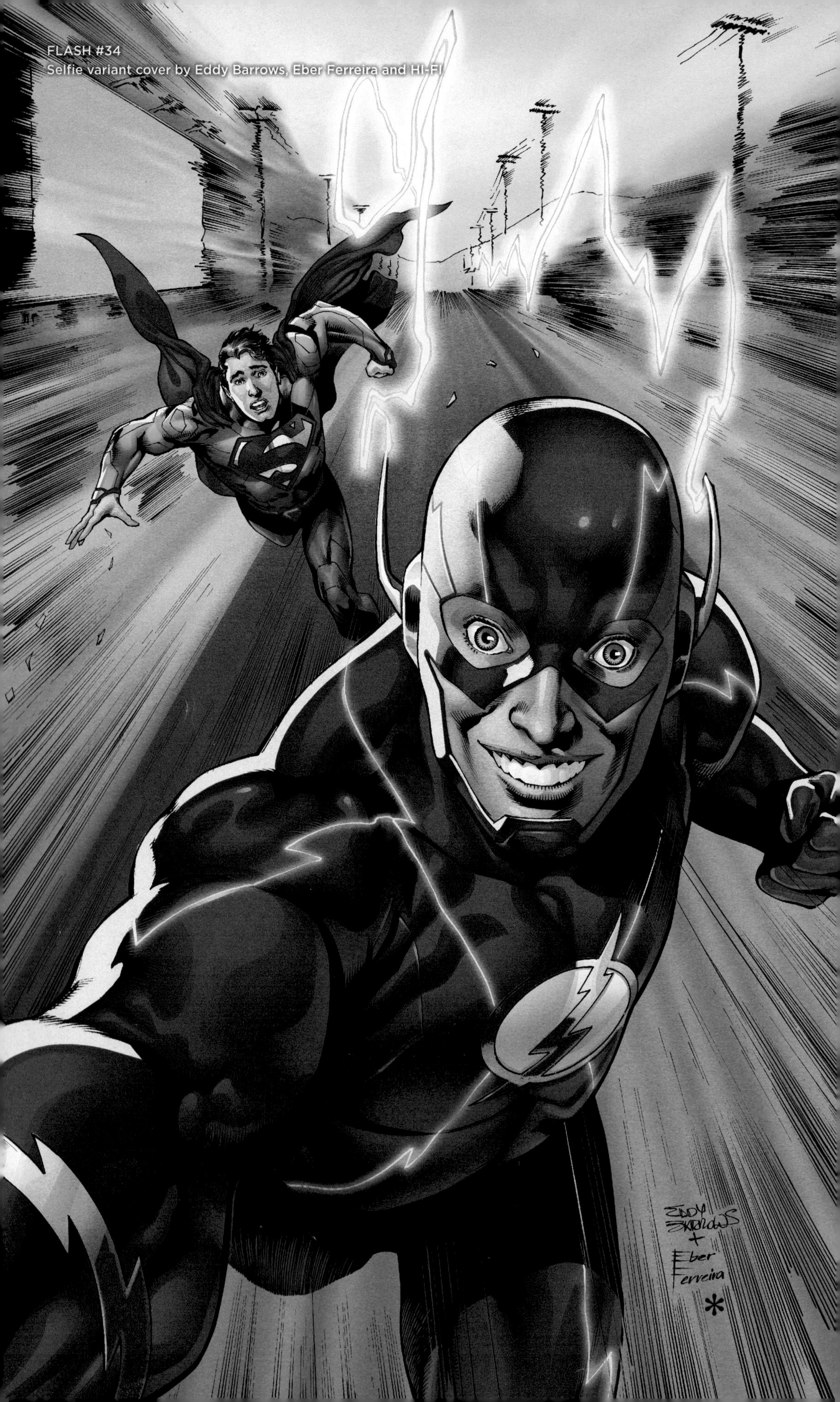
Eddy Barrows
+
Eber Ferreira

FLASH #34
Selfie variant cover by Eddy Barrows, Eber Ferreira and HI-FI

FLASH: FUTURES END #1
Brett Booth, Norm Rapmund and Andrew Dalhouse

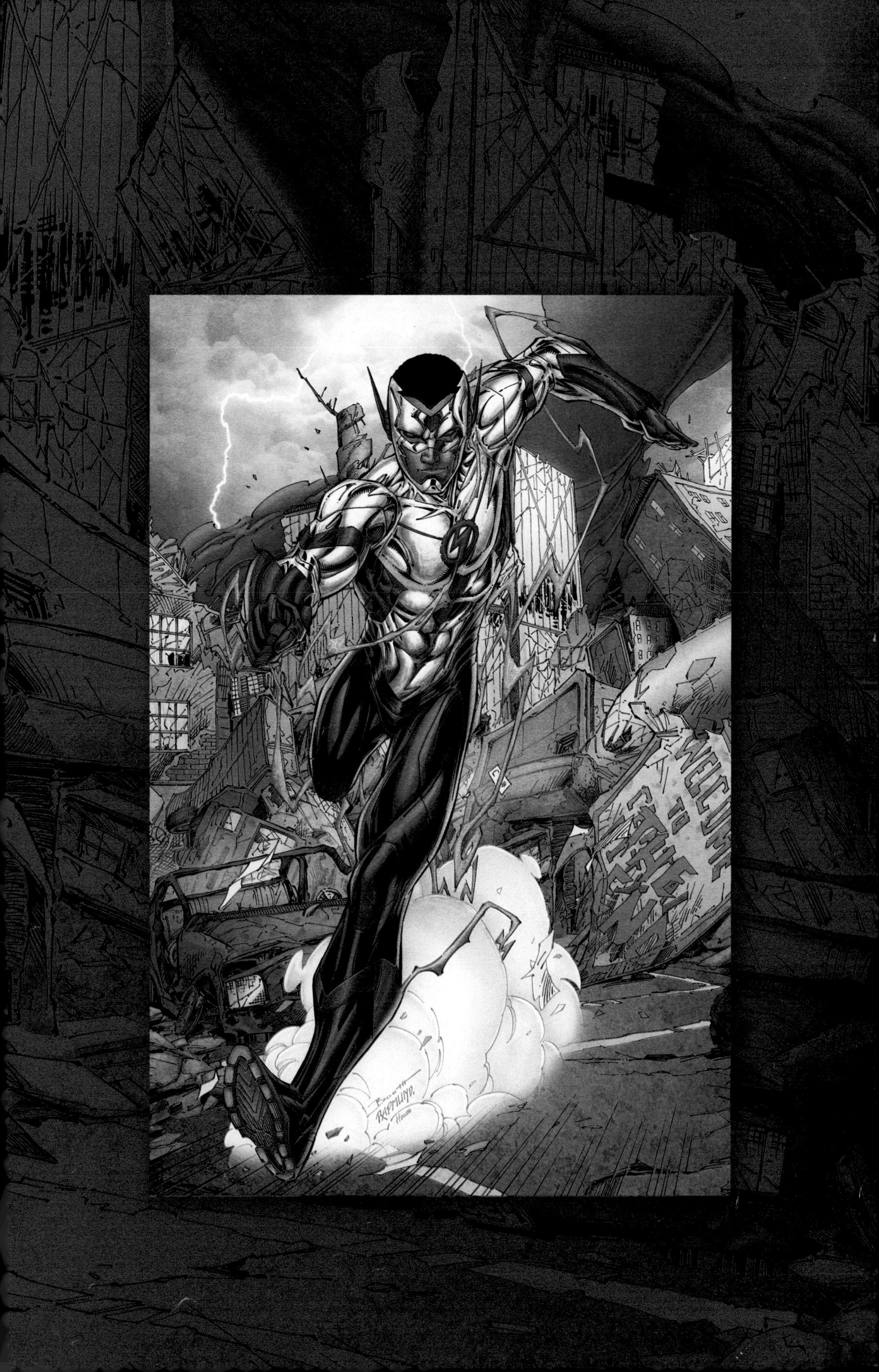

FLASHPOINT
GEOFF JOHNS with ANDY KUBERT

FLASHPOINT: THE WORLD OF FLASHPOINT FEATURING BATMAN

FLASHPOINT: THE WORLD OF FLASHPOINT FEATURING GREEN LANTERN

READ THE ENTIRE EPIC!

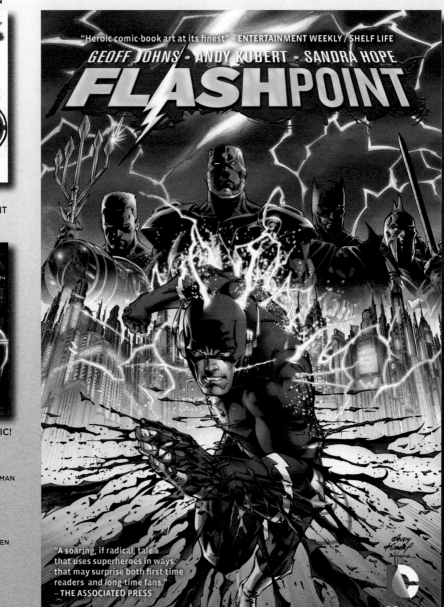

"Heroic comic-book art at its finest" – ENTERTAINMENT WEEKLY / SHELF LIFE

GEOFF JOHNS · ANDY KUBERT · SANDRA HOPE

FLASHPOINT

"A soaring, if radical, tale that uses superheroes in ways that may surprise both first-time readers and long-time fans."
– THE ASSOCIATED PRESS

DC COMICS™

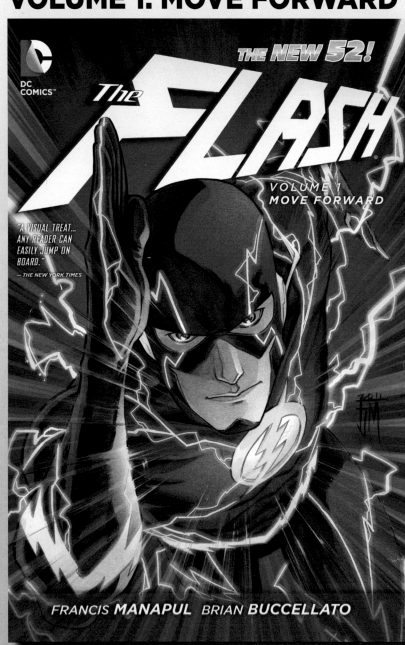